200 Years of American Architectural Drawing

A. J. DAVIS. del. for CUSTOM HOUSE N. Y.

TOWN & DAVIS

NGITUDINAL SECTION.   PREMIUM DESIGN.

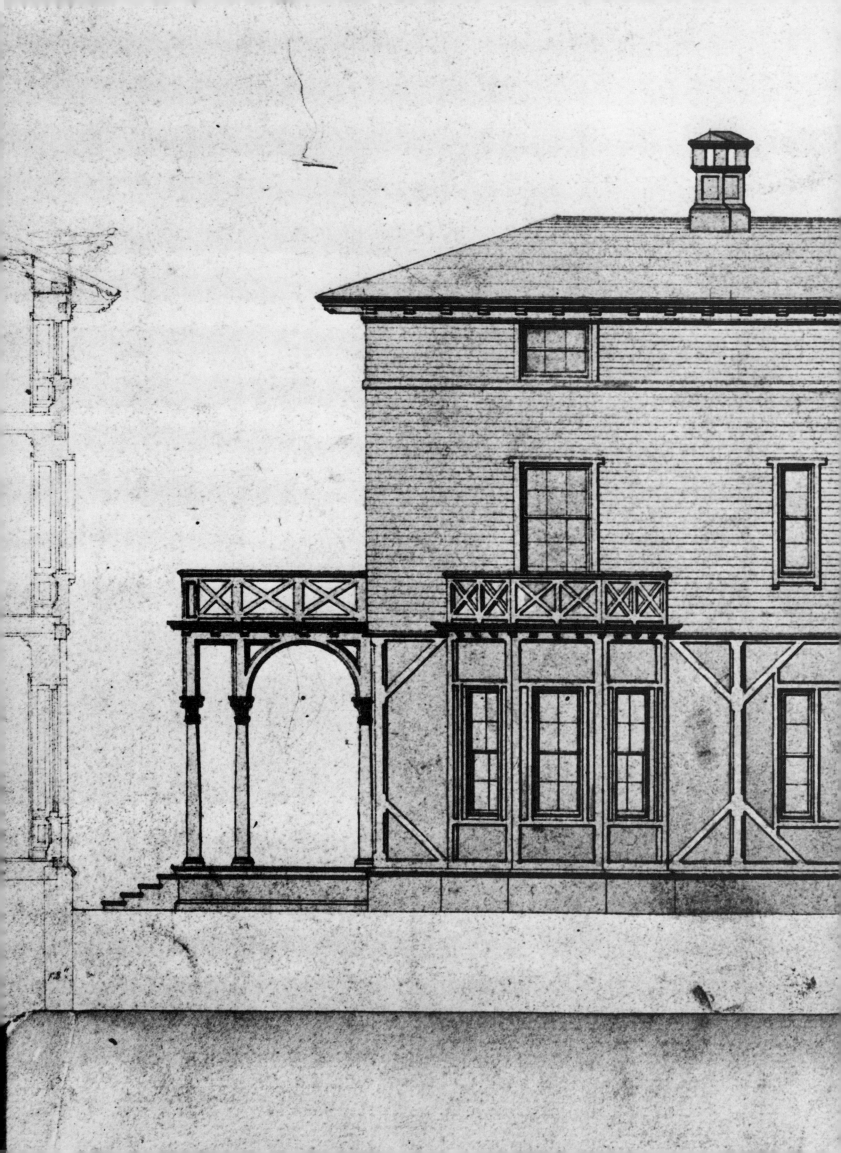

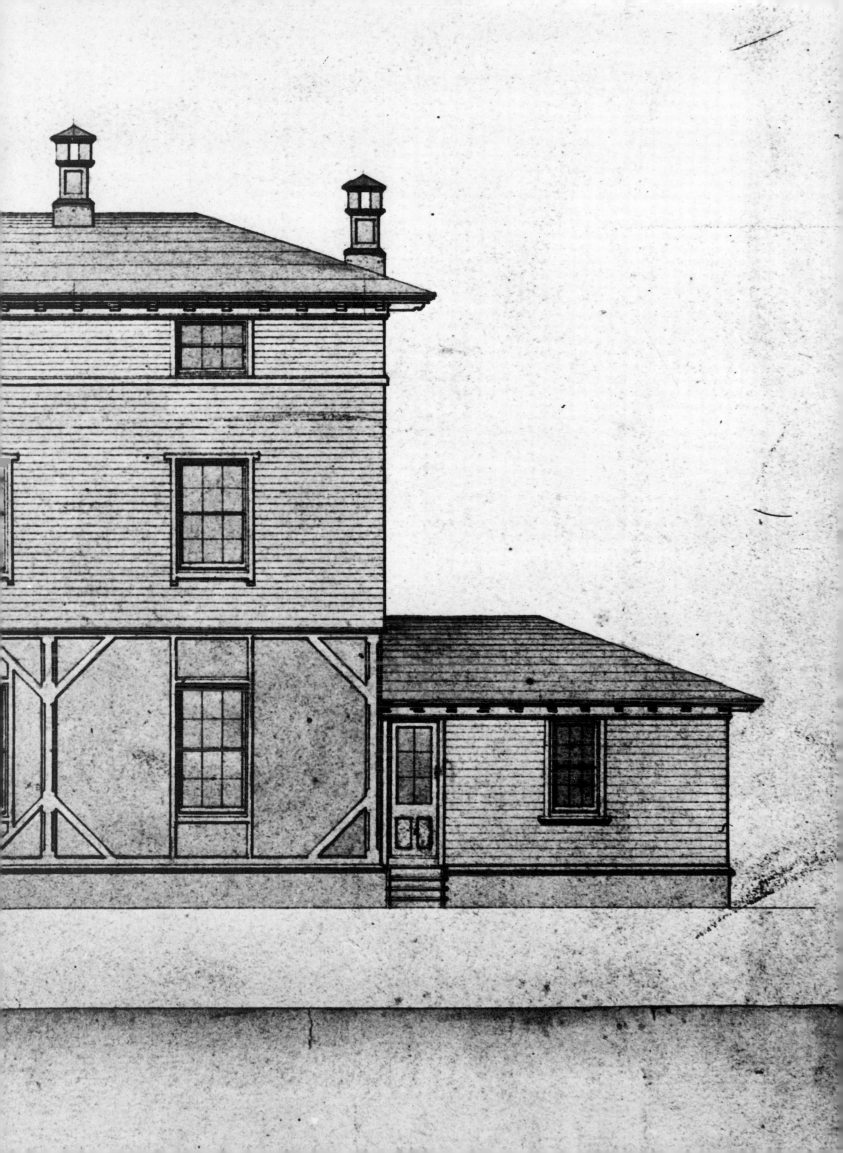

YO REL

L·S·BUFFINGTON ARCHITECT
MINNEAPOLIS MINN· Æ·1888

CIRCLE HALL

200 YEARS OF AMERICAN

By David Gebhard and Deborah Nevins

ARCHITECTURAL DRAWING

Drawings and Intent in American Architecture
By David Gebhard

Commentaries on the Drawings
By Deborah Nevins

WHITNEY LIBRARY OF DESIGN
an imprint of
Watson-Guptill Publications/New York
For The Architectural League of New York
And The American Federation of Arts

Copyright © 1977 by Whitney Library of Design

First published 1977 in New York by Whitney Library of Design,
an imprint of Watson-Guptill Publications,
a division of Billboard Publications, Inc.,
1515 Broadway, New York, N.Y. 10036

Library of Congress Cataloging in Publication Data
Gebhard, David.
    200 years of American architectural drawing.
    Based on an exhibit opening in 1977 at the Cooper-
Hewitt Museum and entitled: 200 years of American
architectural drawing.
    Bibliography: p.
    Includes index.
    I.   Architectural drawing—United States—History.
I.   Nevins, Deborah, 1947–   joint author.
II.   American Federation of Arts.   III.   Architectural
League of New York.   IV.   Title.
NA2706.U6G42   720'.22'2   76-58360
ISBN 0-8230-7470-6

Manufactured in U.S.A.

First Printing, 1977

Edited by Susan Braybrooke and Susan Davis
Set by Gerard Associates/Phototypesetting, Inc.
Printed by Halliday Lithograph Corp.
Bound by A. Horowitz & Son

Designed by Massimo Vignelli

A publication and exhibition organized by The Architectural
League of New York and The American Federation of Arts.
This project was made possible through grants from The
National Endowment for the Arts, The New York State Council
on the Arts, The Graham Foundation for Advanced Studies in
the Fine Arts, and The Architectural League of New York.

In the captions height precedes width. Caption dates indicate
the date of the drawing, not the date of the building to which
it corresponds.

Photographs have generally been provided by the institutions or
private collections that own the illustrated drawings. The fol-
lowing photographers are responsible for the illustrations listed:
Michael Fredericks: 184, 185, 186
Scott Hyde: 172
Sara Cedar Miller: 73, photograph of Deborah Nevins on jacket
Rob Super: 91, 92, 93, 94, 95

Frontispieces, in order of appearance:

*Benjamin Henry Latrobe, design for Bank of the United States,
elevation, Philadelphia, 1818. Courtesy The Library of Congress,
Washington, D.C.*

*Alexander Jackson Davis, United States Custom House,
premium design, longitudinal section, New York City, 1833.
Courtesy Avery Library, Columbia University, New York, New
York.*

*Richard Upjohn, Hamilton Hoppin House, side elevation,
Middletown, Rhode Island, 1856–1857. Courtesy Avery Library,
Columbia University, New York, New York.*

*Harvey Ellis, competitive design for the Indiana Soldiers and
Sailors Monument, project, elevation, Indianapolis, Indiana,
1888. Courtesy Northwest Architectural Archives, University of
Minnesota, Minneapolis, Minnesota.*

*Louis I. Kahn, Alfred Newton Richards Medical Research
Building and Biological Building, perspective, The University of
Pennsylvania, Philadelphia, 1957. Courtesy Department of
Architecture and Design, The Museum of Modern Art, New York,
New York.*

610178

Contents

Throughout architectural history, drawings have played an essential and fascinating role in the architectural process. The Architectural League of New York and The American Federation of the Arts have jointly sponsored this publication and organized an exhibition entitled, "200 Years of American Architectural Drawing," in an effort to delineate this role within the context of America's architectural heritage.

Specifically, this book approaches architectural drawings from two viewpoints. David Gebhard, guest curator, focuses on the character of an architectural drawing and its relationship to the built work. He outlines the history of architectural drawing in America, relating this history to the evolution of the architectural profession, and emphasizes the intimate connection between the drawing's character and its relation to the form of the built work. Deborah Nevins, assistant curator, focuses on the individual architect's career and associates the drawings to the architect's development. Viewed in this context, the drawings appear not only as beautiful objects but also as expressions of the time, the place, and the forces that shaped them and the architects who executed them.

The preparation of this history has been a long, exacting task. Firstly, there is no central repository or complete index of architectural drawings in this country. Although there are some collections notable for their breadth, quality, and documentation, much of the material remains scattered in diverse public and private collections across the country. Secondly, through either neglect or lack of documentation, in the 18th and 19th centuries and even into the 20th century, the careers and the work of many architects remain obscure. David Gebhard and Deborah Nevins have done extensive research, working with scholars across the country to try to remedy this situation. Without their scholarship, patience, energy, and dedication, this book and the accompanying exhibition would not have been possible. It is our hope that this first and thorough effort will open up new directions for scholarly endeavor and will increase our understanding of and respect for the artistic and creative act. In so doing, we hope to expand our society's concern for the built environment, past and present.

Wilder Green, Director, The American Federation of Arts
Robert A. M. Stern, President, The Architectural League of New York

With great appreciation for their foresight and continuing support we thank the Executive Board of The Architectural League of New York who initiated the exhibition on which this book is based and provided the initial funding for this project. The cosponsorship of The American Federation of Arts under the direction of Wilder Green and its extremely able staff—particularly Jane Tai, Assistant Director and Director of Exhibitions; Konrad G. Kuchel, Coordinator/Loans; James Stevens, Coordinator/Scheduling; Melissa Meighan, Registrar—enabled this project to come to fruition. Marita O'Hare, Administrative Director of The Architectural League of New York, played an especially vital role in many of the important administrative aspects of this endeavor. We are grateful to Philip Johnson, who has on many occasions given generously of his advice to The Architectural League and has in a variety of ways enthusiastically supported this project.

On behalf of The Architectural League of New York and The American Federation of Arts we thank The National Endowment for the Arts, The New York State Council on the Arts, and The Graham Foundation for Advanced Studies in the Fine Arts for their generous grants and commitment to presenting an important aspect of our nation's architectural heritage.

We are grateful for the dedication of John Beach, William Cullison, Diane Melish, Susan Slade, Susan Stein, and David Van Zanten who made the preliminary selection of drawings from which final selections came and in later stages of the organization of this project assumed responsibility for the many details necessary for the execution of an exhibition and book of this size. With energy and skill Chris Gray of the Office for Metropolitan History, Judith Paine, Cynthia Rock, and Lindsay Shapiro carried out preliminary research for many of the commentaries on the drawings.

Our editors, Susan Davis and Susan Braybrooke of The Whitney Library of Design, approached this project with expertise, sensitivity, and continuing enthusiasm. Massimo Vignelli, who has for many years been a vital member of The Architectural League, designed this book with the great taste, care, and sense of joy he has brought to all his work.

The staff, many of whom remain anonymous, of numerous libraries, historical societies, and museums throughout the country have given generously of their knowledge and aided in the selection of the drawings. We owe special thanks to the following people who were particularly important in this regard: Sonia Bay, Art and Architecture Library, Yale University; Elaine Dee, Curator of Prints, The Cooper-Hewitt Museum; Arthur Drexler, Director, Department of Architecture and Design, The Museum of Modern Art; Alan Fern, Director, Department of Research, The Library of Congress; Annette Fern, Architectural Librarian, The Burnham Library, The Art Institute of Chicago; Eleanor Garvey, Chief Curator, Houghton Library, Harvard University; Ludwig Glaeser, Curator, The Mies van der Rohe Archive, The Museum of Modern Art; Thomas Hines, The University of California, Los Angeles; Sinclair Hitchings, Keeper of Prints, The Boston Public Library; David Katzive, formerly of the Philadelphia Museum of Art, now Assistant Director of Education and Program Development, The Brooklyn Museum; Daniel Lohnes, The Society for the Preservation of New England Antiquities; Alan Morrison, Fine Arts Library, the University of Pennsylvania; Peter Parker, The Historical Society of Pennsylvania; George E. Pettengill, Librarian Emeritus, The American Institute of Architects; Adolf Placzek, Director, The Avery Library, Columbia University; James Ramsey, Professor of Art History, Vanderbilt University; Wendy Shadwell, The New-York Historical Society; George Talbot, Curator of Manuscripts, The State Historical Society of Wisconsin; Eugene Zep, Department of Prints, The Boston Public Library. The aid of the able staff of Avery Library, Columbia University, where research for the commentaries on the drawings was carried out, made an important contribution to this book, in particular: Charling Fagan, Carole Falcione, Herbert Mitchell, Neville Thompson, and Manfred Ziverts.

We would like to express our thanks to Elaine Hartnett of The Architectural League who typed the commentaries and the bibliography and gave generously of her time when deadlines had to be met; and to Fran Falkin and Mary Ann Monet of The American Federation of Arts who typed the captions for the book, a task requiring great care.

In a variety of ways the following people gave advice and assistance for which we are indebted: Gregory Ain, Carl John Black, Nina Bremer, David Delong, Alden Ball Dow, Anthony Gabriele, Romaldo Giurgola, Michael Graves, Harwell Hamilton Harris, Hans Held, Wheaton Holden, Susan King, Alan Lathrop, Esther McCoy, Elizabeth G. Miller, Sara Cedar Miller, Charles W. Moore, Dion Neutra, Dione Neutra, James O'Gorman, Lynn Orr, Peter Papademetriou, Sara Paulson, Cesar Pelli, Buford Pickens, James Raimes, John Rivers, Cervin Robinson, Michael Rubenstein, Forrest N. Scott, David Shapiro, Susan Siegfried, Rob Super, William Turnbull, Drexel Turner, Robert Venturi, Sally Woodbridge, Lloyd Wright, Cynthia Zaitzevsky, Karoly Zsedenyi.

Howard Lathrop, Francesco Passanti, Susana Torre, and Roger Graham Whidden made important suggestions on the form and content of many of the commentaries; their willingness to extend themselves in this way is immensely appreciated.

Robert A. M. Stern, President of The Architectural League, provided advice throughout the development of this project and insightful, stimulating critiques on the entire text of this book. His exceptional contribution deserves very special thanks.

If you are ready for a mystery adventure akin to those of Nancy Drew or the Hardy Boys, then by all means look into American architectural drawing. Only remember that in the search for American architectural drawings, the good guys do not always win. In all too many ways the subject of American architectural drawings is a sad one. Though there was never a great number of drawings before 1776, only a handful are now known. And the story is not much different from 1776 to the present. If you were to sit down and complete a list of major United States practitioners, from Peter Harrison in the 18th century to William Lescaze in the 20th century, you would quickly discover that we have only a small number of their drawings or in many cases none at all. Some of these collections of drawings will eventually come to light, but most have probably been destroyed. Of Louis H. Sullivan's drawings, we possess only a smattering, and most of these are drawings for ornament; few of them are his remarkable conceptual sketches for buildings.

Especially with the emergence of architecture as a business in the 1890s the propensity of firms to keep anything but their working drawings is very low. Conceptual sketches, which are often the most telling indicators of architectural intent, are seldom retained in a large office or by the small practitioner. To find a William Gray Purcell or an R. M. Schindler who saved a remarkable array of sketches or drawings is highly unusual. And even when they were preserved, what was to be done with them when the architect had ceased to practice? They might be kept for a time in a successor's office or in the garage of a daughter or son. Until recently public institutions—libraries, universities, historical societies, and museums—have not been interested or equipped to house collections of architectural drawings. America has never had an archive of architectural drawings akin to The Royal Institute of Architects' Drawing Collection in London. The Avery Library at Columbia University, the Burnham Library of the Chicago Art Institute, and the Octagon of the American Institute of Architects now have collections of drawings. Elsewhere in the country regional collections are developing. But our present interest in collecting, preserving, and cataloging architectural drawings is in its infancy, and because of this, much of our past—via architectural drawings—is lost forever.

Another obstacle encountered is that many of the collections still remain uncataloged and for all intents and purposes are not available for study or viewing. With a few exceptions the majority of institutions that house collections of American architectural drawings do not sense any obligation to have their drawings exhibited outside their walls. The world of lending for exhibitions elsewhere, which is such an important aspect of the museum art world, has yet to penetrate most institutions that house American architectural collections.

A final limitation has to do with the architects themselves and with the practice of architecture in the United States. Intellectual content has never been a consistent strong point in the practice of architecture in the U.S. The use of drawings to solve theoretical problems has been until recently almost nonexistent. Elsewhere the built building has in the past been only one aspect of the art of architecture and not always its most significant element. Drawings have always occupied a seminal position in the design of a building—regardless of the profundity or lack of profundity of intent. But in the U.S. the illusion of architecture as business has meant that drawing has been played down. The result has been that initial sketches have not been saved, and most architects have purposely eschewed the use of more formal methods of drawing.

Thus, what is presented here in this volume of American architectural drawing is a selection based entirely on existence and availability. We have tried to present as accurate and meaningful a historic picture of 200 years of architectural drawing in America as possible. What we have gathered is, to be frank, not quite what we originally had in mind when we started this project. Drawings by a number of major figures are not represented because they could not be located; we found out that they have been destroyed; or an individual or institution has not been willing to loan them. Since we have tried to include only drawings by the architect of record of a building, several of America's most important architects who have not themselves used drawing as a primary means of developing and communicating their ideas have been excluded from this project. This has been particularly true of architects who practiced during the last century. Often the initial design conception, although formulated by the architect of record for a building, is developed on paper by other designers within the firm. Increasingly during the 20th century the use of models has vied with that of drawing as the primary means of design development. Today many of the most important architectural firms use the model almost exclusively as a means of studying and presenting an idea; others use models as a supplement to drawings.

We feel that this assembly of drawings will provide what we hope will be a stimulation to the collecting and study of American architectural drawings. We also hope that this volume and the drawings themselves will encourage a careful and thoughtful examination of the place of architectural drawing within the discipline and art of architecture.

David Gebhard, University of California, Santa Barbara
Deborah Nevins, The Architectural League of New York

Drawings and Intent in American Architecture

Drawings and Intent in American Architecture

The subject of architectural drawing has enjoyed a highly varied history in our century. The modernists of the 1920s and 1930s, with their uneasiness with history, argued that architectural drawings should be looked upon as documents whose sole purpose is to aid in realizing a built building. Completely opposite that concept is the admiration these same modernist architects and others have felt for the drawings of the late 18th-century French Visionary architects—Etienne-Louis Boullée, Claude-Nicolas Ledoux, and Jean-Jacques Lequeu. These designs were almost exclusively projects for buildings that could never have been realized (structurally or economically) at the time. Here the drawings constitute not a means but an end in themselves.

By their very nature drawings that depict buildings, groups of buildings, urban schemes, and landscape architecture project a complex and in many ways ambiguous world. It is a world, as Reginald Blomfield has pointed out in his *Architectural Drawing and Draughtsmen* of 1912, which demands both "the eye and the brain."[1] And it also brings into play, "knowledge previously acquired . . . the mind jumps from what it sees to much that it does not."[2] Blomfield went on to divide architectural drawings into two types: those that are "objective" (i.e., designs that could be carried out) and those that are "subjective" (i.e., those that produce in the observer "the impression of an architectural idea"[3]). Such a set of distinctions would seem to explain the two types of drawings that we have mentioned—working or contract drawings as opposed to theoretical drawings. But the truth is that all architectural drawings have the potential of being both objective and subjective. A set of working drawings of Bertram G. Goodhue in the early 1920s or by Robert Venturi in the 1970s overflows with architectural ideas; and in contrast loose sketches by Henry Hobson Richardson or Louis I. Kahn have a sure footing in the objective world of a realizable building. Again and again we are aware that theoretical drawings (of unrealized or even unrealizable projects) have often served as a basis for other later built buildings. The tradition of the ideal—of pure geometric forms, such as the cube, the sphere, the circle, which have been so prevalent in architecture from the Renaissance on —owes its persistence to theoretical architectural drawings, not primarily to structures that have been built.

Another distinction that writers on architectural drawings have made is to create a separation between the rendering of architectural subjects by architects and by those whom we would label as painters.[4] But such a distinction is as untenable as the suggestion that we can divide architectural drawings into objective and subjective categories. The portrayal of a building, a city, or a garden in a High Art painting, or in a low art comic strip, has the potential of reality as much as many drawings by "professional" architects. Just as we are aware of the impact of theoretical drawings on later realized buildings, so too depiction of buildings and urban and landscape designs in High Art drawings, prints, and paintings have led to new developments in architecture. We have only to think of the effect of 17th- and early 18th-century French and Italian paintings on the 18th- and 19th-century English Romantic garden or of the episode of the 19th-century Italianate style whose origin is to be found in 18th-century paintings.[5]

In this discussion we will concentrate on drawings by architects, but at the same time we should remain aware that we are treating only one group of architectural drawings. Having stated that we will discuss drawings by architects immediately raises that hoary and in many ways humorous question: who or what is an architect? In the past and up to the moment, there have been three points of reference that have been traditionally employed in defining an architect: first, the designation by a professional body (with or without the sanction of the state); second, all those involved in the production of drawings for built buildings (or anticipated built buildings); third, anyone who does drawings of buildings regardless of his intent.[6]

If we are concerned with American architecture we have to include designs that emanate from all three of these categories, plus the extensive body of work produced by carpenter-builders. The American Classical Revival of the first four decades of the 19th century can only be fully understood when we experience both buildings and drawings of realized and unrealized projects. And by drawings we mean not only the building designs of Benjamin Latrobe and Robert Mills, but the pattern-book schemes of Minard Lafever, the paintings of Thomas Cole, or the color lithographs published by Currier and

Ives.[7] The same would hold true for the episode of the Moderne (Art Deco) architecture of the 1920s and 1930s. Like an iceberg, the constructed buildings of those decades reveal only a small segment of this architectural point of view. We would have to look into the drawings of a nonpracticing architect like Hugh Ferriss and the drawings of the major industrial designers—Walter Dorwin Teague, Raymond Loewy, and Norman Bel Geddes.[8] Equally, we would have to take into account the architectural world of the High Art painters—Charles Sheeler, Stuart Davis, Ralston Crawford—and the low art world of science fiction, *Amazing Stories, Popular Mechanics*, Buck Rogers, and Flash Gordon.

Whether we are involved with the question of the origin and development of a style, or with the events and intent contained in the design of a single building, the availability of drawings always provides us with an insight that can only be partially gleaned from a realized building. To go a step further, it can be forcibly argued that the concept of the architect, in many instances, is far better revealed through the drawings than in executed buildings. The careers of a number of America's architects of the 19th and 20th centuries cannot be comprehended in any depth without a knowledge of their drawings. Even in the case of a personality such as Henry Hobson Richardson who supposedly did not place great importance on his drawings in the realization of a building, a study of his drawings lets us know how he approached a specific design and what was of primary importance to him.[9]

In the 20th century the published and unpublished drawings of Frank Lloyd Wright remain a more revealing testimonial to his remarkable, versatile mind than his realized buildings.[10] Both Richardson's and Wright's deep and long lasting influence on American architecture came about primarily through the publication of drawings, only partially through published photographs, or through other designers' knowledge of the buildings themselves.[11]

Several of America's major architects exist almost exclusively through their drawings. The gifted 19th-century designer-renderer Harvey Ellis, who traveled from one architectural office to another, comes to life through his drawings published in the pages of *The American Architect and Building News, The Inland Architect, The Western Architect*, and *The Craftsman* magazine.[12] And the architectural personality of Hugh Ferriss and his contribution to the 1920s' and 1930s' view of the skyscraper and high-density urban design can only be discovered in his own publications, in his renderings for other architects, and in his drawings used as illustrations for advertisements.[13]

Thus although architectural drawings are generally conceived of as a means to an end (a realized building), they also exist as their own end. Because a building depicted in a drawing was not built or could not be built should not be seen as a limiting factor for the world of architectural drawings. The architect, the urban designer, the landscape architect seek to reorder a segment of the environment. The spaces they create, the symbols they employ reveal their own personal view of how space should be ordered. The depiction of their ideal of reordering can be much more forcibly asserted through the convention and symbolism employed in drawings than by the actual construction of a project. A realized project, a building, a garden can by its very nature only hint at the reordering ideals of the architect. Even assuming the most ideal circumstances—an open, sympathetic client, unlimited budget, committed contractors and workers—the moment a project is completed, it begins to be transformed. The constructed project exists in time; as a physical object it immediately begins to be modified by nature and by our use of it. More importantly, our reaction to it continually undergoes a metamorphosis: it cannot, nor does it, remain static.

Drawings, however, remain fixed; we experience the project through the selective eye of the architect. He or she draws our attention to the symbols and spaces that he feels are significant; he deemphasizes or eliminates that which for him is unimportant. This is the reorganized world as it should be. Admittedly our response to a drawing will not remain set, but the object itself (i.e., the project as depicted in the drawing) remains unchanged.

A major error that historians have made in their study of past architecture is that while they always considered the question of style, they have seldom looked into the question of changes in drawing conventions. Each period in architecture has developed not only its own style, but its own style of drawing. These styles say as much about the period as do the styles themselves. Why in one period are buildings depicted almost exclusively via orthographic projections (elevations and plans) while in another period perspective or isometric drawings are preferred? Why does the architect select this or that point for us to view the project? Equally fascinating is the perplexing, and perhaps not fully answerable, question of how drawings affect the design of buildings. American architectural drawings of the 18th and 19th centuries tend almost exclusively to be renditions of elevations and floor plans. In the later 19th century, the Romantic Picturesque styles—the Eastlake, Queen Anne (including the Shingle Style), and the Richardsonian Romanesque—were most effectively conveyed through perspective drawings. The techniques of rendering entailed in the turn-of-the-century Beaux-Arts style, particularly in its rendering of site plans and cross sections, say more about the Beaux-Arts architects' intent than do their impressive elevational drawings! And in our own contemporary period it is not by accident that Charles W. Moore, William Turnbull, Robert Venturi, and others have turned to isometric drawings (including cutaway sections)—a rendering technique closely related to the use of cardboard models as conceptual design tools.

The selection of drawing conventions is then not just a result of the architectural view of a period, but the style of drawing has decidedly affected the product, i.e., the building. In her perceptive paper, "Late Nineteenth-Century Published American Perspective Drawings," Eileen Michels points out in her discussion of the Shingle Style, "one can go a step further and observe that in certain cases the sketch or drawing actually determined some of the fundamental architectural facts."[14] The path that leads from the abstract architectural concept to the finished product of a built building is generally not an easy one to follow. The stylistic conventions employed in architectural drawings almost always tend to be borrowed from outside architecture, especially from painting, later from photography and various aspects of technology. These outside values are built into design via the drawings at an early stage, and they are carried on through the design process, eventually to be incorporated into the constructed building.

Equally fascinating to study is how drawings function as tools in the realization of a building. Generally, drawings produced before the mid-19th century consisted of just a sheet or a few sheets containing (usually in very small scale) the principal floor plans and one elevation. On occasion these might be accompanied by one or two additional elevations, by a cross section of a principal part of the building, plus a few details. Although all these would be drawn to scale, their dimensioning was often not precise. Such cursory "working drawings" served their purposes well since those involved with building were operating in a highly traditional world of technology (in terms of structure and materials) and an equally traditional world of design. Where there is general agreement as to proportions, scale, structure, and detailings, there is little need to produce elaborate drawings to explain all of these.

Though drawings were small and limited in the traditional building world of the 18th and early 19th centuries, the pictorial effect of the drawing was dominant. The emphasis on a principal facade in the built building came directly from the two-dimensional rendition of it on paper. Even in the 18th-century Georgian style—the most robust (three-dimensionally) of the styles of the time—the facades are flat and only become three-dimensional through sculptural ornamentation. The later styles of the 18th and early 19th centuries, the Federal and the Greek Revival, placed increased reliance on drawings, at the expense of traditional esthetic values. This increased dependence led in several different directions. In the Federal style the thin surface articulation was akin to the style of drawing utilized in publications on Roman art and architecture and in the published pattern books that were coming into their own.[15] With the fewest of exceptions these 18th-century drawings of Roman antiquity (especially the influential ones published on Pompeii and Herculaneum) and the drawings presented in pattern books depicted elevations, floor plans, and details.[16] Perspective or isometric drawings were avoided, and the buildings were shown as abstract entities unrelated to site and landscaping.

At first the Greek Revival was, like the earlier Federal style, a two-dimensional surface style, but by the mid-1830s it had taken over the picturesque values of the English Romantic garden tradition, and therefore it became three-dimensional. Stuart and Revett's *Antiquities of Athens*, published in 1762, 1787, and 1794, placed its prime reliance on impressive elevational drawings and plans.[17] By the second decade of the 19th century adaptations of Greek architecture were being presented by J. C. Loudon in London and even by the Gothic Revival-oriented A. J. Downing in America in perspective as three-dimensional volumes set in the landscape.[18] Though working drawings of the 1820s through the 1840s still remained quite simple, they did in part seek to mirror this new desired image. As has happened continuously in the history of architecture, the pictorial ideal asserted in the perspective drawings could not be fully sustained in the reality of the working drawings and in the constructed buildings. In the case of a good number of those buildings, if they work ideologically, it is because of independent fragmented episodes, not because of the unity of purpose of the whole.

As this discrepancy increased in the mid-19th century, architectural design shifted to respond to it. American architectural styles after 1860 were established by fragments—separately conceived historical remembrances. The Eastlake makes a nod to the Gothic through a few details. But the details are in fact of a linear nature taken from the drawing and then realized with 19th-century technology—the jigsaw, router, and the lathe. The Queen Anne and the later Colonial Revival (including the Shingle Style) carried on a similar approach. Even the Richardsonian Romanesque, which came the closest of any to evolving a style, simply ended up by using larger-scaled details.

To a considerable degree the character of these later 19th-century styles did indeed result from the drawing process. These styles were also an outcome of several other factors: the economics and technology of construction, the nature of architectural practice at the time, and new influences affecting drawing. Both photography and the introduction of photolithography strongly affected the conceptual image in the minds of both client and architect. The introduction of new methods of reproducing architectural working drawings in the 1870s (the blueprint process) and the increased reliance on drawings as a specific legal document among the architect, client, and contractor(s) meant that working drawings (together with the written specifications) assumed an importance that they never had before.[19]

Before the 1870s the publication of architectural drawings was generally limited to pattern books. Except in the case of basic carpentry manuals, the illustrations found in these pattern books were meant to supplement the written text. With the introduction of many periodicals in the 1870s, drawings of buildings and details assumed a major importance. Because of the format of many of these magazines, large page sizes were often available. In the more pretentious of these publications, like *The American Architect and Building News*, the drawings were arranged separately in a plate section, similar to the layout of many art publications of the time.

In the 20th century an additional demand was made on working drawings; they had to indicate that the proposed building would satisfy certain public needs, such as "adequate" plumbing, electricity, and structure. In the 1970s those public aspects have been tremendously expanded, so that the drawings as a document must now, for example, contain an analysis for environmental impact reports and indicate how various energy conservation questions will be answered. Each of these new demands has meant either the tightening up or expansion of information that must be contained in a set of drawings.

Another purpose that today's architectural drawings serve is as an answer to the increasing demand made by communities through appointed bodies that new structures take into account the scale and nature of the buildings that exist in proximity to the new project. In some instances buildings must go a step further and reflect a generally established architectural style already present in a community. The drawings prepared for this process combine the conceptual/presentation modes, which in most instances are quite different from the form used for a client presentation drawing and from the "finished" set of working drawings that previously constituted the sole document deposited with a public body (i.e., the planning and/or building department). Thus it is readily apparent that the architectural drawing as a document is currently undergoing major changes.

As a document it is becoming increasingly significant within the current bureaucratic complexities of government.

Anyone who has ever had the experience of working in a 20th-century architectural office of reasonable size will realize how difficult it is in many instances to precisely trace the evolution of a design, from the idea through the production of working drawings and specifications. From the late 19th century on, medium to larger offices have employed delineators and designers who have occasionally used the drawing process as a means of affecting the finished design. When these pieces of evidence are present, we can analyze the process of design and come up with some reasonable conclusions about how the design developed, who contributed what, etc. Even in the instances where we possess a rich variety of drawings relating to a single project, an intimate knowledge of how the architectural office operates, a deep awareness of the personalities involved, etc., will make our historical reconstruction more accurate.

A building can, as we are aware, be realized without drawings. The abstract imagery, plus the facts of a building, may be handed on by tradition. One can build by referring to what has been and what is. Such vernacular methods of design dominated much of the building scene until the mid-19th century. When intent remained an accepted, agreed-upon convention, such a vernacular approach to design was entirely adequate. When intent became increasingly complex and abstract (experienced only by an elite within society), then it became necessary to devise a symbolic method of conveying these intentions.

In addition to architectural drawing, another method has been utilized—architectural models. From what we know historically, models and drawings have always existed side by side.[20] The subject of the historical connection between drawings and models is another aspect of architecture that has never been adequately explored. Models, like drawings, have several diverse purposes in architectural practice. We know that models have been used from classical Greco-Roman times on as instructional design tools, much as a full set of working drawings are used today.[21] Models have also been used throughout history to reveal and sell a design, serving a similar function as a presentation drawing.[22] Finally, models have been used like sketches and other drawings as a pure design tool.[23]

Experiencing a model is as different from the special experience of a built building as is the world of a drawing from an actual building. A model becomes understandable through reference to architectural drawings, not to the built building. In the area of architectural style, models closely mirror the current fashions employed in drawings. Thus in the 20th century, models of clay and plaster of the teens and twenties display a quality identical to that of the corresponding drawings.[24] In much of contemporary architectural practice we find that models have been extensively employed for study purposes, which seems to imply that they have taken the place of the more traditional use of architectural study-sketches.[25] Such, in fact, is not the case. The current fashion of thin cardboard models must be read against a long 20th-century sparse linear drawing technique, especially the present use of isometric and cutaway isometric drawings.[26] It is intriguing to note that those models assume a major impact when they are yanked from their own dollhouse, just pretend world through the photograph. For in the photograph they again take on the values we associate with drawings.

We have already touched on the question of the relationship between architectural drawing and High Art painting. As with so much of architectural history this is an area awaiting detailed historical studies. The critical connective link in most instances is the drawing.[27] The drawing stands midway between the two-dimensional world of painting and the realized building. On the surface the allegiance of the drawing to the two-dimensional realm of High Art drawing, printmaking, and printing would appear to be extremely close. Technically both share media and method, and both often utilize shared images. But intent is what divides them, and intent links the architectural drawing to the quite different world of architecture. The architectural drawing seeks to portray humanity's seizure and reorganization of a segment of the environment. The drawing states this ideal; the building gropes for its realization in the actual world.

Painting, then, can supply both techniques and specific configurations of images, but those images assume quite a different reality in an architectural drawing. Several general observations are of value in any discussion of the relationship of

High Art and architectural drawings. First, the techniques of renditions encountered in architectural drawings have remained quite conservative.[28] Second, the imagery employed in architectural drawings has in many major episodes of style in the 19th and 20th centuries been taken directly from painting and/or sculpture. But it can well be argued that a number of major esthetic/ideological movements in America of the 19th century reached their culmination not in High Art, not in written ideologies, not in built buildings, but in architectural drawings. The pictorial Romanticism of the late 19th century found its height of achievement in the drawings of Eastlake, Queen Anne, and Romanesque Revival buildings, published in the pages of *The American Architect and Building News* and elsewhere.[29] In the 20th century we do not have to go to see the works of European or American Expressionists or the later Surrealists; the concepts of these two closely related 20th-century movements are most fully explained in the drawings of Frank Lloyd Wright, R. M. Schindler, Bruce Goff, or John Lautner.[30] Equally, Cubism and the later episodes of post-Cubism (such as the American Immaculates), and in our current art scene the marriage in various movements of the past 10 to 15 years of the commercial vernacular with traditional Cubist/post-Cubist principles, find their greatest strength in the architectural drawings of Charles W. Moore, William Turnbull, and Robert Venturi.

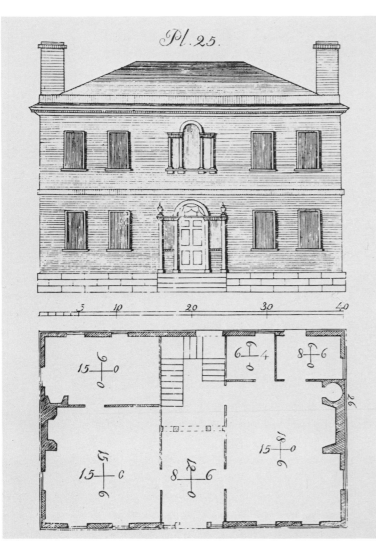

1

The Early Years: 1700–1820

The actual number of American architectural drawings that survived from the 18th century is small in number. In part this is because few drawings were produced and utilized. Buildings were erected on the agreed-upon tradition of provincial Georgian design, coupled with the use of carpenters' manuals and pattern books.[31] Although many aspects of 18th-century American architecture have been studied and written about, it is surprising how little is known about architectural drawings and the specific function of drawings of these decades today. We do not possess anything in the way of drawings, let alone the name of the architect, for many of the major buildings of this century. Some of these buildings conceivably did not have an architect; their designs were probably worked out by client and master carpenter using a plan book, as was supposedly the case of Stratford, c. 1725, the Lee house in Westmoreland County, Virginia. But others were most certainly designed by architects, and in most instances drawings were unquestionably made. With recent research we are learning more about these architects. Two people recently discovered are Richard Taliaferro, the gentleman architect of Virginia, who may have designed Westover of 1726–1730 in Charles City, Virginia; and John Ariss, to whom is attributed the Palladian design of Mount Airy of 1755–1767 in Richmond County, Virginia.[32] We do not possess any drawings by either Taliaferro or Ariss.

Among the losses of early 18th-century architectural drawings particularly to be regretted are those of one of America's first "professional" architects, Peter Harrison whose architectural record was destroyed.[33] As a result we are forced to know Harrison's intent only from early illustrations and his surviving buildings. In the case of the late 18th century we are in a much better position to study architectural intent through drawings. Thomas Jefferson has left a sufficient number of drawings so that we can appraise what part drawings played in his design process.[34] The same is fortunately the case for Boston's Charles Bulfinch, Salem's superb carpenter-architect Samuel McIntire, and New York's John McComb, Jr.[35]

Coupled with drawings that have survived is our remarkably detailed knowledge of the architectural books intensively utilized throughout the 18th century.[36] According to Helen Park, there were 106 books on architecture available in the English colonies before 1776.[37] With the exception of eight titles, all were English, and a majority were organized as practical carpenters' manuals.[38] As should be expected, the first American book on architecture, Asher Benjamin's *The Country Builder's Assistant* of 1797, was itself such a practical do-it-yourself volume. In studying 18th-century American architecture (and much of 19th-century architecture for that matter), we should approach those pattern books in the same fashion as we might examine drawings for specific buildings. The design ideals of that century came to be expressed through the drawings presented in their pages as well as in the buildings inspired by them.

A number of observations can be made about the drawings contained in these pattern books. First, we must note that these books, and the several revisions through which many of them went, reflect the changes that occurred in English architectural fashions during the 18th century, ranging from the late Baroque, through Palladianism, the late Georgian, and the Regency. Second, it is remarkable how these various architectural fashions were only tenuously related to the English picturesque garden tradition. Although any of these classically derived English buildings could pose as an object of historical romance in the informal English garden, they were no more adequately related to the landscape than such nonclassical styles as the Gothic or those imitating the Chinese or Moorish.

The design of those classical-inspired buildings without regard for landscape setting is effectively conveyed in the plates of Betty Langley's *The Builder's Jewel, or Youth's Instruction, and Workman's Remembrances*, published in London in 1741, or in Abraham Swan's *The British Architect* or *The Builder's Treasury of Staircases*, published in London in 1745.[39]

The plates of drawings in these 18th-century pattern books almost universally rely upon orthographic projection—in most instances a portrayal of the major floor plans together with the principal elevation.

In a few examples these two types of projection are accompanied by a cross-sectional drawing. Although all these drawings are to scale, they are seldom dimensioned. Generally

1 *Asher Benjamin. From* The Country Builder's Assistant, *1797.*

2 *Andrew Hamilton and Edmund Woolley, Pennsylvania State House (Independence Hall), Philadelphia, 1732–1753. Courtesy The Historical Society of Pennsylvania.*

3 *Samuel Rhodes, study no. 21 for a facade, c. 1750. Courtesy The Historical Society of Pennsylvania.*

4 *Richard Munday, Ayrault House, Newport, Rhode Island, 1739. From Sidney Fiske Kimball,* Domestic Architecture of the American Colonies and of the Early Republic, *Charles Scribner's & Sons, 1922; reprint, Dover Publications, 1950.*

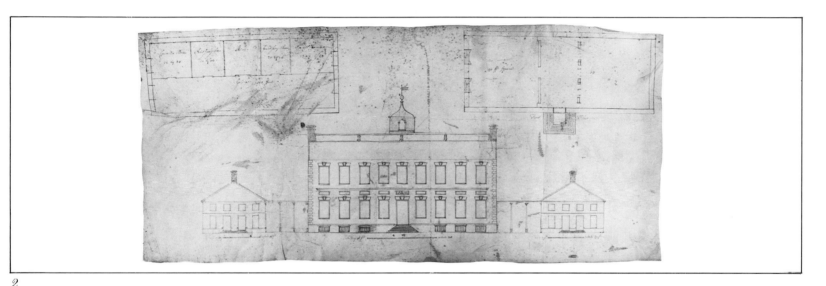

2

3

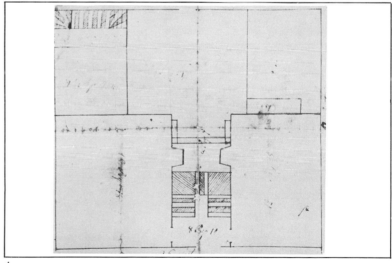

4

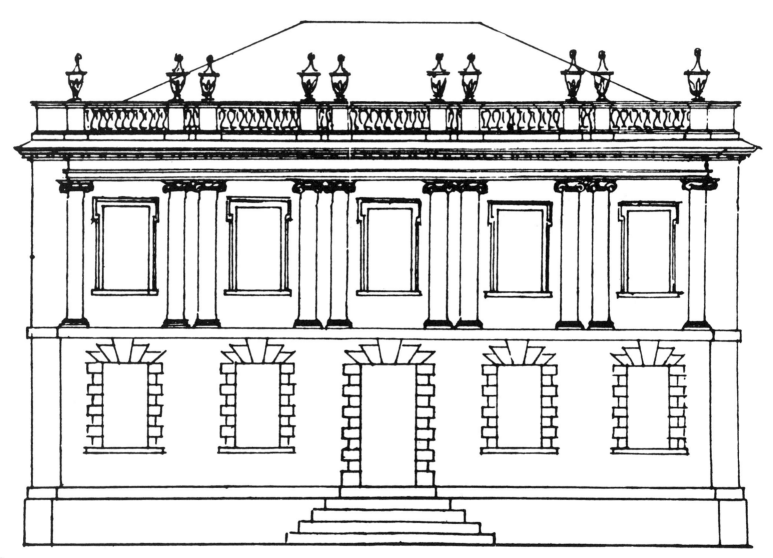

5

*5   Samuel McIntire, Lyman House, Waltham, Massachusetts,
c. 1793. From Sidney Fiske Kimball*, Mr. Samuel McIntire,
Carver, the Architect of Salem, *The Southworth-Anthoesen
Press, 1940.*

these drawings use line to establish planes that tend to be decidedly flat. The planes are differentiated from one another by the suggestion of shallow shadow patterns and by the dark and light effect of close and widely spaced parallel lines. The suggestion of light is usually handled ambiguously; if a source of light is revealed, it is generally from the upper left, falling in the lower right. But even when such a source is indicated, other surfaces and their relationships may be articulated by a light/dark effect that is nondirectional.

The light/dark relationship found in these elevational drawings tends to reinforce that classical design principle of the column—base, shaft, and capital. The raised basement will be very dark; the main body of the building will be light; and finally the roof/attic/balustrade will again be dark, but lighter than the base. These elevational drawings seldom give any indication of surface materials (except occasional references to quoining or a rusticated basement); and they do not describe any depth or projections. Openings are treated as dark blanks, i.e., a recessed plane, just back of the plane of the facade.

The plans, which generally were printed below the elevations, are composed of parallel lines filled in with a 45° parallel line or a dark wash in some instances. These lines portray surfaces, which in turn suggest volumes. Of prime importance, their double lines with infill suggest the idea-relationship of the interior—symmetry, axis, and balance. When cross sections are present they almost exclusively make the plan more readable than does the elevation.

As historians have pointed out, the drawings that are not presented are as important as those that are.[40] Site plans are literally nonexistent; so too perspective, oblique, isometric, and axonometric projections. These orthographic designs carry on the Classical/Renaissance tradition of thinking of architecture in terms of the two major parts: elevations, on the one hand, and plans, i.e., interior spaces, on the other. In a way the built American examples come even closer to the intent of the corresponding drawings than do their European counterparts. The general use of wood for structure and surfaces and the provincial simplicity of surfaces enhance the two-dimensional nature of these designs and the spaces revealed in the plans. To comprehend the building based on these drawings, we must respond to each elevation separately, and we must think in terms of elevations viewed at a midpoint, not from a position on the ground. Equally, we can read each individual chamber, but to understand the interior space we must carry the idea of the plan with us.

All that we have said about these English pattern books applies to Asher Benjamin, the author of America's first pattern book, *The Country Builder's Assistant* (first published at Greenfield in 1797), and the subsequent volumes that he published—*The Rudiments of Architecture* in Boston in 1814 and *The Practical House Carpenter* in Boston in 1830.[41] Following the approach of the earlier English pattern books, his publications were organized, first, with a presentation of design detail, ranging from columns and staircases to stairs and fireplaces, and then these detail drawings were followed by plans and elevations.

The culmination of the 18th-century pattern book tradition occurred in the designs of Samuel McIntire of Salem. Here is one instance where we, fortunately, possess a number of drawings, and we have a close knowledge of McIntire's work as a designer, master carpenter, and wood carver.[42] McIntire's drawings reveal how important drawings could be, even when the architect was in essence his own contractor/craftsman/workman. The uses to which he put his drawings fall into the traditional classical pattern—study plans and elevations, drawings to sell the project to the client, and drawings (particularly details) that in essence are working drawings. The latter two functions were probably combined on occasion: i.e., the client-presentation drawings likely served as basic working drawings. Though as a carver McIntire was intensely interested in ornament, the surfaces of his buildings remain as paper-thin planes. Horizontal floor lines, entablatures, engaged columns, and sculptured details, which are highly prominent in the elevational drawings, end up still reading as delicate pencil lines on the buildings themselves. As with other designers, before and after, McIntire's drawings provide a much more detailed view of his intent than his completed buildings do. His most important works—the competition design for the United States Capitol of 1792 and his many early studies for the Elias Derby Mansion in Salem of c. 1795-1799—exist only in drawings. Such major designs as the Lyman House at Waltham of 1793 or the Assembly House in Salem of 1796 are much more readable in drawings than in the built buildings.

The transition from the pure Georgian style to a purer version of the classical can be seen in the drawings of the physician-turned-architect William Thornton and in the architectural drawings of the painter John Trumbull.[43] Trumbull's design for an art gallery at Yale University in 1831 to house his collection of paintings places us fully in the Jeffersonian neo-classic tradition. His projected building is no longer a frontispiece in the 18th-century tradition of orthographic projection. It is presented as a piece of classical sculpture set in a landscape, similar in intent to folly or garden structure in an 18th-century English garden. Not only has the style changed, but so has the method of presentation.

The major American figure whose drawings and buildings carry us from the late 18th through the early 19th century was the Boston architect Charles Bulfinch.[44] His drawings run the full gamut of elevation/plans, cross-sectional drawings, and perspective drawings of both interior and exterior. In each of these types of drawings he changed appreciably from the earliest to the last, reflecting the general changes that occurred in rendering techniques. The linear-descriptive technique employed in the drawings for the principal facade of the Joseph Coolidge, Sr., House in Boston of 1791–1792 is really not much different from a Samuel McIntire drawing of the same period, though the esthetic intent is indeed different.[45] A later drawing, such as Bulfinch's various elevational studies for the Unitarian Church in Washington, D.C., of 1821–1822, delineates not surfaces as such, but planes, which when read together present articulated volumes. Bulfinch's perspective drawings seem to undergo a similar change: from early drawings that convincingly present a major facade to structures that are set in a landscape.[46]

The paramount importance of drawings, especially to the gentleman architect, is beautifully illustrated in the architectural career of Thomas Jefferson. For a self-trained draftsman, Jefferson produced a number of remarkably sophisticated drawings—sophisticated in technique and sophisticated as an index of his intent in design.[47] His elevational drawing and floor plans of 1771–1772 for his first Monticello illustrate how fully he had absorbed the principal lessons of Palladio.[48] His fascination with questions of pure forms, of proportions and ratios, cannot be fully appreciated in his realized buildings; but it can be sensed in his drawings. The sphere and the circle as a conditioner of ideal forms is revealed in his c. 1778 study for a decorative outchamber and again many years later in the design for the Rotunda (library) at the University of Virginia c. 1821. In all his drawings Jefferson relied on line, on occasion reinforced by 45° parallel lines to emphasize wall thickness. His lines though, even more than Bulfinch's, represent highly abstract three-dimensional intensions, not representations of frontispiece facades.

During his stay in Paris in the 1780s Jefferson became one of the first designers to adopt the use of lined graph paper.[49] The squared graph paper provided him with a preordered world within (not onto) which he could create his own definitions of space. Peter Collins has pointed out that Jefferson's use of squared graph paper was one of those 18th–19th-century steps that lead onward and upward to the modular systems employed in our century.[50] But in Jefferson's case (like that of Le Corbusier), the graph paper acts as a pair of glasses through which we see the underlying order.

The complexity and subtlety of Jefferson's intentions can only be surmised in his realized buildings. In his drawings it is all set out in the open, and it is so clear. For Monticello of 1768–1809; Barboursville, Orange County, Virginia, c. 1817; and the University of Virginia in Charlottesville of 1817–1826, we possess drawings that make it possible for us to understand the abstract ideas that interested him. In the case of the octagonal design for his own retreat of Poplar Forest, near Lynchburg of 1806, we have only the drawings attributed to Cornelia R. Randolph and a house that was rebuilt after a fire in 1845.[51] Knowing Jefferson's other drawings, it is apparent that we can only speculate as to how he envisaged the centralized octagonal form to realize what was surely an intricate series of ideas.

It was Benjamin Henry Latrobe who took Jefferson's ideologically oriented designs and carried them over into the realm of professional architecture.[52] Latrobe also bridged other

6

7

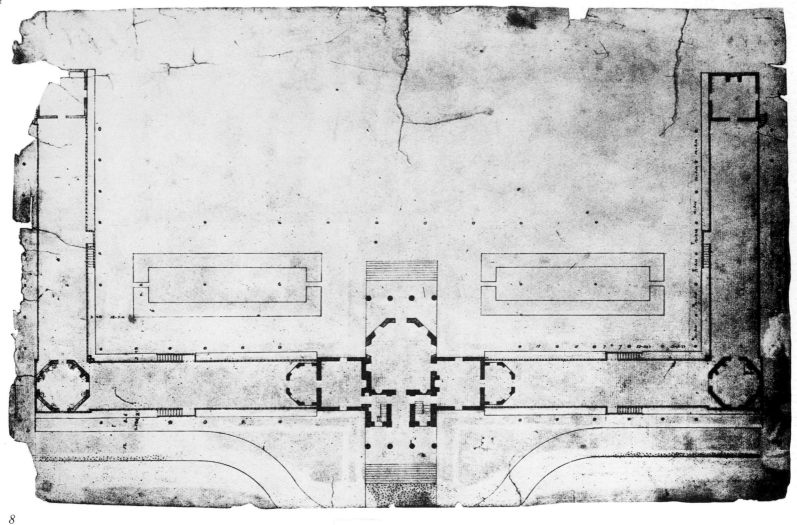

8

8 *Thomas Jefferson, Monticello, first floor plan and dependencies, Charlottesville, Virginia, c. 1771–1772. Courtesy The Massachusetts Historical Society.*

9 *Thomas Jefferson, a decorative outchamber, c. 1778. Courtesy The Massachusetts Historical Society.*

10 *Benjamin Latrobe, Robert Liston House. From Sidney Fiske Kimball,* Domestic Architecture of the American Colonies and of the Early Republic, *Charles Scribner's & Sons, 1922; reprint, Dover Publications, 1950.*

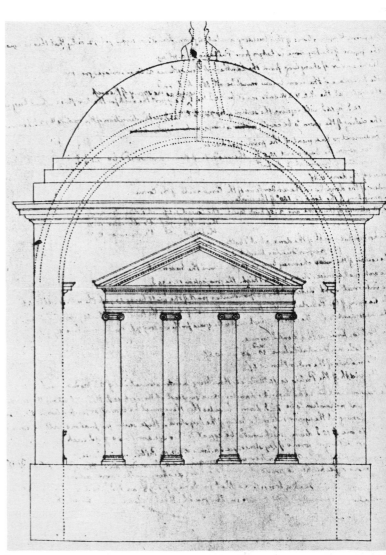

9

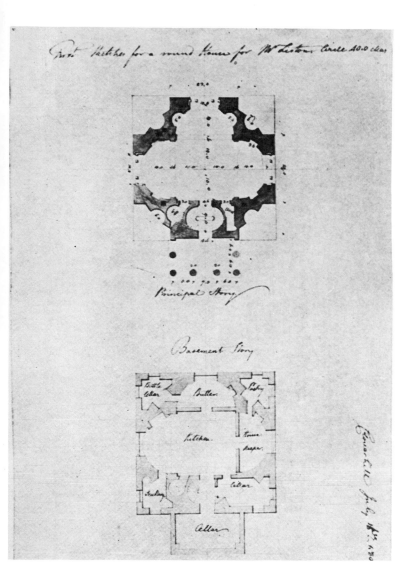

aspects of 18th- and 19th-century architecture. He was the first major American figure to utilize the Greek and neo-Classical Revivals, making them an integral part of the English picturesque tradition. Many of his designs mirror the same concern with abstract shapes and spaces as in the work of Etienne-Louis Boullée, Claude-Nicholas Ledoux, and Jean-Jacques Lequeu in France or of Joseph Gandy and John Soane in England.[53]

But there was a major difference. Latrobe's drawing indicates that his ideals of form and space were conceived as being situated in a landscape—and in most instances, in a specific landscape. The building set in a landscape occurs not only in his many perspective sketches and drawings, but also in many of his elevational and even cross-sectional drawings. His studies of interior spaces, whether perspective or orthographic, are in essence enclosed spatial landscapes. But it should be noted that his involvement with the landscape tradition was not fundamentally a romantic one. The element of landscapes provided him with a tool to indicate the specific place where his intellectual exercise would take place. A study of Latrobe's drawings indicates that for him architecture was an intellectual process; the visual (shapes, forms, spaces) was a means to express formal ideas. This primary intent on his part is only partially apparent in his built buildings, whereas it openly confronts us in his drawings.

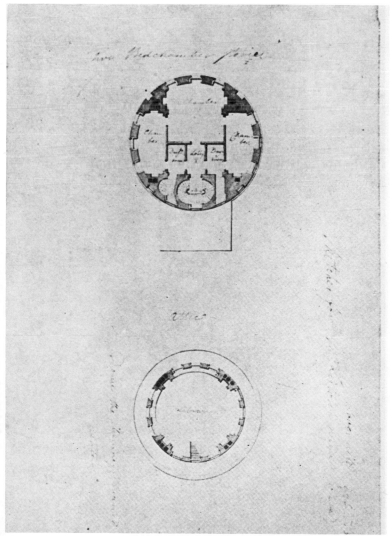

11 *Alexander Jackson Davis and John Notman, a gardener's cottage, c. 1837. From A. J. Downing,* A Treatise on the Theory and Practice of Landscape Gardening, *Saxton, 1849.*

1820-1861

Perhaps the most potent of the architectural ideals of the first half of the 19th century is beautifully summed up in A. J. Downing's comment that "*Architectural beauty* must be considered conjointly with the *beauty of the landscape* or situation."[54] The architectural drawings that A. J. Davis and John Notman provided for Downing's influential *A Treatise on the Theory and Practice of Landscape Gardening* (first published in 1849) carried out the Romantic picturesque tradition for which Downing was arguing.[55] The buildings depicted in these drawings are subservient to nature. Atmospheric conditions expressed by dark, forbidding clouds and approaching storms suggest not only situation but time. The presence of occasional animals and above all human forms is a device used to draw the viewer into the projected scene. The building emerges as one and only one element in an emotional scene. The drawing demands our attention through two devices: the painterly pictorial scene (visual) and the use of historic remembrances in the building. Such a use of architecture, and above all of past architectural symbols, is completely the opposite of Jefferson's or Latrobe's intellectualism.

In an actual urban situation Downing's picturesque mode was appreciably compromised. Although it could be argued that there is a reasonable relation between a Tuscan villa by Town & Davis and the drawing for it, there could not be the same relationship of a drawing to a building placed in an urban environment. To comprehend what Town & Davis intended in their amphiprostyle Doric temple that posed as the United States Custom House of 1833–1842 in New York, we must look at their perspective and cross-section drawings.[56] In the perspective drawing the delineator hinted at the urban scene by his reference to the stone streets surrounding the structure, its lack of any reference to nature (i.e., terrain and vegetation), and the importance of a dark, brooding sky. Accentuated darks and lights provide us with the suggestion of a romantic passage through the interior spaces of the building. Neither of these experiences could ever have been possible in the completed building, even if the building had been completed as Town & Davis had originally designed it. Yet the building for the urban landscape was not rendered differently from the villa in the garden.

The drawings of William Strickland and Robert Mills occasionally serve a similar purpose.[57] While Strickland's competition drawings for the Egyptian Gate to Laurel Hill Cemetery in Philadelphia, c. 1836, concentrate our attention on the structure, its foreground and forested background is pure Downingesque. His perspective drawing for the Girard College Competition of 1833 is less successful as a Romantic picturesque statement than Town & Davis's drawings for the New York Customs House. Still Stickland's intent is basically the same as that of Town & Davis. His Romantic picturesque intent comes through strongly in his drawings. His low horizon line and distance from the viewer create a strong although not specific reference to an object in space.

The Romantic picturesque tradition just touched upon, which was so clearly expressed in many architectural drawings, did not entirely supersede the ideological idealism of Jefferson or the surface orientation of Bulfinch and others. Robert Mills, who had been associated with Jefferson, took his ideological forms through the decades after 1820. But like Latrobe his involvement was with the abstract form, not the abstract content. His intent was singularly architectural. On first glance his drawings for the octagonal Unitarian Church in Philadelphia, c. 1813, or his drawing for the Washington Monument in Washington, D.C., of 1833, seem to share intent with Jefferson and Latrobe. But his purpose, which comes close to being academic, is in the correctness of the forms, not of the idea that lay behind them.

Thomas U. Walter, whom we know primarily for his work on the dome of the U.S. Capitol in Washington, mildly adhered to Downing's picturesque intent.[58] Stronger in commitment were the designs of Calvert Vaux and the pattern book drawings of Minard Lafever.[59] Lafever in his *The Architectural Instructor*, published in New York in 1856, employed both elevational drawings with plans and perspective drawings to convey his intent. His orthographic drawings seldom denote place, but his use of shadows and of gradation washes went a long way to create a romantic mood, which alludes to the drawing more as a

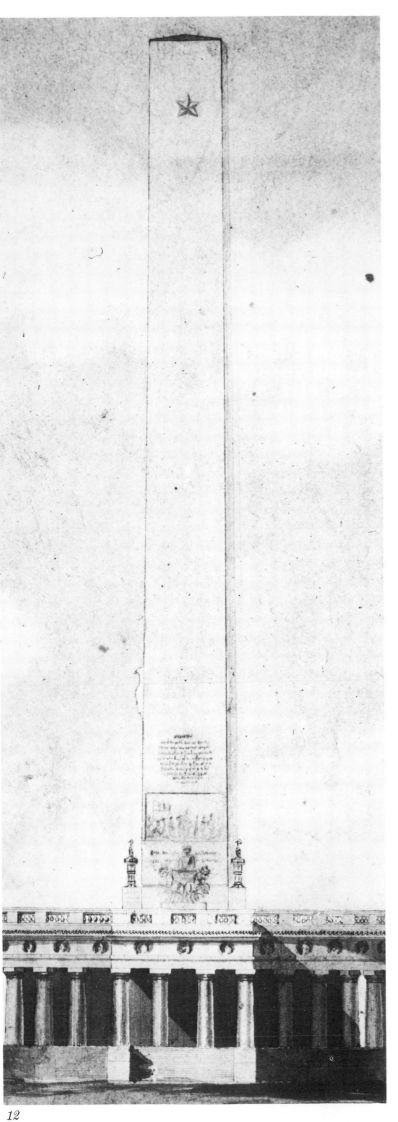

12

13

12 *Robert Mills, first scheme for the Washington Monument, Washington, D.C., 1833. Courtesy The Library of Congress.*

13 *Minard Lafever, design for a monument to George Washington, 1847. From Jacob Landy,* The Architecture of Minard Lafever, *Columbia University Press, 1970.*

picture than as a building. Lafever's perspective drawings fully embrace the Romantic picturesque tradition. He poses his "Design for a Monument to George Washington" of 1847 in the Egyptian Revival style in a forlorn field with a threatening sky; dusk seems to be falling in his drawings for the Brooklyn Savings Bank of 1846–1847 and for Packer Collegiate Institute in Brooklyn of 1854–1856.

Just as Latrobe bridges the late 18th and the first decades of the 19th century, so Richard Upjohn performs a similar function between the pre- and post-1850 decades.[60] Like Latrobe, Upjohn's intent was exclusively architectural (i.e., visual). Also as with Latrobe his drawings are highly varied both in technique and in intent. Upjohn's perspective drawing for Trinity Church in New York of 1846, with its moody graveyard and forested landscape, could well illustrate a macabre story of his contemporary, Edgar Allen Poe.[61] Other of his drawings seem to suggest a far away fairytale land. This implication of a more idyllic, far distant land is revealed in such drawings as his elevational studies for Dr. Polter's Presbyterian Church in New York of 1844, for Jubilee College in Robin's Nest, Illinois, of 1844, and for St. Paul's Church in Buffalo of 1850–1851.

After 1850 intent in American architecture took another direction; this change was mirrored in Upjohn's work and drawings. In his earlier drawings and completed buildings Upjohn advocated his own personal version of the Downingesque principles of the Romantic picturesque. These earlier designs of Upjohn were conceived as a unified whole, which was subservient to the site and nature. In the 1850s he began to produce buildings that emphasized a thin, volumetric enclosure with historic details seemingly hung on their surfaces, as one might fill a bric-a-brac whatnot or hang an ornate framed easel painting. This is apparent in the drawings presented in his 1852 *Upjohn's Rural Architecture*, published in New York. The churches and other buildings presented in this book appear to float lightly over their sites, in the fashion of a mid-20th-century mobile home, to be as and not as parts of romantic landscapes. Though Upjohn's favored style in these drawings was Gothic, the approach that he (and even more the later work of his son Richard M. Upjohn) came to characterize was the Stick, Eastlake, and Queen Anne Revival styles of the later 19th century.[62]

14

14 *"Suburban Architecture," 1888. From* Carpentry and Building, *April 1888.*

15 *Charles Edward Parker, "Chapel Near Boston," c. 1878. From* American Architect and Building News, *June 1, 1878.*

16 *H. Hudson Holly, "Design No. 11," 1878. From H. Hudson Holly,* Modern Dwellings for Town and Country, *Harper, 1878.*

1862-1889

For the American architectural profession the three decades from the mid-1860s on through the early 1890s was a period of immense change. Architecture as a profession became more firmly entrenched. The architect began to create a self-image as the businessperson/designer. The architectural office as a small-scaled bureaucracy (matching what was happening first in business and later in government) came into being. Changes in technology and materials meant that everything had to be outlined and explained. Government, at least on a local level, began to actively get involved with questions of structure on the grounds of public safety. In many instances the client-architect relationship shifted and became increasingly impersonal.

Within the profession the apprenticeship system still persisted, but it slowly began to be supplemented by formal education in architecture and engineering, either here in the U.S. or abroad, especially from the 1880s on in Paris. In New York in 1857, a group of architects organized the American Institute of Architects, and in 1876 the first major architectural journal— *The American Architect and Building News*—began publication in Boston.[63] By the mid-seventies photomechanical methods had been developed so that it was economically possible to publish original drawings. This process was expanded so that by the 1880s it was possible to publish remarkably precise photographs in magazines and books. With the growth of large-sized offices handling a substantial volume of work, it became increasingly advantageous to employ professional renderers who could produce impressive formal drawings used to sell the product to the customer and/or to advertise the firm through publications.

All these changes decidedly affected the uses to which architectural drawings were put. It was in the 1870s and 1880s that the threefold division of architectural drawings became fully solidified. In the larger offices the principal(s) would supposedly produce the underlying concept of the building through sketches. After this had been worked out, formalized presentation drawings would then be made by a skilled draftsperson in the office or by an itinerant delineator; and when this had been approved by the client, working drawings would be produced.[64] As we have pointed out earlier, the working drawings assumed prominence in the drawing world; they became the document that connected the architect, client, government, and contractor.

The first two aspects of drawing—preliminary sketches and especially presentation drawings—continued to have a loose tie with High Art drawing and painting. In the late 19th century, architectural drawings were, like paintings, dramatically affected by the new art of photography as well as methods developed for their reproduction in magazines and books.

The magazines aimed at carpenter/builders, such as *The Builder and Wood-worker,* published in New York beginning in 1868, and *Carpentry and Building* started in 1877 in New York, followed the same pattern as the more pretentious "professional" journal, *The American Architect and Building News,* by relying primarily on a formal perspective drawing. The popular magazines had a tendency either to supplement or to rely more heavily on elevational drawings and plans. Quite often all four elevations plus the roof plan and some interior detailing would be illustrated—bringing the world of presentation drawings very close to that of working drawings.

The ever-increasing number of pattern books kept up remarkably well with changes in architectural drawing fashion. Those of the 1860s like George E. and F. W. Woodword's *Country Homes,* published in New York in 1866, or Samuel Sloan's *Homestead Architecture,* published in Philadelphia in 1861, continue Downing's basic reliance on perspective drawings.[65] Later pattern book authors went off in several different directions. Some continued to use numerous perspective drawings to convey the sense or the atmosphere of their designs. H. Hudson Holly's *Modern Dwellings for Town and Country,* published in New York in 1878, employed only perspective drawings with plans, and both text and drawings seem to be aimed at potential clients rather than the carpenter/ builder architect. Though Louis H. Gibson entitled his popular volume *Convenient Houses with Fifty Plans for the Housekeeper,* published in New York in 1889, it was essentially directed to the builder. Gibson put his primary reliance on elevational drawings and floor plans; in addition his volume was one of the earliest pattern books to use photographs.[66]

15

16

17

The characteristic method of presentation in the pages of *The American Architect and Building News* was a perspective drawing, usually accompanied by a small insert drawing of the principal floor plan. The point (or points) employed in the perspective drawing was at eye level—as it would normally be seen. The principal facade was given prime emphasis in most cases, and a suggestion was always made about the specifics of place. Though most of the buildings could well be considered Romantic, the drawings tend toward dryness and neutrality. Dark and light areas are there, but minimized; atmospheric effects are not present. Although the location of the building is indicated, nature as such is basically ignored. Compared with architectural drawings published during the first half of the 19th century, later drawings placed greater emphasis on interior space and upon an assembly of details. In the 1870s and 1880s elaborate drawings of interiors were published; interior details and elevations often occupied entire pages.

By 1890 several changes had occurred. Many of the perspective drawings of Colonial Revival/Shingle Style dwellings were purposely sketchy and far less descriptive of specifics than had generally been the case before. Nature returned as an important ingredient—the delineated building is reduced in size within the drawing and an emphasis placed upon the site, vegetation, and sky—and the observer in many instances viewed the building and its site from an appreciable distance. Atmosphere also began to reenter the drawings, especially those delineated by Harvey Ellis. Some of Ellis's drawings seem to inhabit a Pre-Raphaelite, almost proto-Art Nouveau space.[67] Finally, as we have already noted in later pattern books, photographs were introduced in *The American Architect and Building News* and other journals. At first these photographs were composed and then printed in a fashion similar to that of drawings. The photograph itself reflected the approach that a draftsperson might take when producing a perspective drawing. The buildings were shown obliquely, with an emphasis on one facade. Dark and light shadow contrasts were low keyed, and the skies were generally removed.

How effective an elevational sketch can be in formulating and revealing a highly sculptural architectural image can be seen in the drawings of Frank Furness.[68] His small conceptual elevational drawings reveal his intent as powerfully as the built product. In the finished product his bold, heavy masses are defined by smooth surfaces into which and out of which shapes were sharply gouged or projected. In his drawings the surfaces are as agitated as the details, and the brittle, sharp, angular quality present in his constructed buildings is only one of many elements found in his conceptual drawings.

The presentation drawings of the Furness firm (Furness & Hewitt) occupy a strange middle ground between the conceptual sketches and the realized building.[69] Neither the presentation drawings nor the working drawings make the architect's intention readily apparent. Furness's often reproduced colored ink and wash drawing of the Broad Street facade of the Pennsylvania Academy of Fine Arts of 1873 or of his 21st Street Armory in Philadelphia of 1874 certainly does not disclose what greets the viewer who experiences the buildings. Furness then appears to have used the formal presentation drawing (usually an elevation, rather than a perspective drawing) as a neutral contract tool—between his highly important conceptual sketch and the realized building.

Harvey Ellis takes us directly into the complexity of the 19th-century architectural office and the problems that such offices pose in trying to establish responsibility for design.[70] In the usual 19th-century offices we should be able to assume that the principal(s) exercised sufficient control over the designs and their production process so that whatever was produced was indeed theirs. But in the case of itinerant designers/draftsmen such as Ellis, it is apparent that their presence in an office injected a new architectural point of view that often came to dominate the designs from that office.[71] Ellis and others like him were brought into an architectural office for two purposes: to design and to produce presentation drawings that would help sell the product. In his work for the Minneapolis architect LeRoy Sunderland Buffington and for several other midwestern firms, Ellis ended up being in fact the principal designer. His beautiful presentation drawings brought these firms national attention, because of both the quality of his design and his finesse as a delineator.[72]

Ellis's mode of participating in design meant that his

18

17   *Frank Furness, Guarantee Trust and Safe Deposit Co.,
Philadelphia, 1873. From James F. O'Gorman,* The
Architecture of Frank Furness, *Philadelphia Museum
of Art, 1973.*

18   *Harvey Ellis for LeRoy S. Buffington, "A Study for a
Dining Room," 1888. Courtesy Northwest Architectural
Archives, University of Minnesota, Minneapolis, Minnesota.*

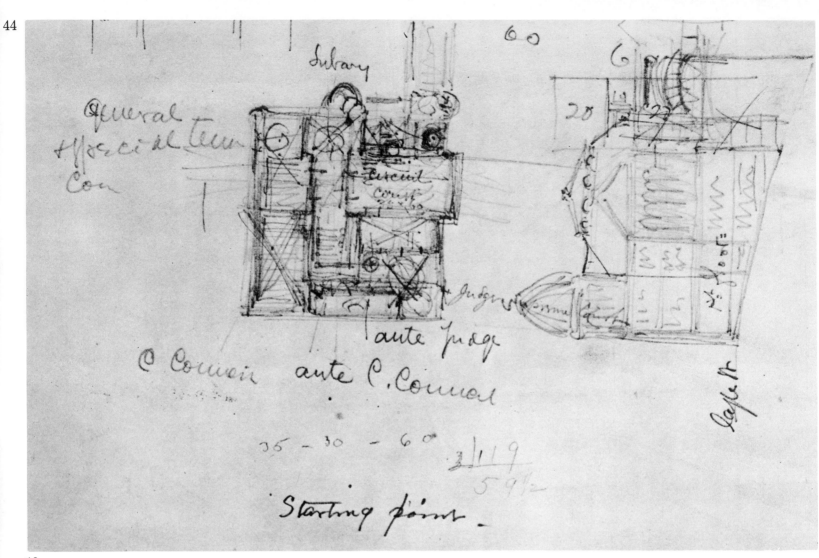

19

19 *Henry Hobson Richardson, Albany City Hall, Albany, New York, 1880–1882. From James F. O'Gorman,* Henry Hobson Richardson, *Harvard College Library, 1974.*

architectural intent must be judged solely through his drawings and not in the buildings derived from his designs. Not one of the buildings constructed from his designs for the Buffington office or the St. Paul offices of J. Walter Stevens or Mould & McNichol conveys anything approaching the vigor of his designs as shown in his drawings. The reason for this discrepancy is complex. In his drawing Ellis created an overall atmosphere that is not of the real, everyday world. He suggested sculptural masses that could have been built in the 1880s, if cost were of no consideration. But perhaps the major reason for Ellis's inability to realize his intent in a finished building was that he was apparently not in control of the design process as it flowed through the office. Elements of design that were of major importance in a project were watered down and eliminated. In fact this may be due to the nature of Ellis's position in the architectural office, but in part it was probably an outcome of the lack of staying power. The minute attention needed to pursue the design through working drawings and specifications, and then closely supervise construction, did not seem to be the sort of activity that appealed to or was within Ellis's grasp.

A person who is in striking contrast with Ellis is the Boston architect Henry Hobson Richardson, who was the most influential figure of the 1880s in American architecture. From his office stemmed the Romanesque Revival, which established such a strong hold on America at that time. Equally important were his contributions to the Queen Anne Revival and the Colonial Revival/Shingle Style.[73] In the case of Richardson we are fortunate to possess two superb monographs on the architect and his work; in addition we have a fairly full array of his architectural drawing.[74] His office practice and its use of drawings has been the subject of a recent exhibition and catalog, so we now have a reasonable knowledge of his work.[75] Here we have one major American architect from whom we can gain a close look at how architectural drawings were used.

Though Richardson was trained at the École des Beaux-Arts in Paris, formal presentation drawings were of little interest to him, nor did they loom large in the office practice. Within his office Richardson established each of the designs, first by his conceptual sketches and then by his ability to follow the design through the process of presentation drawings, working drawings, and final construction. James F. O'Gorman, who organized the 1975 exhibition of Richardson's drawings, convincingly argues that we should view all the office drawings as an expression of Richardson's intent, whether he in fact put pen and pencil to paper or not.[76] In a sense this is true, especially if we are to judge Richardson's intent exclusively through his built buildings. But once again a strong case could be made that Richardson's small sketches of floor plans and elevations say more about his intent than any one of his impressive completed buildings. His 3¼ x 6 inch/7.6 x 15.2 centimeter pencil and ink sketch of the plan for Trinity Church in Boston of 1872–1877 discloses a sense of strength, solidity, and spatial organization only partially present in the finished building. That Richardson and his staff could proceed from a small conceptual sketch and maintain much of its integrity through the elaborate drawing and supervision process to produce monuments such as Trinity Church, the Ames Gatehouse of North Easton in 1880–1881, or the Crane Memorial Library at Quincy in 1880–1883 was a remarkable feat. But this fact does not in any way diminish the primacy of the original conceptual sketch.

The drawings from Richardson's hand also belie another myth about design that has been applied to him and others. Namely, that he established his design exclusively through the plan and then went on to elevation studies.[77] In Richardson's case the argument for the primacy of the plan is based on two considerations. First, if emphasis is placed on the plan, a strong argument could be made that the design was an outcome of functional considerations. Second, among Richardson's conceptual sketches, drawings of plans predominate over elevations. But a close study of the plans shows that when Richardson drew them he was thinking of the whole building — of interior spaces and the building existing in space. As a vehicle the plan can convey the intent and its ramifications to a greater extent than any other drawing type. Richardson's reliance on the plan should not then be thought of as an indication of the primacy of functionalism in his interests. The close relationship between plan and elevation is evident in those instances where both occur in a single drawing. In his sketch for the Albany City Hall of 1880–1882, the Crane Memorial

Library, and the North Easton Railroad Station in Massachusetts of 1881–1884, the plan and the elevational studies are molded into a single statement.

Drawings for Queen Anne/Shingle Style houses closely mirror what happened to the style itself. The first examples of the style realized in Henry H. Richardson's Watts Sherman House of 1874 in Newport, Rhode Island; McKim, Mead, & Bigelow's House on Long Island in 1879–1880; or "The Craigs" of Bruce Price at Mount Desert, Maine, of 1879–1880 were published via precise, crisp elevational and perspective drawings.[78] The sites were indicated in these drawings, but the buildings predominated. None of the buildings is one with its site; rather in the fashion of most Eastlake and Queen Anne buildings, they float gently on top of the contoured site. By the 1880s looser drawing techniques for suburban dwellings are found more and more often in the pages of the architectural journals. William Ralph Emerson, Wilson Eyre, Bruce Price, and John Calvin Stevens conveyed their nostalgic and Romantic dwellings through sketches that were in themselves informal.[79] The sketches were not meant to be read as drawings for proposed buildings, but as picturesque sketches of buildings in a landscape. These published drawings are similar in mood to drawings that were then being published of examples of 18th-century American "Colonial" architecture.

PLAN AT STREET LEVEL
ONE INCH SIXTY FOUR FEET

McKIM, MEAD AND WHITE
ARCHITECTS

·NEW YORK TERMINAL STATION – PENNSYLVANIA RAILROAD·

20

20 *McKim, Mead, & White, Pennsylvania Station, New York City, 1906. From* The American Architect, *October 1910.*

21 *John Russell Pope, "Competition for Newark Memorial Building," Newark, New Jersey, 1915–1916. From* The American Architect, *October 11, 1916.*

22 *John Russell Pope, "Competition for Newark Memorial Building," Newark, New Jersey, 1915–1916. From* The American Architect, *October 11, 1916.*

1890-1919

We tend to think of the 1890s as the beginning of the strong Beaux-Arts movement in American architecture. The classical "White City" created for the World's Columbian Exposition at Chicago in 1893 did indeed set the stage for what was to follow, particularly for large-scale buildings for business and government. But the openly Romantic tradition of the 1880s continued on through the next decade, and it provided a basis for the Craftsman movement that developed after 1900. By the early years of this century each of these architectural points of view had arrived at an essentially set series of conventions for conveying their ideas through architectural drawings. The drawings of these years also illustrate the intensity of interchange that occurred between the supposedly opposite points of view of the urban Beaux-Arts and the suburban Craftsman movement.

The Parisian Beaux-Art educational system placed its major emphasis on drawing, as an instrument to express a concept fully and quickly, as well as to produce a highly polished formal drawing.[80] Within the Beaux-Arts system it was the plan that conveyed the governing intent. If the plan was adequately conceived, then everything else would logically fall into place. Since logic, in fact everything rational, was a cardinal principle of the Beaux-Arts, the orthographic projection of the plan provided the best vehicle to assert these abstract ideas. The students at the Ecole des Beaux-Arts in Paris were taught through the plan, supplemented in a minor way by elevational studies. Perspective drawings were seldom used. Only when the student had graduated and gone out into the real world of building did he or she begin to rely on perspective drawings. And then the perspective drawing was almost exclusively a sales device aimed at the client. Superb elevational, cross-sectional drawings and plans continued to be produced, but these were directed to other architectural professionals, not the general public. The major American Beaux-Arts architectural firms—McKim, Mead & White and Daniel H. Burnham & Company—came to depend not on drawings, but on photographs to present their work in the architectural journals.[81] When these prestigious firms did publish drawings, they tended to be floor plans and elevational drawings that could accompany the photographs.

Until quite recently we have reconstructed the architectural history of the three decades after 1890 as a world peopled by the Beaux-Arts reactionaries (the "bad guys") versus the Midwest and West Coast progressives (the "good guys"). Visually and conceptually we now sense that such a simplistic view of this period creates a world that simply never existed. The drawings produced by these architects show how many ideals were commonly shared by all the practitioners. Louis H. Sullivan, himself a product of the École des Beaux-Arts, used drawings in a fashion identical to that of his supposed adversaries McKim, Mead, & White, among others. The few conceptual sketches we possess of Sullivan's are remarkably close to those of H. H. Richardson. His drawings for ornament carry on the Parisian Beaux-Arts technique and purposes; i.e., they seek to complement the building and its decoration. The publication of drawings of the firm of Adler & Sullivan followed the usual pattern of the 1880s and early 1890s—perspective drawings accompanied by plans. By the 1890s (the firm was dissolved in 1894) elevational and cross-sectional drawings were published either alone or with photographs. The late work of Sullivan produced after 1900 was almost exclusively published via photographs. His famous National Farmers' Bank at Owatonna, Minnesota, of 1907–1908 or his Babson House at Riverside, Illinois, in 1907 were presented not by drawings (except the floor plans), but by interior and exterior photographs.

The younger Midwestern progressives, centering around Frank Lloyd Wright, placed a far greater emphasis on drawing than did Sullivan or the out-and-out proponents of the Beaux-Arts. It was almost as if they were going to out–Beaux-Arts the Beaux-Arters, though it must readily be pointed out that the drawings themselves, their reason for using them, and their content were not solely classical and academic. Yet in Wright's work, the plan occupies the same preeminence as it does in the Beaux-Arts. His classic Prairie House of the years 1900 through 1910 lets the axis and cross axis govern his design just as a student at the Beaux-Arts would. Wright's drawings of plans end up being both visual and conceptual documents that do not need either drawings or the built building to explain them. On

21

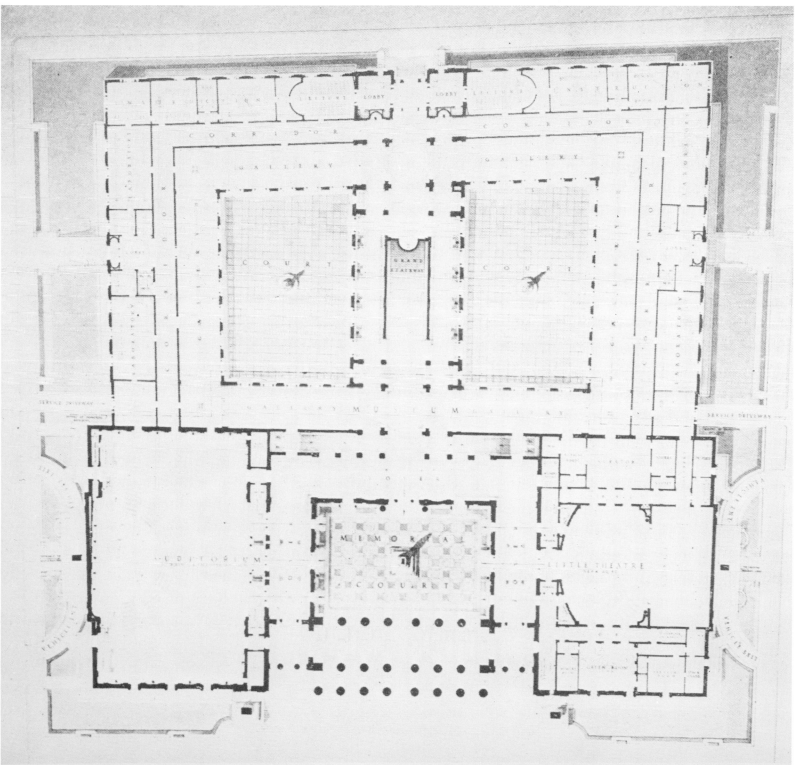

22

23   Louis H. Sullivan, design for a screen for Andrew
O'Connor, Jr., Sculptor, 1922. Courtesy University of
Michigan.

24   Louis H. Sullivan (George G. Elmslie), Bayard Building,
New York City, 1897–1898.

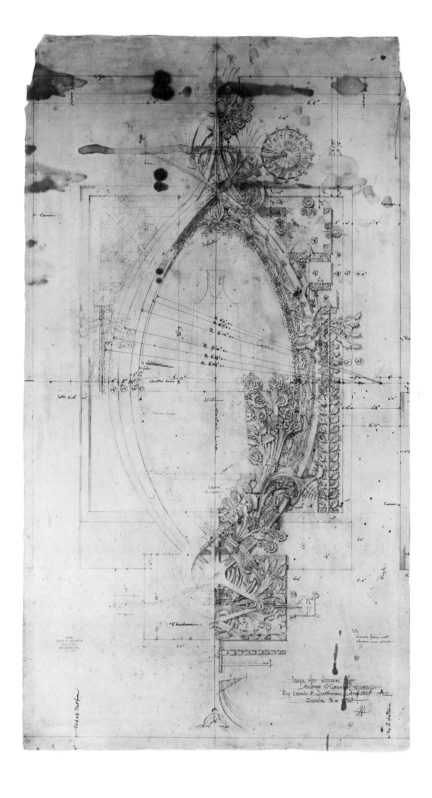

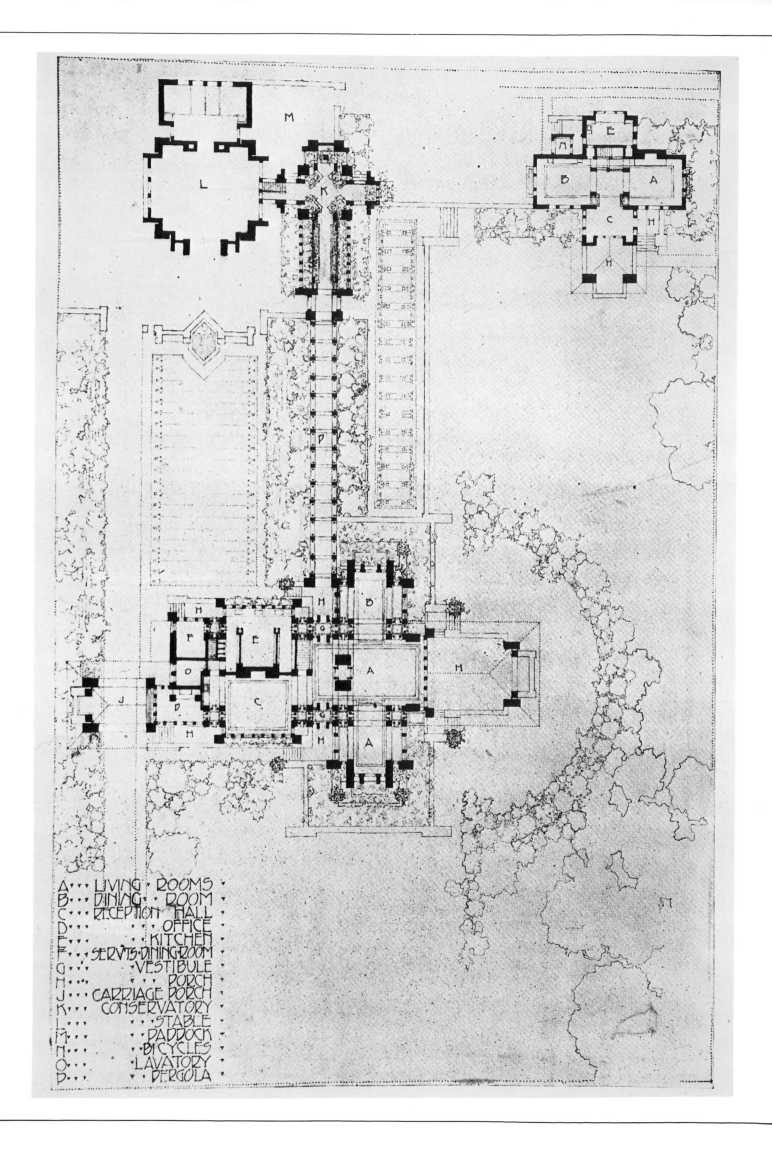

A···LIVING·ROOMS·
B···DINING·ROOM·
C···RECEPTION·HALL·
D···········OFFICE·
E···········KITCHEN·
F···SERVTS·DINING·ROOM·
G···········VESTIBULE·
H···········PORCH·
J···CARRIAGE·PORCH·
K···CONSERVATORY·
L···········STABLE·
M···········PADDOCK·
N···········BICYCLES·
O···········LAVATORY·
P···········PERGOLA·

the contrary the built building, whether the Martin House of 1904 in Buffalo or the Coonley House in Riverside, Illinois of 1908 can only be fully understood when we are aware of the plan and the site plan.

In the extensive 1901 presentation of Wright's design in *The Architectural Review* of Boston, he relied heavily on drawings.[82] In his 1908 *Architectural Record* article, "In the Cause of Architecture," Wright followed the fashion of the time by illustrating his buildings primarily with photographs.[83] But when it came to stating his basic conceptual views in the sumptuous Wasmuth portfolios, drawings were used exclusively.[84]

In a similar way drawings came to be used by Wright's progressive colleagues—William Drummond, Marian Mahony and Walter Burley Griffin, and Purcell & Elmslie.[85] In the three issues of *The Western Architect* devoted to their work, Purcell & Elmslie employed photographs and drawings, and these were arranged as a two-dimensional design on each page. Within these page designs the photographs act as, and take on many of the characteristics of, a drawing. As with Wright the most revealing element within these pages is the plans: they express the concept, and they govern the design. George Grant Elmslie's small freehand sketches for ornament, like those of Louis H. Sullivan, tell us how he began each design, how the motifs were slowly added, and how they were intertwined with one another. Without belittling the actual ornament in terra cotta, wood, or metal, these delicate freehand drawings are by far more revealing of intent. Purcell & Elmslie carried their concern for drawing—as both means and ends—into their working drawings. Along with the Greene brothers, the Griffins, and Wright, they composed contract documents so that their intent was revealed, not only in the facts openly stated, but in the total layout of each sheet. Many details were repeated to bring added emphasis, and colored inks were used —inks that would end up reading as gradations of white in the printed blueprint.

Marian Mahony Griffin and Walter Burley Griffin arranged their drawings and photographs, like Purcell & Elmslie, so that the printed page emerged as the conceptual assertion of the design. In the August 1913 issue of *The Western Architect* given over to their work, it is again the drawings that are far more effective than the photographic illustrations.[86] Their characteristic full-page drawings usually are much fuller in what they say about the design than those of either Wright or Purcell & Elmslie. The Griffins normally provide us with a perspective study, plans, elevations, and cross sections laid out as a narrow, long Japanese scroll.

Wilson Eyre is one of those figures who served as a direct bridge between the Colonial Revival/Shingle Style of the 1880s and the post-1900 Craftsman movement.[87] Eyre's designs of the 1880s, and his drawings for them, fall only marginally within the Shingle Style. These designs are picturesque, they sometimes employ shingle sheathing and Colonial detailing, and their plans are often organized around a living-hall, but they always turn out to be quite different in spirit. In part this would appear to be due to the strong English character of Eyre's designs. The real difference, though, was the outcome of his delight in a vernacular primitivism that by comparison makes the designs of John Calvin Stevens or William Ralph Emerson appear academic and sophisticated. Though Eyre was an accomplished draftsman, many of his sketches and presentation drawings seem to deliberately cultivate a feeling of crudeness, a crudeness dramatically apparent in his plans and elevations.

Cultivated primitivism was a hallmark of the American Craftsman Movement, and as was the case with Wilson Eyre, this open crudeness was expressed in most Craftsman drawings. The ink and wash presentation drawings utilized by Gustav Stickley in his magazine *The Craftsman*, published from 1901 to 1917, or in his *Craftsman Homes*, published in New York in 1909, appear to have been delineated by a home builder or carpenter.[88] Back to nature meant back to the home craftsman. Drawings of these buildings, interiors, and furniture should not be overly sophisticated. Just enough was conveyed in these drawings that no potential client of the simple life would be frightened away and think that the realization of such a dwelling would be too difficult a task.

Drawings and their place in the production of buildings was in many ways more confused and varied on the West Coast than it

26

25 *Frank Lloyd Wright, Martin House, Buffalo, New York, 1904. From* Architectural Record, *1908.*

26 *Frank Lloyd Wright, project: "Fireproof House for $5,000,"* The Ladies' Home Journal, *1907. From* Ausgeführte Bauten und Entwürfe von Frank Lloyd Wright, *Wasmuth, Berlin, 1910.*

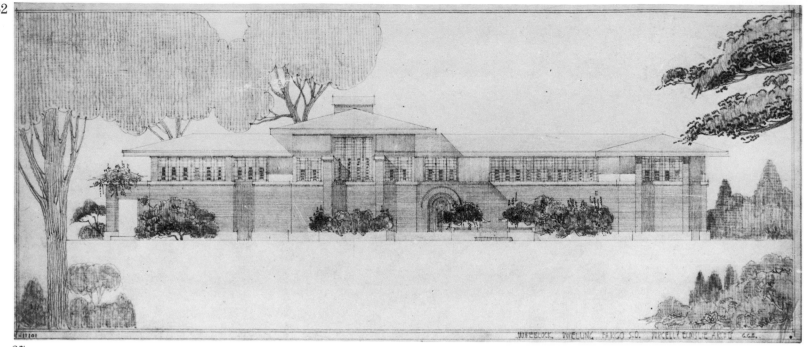

27

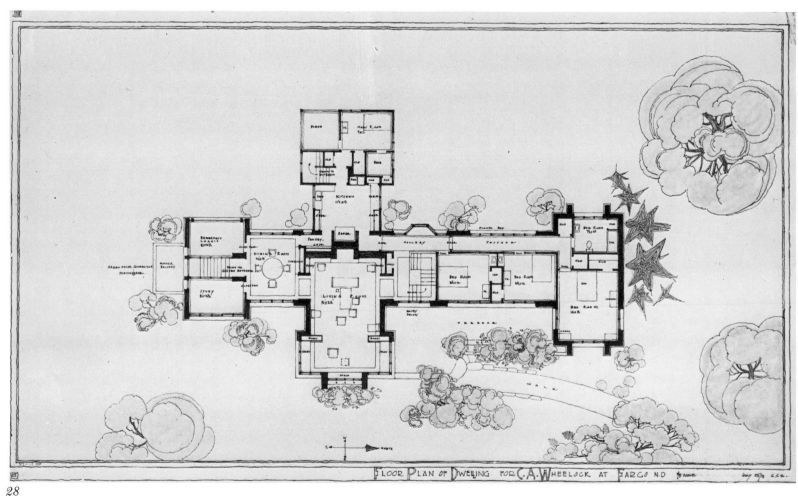

28

27 Purcell & Elmslie, project: G. A. Wheelock House, Fargo, North Dakota, 1913. Private collection.

28 Purcell & Elmslie, project: G. A. Wheelock House, Fargo, North Dakota, 1913. Private collection.

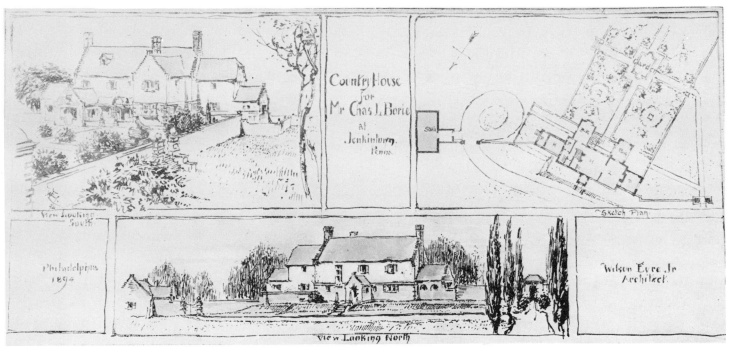

29

30

29 *Wilson Eyre, Jr., Borie House, Jenkintown,
Pennsylvania, 1894. From* The Architectural Annual,
Philadelphia, 1900.

30 *Gustav Stickley, "Open Air Dining Room," 1906. From*
Craftsman Homes, *Craftsman Publishing Co., 1909.*

54 was in the Midwest and East. The older practitioners, like the English-trained Ernest Coxhead or John Galen Howard and Willis Polk, tended to mix the pictorial tradition of the 1880s and its reliance on perspective drawings with the Beaux-Arts mode of the 1890s and 1900s.[89] Coxhead continued to carry on the Romantic pictorial intent of the 19th century. The key to his designs is to be found in his perspective and elevational drawings, not in his plans. Even after 1900 when he took over the academic Beaux-Arts as a style, his intent remained pictorial, and his sketches and presentation drawings attest to this.

Willis Polk and the younger Bernard Maybeck shared Coxhead's pictorial intent in architecture, and this is revealed in their drawings.[90] Polk, who had worked briefly in Coxhead's Los Angeles office, was an accomplished draftsman/delineator. In his own work, Polk's technique of rendering—his suggestion of a quick, loose line, his selective processes of emphasis and elimination, his strong contrasts of light and dark—closely connect him to Harvey Ellis and other delineators of the 1880s. His preferred drawing, both conceptually and as a formal rendering, was a perspective delineation of a building, placed well within the landscape. How the building established its roots in the site was obviously of paramount importance to him.

As a product of the École des Beaux-Arts, Bernard Maybeck was a skilled draftsman, but presentation drawings were insignificant in his work. What few of his buildings were published were presented by photographs accompanied by text.[91] His conceptual sketches, though, are remarkably complete in what they tell us about his concept and the process he went through to realize his designs. While there are some exceptions, a majority of his first sketches were elevations and/or perspective drawings, not plans. Maybeck's presentation drawings occupy a strange position between those vital and provocative first conceptual sketches and the final building. His presentation drawings are perfectly correct Beaux-Arts rendering. The ink lines and the intonations of wash are maneuvered in a highly competent but bland and neutral manner. No one could guess, looking at these presentation drawings, that a pictorial Romantic product would finally emerge in the completed building.

Two other West Coast figures, John Galen Howard and Julia Morgan, also fit comfortably within the turn-of-the-century Beaux-Arts tradition. Howard had, like Polk, been in Los Angeles in the late 1880s, and his sketches and presentation drawings seem to share the same pictorial attitude as those of Coxhead.[92] After his experience in the New York office of McKim, Mead, & White, he turned to the Beaux-Arts, not only as a style, but as the approach that he took to drawings.

Julia Morgan, the first woman graduate of the Beaux-Arts, was, on the surface, the complete professional Beaux-Arts architect.[93] But there was a significant limitation in her practice of architecture, and this is disclosed in her drawings as well as in her building. In contrast with the Beaux-Arts ideal, the plan was in most instances not the point of departure for her architectural ideas. An examination of her drawings reveals that the elevation was the element most carefully worked out and it was of prime importance. In abandoning the primacy of the plan she did not transfer ideological significance to these elevational studies. Thus we are left with a thoroughly competent architecture that comes quite close to being devoid of intent—or perhaps we should say an intent of substance.

Another Californian, Irving J. Gill, eschewed, as far as intent is concerned, the entire process of drawing. All the drawings from his hands—whether sketches, presentation drawings, or working drawings—are technically and conceptually poor. None of his drawings reveals his intent with the force of his realized buildings. One has to assume that his abstract concept was formed as an idea, and the drawing process generally served, like written specifications, as an objective document that one had to agonize through to realize the building.

The intent of Charles and Henry Greene of Pasadena is known to us exclusively through their built buildings or photographs of them. The publication of these woodsy bungalows of the 1900s in *The Western Architect*, *The Architectural Record*, and *The Craftsman Magazine* was with photographs accompanied once in a while by simple, nondescript drawings of plans. They did on occasion prepare presentation drawings, such as Charles Greene's drawing for the Tichenor House in Long Beach of

31

32

33

34

31 *Ernest Coxhead, study for a house, c. 1895. Courtesy John Beach, Berkeley, California.*

32 *Bernard Maybeck (Maybeck & White), project for a church complex, c. 1904.*

33 *Cass Gilbert, project: Railroad Station, New Haven, Connecticut, 1907. From* The Architectural League of New York Yearbook, *1909.*

34 *Bertram B. Goodhue, Nebraska State Capitol Building, Lincoln, Nebraska, 1916–1928. From* American Architect, *July 21, 1920.*

1904. These presentation drawings by Charles Greene are painterly rather than architecturally pictorial. Far more revealing are their working drawings into which they lavished a care for composition and detail that went far beyond the strictly utilitarian needs of a constructional document. The concern for completeness, for detail, in their working drawings is precisely the same as one finds in their built buildings. These drawings can serve as an introduction to the realized building, but they are not a substitute for the richness of intent conveyed by the buildings themselves.

As the Beaux-Arts method gained prominence in the United States after 1900, it tended to conceal from the outside world the crucial nature of drawing in the realization of a design. The preeminence of drawings remained, but with the urge to create a businesslike, practical appearing architectural practice, drawing emerged as either a selling device or as a contractual document. The great Beaux-Arters of the time—Henry Bacon, Arnold Brunner, Harold Van Buren Magonigle, Whitney Warren—all employed the plan as the generator of the design.[94] Except for large-scale competition drawings, their work was generally presented to the public or even to their colleagues through photographs.

Two major exceptions to this approach were Cass Gilbert and Bertram G. Goodhue, both of whom continued to rely on drawings to formulate their ideas and to present themselves to their professional colleagues and the public.[95] It is easy to speculate that Gilbert's and Goodhue's view of architecture and of the place of drawings within the architectural process was due to the strong hold the 19th century had on them. Cass Gilbert's designs for the Woolworth Building in New York in 1913, the earlier Minnesota State Capitol in St. Paul of 1895–1905, or the Detroit Public Library of 1921 come to life more effectively in his drawings than in the built buildings.[96] Goodhue's drawings are even stronger. His effort to contemporize both the classical and medieval traditions is brilliantly displayed in the published presentation perspective drawings for the State Capitol of Lincoln of 1916–1928, the Public Library in Los Angeles of 1925, or his many early 1920 designs for skyscrapers.[97]

Goodhue's facility with drawings was not, interestingly enough, shared by his earlier partner Ralph Adams Cram and some of the other 20th-century exponents of Medievalism. Cram's early drawings were adequate expositions of the pictorial mode of the 1880s.[98] But neither these early drawings nor his later conceptual sketches give us the slightest hint that he was a major American designer. As a Medievalist it was the built building and the craftsman process that went into the building which counted for Cram. It could well be argued that the general dryness of Cram's Gothic designs had to do with his being forced to rely on drawings, which he didn't really believe in, and on ordinary American unionized labor to realize his buildings.

35

35 *Raymond Hood (Howells & Hood), Chicago Tribune Tower Competition, Chicago, 1922. From* Tribune Tower Competition, *The Tribune Company, 1923.*

36 *Eliel Saarinen, Chicago Tribune Building Tower Competition, Chicago, 1922. From* Tribune Tower Competition, *The Tribune Company, 1923.*

1920–1944

Though eventful changes occurred in architectural design and practice between the end of the First World War and the beginning of the Second, the uses of architectural drawings changed very little. Throughout the 1920s and 1930s the Beaux-Arts, with its emphasis on drawing, remained as the central mode for architectural education and practice. Those who received their architectural education during those years emerged with a great respect for drawing. The intent of the designer was still to be realized in the initial sketches. Presentation drawings remained of major importance in selling the design, and working drawings and their accompanying written specifications became increasingly detailed and complex.

Because the 1920s was an opulent period for American architects, it should not be surprising that an increased number of firms hired professional delineators to prepare their presentation drawings. A few innovations crept in, such as the increased use of the air brush. With the higher cost of draftsmen's wages, most firms abandoned producing working drawings in ink on waxed linen. They substituted pencil on velum, which, because of the quality of reproductions available in the blueprint process, could now produce excellent copies. We have previously noted that after 1900 photography began to be the major vehicle for reproducing architecture in the major architectural magazines. The principal magazines of the twenties and thirties—*American Architect, Architectural Forum,* and *Architectural Record*—printed very few drawings. The one exception was *Pencil Points,* which was intended, as its title indicates, to be a magazine devoted primarily to architectural draftsmanship.[99] Drawings continued, of course, to be the method of presenting designs in the pattern books of these years, and drawings were extensively employed in architectural advertising.

The 1922 International Competition for the Chicago Tribune Tower provides a revealing indication of how presentation drawings were used to convey architectural intent.[100] While plans, elevation, and a cross-sectional drawing were required in the competition program, it was the exterior perspective drawing that was of paramount importance. The perspective drawing of the winning design by John Mead Howell and Raymond M. Hood employed a number of drawing techniques that beautifully conveyed the vertical linear sweep of their Gothic design. The viewer's position is at ground level, looking up at the tall, vertical tower. The thin lines and the light shading established the delicate linearity of the design. Eliel Saarinen's second prize design employs an even finer line, almost but not quite taking the building out of the real and possible world. As a drawing, the Saarinen piece is by far the finer; perhaps because it is so fine, it exists too much in the world of drawing.

The only other drawing in the Chicago Tribune Tower Competition that has the strength of Saarinen's was that submitted by Bertram G. Goodhue. His architectural intent was very different from Saarinen's. His design for a monumental structure looked at once toward the Classic, the Byzantine, and the Moderne. Instead of relying on line, Goodhue emphasized surface, using thin washes, which resulted in as subtle an effect as that achieved by Saarinen with a pen. The remaining competition drawings realized their design through a combination of washes and line or by the exclusive use of line. The selection of a linear or a painterly approach did not on the whole seem to have been equated with architectural intent, nor did the selection of the viewing point always bring out the salient characteristics of the design.

As in France and other European countries the Beaux-Arts design tradition underwent a number of changes in the two decades between the wars. The most noticeable shift was one of simplification, which led directly to an emphasis on the abstract qualities inherent in the Classical tradition. This abstracting process had begun in the early 1900s in the work of Josef Hoffmann in Vienna and Peter Behrens in Berlin, and in England in the buildings of Edwin Lutyens. In the U.S. it was Bertram G. Goodhue who after 1910 began to explore a similar approach to Classical-oriented design.

In the twenties the Beaux-Arts design approach proceeded along two principal paths. The first of these, beautifully exemplified in the work of John Russell Pope, followed a Jeffersonian course where the Classical ideals of the orders,

37

37 *Paul Cret, Pan American Union Building, Washington, D.C., 1912–1913. From* Architectural Record, *November 1913.*

proportions, and ratios were strongly adhered to.[101] The second, and by far the most widespread course followed by the Beaux-Arts, was to modify the Classical-derived imagery so that it could encompass other traditions (such as the Medieval and Byzantine), and above all so that it could absorb some of the "feel" of Moderne architecture. Paul Cret and Harold Van Buren Magonigle retained the primacy of Classical principles in their increasingly stripped designs, while Raymond M. Hood, Ely Kahn, and others let the Classical design ideals underlie their Moderne (Art Deco) buildings.[102]

As a graduate of the École des Beaux-Arts and as a teacher at the University of Pennsylvania, Paul Cret relied heavily on drawings to realize his intent.[103] His conceptual drawings include freehand sketches, measured plans, and site plans as well as elevational studies and small perspective drawings. On the conceptual level the most telling of these drawings are the site plans. The elevations and the freehand perspective drawings appear to follow the plan drawings in his design system. In contrast with many American graduates of the École des Beaux-Arts, Cret's most impressive presentation drawings are elevational, rather than perspective. These elevational drawings, dramatized by a polished finesse of lines and washes, are so impressive that it is easy to forget that they are elevational drawings. When he did present his designs through perspective drawings, they, like the completed buildings, are never as impressive as the elevational renderings.

Another index during the 1920s of American drawing and design was the competition held for the Liberty Memorial at Kansas City of 1920–1925.[104] Bertram G. Goodhue submitted elevational renderings that powerfully convey the monumentality of his approach to stripped Classical forms. Deep shadow patterns show us how each of the masses is broken up into projecting and receding blocks and how each of the principal blocks is sculpturally related to one another. The winning design by Harold Van Buren Magonigle takes this abstraction process further so that the design intent crosses over from the monumental Classic to the monumental Moderne.[105] Magonigle's presentation drawings reflect this different attitude, with surfaces emphasized as containers of volumes through strong contrasts of highlighted and dark shadow areas.

Several of Magonigle's presentation drawings for the Liberty Memorial were dramatic perspective drawings, which in themselves are really conceptual and highly abstract. They suggest some mythical world where select surfaces of the building were artificially lighted, while other surfaces remain dark, and the thrust of the building into the sky seems endless. This type of theatrical technique was utilized by a number of architects and delineators in the 1920s; foremost among them was Hugh Ferriss. This delineator, like Harvey Ellis in the late 19th century, set a fashion for presentation rendering in the 1920s that ended up strongly affecting the course of urban architectural design.[106] Ferriss's charcoal and pencil drawings have the remarkable characteristic of making the dullest project appear plausible and romantic. By highly contrasting the black and white areas of his drawing, he could emphasize certain aspects of the design and in effect eliminate or play down the rest. His sense of a highly charged atmosphere puts to shame the atmospheric effects found in the presentation drawings of the 1880s. Though Ferriss was himself an architect and occasionally served as a consulting designer, his extensive influence came about through his effective statements of design ideas published with his many drawings.[107] There is a Hollywood stage set quality about these renderings that suggest both the present world of science, technology, and business and the Buck Rogers world of the future.

Another figure who had a strong impact on the design world of the teens and twenties was the architect turned stage designer, turned mystic, Claude Bragdon. Bragdon's own architectural designs, many of which were built in Rochester, New York, in the first two decades of this century, were at best a competent but uninspired variation of the Beaux-Arts theme. But it was in the teens and twenties that he published several volumes which contain drawings that had a decided impact on the "Zigzag" Modernes (Art Deco) of the twenties.[108] The text of such a volume as Bragdon's *The Frozen Fountain*, published in New York in 1924, is pretentious and supposedly mystical, and was probably read by few people, especially not architects. But the drawings, based upon interwoven geometric shapes, contributed to motifs extensively utilized in Zigzag Moderne

38

39

40

38   *Harold Van Buren Magonigle, Liberty Memorial, Kansas City, Missouri, 1920–1921. From Talbot Hamlin,* The American Spirit in Architecture, *Yale University Press, 1926.*

39   *Hugh Ferriss, "Crowding Towers," c. 1929. From Hugh Ferris,* The Metropolis of Tomorrow, *Ives Washburn, 1929.*

40   *Claude Bragdon, "Interior," 1924. From Claude Bragdon,* The Frozen Fountain, *Alfred A. Knopf, 1932.*

41

architectural decoration and in designs employed in magazines and books.

By the end of the twenties Raymond M. Hood, whose name was so closely associated with the skyscraper frenzy of the twenties, took the design principles of the Beaux-Arts on into the Moderne without, it should be noted, letting go of any of its principles.[109] With his background in the Cram, Goodhue, & Ferguson office and at the École des Beaux-Arts in Paris, he could vary his rendering according to his architectural product. Hood could produce Beaux-Arts Classical composition through polished ink and wash drawings, or he could veer off toward the Gothic with a rendering that was thin and linear. His first sketches for the Chicago Tribune Tower Competition established a strength that was lost in his later studies, formal presentation drawings, and the building itself.[110] In Hood's first studies for the Moderne Daily News Building in New York in 1930, he laid out the design on grid paper.[111] In this grid study for the Daily News the cruciform Beaux-Arts plan dominates, and the elevational studies and small perspective sketches amplify the plan. The vertical fenestration of this building, which we today think of as such an important aspect of the building, is not suggested in this drawing.

The usage of fragments of the historic past was especially intense in the work of domestic architects of the 1920s. Whether the image was American Colonial, English and French Medieval, or Spanish and Mediterranean, it was clearly meant to fit itself into a suburban environment. Initial sketches and presentation drawings for this architecture assumed a set technique. Such drawings were loose and free, suggesting the architect's quick, sensitive, and therefore romantic effort to symbolize a nonurban world. These suburban dwellings were generally illustrated in the professional journals and popular home magazines by photographs and line plans, rather than by drawings. If one considers how completely the drawings of Mellor & Meigs, George Washington Smith and Lutah Maria Riggs, or Horace Trumbauer reveal their intent, it is surprising how few were published at the time.

The popular pattern books of the twenties and thirties normally combined photographs with perspective, elevational, and detail drawings and plans. As drawings the high point was reached in the 1940s in the pattern books published by the Boston architect Royal Barry Wills.[112] These perspective drawings for charming Cape Cod cottages and clapboard or shingle salt boxes are so enticing that even the most avid exponent of modern imagery would find it difficult to resist them. The charm together with a strong hint of nationalism of the Colonial was presented during these decades in the drawings and later the photographs of Samuel Chamberlin.[113] Chamberlin's drawings, and the many measured drawings of 18th-century American buildings published at the time, provided a frequently used source for architects, carpenter/builders, and clients.

There were very few changes in the technique and usages of drawings by those who had come to the fore as Modernists before 1920. George Grant Elmslie continued to produce his delicate linear elevational drawings, as can be seen in his design for Humboldt Park Distribution Center in Chicago c. 1924.[114] Such elevational studies, though, were based upon the plan in a full and complete Beaux-Arts manner. Elmslie's former partner, William Gray Purcell, whose intent had always remained pictorial, worked out his designs by elevations, cross sections, and then the plan.[115] His formal rendering, in contrast with Elmslie's, continued to be perspective drawings, with the building convincingly set in its environment.

Some of the most exciting drawings that came from this period were the sketches by Barry Byrne, the young Bruce Goff, and Lloyd Wright.[116] The work of all three could, at least at the beginning of the twenties, be labeled as Expressionist. Their sketches have some of the same qualities of agitation and unreality found in the drawings of Claude Bragdon. What is openly apparent in their drawings is that the Expressionistic element is an overlay underneath which the Beaux-Arts plan continues to dominate.

Frank Lloyd Wright's drawings of the twenties share this Expressionist atmosphere.[117] A significant difference, though, was Wright's continued heavy reliance on the T square and the instruments of the drafting board. If one looks at his sketches for the Barnsdall House in Los Angeles of 1917–1922, or his later projects for the desert near Chandler, Arizona, in 1927,

42

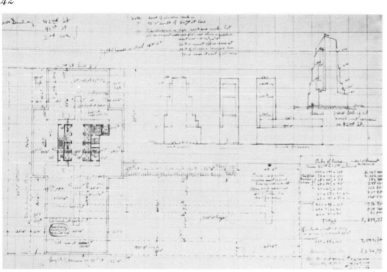

43

41　*Raymond Hood (Howells & Hood), Chicago Tribune Building, Chicago, 1922–1924. From* The American Architect, *May 1928.*

42　*Royal Barry Wills, "15,870 Square Foot Cape Cod House," c. 1944. From R. B. Wills,* Houses for Homemakers, *Franklin Watts, Inc., 1945.*

43　*Raymond Hood (Howells & Hood), Daily News Building, New York City, 1928. From* The American Architect, *May 1928.*

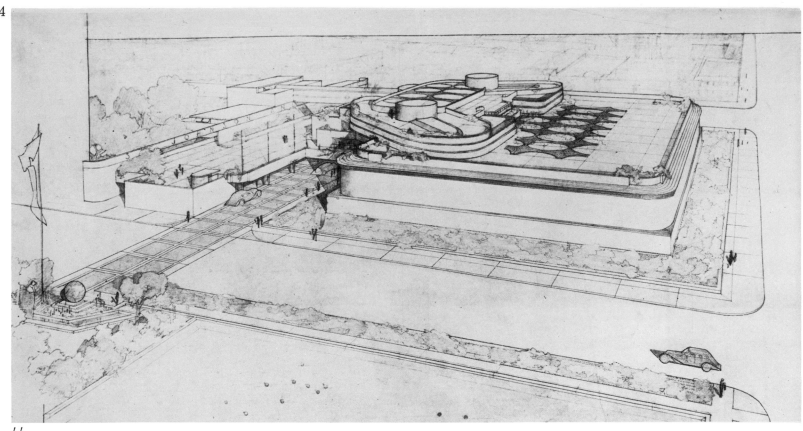

44

44   *Frank Lloyd Wright, Administration Building, Johnson's Wax Co., Racine, Wisconsin, 1936–1939. From* Architectural Forum, *January 1938.*

45   *Edward D. Stone, Goodyear House, Old Westbury, Long Island, New York, 1939. From John McAndrew,* Guide to Modern Architecture: Northeast States, *The Museum of Modern Art, 1940.*

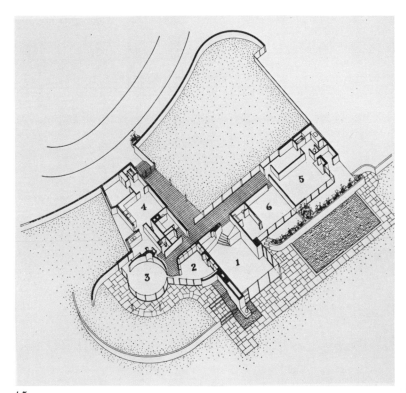

45

one feels that they are an intriguing expression of the doodles of an architect seated before his drafting board. The more developed sketches and presentation drawings seem to have needed the straight edge of the T square and triangle to enlarge and make the design more precise. Even though a number of these drawings are tinted with watercolor in a highly decorative manner, they still remain as linear products of the drafting board.

As Wright's work emerged into the 1930s his drawing board technique lent itself very effectively to the new International Style of Modernism, which he partially embraced. His lines came to describe broad, plain, cardboard-thin surfaces; they no longer concentrated on suggesting the rich, tactile quality of wood, stone, or concrete blocks. As in his Prairie years the generator of his idea remained the plan. The "Streamlined" Moderne nature of many of his 1930 designs was beautifully mirrored in many of the presentation and working drawings delineated under his direction by members of the Taliesin Fellowship.[118] Though these drawings were not produced by airbrush and ink line, they exist in the same world as the drawings of such industrial designers of the time as Norman Bel Geddes and Raymond Loewy.

Like Wright two of the early California Modernists—Richard J. Neutra and R. M. Schindler—thought in terms of the precision of the drafting board.[119] Schindler shared Wright's devotion to the plan as the governing element of design. The plan for his own house of 1921–1922 on Kings Road in Hollywood states the whole revolutionary concept of this design. No elevation, cross section, or perspective drawings are really needed to understand it. Neutra's drawings of plans point in another direction. As with many of Ludwig Mies van der Rohe's plans of the 1920s and 1930s, Neutra's pencil or ink drawings of plans come close to existing as decorative de Stijl designs. Architecturally they seem to refer to fragments, not the whole, and they are limited and marginal in what they have to say about the architect's intent. Though Neutra's sketches and drawings are accomplished and fascinating in and of themselves, they do not state his concept as well as the built building.

Because of the initial lack of commissions, study and presentation drawings assumed a major importance for young architects who began to practice during the Depression years of the 1930s. Gregory Ain, Harwell Hamilton Harris, and Raphael Soriano worked with Neutra at the beginning of the 1930s.[120] Ain and Harris, working under his direction, produced many of the drawings for Neutra's Rush City Reformed.[121] Ain's sparse, highly linear perspective presentation drawings of this decade are often similar to Schindler's in his use of a dramatic viewpoint, but they are more delicate and lighter in feeling, beautifully reflecting the fragile nature of his building. Harris had a fondness for aerial perspective views of his projected buildings, which enabled him to abstractly comment on building and site.[122] Few of the drawings of Ain, Harris, or Soriano were published, but a study of them reveals a far richer design world than is apparent in their built buildings.

In the Midwest and East the exponents of the International Style, ranging from William Lescaze, Edward D. Stone, Oscar G. Stonorov, and such Romantic Modernists as Alden Dow, published drawings rather sparingly, though conceptual sketches were still a key device in expressing their intent. Lescaze's presentation drawings varied appreciably in technique. Some employ normal eye level perspective and are almost photographic descriptions, like his drawing for the Brooklyn Children's Museum of 1937. In his published drawing for the Porter House in Ojai, California, c. 1929, his aerial view is more linear and European in feeling.[123] One of the favored presentation devices in the late thirties and forties of the Modernists was the isometric or axonometric cutaway drawing, which looked down at the building from above. The effect of these drawings is peculiar. Such drawings are not able to convey the abstract content of a plan, nor can they perform the function of either an elevational or a perspective drawing. The space that they suggest ranges somewhere between that asserted through the drawing of a plan and that revealed in a perspective rendering. The ideal of the machine and the mechanical is as much the content of these drawings as anything directly architectural.

With the coming of Mies van der Rohe to this country in 1938, some of the same qualities revealed by the cutaway isometric and axonometric drawings could be obtained by viewing the

building's interior through a glass wall. Carl Koch did this in his published drawings for his own house at Belmont, Massachusetts, in 1940.[124] The most elegant of this form of drawing was Philip Johnson's view of his own 1942 Cambridge house where he lifted the viewer above the walled courtyard and allowed a look into the whole expanse of the house through its glass wall facing south.[125] Mies' own drawings of the late thirties and early forties are far less linear than those of his American contemporaries. For the Illinois Institute of Technology he produced both elevational and perspective drawings, with the elevational drawings by far the most effective.[126] It was also in the late 1930s that Mies took over Herbert Bayer's 1920s photomontage technique, so that in his drawing for the Resor House in Jackson Hole, Wyoming, of 1938, the area of the glass infill between the vertical and horizontal steel members was filled by a photograph of the Teton Mountains. As with the cutaway isometric and axonometric drawings, the use of such a technique blurs the architectural intent by spilling over ideologically into High Art. These drawings come close to commenting more on High Art than they do on architecture.

1945-1976

The triumph of the Modern Movement after World War II
ended up producing an architectural style that while
superficially related to the earlier International Style and to the
Streamline Moderne came reasonably close to being barren of
content. The European International Style of the twenties and
thirties and its American offshoot never lost sight of the basic
allegiance of architecture to content. Those who developed the
International Style—Gropius, Le Corbusier, and Mies—were
after all products of a pre-World War I architectural education,
and while they might argue for machine production in
architecture, their real interest was that of symbolically
expressing this and other abstract concepts. The Streamline
Moderne of the industrial designers of the thirties—of Norman
Bel Geddes, Raymond Loewy, and Walter Dorwin Teague—
evolved an aerodynamic styling that while symbolizing the
anonymous in drawings and products was still heavily overlaid
with a science fiction view of the future.

The new architecture of the late forties and fifties seized upon
the element of machine anonymity, and out of this emerged
an architecture whose principal content was neutrality and
blandness. This blandness could be elegant as it was so often in
the work of Skidmore, Owings, & Merrill. But in the hands of
less skilled designers its stark interior volumes, its cardboardlike
box form, and repetitious metal curtain walls were simply a
bore.

The proponents of the 1950s Modern successfully revamped
architectural education with the Modern, seen as the sole
legitimate style at the major schools across the country.[127] The
two elements of the traditional core of pre-Modern architectural
education were the studio, where drawing was the means of
realizing a building, and the study of history, so that the
traditional, recognized images of the past might continue into the
present. One would have assumed that with the ascendancy of
Modern, both drawings and history would no longer occupy a
central position in architectural education. But, surprisingly,
this did not occur. Bannister Fletcher was simply replaced by
Siegfried Giedion, and the past to be emulated was now the
near-past of the 1920s and 1930s.

The studio phase of architectural education with its emphasis on
design remained as the core of the program. And although
students might be encouraged to make study models, drawing
remained as *the* device to express architectural intent. Certain
drawing skills were all but eliminated, especially freehand
drawing, but the formal use of drawings—as sketches and via
the drafting board—still remained. The Beaux-Arts' primacy
of the plan remained, though the Beaux-Arts' principles of
balance, symmetry, and axial organization were now eschewed
for equally inflexible Modern principles of nonsymmetry and
flowing rather than contained space. But perhaps one should
not use the term "plan," at least as it has been thought of
traditionally. The characteristic post–World War II Modern
plan concentrates on what happened to the exterior parameter
of the rectangular box and the siting of the box. The ideally
internal spaces described in the drawings were repetitious
rectangles and/or cubes, as if the repetition of the metal curtain
wall had been laid down to form the plan. The repetition of
recognizable elements is of course an old, time-honored device
in architecture. But in the past the repetition expressed in the
plan was related to the whole and to the elevations by the
abstraction of proportions and ratios. An awareness of
repetition in post-1945 Modern design then was not an open,
visual matter, but a structural one, gained primarily from
information conveyed in the drawings.

Two other characteristics were involved with repetition in
post-1945 Corporate International designs, and both of these
were well expressed in drawings of plans, elevations, cross
sections, and details. Pre-Modern design, whether Classical,
Medieval, or anything else, had been quite clear in stating that
a building must be horizontally and vertically terminated. The
denial of termination became a governing tenet of the Corporate
International Style. Now one could, at will, take out a pair of
scissors and snip off or glue on to the length, width, or height of
a building. Any terminating point was as logical as any other.

The other characteristic of repetition insisted upon by the
modernists concerned the structural form itself. Although the
argument of structure as *the* determinant of design was always
advanced as one of the pillars of the Modern Movement, it
was involved in numerous contradictions. The presence of
repetitious vertical and/or horizontal structural members was

readily apparent in the plan, but in most instances it could not be read externally or internally in the building itself. Horizontal members of a steel or reinforced concrete structural frame might occasionally be hinted at, but to really see them one would have to examine cross-sectional and other detailed drawing. Since the hallmark of the Corporate International Style was the curtain wall hung outside the frame, a knowledge of the modular repetition of structural elements usually had to be gained from the drawings, not from what one visually might see.

An examination of most preliminary sketches and typical Modern architectural drawings of the post-1945 decades reveals little of the basic architectural intent of the designers, nor do either formal perspective renderings or working drawings have much to say about content. Generally, the key drawings are orthographic projections of plans and elevations drawn exclusively with the drafting board or a machine. Since the Corporate International Style was not interested in traditional space, but in transparency and thin, defining surface planes, drawings of plans (with an indication of their governing structural system) and elevations probably provide more information about the design than the built building. Though the machine ideal was supposed to be the theme of these typical metal and glass curtain-walled buildings, their main concern seems, more often than not, to be that their patterns come directly from the drafting board.

The economic expansiveness of the 20 years from 1945 to 1965 led to the greatest architectural boom this country has ever experienced. The architects who profited the most were those who were members of the large architectural firms, which strove to imitate the size and complexity of a business corporate office. Within such an atmosphere architectural drawings increasingly became architectural drafting; for the increased complexity of construction and of the mechanical core of a building placed a heavy demand on working drawings. As government at various levels became more deeply involved in financing, planning, and public safety, more detailed preliminary and finished working drawings were needed to explain and justify a project.

The two decades following the Second World War were momentous ones in the history of High Art, encompassing the evolution of form from the personal gesture of Abstract Expressionism through the cool, ironic commentary of Pop Art. The technical styles employed in architectural drawings of that period indicate an obliviousness to what was going on in High Art; or perhaps we should say that since the intent of High Art was so different from that of architecture, this difference was actively mirrored in their visual imagery. The style of these elevational and perspective drawings (the latter usually labeled "an artist's rendering") does have a very decided character of its own, but that character refers back to Moderne architectural drawings of the 1930s. The two preferred techniques for renderings were a mixture of thin and soft line pencil and a repetitious linear use of thin lines. Both these techniques could produce drawings that rise out of mediocrity in the talented hands of such practitioners as Louis I. Kahn, Mies van der Rohe, or Richard J. Neutra, but with others they seldom did. Most of the formal presentation drawings were bright, grossly colored perspective drawings that seem to insist that they are a product of the world of commercial art rather than that of architecture. The best of these gross renderings merge into the world of Pop; the rest are often as embarrassing as the buildings they describe.

The older Modernists continued to express their architectural ideas in revealing conceptual sketches. Eric Mendelsohn's pencil and crayon sketch for the Russell House in San Francisco of 1948–1951 or for the Maimonides Hospital in San Francisco of 1946–1950 exhibit his design intent, as well as his famous studies drawn between 1917 and 1920.[128] Mies worked out variations in his use of the collage technique in drawings that anticipate the Pop High Art environment of the mid-1960s, and in the 1970s Hardy Holzman Pfeiffer Associates and other designers have worked out new uses of the collage technique. America's own crop of younger Modernists often produced highly descriptive conceptual sketches and on occasion perspective presentation drawings. Edward D. Stone's sketches for the design of the United States Embassy in New Delhi of 1954 or for the Huntington Hartford Gallery in New York in 1958 are traditional conceptual drawings that are more valuable

to study than the built buildings.[129] Generally, drawings such as these were seldom published. Polished presentation drawings (almost always perspectives) were occasionally published in small halftone cuts in the news section of the principal architectural magazines. There were occasional exceptions; such as when Matthew Newicki died in an accident in 1949, a number of his sketches were published.[130]

One of the favored devices used to present larger projects to the client and to the public were photographs of a highly finished architectural model. The photographs of a finished model tended to take design (and the architect) one step further out of architecture as art and into architecture as a practical building enterprise. Even gifted delineators like Eero Saarinen seemed enamored with this method of presentation.[131] The photograph of the model became a standard sales device with the major firms—Welton Becket, Harrison & Abramovitz, I. M. Pei, William L. Pereira, and Minoru Yamasaki.

Within the Modernist tradition of the 1950s and 1960s, the Case Study House program of John Entenza in his magazine *Arts and Architecture*, published between 1945 and 1964, made consistent use of architectural presentation drawings. Esther McCoy has gathered much of this material together, and now we can carefully study the relationship between the published sketches and drawings and the completed projects.[132] Several of the first Case Study Houses were not built because of the economic conditions of the immediate post–World War II period. So for several designs by Neutra, as well as one each by Ralph Rapson and Whitney R. Smith, we have only the evidence of the drawings. Charles Eames's Pacific Palisades Case Study House of 1949 provides a characteristic look into how drawings were used alone or in conjunction with photographs to present the design. The first scheme for this house was as an elevated bridge house of 1947, which reached a sufficiently finished design stage that it could be depicted by a formal perspective drawing. This design was abandoned, and one consisting of two separate rectangular volumes (house and studio) was finally adopted. No formal perspective drawings were published for this design; instead it was published via exterior elevational drawings, plans, and interior perspective drawings.[133] Eames's special emphasis on line in these drawings is identical in feeling with the drawings for his wire furniture, which was being produced at the same time. Though these drawings comment extensively on the concept of the building, they do not indicate how different this house is from a pure Miesian design. Here we have an instance where the built object reveals intent far better than the drawings do.

The later drawings of steel structures in the Case Study House Programs by Craig Ellwood, Pierre Koenig, and Raphael Soriano are also of a sparse, minimal linear nature, but in these drawings the lines define planes. They do not, as in the Eames drawings, say anything directly about modular construction or the steel frames themselves. In contrast with the Eames presentation these later Case Study House drawings tend to be angular, close-up perspectives rather than elevational drawings.

The Bay Area architects, such as Gardner Dailey, Joseph Esherick, and William Wurster, freely continued to use drawings to arrive at their initial concept of design. These sketches are traditional freehand productions, and so too were some of the presentation drawings used to sell the design to the client. With his skill at drawing, Joseph Esherick occasionally delineated large-scale perspective drawings entirely freehand, as in his view of the 1952 Bewley House in Stockton. Most, though, of the Bay Area drawings were produced on the drafting board. Many of the perspective drawings were aerial views with a highly stylized series of motifs of vegetation, hills, clouds, and sun within which hides the building. The best and most revealing of these drawings are the site plans proposed with great sensitivity by landscape architects such as Thomas Church and Lawrence Halprin.[134]

Frank Lloyd Wright continued to occupy his normally unusual position in American architecture. His well-cultivated image as the artist-architect was completely opposite that which a typical AIA member was then seeking to cultivate. Although Wright's highly personal style of design had little influence on the Corporate International Style of these years, his prestige among younger architectural students was higher than ever (though his influence can hardly be seen in actual work); and in the world of High Art in art and architectural history and museum circles, he remained as a major god-figure.

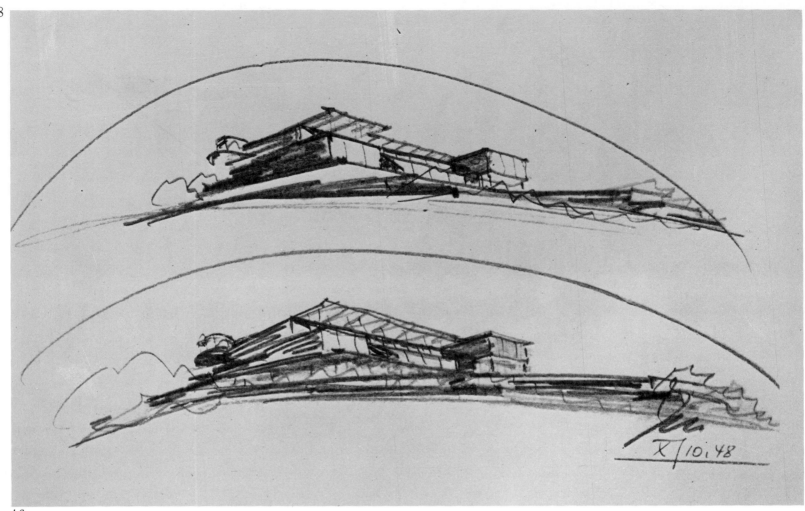

46

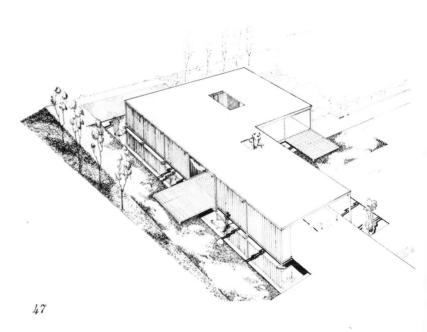

47

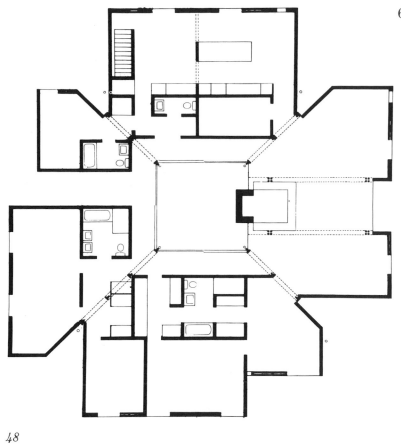

Much of Wright's continued preeminence had to do with the flow of drawings that he published during these years.[135] In 1948 *Architectural Forum* again devoted an entire issue to his work, and as he had always done earlier, drawings, not photographs, were the principal means he used to convey his buildings.[136] In 1953 when the completed Price Tower in Bartlesville, Oklahoma, of 1952, was published in *Architectural Forum*, the full-page color rendering executed by the Taliesin Fellowship explains far more about the design than any photograph could possibly do.[137]

Another maverick figure in American architecture, Bruce Goff, placed a high premium on presentation drawings to exhibit his personal version of Buck Rogers futurism.[138] Goff's beautiful color and black and white drawings occupy a place identical to that of the late 18th-century French Visionary architects—Boullée, Ledoux, and Lequeu. While Goff's built buildings attempt to conjure a world that is at times beyond our conscious grasp, his drawings go further. Some aspects of his Bavinger House in Norman, Oklahoma, of 1950 are in the nature of a folk folly, but his drawings for this house state a complex intent that is anything but folk oriented. Since Goff's unbuilt buildings make up much of his production, drawings assume a major importance in understanding his work.

With the exception of Goff, Louis I. Kahn, Paul Rudolph, Eero Saarinen, Wright, and a few others, the American architectural scene of the fifties came terribly close to being devoid of intent of any substance. The drawings of the time exquisitely expose this emptiness as clearly or more so than the built buildings do themselves. The Moderne of the twenties and thirties took the symbolic and factual argument of Functionalism (via machine imagery) and evolved an impressive means of expressing it. The Corporate International Style of the fifties took over parts of this vocabulary as style—a style stripped of any content. In contrast, many of the major European designers who practiced in the fifties never lost sight of content. As in the 1920s and 1930s Le Corbusier was there and was as strong in his insistence that architecture be valued as High Art as ever. In England Alison and Peter Smithson saw to it that the British tradition of expressing architectural intent through the written word, not the image, was well maintained. A few American designers took content seriously, especially Paul Rudolph and Eero Saarinen. Though both Rudolph's and Saarinen's drawings are crucial to an understanding of their view of order, their products and those of others often seem primarily concerned with order as a device to realize the picturesque.[139] In Saarinen's case his models probably end up saying more about how he has employed theatrical forms and equally theatrical structure to express his romantic view of the machine and technology. The reverse is true of Rudolph, for it is his drawings that make plain how he has imposed an order on each of his compositions.

The one American personage of the 1950s who can unquestionably be credited with bringing content back into American architecture was Louis I. Kahn.[140] The return to content also meant a return to the primacy of the drawing as *the* vehicle to assert intent. Kahn's Yale University Art Gallery in New Haven, Connecticut, of 1951–1953 is essentially a dull building as a building. But a study of his plans—and specifically the ceiling plan of the gallery—reveals the visual/intellectual order that was of such deep concern to the architect. In the mid-1950s Kahn concentrated on the cube as a governing element in design. The classical square had already inspired elements of his design for the Yale Art Gallery, and it came into strong play in his drawings for the projected De Vore House of 1955, the Bath House at Trenton, New Jersey, of 1955–1956, and the projected library at Washington University in St. Louis of 1956. Later he expanded his vocabulary to utilize other pure geometric forms: the triangle, circle, half-circle, etc. By the end of the fifties he had begun the process of establishing the contained geometry of his forms and then deliberately breaking it, most often with a strong single or multiple diagonal.

It is not simply Kahn's drawings but his plans that are the crucial elements to forming an understanding of his intent. His designs refer directly back to the mid-16th-century designs of Andrea Palladio, not only in content, but in their insistence that content be made known exclusively through drawings. Kahn made drawing once more respectable and crucial for the American architectural scene. Kahn took the traditional drawing processes off the two-dimensional sheet and extended

48

46   Eric Mendelsohn, Russell House, San Francisco, California, 1948. From Susan King, The Drawings of Eric Mendelsohn, *University of California, Berkeley, 1969.*

47   Pierre Koenig, Case Study House, Los Angeles, California, 1958. From Arts and Architecture, *May 1958.*

48   Louis I. Kahn, Goldberg House, Rydal, Pennsylvania, 1959. From Vincent Scully, Louis I. Kahn, *Braziller, 1962.*

them into the cardboard study model. Except for some formal presentation models Kahn's cardboard study models are an expansion of drawing, which read most completely in photographs where the drawing once again is brought back to the two-dimensional sheet.

The Palladian/Beaux-Arts roots of Kahn's architecture became the point of departure for a number of the younger American practitioners of the sixties. The content of Kahn's architecture and its use of drawings were so rich and so abstract that others could and did take off from them in various directions. Peter Eisenman employed the plan, elevation, cutaway isometric drawing, and model to establish his own obtuse formal spatial orders.[141] To understand what Eisenman is about, one must sit down and slowly go through the sequential arrangement of his drawings. When this has been done and the information digested, then we are in a position to experience the building itself. Eisenman's approach has just a hint of esthetic medieval scholasticism about it; obscure learning may perhaps be its end, and his architecture like his writings may be a means not an end.

Other practitioners of the late sixties and seventies—Michael Graves, Charles Gwathmey, and Richard Meier—have, it would seem, only marginally looked at Kahn. In relation to content, Gwathmey has learned the most, but all turned to drawing and the cardboard cutout model as their most telling means of expression. The same steps are repeated in each of their projects: the drawing, the model as an extension of drawing, and the built object as a mode in full scale. Their intellectual content, in contrast with Kahn or Eisenman, is in their High Art reference to the near-past of Cubism, Purism, and Le Corbusier. This continual side glance into the past pushes them over into the picturesque, which is best revealed in elevations, isometric, and perspective drawings, not in the plan.[142] Of the "New York Five" John Hejduk has on occasion been inspired by Kahn's geometry. The half circle, half of a double square, and half of a diamond (a triangle) in his projected "One Half House" of 1966 obviously looks to Kahn's vocabulary of pure shapes and to his use of a connecting spine. Hejduk's transparent axonometric-plus renderings are remarkable drawings, but are not readable without the plans. In such later 1970s schemes as his "Wall House" and Diamond, Canal, and Bye houses, the Kahnian spine remains, but the clarity of order has now been replaced by a picturesqueness which is not that of traditional architecture, but of High Art painting and sculpture.[143] His picturesqueness becomes most readable in his colored cardboard models as drawings. One is thrust right back to the early colored drawings for architecture and models of Theo Van Doesberg and de Stijl.

Though order was Kahn's underlying concern, his drawings and built buildings often evoke a picturesque image; and the intense play between order and the picturesque is strongly apparent in many of the architectural products of the 1970s. The Philadelphia firm of Mitchell/Giurgola Associates has pursued both themes in its work.[144] Their MDRT Foundation Hall at Bryn Mawr, Pennsylvania, of 1970–1971 reads most clearly as a picturesque composition through the building itself. It is not necessary to look at preliminary drawings or plans to make it out. However, their South End Branch Library in Boston of 1967–1971 or their glass 8th Street Subway in Philadelphia of 1970 become clear through drawings, not through the realized building. Although much of Kahn's vocabulary is present in Mitchell/Giurgola's plan for the 1969–1974 Student Union at the New York State University College at Plattsburgh, photographs of the building or the building itself illustrate how their Kahnian devices were basically employed for internal and external picturesque effects.[145]

Another of the prominent, well-publicized firms to emerge in the past 10 years, Hardy Holzman Pfeiffer Associates of New York, has taken the Kahnian picturesque and mixed it with a smattering of English New Brutalism of the mid-1950s.[146] In the process of transforming the intense seriousness of the English New Brutalists, Hardy Holzman Pfeiffer Associates have closely related both their collage drawing technique and their realized buildings to the High Art scene of the late 1960s and 1970s—of Pop, of Op, of Hardedge, and of Minimal. Although this firm's drawings are fascinating—almost in the nature of a playful game—their intent is best registered in their built buildings. Vestiges of Kahn through Charles W. Moore and Robert Venturi are to one degree or another all around us

today. Most of these designs end up as a kind of parody. Some designs, like that of John S. Hagemann and Robert A. M. Stern in their 1974 Lang House in Washington, Connecticut, evoked a learned picturesqueness that is more apparent in the built building than in their published drawings.[147]

How drawings are viewed in the practice of architecture in the seventies can be illustrated by examining the practice of two Los Angeles designers—Cesar Pelli and Frank O. Gehry. Pelli, with his large-scale practice first as a designer with DMJM and later at Gruen Associates, plays down the importance of drawings. Yet the order of geometry that underlies schemes like the Sunset Mountain Park Housing Development in the Santa Monica Mountains (designed with Anthony J. Lumsden in 1965) or the rocket-ship imagery of the El Monte Busway Station of 1973–1975 can be completely read only via drawings.[148] Frank O. Gehry, with his personal involvement in High Art, is conscious of the importance of drawings in the history of architecture. His rapid sketches, like those for a projected house in West Los Angeles of 1972 or his elevational study for the Gemini Building in Los Angeles of 1975–1976, are as important or more so than the completed buildings.[149]

It is surprising that drawings have been so unimportant for several of America's major architects of the 1960s and 1970s. One would have expected that Philip Johnson, with his eye always turned toward history, would have continued to place great emphasis on drawings, but such has not been the case. The glossy published renderings from his office have none of the strength and weakness that exist in his built buildings. The published presentation drawings of Edward Larrabee Barnes and I. M. Pei hint at substance, but are still disappointing. The slick, pretentious presentation drawing equated to the slick, pretentious building is what we expect of nearly all the work of Charles Luckman, William L. Pereira, and Minoru Yamasaki, but with Barnes, Johnson, and Pei, there is at least a suggestion of content—but it is certainly not revealed in their published drawings.

However, drawings and models functioning as drawings have been a major device to convey intent of the two leading figures of our contemporary scene—Robert Venturi and Charles W. Moore. In his work of the late 1960s the multiple ideas with which Venturi was concerned meant that a full understanding was only possible by carefully consulting both the drawings and the written word.[150] His controversial Friends' Housing for the Aged in Philadelphia of 1960–1963 is indeed (as Venturi insists) a commonplace, dull building as a built object. The drawings for it, though, accompanied by the written text, transform it into an intellectual statement that plays off a vocabulary of the vernacular, low art against the traditional. Venturi's later work, his two vacation houses at Nantucket of 1972 or his Brant-Johnson House at Vail, Colorado, of 1975–1976 rely less on the written word and more on the relationship between the drawings and the built building.[151]

For Charles W. Moore and his colleague William Turnbull of MLTW drawings serve a function different than those of Venturi.[152] The characteristic Moore product—whether the well-publicized condominium at Sea Ranch, California, of 1965–1966, the Burns House in Los Angeles of 1974, or Kresge College at the University of California at Santa Cruz of 1966–1973—is fully within the early 19th-century Downingesque tradition of the picturesque. The subtlety and humor of intellectual intent that lies behind so many of Moore's designs is not readily apparent in the realized building. The intent must to a considerable extent be gained from the drawings, and in Moore's case from isometric cutaway drawings or the model as a medium of drawing. Moore's three-dimensional version of internal spatial order does not come through well in his plans, but it is apparent in the isometric drawings.

American architecture of the mid-seventies is in a much more splintered position than in any period since the 1930s. Though this division exhibits itself through style, its actual basis is due to a diversity of intent. And if the intent has intellectual substance, drawings remain, as in the past, the principal means to convey it. Most contemporary architects, historians, and critics would either deny or feel uneasy about claiming the primacy of the drawing, but if they are uneasy with what has been termed "paper" architecture as opposed to "real" architecture, they may well be indicating that their primary allegiance is to building, not to architecture.

49

49   Charles W. Moore (MLTW), first scheme for the Faculty Club, University of California, Santa Barbara, 1969. Courtesy Architectural Archives, University of California, Santa Barbara.

1776/1819

74 *1   House, Suffield, Connecticut*
Architectural details, c. 1795–1798
Ink on laid paper, 14¼ x 12⅜" (36.2 x 31.5 cm)
Society for the Preservation of New England Antiquities
Boston, Massachusetts

2   Meeting House
Elevation, 1810
Ink with gray and green coloring on laid paper
16½ x 10¼" (41.9 x 26 cm)
Society for the Preservation of New England Antiquities
Boston, Massachusetts

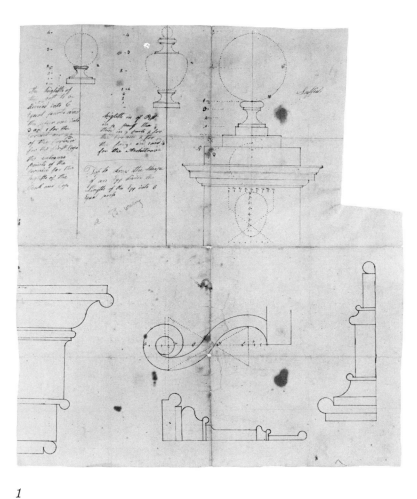

1

Asher Benjamin (1773–1845)

At the time of the Revolution there were no architects in the colonies who regarded architecture as at once an arena for individual artistic expression and as a principal means of earning a living. From the 18th through the mid-19th century, the American builder often relied on architectural pattern books for technical guidance and esthetic inspiration. The standard content of these books was a series of plates that provided plans for the fabrication of the classical orders, building details, stairways, fireplaces, and doorways. Compendiums of Greek and Roman antiquities and the treatises of Vitruvius and 16th-, 17th-, and 18th-century architects were used by the more sophisticated builder/architects as pattern books for formal inspiration.

In 1797, Asher Benjamin, born in western Massachusetts in 1773 and trained as a carpenter, published *The Country Builder's Assistant*, the first of his seven builder's guides and the first architectural book both authored and published in the colonies. His most popular guide, *The Practical House Carpenter*, went through 17 editions from 1830 to 1856. His last book was published in 1843. Although his first book relied heavily on English books such as those by William Chambers (1723–1796) and Peter Nicholson (1765–1844), Asher Benjamin was no slavish copyist. He made significant changes in his English models to adapt them to the needs of Americans. By substituting construction methods and building materials better suited to American technology and resources, simplifying architectural detailing, and sanctioning a nonarcheological use of the orders in all but the most monumental structures, Benjamin created designs that could be easily reproduced by thousands of his compatriots. Passages in his books reveal that he was completely cognizant of the implications of his adaptations.

Asher Benjamin's enormous influence on the American environment came not from the forty-odd buildings attributed to him, such as the West Church in Boston of 1806, the Old South Congregational Meeting House in Windsor, Vermont, of 1798, and many domestic structures in New England, but rather from the 30,000–40,000 copies of his books that were in circulation in 1862. It was in part through these books that the Federal style and later the Greek Revival were disseminated throughout the North. His influence on the South was less important. Like a chameleon, Asher Benjamin reflected changes in his environment or in the national taste almost immediately in his books. For example, in 1803 he moved to Boston, where he was able to observe the work of Charles Bulfinch (page 76) at first hand. The latter's influence on Benjamin is evident in his second pattern book, published in 1806. Through the mid-1820s, Benjamin's work was characterized by the thin proportions and delicacy of the Federal style. During the 1820s, as the national taste was changing, his designs took on the heavier proportions and the detailing of the Greek Revival.

Asher Benjamin's simple drawing style, with its thin lines, limited shading, and avoidance of perspectives, is typical of the period. The drawing of architectural details for the Suffield, Connecticut, House (1) c. 1795–1798 is similar in the arrangement of the details on the sheet to many pages of his pattern books. The notations on the drawing describe the proportional relationships among the parts of several details.

The Meeting House (2) elevation of 1810 is similar to hundreds of contemporaneous designs for New England churches. Characteristic of the type is the multilevel steeple and pedimented entry. Among the inspirations for these churches were the plates in Englishman James Gibbs's (1682–1754) *A Book of Architecture* of 1728 and particularly those of his St. Martin-in-the-Fields in London of 1722–1726. The steeple of Benjamin's 1810 Meeting House is, however, closer to that of Gibbs's Marybone Chapel, also published in *A Book of Architecture*.

Drawn from a scale of 8 feet to one Inch
by Asher Benjamin 1811

3

3 *University Hall, Harvard University*
Cambridge, Massachusetts
Elevation study for cupola, 1813–1814
Brown ink on paper mounted on linen, 18½ x 10″ (47 x 25.4 cm)
Harvard University Archives
Cambridge, Massachusetts

Charles Bulfinch (1763–1844)

Synonymous with the city of Boston are the Massachusetts State House, the Boston Common, and the elegant row houses of Beacon Hill. The form of all three is directly or indirectly connected with the name of Charles Bulfinch, who was chairman of the Board of Selectmen for 20 years, architect of the State House, first planner of the Common, and designer of elegant townhouses that would serve as models for Boston's builders. Among the most notable of Bulfinch's Boston houses are the three constructed between 1795 and 1806 for the Harrison Gray Otis family. Bulfinch also worked outside Massachusetts, and in 1817 he replaced Benjamin Latrobe (page 82) and assumed responsibility for the completion of the United States Capitol, which included the restoration of the wings destroyed by the British in the War of 1812, and construction of the central section, including the dome, which was much taller than that intended by Latrobe or desired by Bulfinch. Congress called for both a loftier dome and a Gothic form. Bulfinch complied only with the first request. Bulfinch was the first professional architect born in America and one of the most elegant practitioners of the Federal style, which relied heavily on English 18th-century architecture, particularly the work of William Chambers (1723–1790) and Robert Adam (1728–1792). Chambers' Somerset House of 1786 in London was a source for the elevation of the State House. The delicacy of Adam's decorative details, the clarity of the relationship of the parts of the decoration to each other, and the rich and varied spatial organization of Adam's plans—based not just on esthetics, but on functional needs—all left an imprint on Bulfinch's work. Bulfinch's work was used as a source for American pattern books, and it was in part through these that the Bulfinch-Adam style spread through the East.

The Massachusetts State House (5) of 1795–1797 is one of Bulfinch's first projects. The source of the central portion of this building is the river side of Somerset House. However, the building is lighter in scale, and its decorative elements are thinner and flatter than the very sculptural detailing of the English building. This lightness of scale comes from Adam, as do aspects of the plan. The centralized form of the representatives' chamber flanked by rectangular rooms sets up a sequence of changing spatial forms typical of Robert Adam.

In November 1812, Bulfinch received the commission to design University Hall(3, 4) for his alma mater, Harvard College. It was constructed between 1813–1814. He submitted three sets of plans, but the drawings for the third and final scheme are lost. Both the drawings illustrated here represent aspects of the building that were never constructed. The design for the cupola was first used by Bulfinch in the Worcester County (Mass.) Courthouse, designed in 1801–1803 and demolished in 1898, and later at the Lancaster Meeting House in Lancaster, Massachusetts, 1816–1817. The templelike front raised above the ground on a basement story is a typical Federalist facade. The cupola was never built, and the facade illustrated in the drawing was constructed without the templelike portico entrance.

University Hall was built of granite with smooth ashlar walls and a rusticated basement. The use of stone with but a few important exceptions was rare in Boston until after 1800. Its use is indicative of changes in Bulfinch's work toward a more monumental style. This work belongs to a development in neoclassical architecture that has been called its "rational phase" (see page 82). The two most notable examples of this phase of Bulfinch's career are the New South Church of 1814 in Boston and the Lancaster Meeting House. In both buildings internal volumes are given expression in external massing. Volume is emphasized over surface by a planar treatment of the wall. Ornament is kept at a minimum and is primarily used as part of the structure or to emphasize the interrelationship of the volumes.

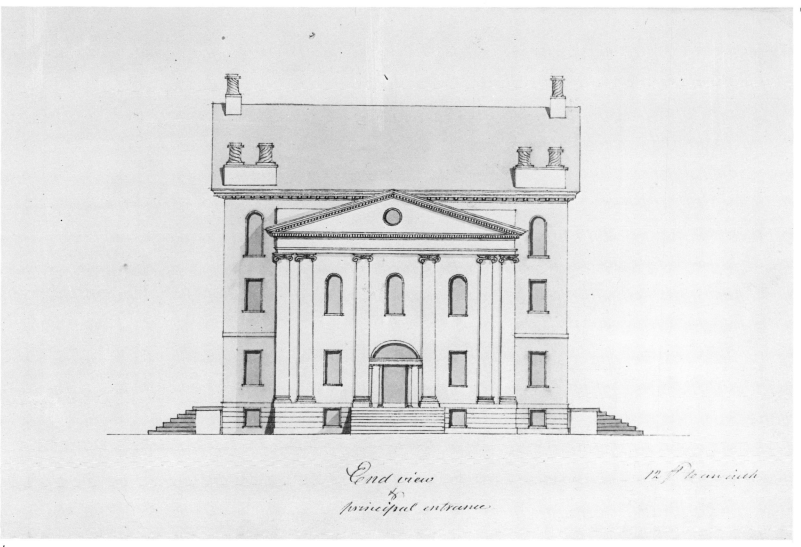

End view
of
principal entrance

12 ft to an inch

4

4   *University Hall, Harvard University, Cambridge,*
Massachusetts
End view of principal entrance, an alternative elevation
1813–1814
Watercolor and ink on wove paper, 9 x 15" (22.9 x 38.1 cm)
Harvard University Archives
Cambridge, Massachusetts

5   *Massachusetts State House, Boston*
Elevation and plan of principal story, 1795–1797
Sepia ink and gray wash, 11.8 x 8.14" (30 x 20.7 cm)
The I. N. Phelps Stokes Collection
Prints Division
The Astor, Lenox, & Tilden Foundations
The New York Public Library
New York, New York

Representatives

Senate

Governor
&
Council

...ation and plan of the principal Story of the New State House in ...

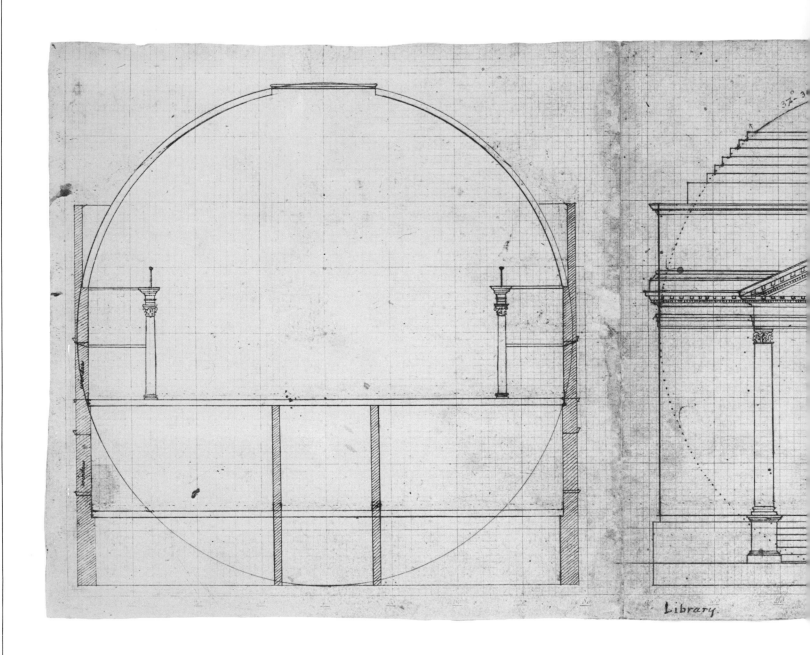

6

6   Rotunda, The University of Virginia, Charlottesville, Virginia
Elevation and section, probably 1821
Ink on laid paper, 8¾ x 17¼″ (22.2 x 43.8 cm)
Alderman Library
The University of Virginia
Charlottesville, Virginia

7   Rotunda, The University of Virginia, Charlottesville, Virginia
Plan, probably 1821
Ink on laid paper, 8¾ x 12¼″ (22.2 x 31.1 cm)
Alderman Library
The University of Virginia
Charlottesville, Virginia

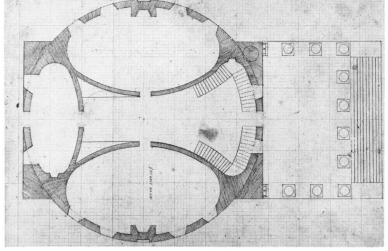

The buildings of Thomas Jefferson, lawyer, statesman, naturalist, architect, are exquisite creations of a brilliant and fertile 18th-century mind. Their beauty and originality are reflections of Jefferson's statement to James Madison in a letter of 1785: "You see I am an enthusiast on the subject of the arts." Jefferson believed that the arts and especially architecture had an extremely important role within society. He believed that architecture had a didactic, propagandistic, and political value beyond esthetic delight and shelter. If a building was reflective of the cultural values of the nation in which it was constructed and if it was also beautiful, Jefferson contended that it would reinforce the ideals of that country, improve the taste of its citizens, and raise its esteem in the world's eyes. It is in this context that Jefferson's work should be considered, and it is in this context that he designed some of America's most powerful architectural symbols: Monticello, begun in 1768 and largely completed by 1809, and the University of Virginia of 1817–1826, both in Charlottesville, Virginia; and the Virginia State Capitol in Richmond, completed in 1796.

Jefferson's architectural theory and the buildings he designed are directly related to his education and personal political philosophy. He studied law with George Whyte, one of the outstanding lawyers and classical scholars in Virginia. It was through this contact that Jefferson's connection with classical literature and the writings of Renaissance humanists must have developed from that of general familiarity to deep personal involvement. Many of the formal as well as programmatic aspects of Jefferson's architecture and site planning derive from classical models, both extant buildings and literary descriptions of others that did not exist in the 18th century. Important additional sources for Jefferson were Renaissance architecture and theory, inspired, like his own, by classical artifacts and literature, and 18th-century European architecture, mainly French.

The design for the first Monticello, built on a hill, was begun in 1768 and continued in construction until 1782. Jefferson was in France from 1784 to 1789 and on his return he began to radically alter the house, which arrived by 1809 at the form reproduced on the United States nickel. The first floor plan for Monticello, which includes the dependencies (9), was drawn and reworked between 1772 and 1784. The final design of the estate is essentially derived from this scheme, with the exception of the octagonal outbuildings, which were not built.

The plan of the house and estate are illustrative of the eclectic manner in which Jefferson always designed, using sources from a variety of periods and combining them into something that has a unity and meaning of its own. Jefferson may have used plate 37 from an English source, Robert Morris's *Select Architecture* of 1755, for the cross-axial plan of his house. The facade was derived from Andrea Palladio's *Four Books of Architecture* of 1570. After Jefferson returned from Europe with first-hand observation of modern French architecture, he altered the facade using as inspiration the Hôtel de Sâlm, which was under construction while he was in Paris.

Palladio is an important point of departure for the site plan of the estate as many of the villas in Palladio's book are situated at the center of projecting terraces. Other important sources for Monticello were the descriptions by the Roman authors Pliny and Cato—both read by Jefferson—of the ideal villa. Both writers describe the prototype, situated on a hill, as a house combined with a hippodrome-shaped garden defined by terraces superimposed on underground passages and rooms. These are all features of Monticello and unique in American architecture of the era.

Jefferson had a romantic attitude toward nature that, like his reliance on the sources described above, was very much a product of the 18th century. His letters contain highly romanticized, idealized descriptions of the environment. The siting of the estate on the crest of a hill provides some of the most spectacular views from any totally planned estate in America and a dramatic vantage point from which the seasonal and daily changes in nature could be seen.

The drawing for the decorative outchamber at Monticello (8), conceived before 1778, is tied to the same sources as the plan of the estate. The idea of including outbuildings is present in many of the descriptions of classical villas as well as European estates of the 18th century but is unusual in America. The notes on the back of the drawing provide specifications for the building and list some of its formalistic sources—Inigo Jones, Palladio, and descriptions of similar classical buildings.

The Rotunda of the University of Virginia (6, 7) of 1817–1826, originally serving as a library and lecture hall, is derived from the Pantheon in Rome. It was situated by Jefferson at the end of a long lawn and flanked on either side by double rows of pavilions. As indicated in the section the building had three levels: a basement with four oval rooms; the principal floor with center hall flanked by ovoid rooms; and the domed room lit by a skylight. Jefferson intended the dome to be painted blue and decorated with gilt stars although there is no evidence to suggest that this conception was executed. The ten pavilions bordering the lawn in front of the Rotunda were based on Roman, Renaissance, and 18th-century French sources and were intended as was the Rotunda to serve as models for instruction in the history of architecture. The Rotunda, modified by Jefferson in the interest of practicality as well as esthetics, is not a literal copy of the Pantheon. His building is exactly half the size of its model while retaining its general proportions; its back wall is flat, not round; the number of columns is reduced from eight to six; the entablature of the portico is drawn around the drum of the dome, as it is not in the Pantheon, to link the two parts of the massing more closely; and windows are inserted into the wall, with only an oculus in the model.

Jefferson chose the Pantheon, which he must have considered one of the most perfect buildings, as a model for the most important building on the campus. The plan of the rotunda is a circle; its volume would be a sphere if the circumference of the dome were extended in three dimensions. Jefferson was aware that the circle was held by Plato as well as Renaissance theorists to be the ideal form in nature. Palladio describes the circle as the most perfect geometric form, the direct reflection of the universe and of the unity of God—therefore the form to be used for sacred architecture. To humanist Jefferson the most sacred building in a university was the temple of learning, the library.

Working in his accustomed manner of using many sources, Jefferson may have been stimulated to incorporate the Pantheon into his university by a project for a Baptistery derived from the Pantheon by Joseph Bernard that was published in 1787 while Jefferson was in France. Its plan, however, is different from Jefferson's building. The Rotunda's first floor plan may well have come from a plan in Jefferson's copy of C. L. Steiglitz's *Plans et Dessins Tires de la Belle Architecture*, published in Leipzig in 1800, which contained a plan of a building much like the Rotunda's first floor. Another source could have been the ovoid rooms of the Désert de Retz in France that Jefferson had visited with his close friend Maria Cosway and that he recalls in his famous "Head and Heart" letter to her.

The Rotunda burned in 1895, was rebuilt and altered by Stanford White, and has recently been restored to Jefferson's original design.

8 *Monticello, Charlottesville, Virginia*
Decorative outchamber elevation, before 1778
Ink on laid paper, 8 x 6½" (20.3 x 16.5 cm)
Massachusetts Historical Society
Boston, Massachusetts

9 *Monticello, Charlottesville, Virginia*
First floor plan with dependencies, 1772–1784
Ink on laid paper, 13½ x 20¼" (34.3 x 51.4 cm)
Massachusetts Historical Society
Boston, Massachusetts

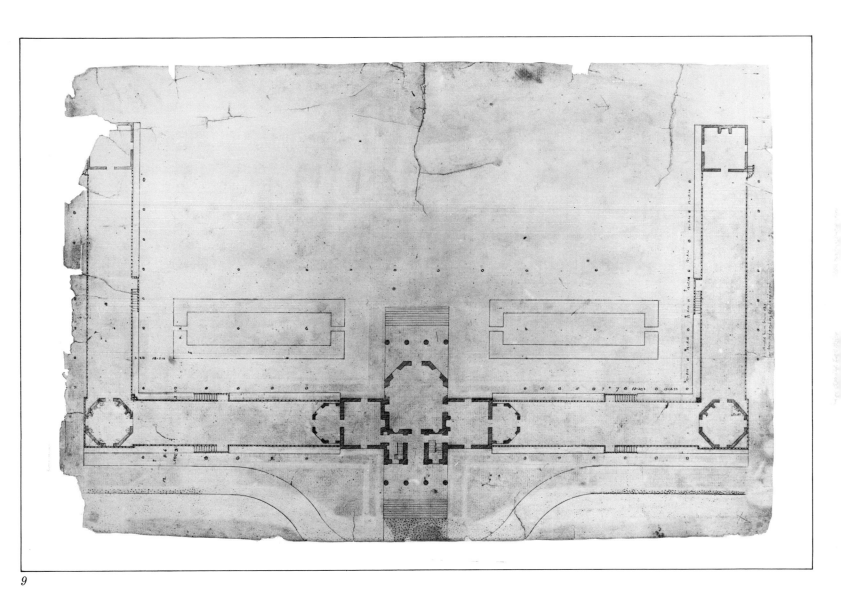

9

10 *United States Capitol, Washington, D.C.*
North wing, principal floor: section, plan, and elevation details,
1817
Ink and gouache, 19 x 15" (48 x 38 cm)
Library of Congress
Washington, D.C.

11 *The White House, Washington, D.C.*
Plan of principal story as proposed to be altered, 1807
Ink and watercolor, 19 x 15" ((48 x 38 cm)
Library of Congress
Washington, D.C.

12 *United States Capitol, Washington, D.C.*
West elevation, February 4, 1817
Ink and gouache, 20½ x 30" (52.1 x 76. 2 cm)
Library of Congress
Washington, D.C.

Benjamin Henry Latrobe (1764–1820)

Englishman Benjamin Latrobe arrived in America in 1796. He helped Jefferson complete the Virginia Capitol, and by 1798 he settled in Philadelphia. Latrobe introduced a new architectural esthetic and a technical competence and engineering skill not displayed in America before. Latrobe's Bank of Pennsylvania in Philadelphia of 1799–1801 was the first entirely vaulted public building constructed here, and he was the engineer and architect for the Philadelphia Waterworks of 1799–1801. Widely acknowledged for his talents, Latrobe received many commissions across the middle-Atlantic states, including the completion of the first United States Capitol in Washington, D.C.; the State Penitentiary in Richmond, Virginia of 1797–1798; the Baltimore Cathedral of 1805–1818, several churches; and many fine domestic structures.

Latrobe's work can suitably be described as belonging to the rationalist phase of neoclassicism. Its intellectual base was in the writings of Antoine Laugier, whose *Essai Sur l'Architecture* of 1753 was translated into English and German 2 years after its publication. Laugier advocated a rational architecture whose forms were derived from programmatic and structural needs. Latrobe's esthetic of domed monumental spaces—cubic masses in which a coherent relationship between structure and space and interior volumes and exterior massing was established—is consistent with Laugier's ideas. Latrobe combines this esthetic with an eclectic approach to the use of sources. The basic form of the Bank of Pennsylvania is derived from a Roman podium temple. Latrobe integrates this with a Roman domed interior space and the first use of a Greek order, the Ionic, in America.

Latrobe was conscious of the need to create monumental spaces for public edifices in America. His attitude can be summarized in a letter he wrote to his friend and fellow architect, Thomas Jefferson (page 79). Latrobe expresses his general preference for Greek architecture but writes that "our religion requires a church wholly different from the [Greek] temples, our legislative assemblies and our courts of justice, buildings of entirely different principles from their basilicas; and our amusements could not possibly be performed in their theaters and amphitheaters." The recognition of this situation led Latrobe to Roman architecture for inspiration as well as to the Greek.

The three drawings shown here can be used as tools to understand Latrobe's particular approach to neoclassicism and his attitude toward the creation of public space. In 1803, Latrobe, the personal choice of President Jefferson, was appointed Surveyor of Public Buildings, and he held this position until 1812. Latrobe was called specifically to supervise the construction of William Thornton's plan for the United States Capitol, the winning entry in the 1792 Capitol Competition. The central portion of the interior of the Capitol as it exists today is essentially the work of Latrobe; the exterior is primarily the work of Charles Bulfinch (page 76) and Thomas U. Walter (page 122).

The west elevation (12) of 1817, one of several Latrobe conceived in his tenure, is based on several sources: the dome like that of his Baltimore Cathedral derives from the Pantheon; the tall rusticated basement with double height columns is not unlike the elevations of many 18th-century English public buildings; the entrance is derived from the Athenian propylaeum. Latrobe's facade is a combination of massive forms juxtaposed to each other: dome, rectangular volume, templelike entry. The almost complete lack of decoration underlines this monumental composition.

The page of details of the north wing of the Capitol (10) contains studies for the plan, dome, and staircase of the Senate wing. The studies for the section of the domed space and the plan of the lantern reveal Latrobe's fascination with the effect of dramatic light in a vaulted interior space. [This involvement with dramatic light, as well as other aspects of Latrobe's work, must have been derived in part from the work of John Soane (1753–1837), who was producing some of his most innovative buildings in London and its environs while Latrobe was still practicing there.] Chimneys from the many stoves needed to heat this section of the Capitol are consolidated in the lantern. This Latrobe defended against Jefferson's objection as being more functional than spreading the chimneys all over the roof. Moreover, the pure volume produced by this course must have

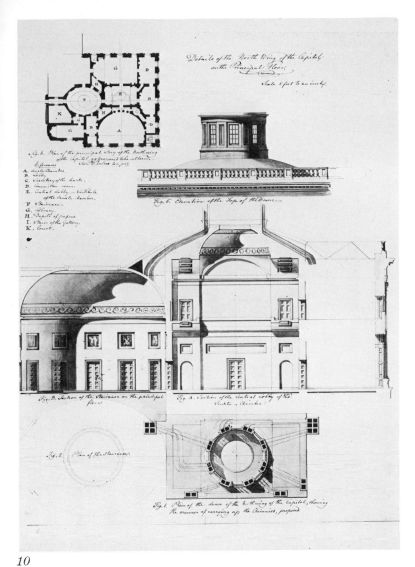

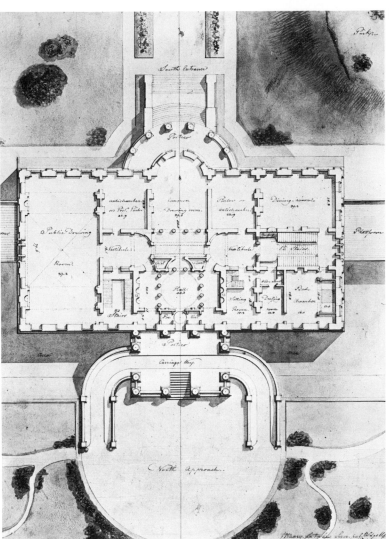

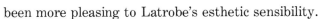

10

11

been more pleasing to Latrobe's esthetic sensibility.

Only the porticoes of Latrobe's scheme (11) for the alterations of James Hoban's (c. 1762–1831) plan for the White House of 1807 were ever executed. The use of light and shade in this drawing and in those for the Capitol reveals the details and mass of the structure in a graphic manner and conveys the sensuous effects created by light pouring through the windows and reflecting on classical forms.

13

13   John McComb, Jr.
City Hall, New York City
Elevation of cupola, c. 1803
Ink and wash, 33¾ x 20⅞" (85.7 x 53 cm)
The New-York Historical Society
New York, New York

14   Joseph Mangin
City Hall, New York City
Elevation, 1802
Ink and wash, 24¼ x 38" (61.6 x 96.5 cm)
The New-York Historical Society
New York, New York

15   Joseph Mangin
City Hall, New York City
Section, 1802
Ink and wash, 17 x 29" (43.2 x 73.7 cm)
The New-York Historical Society
New York, New York

John McComb, Jr. (1761–1853)
Joseph Mangin (dates unknown)

John McComb, Jr., and Joseph Mangin were the architects for the New York City Hall of 1802–1811. The important role of each architect in the development of this building can only be comprehended by understanding their very different biographies. John McComb, Jr., was the son of John McComb, Sr. (d. 1811), an outstanding pre-Revolutionary architect in New York whose work, relying on English neo-Palladian architecture, included the Old Brick Church of 1767 and the North Dutch Church of 1769. This reliance on English forms was passed from father to son, whose churches, such as St. John's on Varick St. of 1803–1807 designed with his brother Isaac and the Bleecker Street Church of 1822, derive their inspiration from the work of the English architect James Gibbs (1682–1754). Their domestic buildings have the delicacy of scale and spatial variety of the work of Robert Adam (1728–1792). McComb, Jr., is responsible for the lighthouses at Montauk of 1795, Eaton's Neck, and Cape Henry, Virginia; the Fort at Castle Garden, New York; Alexander Hall at Princeton Theological Seminary of 1815 in New Jersey; and the Queen's Building at Rutgers University in New Jersey of 1809–1812.

Joseph Mangin, born and educated in France, came to America in the mid-1790s to join his brother Charles, also an architect. Buildings attributed to Joseph Mangin in New York City are the State Prison of 1797 built north of Christopher Street and the Gothic Revival St. Patrick's Cathedral of 1809–1812. He is also responsible for the Mangin-Goerck map of New York. Prior to 1817 he left New York; little else is known about him.

The cornerstone for the New York City Hall proclaims only John McComb, Jr., as its architect, but in actuality Mangin probably had the major role in its initial design. Mangin does not seem to have been associated with McComb during the construction of the building, which may in part explain this error. The commission for the City Hall was won by Mangin and McComb in a competition of 1802 entered by 26 competitors, among whom was Benjamin Latrobe (page 82). Latrobe's fine Greco-Roman scheme did not win, perhaps because Latrobe, supported by Aaron Burr and Thomas Jefferson, both Republicans, would have been unacceptable to the judges, the Federalist Common Council. McComb, however, was supported by the Federalists Rufus King and Alexander Hamilton whose country mansion, The Grange, McComb had built in 1801 in upper Manhattan.

From the time the cornerstone was laid, Mangin's defenders called for acknowledgment of his vital participation in the project. Montgomery Schuyler at the beginning of this century and more recently Clay Lancaster and Damie Stillman have attributed the overall conception of the design to Mangin; the design of the cupola, most of the interior details, and the supervision of the entire construction to McComb. The evidence for this conclusion rests primarily on an examination of the careers of both these men and only secondarily on the fact that Mangin's name, placed above McComb's, was erased on the competition drawings.

The general design for City Hall is inspired by French 18th-century architecture and is unlike any building McComb executed before or after its construction. The rendering style of the front (14) and back elevation and section (15) drawings for the competition is likewise unlike McComb's drawings as, for example, that for the cupola. The facade and sections for City Hall are based on an intimate knowledge of French sources, which Mangin, probably related to an important family of French architects, would have been familiar with. The arcaded lower story, each arch separated by pilasters, combined with the rectangular second-story openings and the projecting one-story central section without a pediment is very close in conception to A. T. Brongniart's Hôtel de Monaco in Paris c. 1774. The domed rotunda with its double flight of stairs recalls the Hôtel de Ville in Nancy designed by E. Héré de Corny and J. Lamour c. 1752–1755.

McComb's major contribution to the facade was the design of the cupola (13), for which he also did the drawing. McComb's scheme is higher and lighter in scale than Mangin's original conception. Some exterior details and many important interior elements are attributed to McComb and are ultimately derived from English sources. McComb's copy of William Chambers' *Treatise on Civil Architecture* of 1759 contains notes in

14

15

McComb's hand, indicating figures in the book used by him as sources for elements in the City Hall design. McComb derived from Chambers the Ionic pilasters on the exterior and in the Board of Estimate Chamber; the exterior second story Corinthian order, with the frieze omitted; and many details of exterior and interior capitals. McComb was also influenced by Robert Adam and his followers. "Adamesque" describes the curved screen of columns in the Board of Estimate Chamber, which transforms the room from a rectangular space to a semicircular one; the many-lobed shell of the Committee Room dome; the delicacy of the interior detailing; the fanlights; and the combination in the interior of Ionic capitals with the triglyphs and metopes of a Doric frieze.

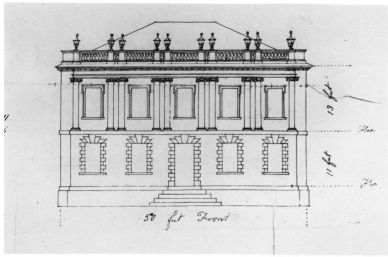

16

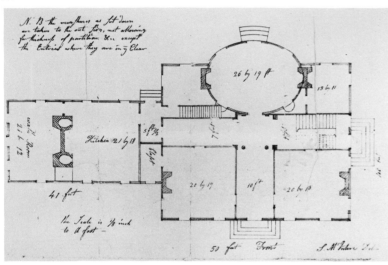

17

16 *Lyman House, Waltham, Massachusetts*
Elevation, 1793
Pen and ink, 7½ x 11" (19.1 x 27.9 cm)
The Essex Institute
Salem, Massachusetts

17 *Lyman House, Waltham, Massachusetts*
Plan, 1793
Pen and ink, 7½ x 12¼" (19.1 x 31.1 cm)
The Essex Institute
Salem, Massachusetts

18 *United States Capitol Competition, Washington, D.C.*
Elevation of back front and plan of lower floor, 1792
Pen and iron gall ink, scored guidelines
13¼ x 17⅞" (33.7 x 45.4 cm)
The Maryland Historical Society
Baltimore, Maryland

19 *United States Capitol Competition, Washington, D.C.*
Plan of second floor and elevation of principal front, 1792
Pen and iron gall ink, pencil underdrawing
14⅛ x 18⅜" (35.9 x 46.7 cm)
The Maryland Historical Society
Baltimore, Maryland

Samuel McIntire (1757–1811)

Samuel McIntire, "architect of Salem" as the Salem town clerk called him at his death, was also called "carver" by the historian, Fiske Kimball. Supported by the patronage of rich merchants, McIntire significantly changed Salem from a town of colonial buildings to one of Federal style houses, government and commercial structures, and churches whose delicate interior detailing in wood was designed and often carved by the architect himself.

McIntire developed from a carpenter, the profession of his father, to an outstanding architect. His professional development, although supported by wealthy patrons, was parallel to that of many designers of the period. McIntire's genius enabled him to synthesize the variety of material contained in pattern books and to create an architecture not of major structural or formal innovation, but distinguished by an elegant adaptation and refinement of his models and superb craftsmanship.

McIntire's early work was characterized by heavier proportions and detailing than the work of his maturity. The plans from the early period were generally composed of rectangular rooms arranged symmetrically around an entry hall extending through the length of the building. About 1790 McIntire's work was transformed in feeling and form through contact with the work of Charles Bulfinch (page 76), who after a trip abroad, brought to his designs many of the characteristics of the Adam style in England. Under the influence of Bulfinch as well as pattern books reproducing the details of the Adamesque style, McIntire's carved detailing of geometric and natural motifs became more delicate, with a greater emphasis on the distinction and clarity of each element within the design. William Pierson, who wrote that McIntire's ornament was like the "resilient threads of a spiderweb, across the taut surfaces of the spatial volumes," made a parallel between the composition of McIntire's ornament and the structure of Franz Joseph Haydn's string quartets, which like McIntire's work are composed of precisely defined but closely interrelated parts. Pierson observes that the oldest Haydn Society in the world was established in Boston during this period, and it should be noted that McIntire's prime avocation was music. At this time McIntire also introduced to his plans Adamesque ovoid rooms, subtly interconnected to more traditional rectangular spaces.

The Lyman House (16, 17) in Waltham of 1793, built for Theodore Lyman and his wife who came from Salem, was the only building by McIntire outside the Salem vicinity. The oval room screened from the entry by two columns is Adam via Bulfinch and is clearly influenced by Bulfinch's Barrel House. The rusticated windows and doorway of the facade, derived from Batty Langley's *Treasury of Design* of 1745, counterpoint the delicacy of the Ionic columns of the second story.

In 1792 McIntire submitted designs for the United States Capitol competition (18, 19) won by William Thornton. McIntire's scheme recalls plate 37 in James Gibbs's *Book of Architecture* of 1728; the book was a common source of inspiration for American designers. For his principal elevation McIntire borrowed from Gibbs's scheme the pedimented entry raised on a basement, projecting side bays, and double stairway. McIntire's back elevation, like the garden elevation in Gibbs's plate, is entered through a wide, low stairway. The lower windows on both elevations framed by alternating small and large stone blocks are called "Gibbs surrounds" as this device was frequently used by Gibbs. McIntire added a roof balustrade and sculpture to Gibbs's conception.

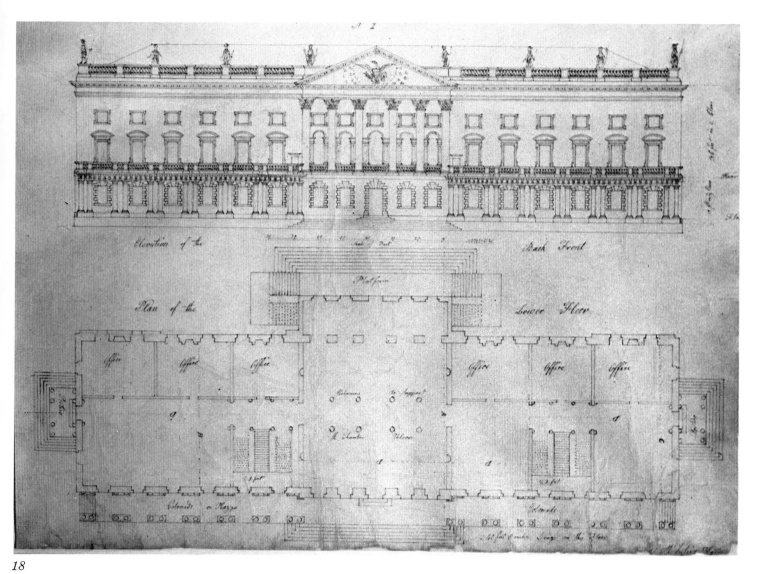

Elevation of the .... Back Front

Plan of the .... Lower Floor

18

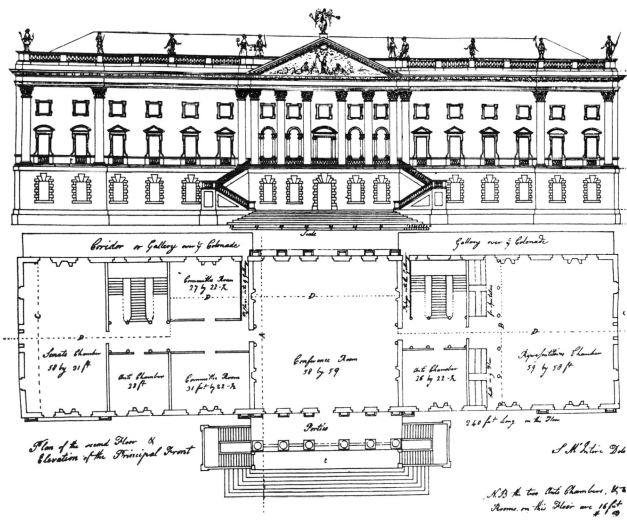

Plan of the second Floor &
Elevation of the Principal Front

S M'Intire Del

N.B. the two Anti Chambers &
Rooms on this Floor are 16 f.t

19

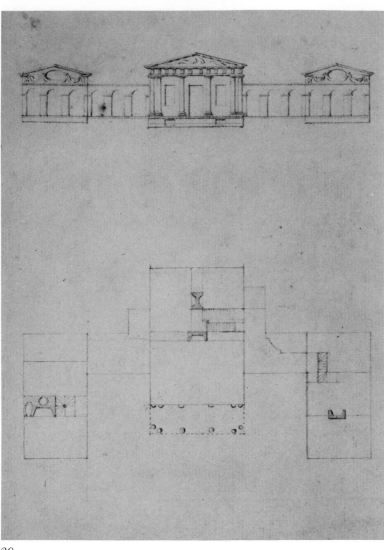

20

John Trumbull (1756–1843)

John Trumbull, son of the governer of Connecticut, was one of the finest and most sophisticated American 18th-century painters. He was also an architect, although this career was less important for him than was his career in painting. Trumbull built few buildings but conceptualized many more, as evidenced by his drawings at the New York Historical Society (of which he had been a vice president), Yale University, and the Cooper-Hewitt Museum of Decorative Arts and Design. However, to date his work has not been adequately discussed. His most famous building, the Greek Revival style Yale University Art Gallery, built in 1831–1832 and destroyed in 1901, was the first university-connected art gallery in the United States and was designed to house his own painting collection, which he had just given Yale in exchange for an annuity. He was advised on the project by the firm of Town & Davis, but his completed design differed in many details from their suggestions (page 100). His other important building, also Greek Revival in form, was the headquarters of the American Academy of the Fine Arts of 1831 in New York, of which he was a founder.

Trumbull's work before the Yale Art Gallery was tied to Anglo-Palladian and French sources. He would have been familiar with the Palladian revival through publications before 1781, the year of his first visit to England. From 1781 to 1815 (when he returned to America on a permanent basis) Trumbull spent 35 years in Europe, mainly in England. During these years he studied art in Benjamin West's studio where he became friends with West's more mature student, Gilbert Stuart; he worked as an independent artist; between 1794 and 1804 he supervised the Jay Treaty; and he visited France where he stayed with Thomas Jefferson.

Both Jefferson and Trumbull were inspired by the Hôtel de Sâlm in Paris, which influenced Jefferson's second design for Monticello, now reproduced on the U.S. nickel (page 79). A drawing for a house by Trumbull in his sketchbook, now at the New York Historical Society, derives from the Hôtel de Sâlm. Trumbull enclosed an engraving of his French source in the sketchbook.

The drawings for a neo-Palladian country house (20, 21) of 1781 were completed while Trumbull was imprisoned in England between November 1781 and June 1782 under suspicion of being a spy. His confinement ended only through the efforts of his teacher Benjamin West. This design was a compelling one for him, as he sketched variations of it both in 1777 before he went to England and in 1791 when he returned to America. The projecting, pedimented section, with its delicate decoration, the lower side wings, and the symmetrical plan of rectangular rooms, are typical of 18th-century country houses based on Palladian models and the work of Inigo Jones (1573–1652). Trumbull could have been familiar with English houses of the Palladian movement (which extended from 1715 to the mid-18th century) through such books as the architect Colin Campbell's *Vitruvius Britannicus* (volume 1, 1715; volume 2, 1717; supplementary volume, 1725), which illustrates important English buildings of classical inspiration by, among others, John Vanbrugh (1664–1726), Nicholas Hawksmoor (1661–1736), Inigo Jones, and the author.

21

20   *Unidentified country house*
Plan and elevation, 1781
Pen on cream paper, 8¾ x 6" (22.2 x 15.2 cm)
Cooper-Hewitt Museum of Decorative Arts and Design
Smithsonian Institution
New York, New York

21   *Unidentified country house*
Elevation, 1781
Pencil on cream paper, 5¾ x 9⅜" (14.6 x 23.8 cm)
Cooper-Hewitt Museum of Decorative Arts and Design
Smithsonian Institution
New York, New York

1820/1861

Little is known about Andrew Binney except that he studied with William Strickland (page 114) in 1840–1841 in Philadelphia. Andrew Binney's archeologically correct study for a Corinthian order (22) of 1840—the order likened to the proportions of a girl by Vitruvius, called "Virginal" by Vincenzo Scamozzi (1552–1616) and described as "decked like a wanton courtezan [sic]" by the diplomat and author Sir Henry Wotton (1568–1639), who added that the morals of Corinth were bad anyway—can serve as an ideograph for the concern with classicism of American architecture from the 18th century to the beginning of the Modern Movement. The American architect like others before him both accepted the codified orders first established by the Greeks verbatim and invented upon them. The American designer had distinguished predecessors, including such geniuses as Philibert Delorme (1500/15–1570), who invented a new "French" order for the Tuileries Palace in Paris, or Francesco Borromini (1599–1667), who developed his own eccentric and beautiful orders in Rome. Nineteenth-century innovations were supported by the theory of Antoine Laugier (1713–1770), who in his *Essai Sur l'Architecture*, published in 1753 translated into English and German in 1755, advocated the development of new and rational modern orders. In America Benjamin Latrobe (page 82) is famous for his tobacco leaf and corn cob capitals in the United States Capitol. American authors of builders' guides, such as Asher Benjamin (page 74), modified the orders in the interest of practical limitations and economics of American building.

22 Study for the Corinthian Elevation, 1840
Ink and wash on paper, dimensions unknown
Strickland Portfolio
Tennessee State Archives
Nashville, Tennessee

James H. Dakin (1808–1852)

James Dakin began his architectural career in New York working in the large, prosperous, socially prominent firm of Town & Davis (page 100) between 1829 and 1833. Attracted to the South by the impressive economic growth of that region and the success of his brother Charles, who was practicing with James Gallier, Sr. (page 104), in New Orleans, Dakin left New York in 1835 for New Orleans to seek the success he rapidly acquired. Soon after his arrival, he joined in partnership with his brother, who supervised work in Mobile while James remained in New Orleans.

During the 1830s and 1840s alternating in practice both alone and with his brother, Dakin designed some of the finest Greek Revival buildings in America for important private, governmental, and institutional clients. Among these structures are the United States Hotel in Mobile of 1836 and the first buildings for the University of Louisiana, now Tulane, in 1847. He was also associated with the design of the U.S. Custom House in New Orleans, which has a long, complicated history. However, Dakin, who was not tied to one mode, designed some of the first important Gothic Revival buildings in the United States, such as the chapel at New York University in 1833–1835 with Town & Davis, St. Patrick's in New Orleans (completed by Gallier in 1837), and the Louisiana State Capitol at Baton Rouge in 1847, now the State Museum.

Dakin's designs were published by Minard Lafever (1798–1854), the author of many extremely influential builders' guides used as pattern books by carpenters and builders all over the United States. In part through these books Dakin's inventive, not rigidly archeological approach to the use of Greek Revival had a significant impact on the development of that mode in this country. Dakin designed at least one-quarter of the plates in Lafever's *The Modern Builders' Guide* of 1833, and details of Dakin's Bank of Louisville were reproduced by Lafever in *The Beauties of Modern Architecture*, published in 1835. Lafever acknowledges his debt to Dakin in the 1835 volume, and as Arthur Scully quotes from Lafever's description of Dakin in his *James Dakin, Architect* of 1973: "Dakin's philosophy of making his own 'modern combination of parts,' adding his personal flights of 'fancy,' was perhaps his most significant influence."

The Bank of Louisville (24) of 1834–1837 has been reattributed to Dakin by Arthur Scully; for many years it had been credited to Gideon Shryock (1802–1880). Dakin's bank is a free interpretation of Greek and Egyptian vocabularies. He decorates the capitals of the Ionic columns in an unorthodox manner with an anthemion motif, a reiteration of the large anthemion ornament of the acroterion. It is these decorative elements that are reproduced in plate 35 of Lafever's *The Beauties of Modern Architecture*. The Greek-derived details are combined with massing and battered walls that recall an Egyptian pylon. The interior is enclosed by a domed, coffered ceiling lit by an oval occulus.

The undated, unidentified building by Dakin (25) is witness to his skill in setting a building in a cityscape; Dakin in fact illustrated one of the earliest picture books of New York, *Views in New York*, in 1831 by Theodore Fay. This building has a recessed porch with double Ionic columns and the anthemion acroterian ornament of the Bank of Louisville. The tall, thin windows of the side elevation were first used by Dakin's first employers, Town & Davis, and are often called "Davisian" windows. The unidentified "Gothic" church (23) is also characteristic of Dakin's free use of historic forms. The crenelated parapet and the unusual window moldings, used by Dakin in his Louisiana State Capitol designed in 1847, and the general massing of the building reveal a personal Gothic style. An oriental mushroom dome, however, instead of a Gothic spire caps the building.

23

24

23   Unidentified church
Principal elevation, undated
Ink and colored wash, 27¼ x 21¼" (69.2 x 54 cm)
Louisiana Division
New Orleans Public Library
New Orleans, Louisiana

24   Bank of Louisville, Louisville, Kentucky
Principal elevation, 1834–1837
Ink and colored wash, 18½ x 26⅛" (47 x 66.4 cm)
Louisiana Division
New Orleans Public Library
New Orleans, Louisiana

25   Unidentified building
Perspective, undated
Ink and colored wash, 21½ x 30¾" (54.6 x 78.1 cm)
Louisiana Division
New Orleans Public Library
New Orleans, Louisiana

25

26   Pinacotheca for Colonel Trumbull, project
Probably at New Haven, Connecticut
Perspective and two plans, c. 1830
Sepia ink and colored wash, 10 x 6½" (25.4 x 16.5 cm)
The I. N. Phelps Stokes Collection
Prints Division
The Astor, Lenox, & Tilden Foundations
The New York Public Library

27   Suburban Gothic Villa for W.C.H. Waddell
Murray Hill, New York
Perspective and principal floor plan, 1844
Black and sepia ink and colored wash, 8 x 5½" (20.3 x 14 cm)
The I. N. Phelps Stokes Collection
Prints Division
The Astor, Lenox, & Tilden Foundations
The New York Public Library

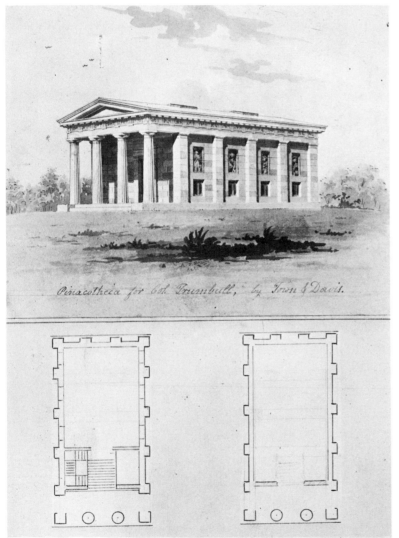

26

Alexander Jackson Davis (1803–1892)

Alexander Jackson Davis is one of the most important romantic, eclectic architects of pre-Civil War America. He was particularly innovative in his application of the various revivalistic modes of the era. It was Davis who initiated the use of the Greek for a state capitol—the Connecticut Capitol on the New Haven Green in 1827–1831, now destroyed. It subsequently became the dominant mode for public buildings until the Civil War. Davis also designed some of the first institutional buildings in the Gothic mode. In 1829, he and Ithiel Town (1784–1844) formed Town & Davis, the first large architectural firm in the United States. Town retired in 1835; however, in the few years of the partnership, the two built such important structures as the New York Custom House, 1832–1842; the Asylum for the Insane on Blackwell, now New York's Roosevelt, Island, 1834; the State Capitol in Raleigh, North Carolina, 1833–1841; and the Wadsworth Atheneum in Hartford, Connecticut, 1842–1844. Alone, Davis had a prosperous practice, which included the Paulding Mansion, now called "Lyndhurst," at Tarrytown, New York, 1838; the Virginia Military Institute, 1852–1859; and Davidson College in North Carolina, 1858. Many of his domestic designs were used as illustrations for a book by Andrew Jackson Downing (1815–1852), *The Architecture of Country Houses*, published in 1850.

Davis was asked by John Trumbull to make suggestions for the design of a Pinacotheca, or art gallery, to house the collection of paintings he had just given Yale University. Davis's design (26) c. 1830 was not used; instead a Greek Revival building designed by Trumbull himself was erected. The model for the Pinacotheca was the small Greek temple adapted by Davis to fit the utilitarian needs of a gallery by adding skylights to the roof and bringing the walls of the building out to the colonnades. Davis's free interpretation of the prototype in this building is characteristic of the classical revival from the work of establishment architects to the structures of village builders.

Another aspect of Davis's vocabulary is exemplified by the house for W. C. H. Waddell (27) in 1844, who was U.S. Marshal of the District of New York under Andrew Jackson. It was the first Gothic castellated villa built in Manhattan. As significant as the new archeological source for this building is Davis's approach to architectural form, which is totally different from that of his Greek Revival buildings. The planning of the building and of the roof line is asymmetrical and picturesque. The building was glassed in dark glass, which created a mysterious and "fairylike" appearance, as it was described by a contemporary author. This esthetic is the parallel in architecture to the Gothic novel, of which we know Davis was enamored.

Davis was certainly influenced by the theorist and landscape architect Alexander Jackson Downing and by English theorists of similar persuasion. Downing favored a picturesque approach to architecture and landscaping and was particularly partial to the Gothic mode. He believed that art should alter nature, but only in ways that were appropriate to a site and in a way that did not formalize nature. These romantic ideas were a reaction to the growing industrialization of the 19th century, but had their roots in 18th-century English theory.

W.C.H. WADDELL, MURRAY HILL, N.Y.   1844.   A.J. DAVIS, ARC'T.

SUBURBAN GOTHIC VILLA.

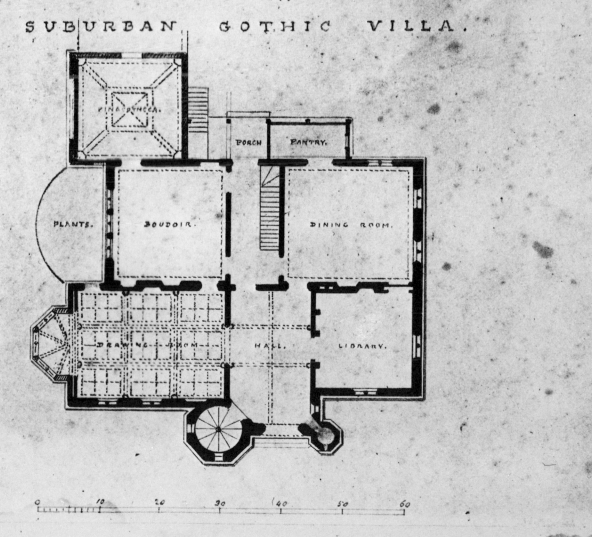

102 28 *Broadway Tabernacle, New York City*
Perspective study of cloister, 1859
Pencil and wash, 14⅝ x 9½" (37.1 x 24.1 cm)
Avery Library
Columbia University
New York, New York

Leopold Eidlitz (1823–1908)

Leopold Eidlitz, born in Prague and educated at the Polytechnic in Vienna, arrived in New York in 1843 and worked for Richard Upjohn (page 118), who was one of the finest and most archeologically correct of the medieval revivalists in America. Upjohn reinforced a predilection for the medieval that Eidlitz had acquired in Europe, yet Upjohn's taste was for the Gothic and Romanesque of England and France, whereas Eidlitz understandably favored that of Germany. Eidlitz's first work, St. George's Church in New York, 1845, built with Otto Blesch, brought him to the attention of the profession and led to a flood of subsequent commissions in New York, including the American Exchange National Bank of 1857–1859, the Church of the Holy Trinity of 1870–1874, and the Dry Dock Savings Bank of 1875.

Today, Eidlitz is perhaps best remembered for his last commission, the reworking of the New York State Capitol in Albany, which was begun in 1867 by Thomas Fuller, who with Herbert Jones was the architect of the Victorian Gothic Capitol of 1859–1867 at Ottawa. Fuller had been dismissed for extravagance, and when Eidlitz and Henry Hobson Richardson assumed the commission in 1875, they were left with a building that had risen only two stories. The design, primarily Eidlitz's, retains Fuller's Second Empire style facade to the last story, which Eidlitz originally designed in the Romanesque. In 1877 the Legislature decided that the building should be completed in the Italian Renaissance mode. Richardson wrote to Olmstead concerning this: "I do believe *entre-nous* that the building can be well finished in Francois Ier or Louis XIV which come under the head of Renaissance." Richardson, not then as well known as Eidlitz, executed most of the Senate wing, while Eidlitz worked on the Assembly. The building was finally completed in 1894 by Isaac Perry.

In 1881 in both New York and London Eidlitz published *The Nature and Function of Art with Special Reference to Architecture* which called for an architecture based on principles of construction and truth to materials. These were the same ideas espoused by the French theorist and architect Viollet-le-Duc (1814–1879) and were important to the work of many distinguished 19th-century architects. Eidlitz does not mention Viollet-le-Duc as a source, but the latter's works were translated in 1875, and his ideas were part of the *zeitgeist* of the time. Many 19th-century architects, and Eidlitz was no exception, were ambivalent about the use of iron in architecture —an issue that produced great controversy in 19th-century architectural circles. Eidlitz felt that to use it beautifully yet truthfully and not represent it as another material would be too expensive. But he believed it was appropriate for what he called "engineering structures," such as his own project for the 1852 Crystal Palace in New York, inspired by Paxton's 1851 building of the same name for the London International Exposition. Eidlitz's Crystal Palace, designed with James Bogardus (1800–1874), had glass walls and a roof suspended by wrought-iron chains from a central tower. Eidlitz was likewise ambivalent about the use of historical sources. He advocated a nonrevivalistic attitude toward architectural style, yet believed that not since the 13th century had there been a style that was ruled by principles of construction. As a result, he built only within the medieval mode.

Eidlitz admired John Ruskin (1819–1900) as "the most analytical mind in Europe," although Eidlitz was a structural determinist, and Ruskin was not. Ruskin advocated the use of nature as a source for ornament and a realistic or truthful use of materials the arch leading to the cloister of Eidlitz's Romanesque Broadway Tabernacle (28) of 1859 is expressive of these attitudes. Much of the ornament is inspired by nature; the polychromatic scheme of the arch emphasized the traditional construction methods of the building. His realism, or truth to materials and nature, is cloaked, as it is in his writings, in the mantle of 19th-century romanticism.

James Gallier, Sr. (1798–1868)
James Gallier, Jr. (1827–1868)

The professional careers of James Gallier, Sr., and his son, James Gallier, Jr., are paradigms of changing architectural taste in America before the Civil War. The father, born in England, was trained in London with various firms, including that of Sir William Wilkins (1778–1839), architect of the Greek Revival National Gallery in London of 1834–1838. He came to America in 1832 with his family and worked for 2 years in New York, first for Town & Davis (page 100) and then as a partner with Minard Lafever (1798–1854), author of *The Modern Builders' Guide* of 1833 and *The Beauties of Modern Architecture* of 1835.

This background made him a confirmed, almost evangelical Greek Revivalist. In 1833 he gave lectures on the Greek style in New York and published his *American Builder's Price Book*, which became a standard volume on the legal, economic, and technological aspects of building. The *Autobiography of James Gallier, Architect*, published in 1864, is a valuable guide to building practice in America before the Civil War.

During the early 1830s New Orleans experienced tremendous economic growth, which attracted Northerners and stimulated building. This brought the enterprising James Gallier and his first partner, Charles Dakin, to Mobile and then New Orleans, where they established a flourishing practice as Dakin & Gallier from 1834 to 1840. They designed commercial and fine residential structures in the Greek Revival mode, including the St. Charles Hotel of 1837. Gallier worked alone to the late 1840s, designing some of the best Greek Revival buildings in New Orleans—the 1844 Mercer House, now the Boston Club, the Commercial Exchange of 1845, and the City Hall of 1845–1850.

The Greek Revival doorway by James Gallier, Sr. (29) c. 1840 typifies the delicacy of Greek Revival detailing whose forms were spread through the United States by builders' guides such as those by Minard Lafever and Asher Benjamin (page 74). Two Doric columns support the small porch in front of the doorway. Delicate rosettes frame the door itself and are similar to the decoration of other doorways in New Orleans.

In the late 1840s Gallier, Jr., took over the firm under the name of Gallier, Turpin & Co., and in 1858 the firm became Gallier & Esterbrook. It was just at midcentury when James Gallier, Jr., assumed control of the firm that the Italianate and Gothic were becoming the dominant modes in America, and his work, largely urban domestic buildings, reflects this change.

The J. J. Warren House (30) in New Orleans by Gallier, Jr., in 1860 contains Italianate decorative details with a cast iron porch typical of New Orleans. Its long plan, almost L-shaped, was typical of both vernacular and sophisticated rural and urban building around New Orleans. Formal suites and master bedrooms are in the front of the house; a long wing of servant's rooms, guest rooms, and children's rooms extends to the back of the lot. This wing traditionally became known as the "garconnière."

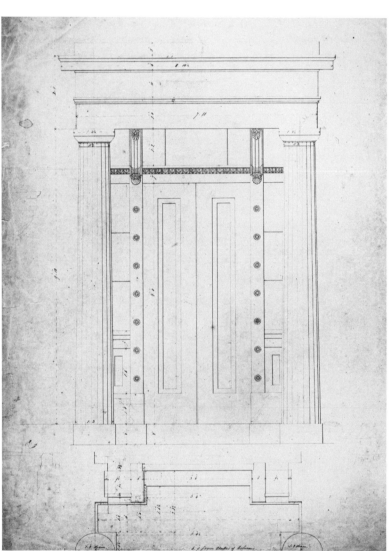

29

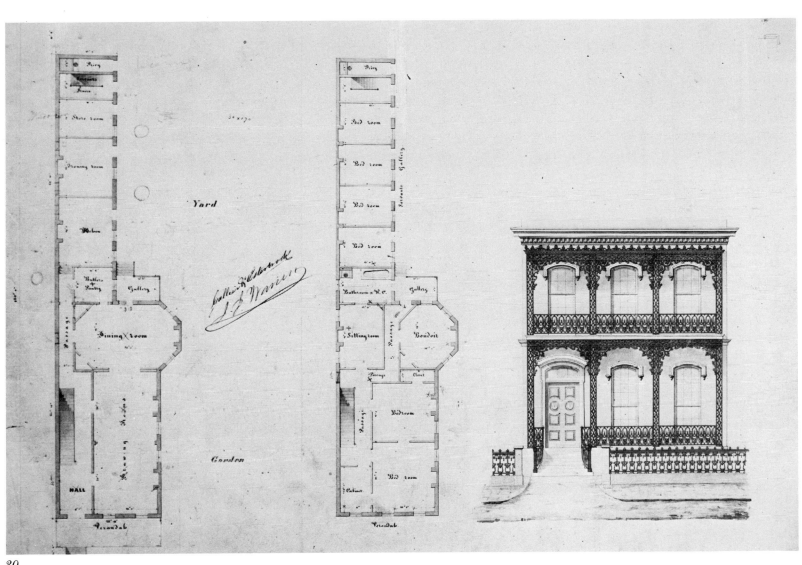

30

29   James Gallier, Sr.
Doorway, New Orleans, Louisiana
Plan and elevation, c. 1840
Ink, 28 x 20¼" (71.1 x 51.4 cm)
Sylvester Labrot Collection
Special Collections Division
Howard-Tilton Memorial Library
Tulane University
New Orleans, Louisiana

30   James Gallier, Jr.
J. J. Warren House, New Orleans, Louisiana
Two plans and front elevation, c. 1860
Ink and watercolor, 20¼ x 26¼" (51.4 x 66.7 cm)
Sylvester Labrot Collection
Special Collections Division
Howard-Tilton Memorial Library
Tulane University
New Orleans, Louisiana

31 Girard College competition entry, Philadelphia
Perspective, 1832
Watercolor, 37½ x 26" (95.3 x 66 cm)
The Historical Society of Pennsylvania
Philadelphia, Pennsylvania

32 Prison studies
Perspective, section, and plan studies, sketchbook, 1831
Pencil, 12¼ x 16¼" (31.1 x 41.3 cm)
Permanent Loan to Charles Patterson van Pelt Library
University of Pennsylvania by Somerset Archaeological and
Natural History Society
Tauton, England

John Haviland (1792–1852)

John Haviland, like many of America's most important pre-Civil War architects—George Hadfield, Benjamin Latrobe (page 82), Richard Upjohn (page 118), and Calvert Vaux (page 120)—was born in England. Haviland made an important contribution to the development of the Greek Revival in America through his many important Philadelphia buildings in the Greek style, such as the First Presbyterian Church of 1820, one of the first religious structures in the United States built in a temple form; the facade for the Asylum for the Deaf and Dumb of 1824, now the Philadelphia College of Art; and the Franklin Institute. In Haviland's builders' guide, *The Builder's Assistant* (3 volumes published respectively in 1818, 1819, 1821), the Greek orders were published in America for the first time. At the same time the book's preface extolled the Greek mode, it also supported the picturesque esthetic. Haviland believed that there should be a close correspondence between a house and a site and that the landscape should be studied before the style of a building was arrived at. It is therefore not surprising that Haviland wrote that a craggy landscape demanded the Gothic and that a flat site required the Greek. Haviland's book had wide circulation in the United States; his preface is one of the elements that promotes the enthusiastic reception for the picturesque in America during the 1840s.

Haviland is acknowledged for his programmatic and esthetic contribution to American prison architecture. He was one of the first architects to construct a radially planned prison block containing individual cells and exercise yards for prisoners who, according to what became known as the "Pennsylvania System," were kept in solitary confinement. The invention of the radial plan is attributed to Sir Samuel Bentham in 1787 and was used on a much smaller scale in Europe. Haviland must have become involved with prison design through his English employer, James Elmes (1782–1862), who published *Hints on the Construction of Prisons* in 1817, the year after Haviland arrived in Philadelphia. Haviland's sketchbook (32) of 1831 shows several studies for radial and rectangular prisons. The first prison in the radial form that he designed was the Eastern State Penitentiary of 1821–1829, destined to be widely copied in Europe. Spread across the sketchbook is a perspective of a prison very close to Haviland's New York Hall of Justice of 1836, better known today as "The Tombs" because of its Egyptian detailing (it was destroyed between 1897 and 1902). The Tombs and the Eastern Penitentiary in the Gothic mode, although based on different stylistic sources, were treated with the planarity and simplicity common to Haviland's Greek Revival works.

Haviland's entry for the Girard College competition of 1832 (31) is a Doric temple connected by covered walkways to four separate smaller buildings. This conception is in distinct contrast with Jefferson's University of Virginia, where the pavilions are unified by colonnades. This design did not place in the competition, which was won by Thomas U. Walter (page 122). With few exceptions, the drawings that exist from the competition are all designed in the Greek Revival style.

31

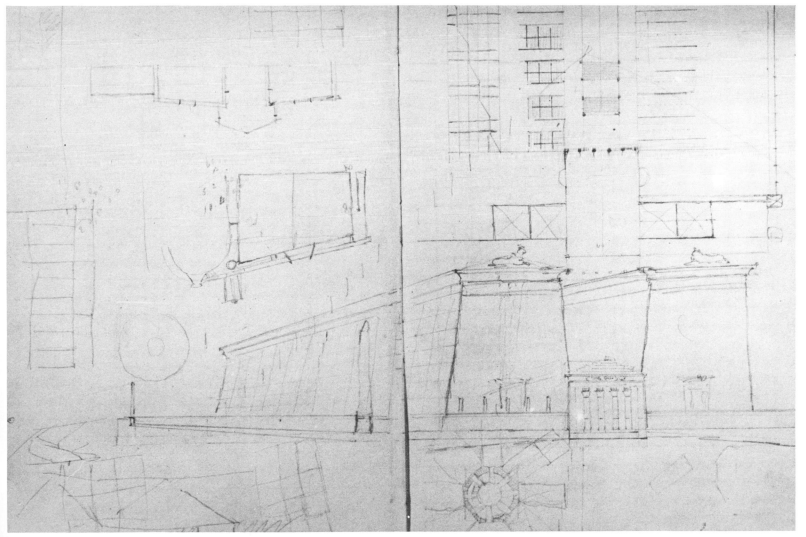

32

Thomas Lewinski was born and educated in London, but it is not known with whom he studied. During the 1840s and 1850s he made an important contribution to the architectural profession in Kentucky, working primarily in Lexington and Louisville for clients such as several members of Henry Clay's family. Lewinski was also involved at this time in the antislavery movement. In the 1850s Lewinski became Secretary of the Lexington Gas Company and effectively ended his career as an architect, except for a few buildings constructed for friends and former clients. His work, primarily domestic, was designed in the Tuscan mode in the 1840s and the Italianate villa style in the 1850s. Buildings designed in the Tuscan style were organized around rigid symmetrical plans reflected in their cubic massing; the Italianate villa mode was organized around asymmetrical plans and irregular picturesque massing not unlike the disposition of elements in a Gothic Revival villa. Both the Tuscan and Italianate villa style had classical and Renaissance detailing. The few churches attributed to Lewinski were designed in the Gothic Revival style.

Lewinski's library included *The Model Architect* of 1852 written by the Philadelphia architect, Samuel Sloan, which contained plates of Italianate villas. Lewinski must certainly have been familiar with the works of the 1840s and 1850s by Andrew Jackson Downing, who advocated that buildings should harmonize with the landscape through materials and massing. This was in contrast with the prevailing mode for domestic design of the previous decade, the Greek Revival, which was not concerned with the unification of nature and architecture or, by implication, humanity and nature through design. Downing criticized the Greek Revival because its predominantly white color and flat materials created a discordance with nature.

Lewinski's home for Dr. Peter (33, 34) c. 1847 in Lexington, Kentucky, is characteristic of the Italianate type. Rooms with a variety of shapes are connected with a servants' wing— the whole forming an irregular perimeter surrounded by three deep porches. The building is composed of volumes of different heights, adding to the picturesque quality. The large brackets, round-headed blind and real windows, interior niches, and arcade are details particular to the Italianate style.

33   *House for Dr. Robert Peter, Lexington, Kentucky*
Northeast elevation, c. 1847
Ink and wash, 5½ x 7½" (14 x 19.1 cm)
Special Collections Division
University of Kentucky
Lexington, Kentucky

34   *House for Dr. Robert Peter, Lexington, Kentucky*
Ground plan, c. 1847
Ink, 7½ x 12½" (19.1 x 31.8 cm)
Special Collections Division
University of Kentucky
Lexington, Kentucky

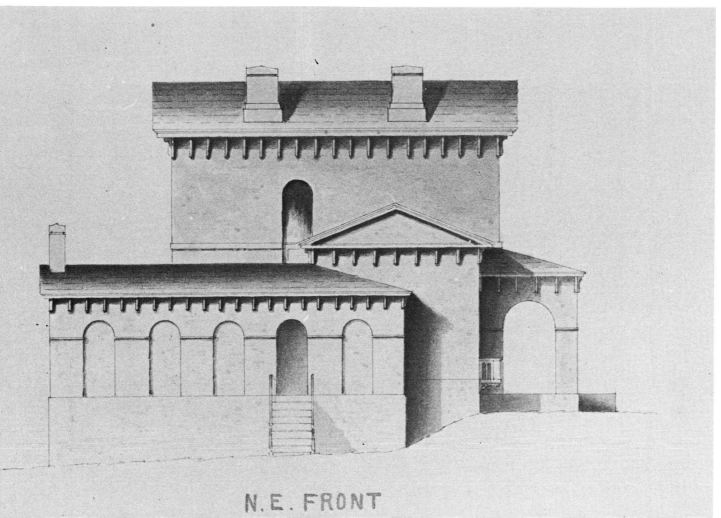

N. E. FRONT

Façade
or
Principal Front of the Church.

Robert Mills (1781–1855)

Robert Mills, architect, engineer, and author, produced some of the finest and most inventive Greek Revival buildings, several of which are the first important government buildings in the nation's capital, including the United States Treasury of 1842 and the Patent Office of 1840. In the competition of 1812 Mills won the commission for the Washington Monument in Baltimore; this was the first column scaled to the height of a building that was erected in the New World and preceded his design for the Washington Monument in the U.S. capital begun in 1848 and completed in 1884.

Mills, born in 1781 in Charleston, South Carolina, was of the first generation of American architects who reached maturity in the postrevolutionary cultural milieu. His education was sophisticated for the period. He studied Classics at the College of Charleston and received his architectural training from the luminaries of the architectural profession in America. In 1800, in apprenticeship with James Hoban, architect of the White House, Mills acquired general technical skills needed for the architectural profession. In 1801 or 1802 he studied with Jefferson (page 79) at Monticello, which gave him access not only to the outstanding architectural library there but to the mind of one of the creative geniuses of the era. Under Jefferson, Mills developed into a superb draftsman. In 1804, furnished with a letter of introduction from Jefferson, he made one of the first known tours of America for the purpose of studying architectural monuments. Between 1804 and 1809 Mills was employed by Benjamin Latrobe (page 82), who was both architect and engineer. Latrobe's rational approach to architecture, his severe language of forms, and his admiration for Greek architecture had a formative influence on Mills.

Mills practiced in Philadelphia and Charleston between 1808 and 1817 and then in Washington, where from 1836 to 1841 he was United States "Architect and Engineer." In this office he was responsible for many custom houses and eight marine hospitals along the Eastern seaboard, as well as his work in Washington. Mills' books include an atlas for South Carolina, the *Guide to the National Executive Offices and Capitol of the United States* published in 1841; *Statistics of South Carolina* published in 1826; and an autobiographical statement printed as an appendix in Helen Pierce Gallagher's *Robert Mills, Architect of the Washington Monument, 1781–1855* of 1935.

Mills had a rationalistic approach to architecture. He derived the form of his buildings from first principles of function and structure. Classical architecture provided a general inspiration for the formal language and symbolism of his buildings. The vocabulary of classical ornament he employed was sparingly applied and used primarily to emphasize structure.

Mills was consciously determined to forge a new American architectural idiom. He writes in his autobiographical notes published in Gallagher that "his [Mills'] considerations were . . . first, the object of the building; second, the means appropriate for its construction; third, the situation it was to occupy . . . ," and further, "the principle assumed and acted upon was that beauty is founded upon order and that convenience and utility were constituent parts." Mills indicates that he believes the origin of all architecture is in natural law and that the Greek mode is to be preferred over the Roman for its simplicity and appropriateness to American ideals. These are notions that parallel those of the French theorist Abbe Laugier (1713–1769), whose ideas may well have come to Mills through his mentors, particularly Latrobe.

In his fireproof building in Charleston, Mills developed a design formula repeated in the Treasury Building in which groin-vaulted cubicles of space, executed in brick and then plastered, at once serve as the structural and functional module for the building, each vaulted bay being an office or cell of space. These cells are interconnected by barrel- or groin-vaulted corridors. In the Treasury Building nearly the only ornament is the half entablature in the corridor, which terminates exactly at the springing of the vault, thus creating a clear articulation of the parts. This "Millsian" solution is determined to a great extent by structure and creates a fireproof construction.

Mills' recognition of the role of program in determining form is exemplified by the development of the "auditorium church," which is round or octagonal in plan. This form developed out of growing demand within all religious sects in the United States for a ritual in which the sermon had an ever-increasing importance. This form provided for seating arrangements that afforded adequate visual and aural contact with the speaker. The best examples of the type were the Sansom Street Baptist Church in Philadelphia of 1809 and the Monumental Church in Richmond, Virginia, begun in 1812.

At a quick first glance the First Presbyterian Church (35) of 1809–1812 in Augusta, Georgia, is basically like the Wren-Gibbs type church of the Colonial tradition (for example, 74), yet its general massing and approach to detail is notably different from that formula. The building exemplifies Mills' severe formal language. It is as if the building were constructed of only a rectangle, a triangle, a polygonal tower, and a conelike steeple.

35   First Presbyterian Church, Augusta, Georgia
Elevation, 1809–1812
Ink and watercolor, dimensions unknown
First Presbyterian Church
Augusta, Georgia

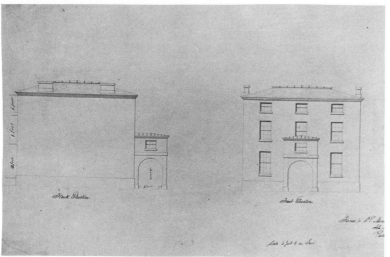

36

36 *Stephen P. Morris House, Philadelphia*
Front and side elevation, 1840
Ink, 16⅛ x 23⅝" (41 x 60 cm)
The Historical Society of Pennsylvania
Philadelphia, Pennsylvania

37 *Stephen P. Morris House, Philadelphia*
Elevation and plan, 1840
Ink and wash, 23 3/16 x 17" (58.9 x 43.2 cm)
The Historical Society of Pennsylvania
Philadelphia, Pennsylvania

John Notman (1810–1865)

The two modes for domestic architecture favored in the quarter of a century before the Civil War were the Gothic and Italianate villa style, the latter inspired by vernacular farm buildings in Italy. John Notman helped introduce the Italianate villa style into the American vocabulary with his house for Bishop Doane in Burlington, New Jersey, in 1837. It was subsequently published by the American tastemaker, Andrew Jackson Downing, in his *Treatise on the Theory and Practice of Landscape Gardening Adapted to North America* published in 1841. Downing recommended the Italianate villa style because its asymmetrical massing at once created the highly valued picturesque effects and was flexible in that it could be made to respond to issues of site orientation and programmatic needs. The asymmetrical massing and planning, brackets, and projecting roof that created this image could be added to easily without altering and perhaps even enhancing the picturesque effect. Notman was also one of the first architects in America to employ the more severe Renaissance Palazzo style in his Philadelphia Atheneum of 1847.

Notman was born in Edinburgh to a family that for four generations had been gardeners and stoneworkers. Before settling in Philadelphia in 1831, he may have studied at Michael Angelo Nicholson's School of Architecture and Perspective in London. M. A. Nicholson was the son of Peter Nicholson (1765–1844), author of influential builders' guides as well as a mathematician. Notman's knowledge of English architecture provided him with precedents for introducing Italianate modes in America; the first English Italianate villa was John Nash's Cronkhill of 1802 near Shrewsbury, and the first 19th-century building in the High Renaissance Palazzo style was Sir Charles Barry's Traveller's Club on Pall Mall in London in 1829.

Notman was distinguished in Philadelphia for his Gothic Revival churches, such as St. Mark's on Locust Street of 1847–1849; Italianate churches, such as Saints Peter and Paul, designed and built in 1846–1864, with the facade completed in 1857, inspired by the Baroque Church of S. Carlo al Corso in Rome; and the Church of the Ascension of 1846, modeled on the Romanesque Saint Ambrogio in Milan. Notman built in several other modes especially for domestic architecture, such as the Oriental (Dunn House in Mount Holly, New Jersey, in 1840, which was published by Downing in 1841), the Tuscan, and the Gothic. A number of Notman's Tuscan villas exist in Princeton, New Jersey: the Stockton House of 1845, "Woodlawn" of 1846, and "Prospect" of 1849. The Harry Ingersoll House, "Medary," of 1847–1848 near Philadelphia is also in the Tuscan mode. Ivy Hall also built in Princeton in 1847 is a Gothic Revival house.

Notman presented two schemes both with a porte-cochere for the Stephen P. Morris House of 1840 in Philadelphia. One (36) is based on Regency models; the alternate scheme (37) is derived from the Swiss chalet type popular at the time, with a deep overhanging roof that creates picturesque shadows. Notman's flexible architectural vocabulary as exemplified by this commission was characteristic of the work of many architects of the period and reflects the eclecticism of the era.

No. 1 Front Elevation of S. P. Morris's House
Southwark
John Notman Archt
1840

No. 2 Principal Floor of S. P. Morris's House
John Notman Archt
1840

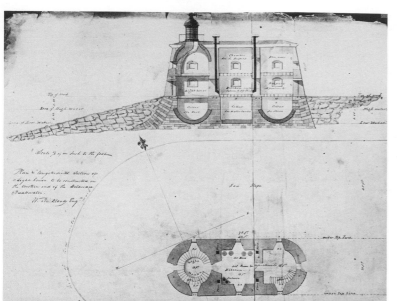

38

38   *Lighthouse for the Delaware Breakwater near Lewtes, Delaware*
Section and plan, 1826–1827
Ink and colored wash, 20¼ x 23¼" (51.4 x 59.1 cm)
Tennessee State Archives
Nashville, Tennessee

39   *Unidentified building*
Principal facade elevation, undated
Ink and colored wash, 11 x 19½" (27.9 x 49.5 cm)
Tennessee State Archives
Nashville, Tennessee

40   *United States Capitol, Hall of Representatives*
Washington, D.C.
Section from the speaker's chair looking north, 1843
Ink and watercolor on paper (now laminated)
40¾ x 26¾" (103.5 x 67.9 cm)
The National Archives
Washington, D.C.

William Strickland (1787–1854)

William Strickland—architect, painter, and engineer—was one of the most important Greek Revival architects in the United States. He, like his contemporary Robert Mills (page 110), was trained by Benjamin Latrobe (page 82), who was one of the first architects in America to be both an architect and an engineer. Decorative refinement, elegance, and formal inventiveness particularly characterize Strickland's *oeuvre*, which includes important public commissions such as the United States Mint in Philadelphia of 1829, the Merchants Exchange in Philadelphia of 1832–1834, and the State Capitol in Nashville, Tennessee, of 1845–1849, where he is buried.

Strickland was the first architect to build a public building entirely in the Greek mode: the Second Bank of the United States in Philadelphia of 1818–1824 based on the Parthenon as reconstructed in Stuart and Revett's *Antiquities of Athens* (volume 1 published in 1762; volume 2 published in 1789). The commission, won through competition, had a program, which stated that the bank's directors "wished a chase (sic) imitation of Grecian Architecture in its simplest and least expensive form." Strickland's bank was the first model for the use of a Greek temple form for a modern function in a milieu ripe to adapt it. Americans associated Greece, as they did their own new nation, with purity and democracy. This was a result of both an idealized view of the Athenian city-state of the 5th century B.C. and the Greek war of independence against the Turks from 1821 to 1829. The Greek Revival was easily accepted because, like the architecture of the Federal period, it had its sources in the classical world. The ease and economy with which this style could be constructed are not to be underestimated in understanding why, between 1830 and 1850, it became the *lingua franca* of the age—the dominant style for public and private buildings for rich and poor.

The undated drawing of an unidentified building on a street front (39) is the other side of the Greek Revival coin from Strickland's imitation of the Parthenon at the Second Bank of the United States. The smooth facade, composed of two Doric columns, a Doric entablature, and two corner piers with Doric details, is based on no specific Greek monument; it is Greek because of its detailing. Strickland recognized the utilitarian problems of employing an ancient Greek model for 19th-century functions; thus he advocated using only the motifs of the Greek style and organizing the plan according to the dictates of programmatic requirements. This is a pragmatic approach; yet the Greek Revival is a pictorial and romantic style, concerned essentially with symbol. It is not concerned, as is the neoclassicism of a Latrobe, with the clear expression of the plan in the massing or with the clear expression of structure in a building. For example, a Greek Revival elevation may front a building whose stories are actually lower than the facade, as in many buildings along the Main Streets of America.

Strickland was asked to study acoustical problems in the House of Representatives' Chamber, for which he produced the illustrated drawing (40) of 1843. This is not the present House Chamber. Strickland recommended creating flat walls in the room and eliminating the niches that Latrobe had designed for this space. He also advised covering these walls with cloth hangings and making the height of the room only one-third its width. None of these ideas was ever implemented.

A complex engineering and architectural project that Strickland supervised between 1826 and 1840 was the building of the Delaware Breakwater. The purpose of this was to provide a safe harbor for Philadelphia. The drawing (38) of 1826–1840 shows the plan and section for a lighthouse in the breakwater.

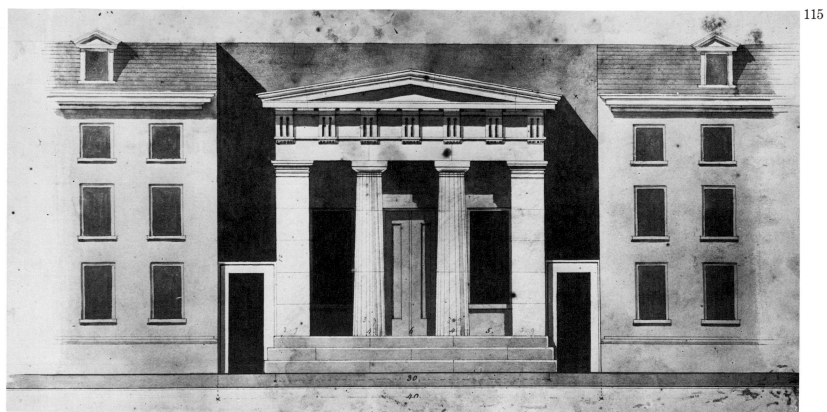

39

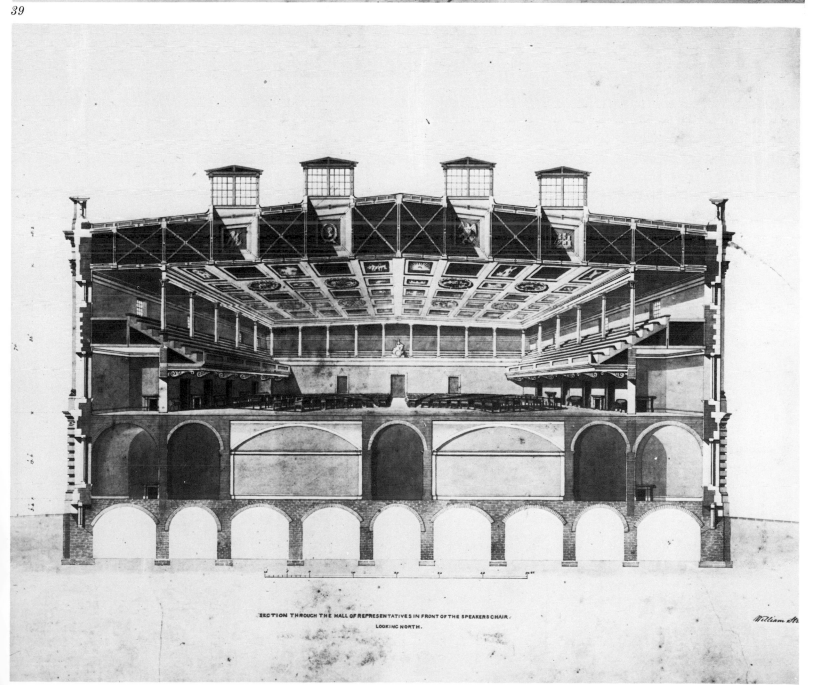

SECTION THROUGH THE HALL OF REPRESENTATIVES IN FRONT OF THE SPEAKERS CHAIR.
LOOKING NORTH.

William St

40

Thomas Alexander Tefft was the outstanding architect of the late 1840s to mid-1850s in Rhode Island. In 1859 he died in Florence while on a trip to study European architectural monuments. He graduated from Brown University in 1851 but before graduation began his architectural career with the firm of Tallman & Bucklin. One of Tefft's earliest works—the Union Depot in Providence, Rhode Island, of 1848 (destroyed by fire in 1898)—was his most notable. Henry-Russell Hitchcock wrote that "Without question it was the finest early [railroad] station in the New World." Tefft designed the red brick building in a Lombard Romanesque style while he was employed by Tallman & Bucklin, the firm that executed the building. The Lombard Romanesque and Renaissance Revival were the modes Tefft favored, although early drawings exist in which he designed in the Gothic mode.

Among his other outstanding works are the Thomas Hoppin House of 1853 and the Central Baptist Church in Providence of 1857. The Hoppin House, like several others Tefft executed in Providence, was inspired by the English architect Sir Charles Barry's (1795–1860) London clubs and mansions, executed in the Italian Renaissance mode. These houses established a local style in Providence that lasted to the 1870s. Tefft also designed the Cannelton Mills in Cannelton, Indiana, in 1849–1850.

Tefft, a school teacher before attending Brown, was a protégé of the educational reformer, Henry Barnard. Several of Tefft's designs for schools were published in Barnard's *School Architecture or Contributions to the Improvement of School Houses in the United States* published in 1848. In addition to his architectural career, Tefft was an energetic advocate of the establishment of a universal currency and both lectured and published on the subject. The Merchant's Exchange of 1856 (41, 42, 43) to be built on Exchange Place in Providence would have been east of the Greek Revival Providence Arcade by Russell Warren and James Bucklin of 1828. Tefft's design was influenced by J. Bunning's (1802–1863) New Coal Exchange in London of 1846–1849, a clipping of which is preserved in Tefft's scrapbook. Tefft's five-story scheme with its Romanesque facade would have contained shops on the lower floors and offices above. The rotunda, vaulted by an iron and glass dome, was to serve as a broker's board.

The union of iron and glass, new to the late 18th and early 19th century, was dependent on advanced technology that revolutionized architecture. The structural properties and esthetic implications of this combination were exploited to their fullest extent for the first time by Joseph Paxton (1801–1865) in his Crystal Palace in London of 1851 for the International Exposition. Its iron and wood structure was totally sheathed in glass. The new, modern image created elicited contempt from John Ruskin (1819–1900), the leading theorist of the High Gothic style in England. Tefft's project, then, is expressive of the two outstanding and often conflicting currents in 19th-century architecture: historical revival and the use of new industrialized building materials.

41   *Merchants' Exchange, project, Providence, Rhode Island*
Plan, 1856
Ink, 8 x 14½" (20.3 x 36.8 cm)
John Hay Library
Brown University
Providence, Rhode Island

42   *Merchants' Exchange, project, Providence, Rhode Island*
Elevation, 1856
Ink, 5¼ x 9" (13.3 x 22.9 cm)
John Hay Library
Brown University
Providence, Rhode Island

43   *Merchants' Exchange, project, Providence, Rhode Island*
Section, 1856
Ink, 6¼ x 14⅜" (15.9 x 36.5 cm)
John Hay Library
Brown University
Providence, Rhode Island

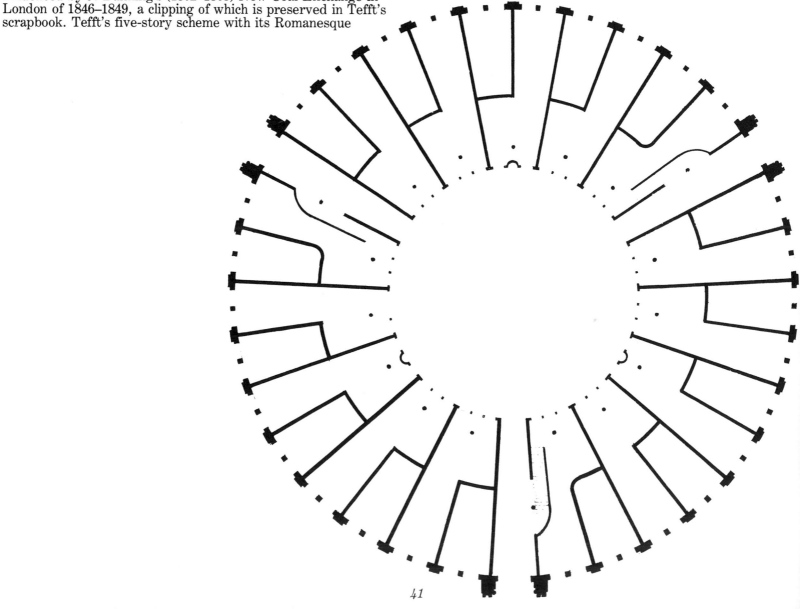

41

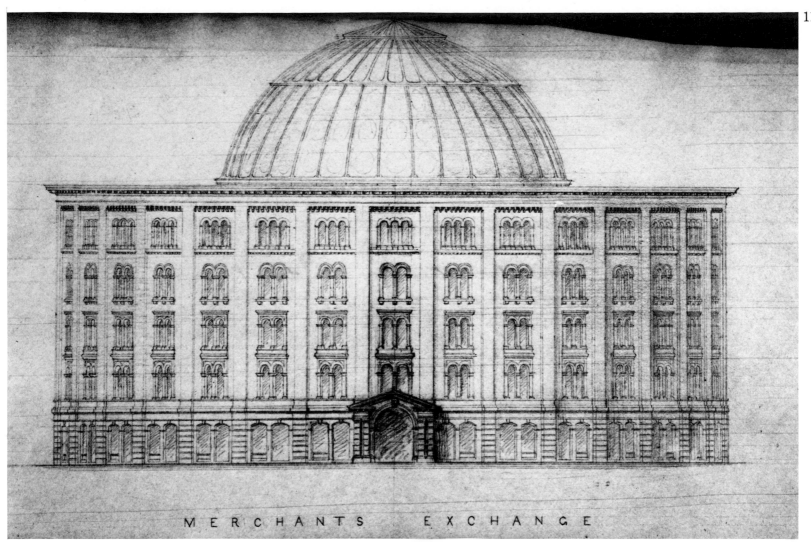

MERCHANTS EXCHANGE

42

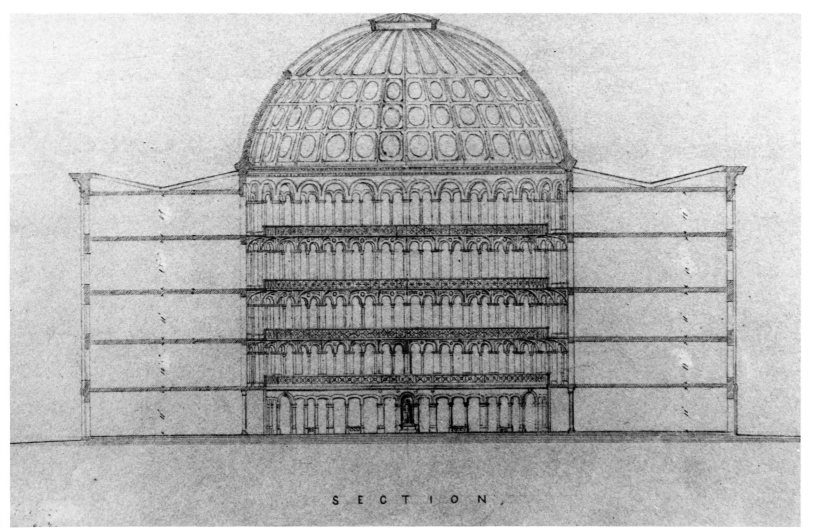

SECTION

43

44 *St. Mark's Episcopal Church, Palatka, Florida*
Four elevations, plan, and two sections, 1852
Ink and wash, 20¾ x 20" (52.7 x 50.8 cm)
Special Collections
Robert Manning Strozier Library
Florida State University
Tallahassee, Florida

45 Hamilton Hoppin House, Middletown, Rhode Island
Elevation, 1856–1857
Ink and wash on paper, 10½ x 14½" (26.7 x 36.9 cm)
Avery Library
Columbia University
New York, New York

Richard Upjohn (1802–1878)

In 1828, the Englishman Richard Upjohn arrived in America, accompanied by his wife and children—one of whom, Richard M. Upjohn (1828–1903), would join his father in 1853 to found Richard Upjohn & Company, one of the most important 19th-century architectural firms. It was the elder Upjohn's distinction to help found the American Institute of Architects (AIA) in 1857 and to remain its president from that time until 1876. The height of the Gothic Revival in America was from the 1830s to the 1860s, and Upjohn built some of its finest secular as well as religious buildings, including what is probably his most famous work, Trinity Church in New York of 1839–1846, designed in the late Gothic perpendicular mode; the George Noble Jones House in Newport, Rhode Island, of 1839, later named "Kingscote"; and St. Mary's at Burlington, New Jersey, of 1846–1854, in the early English Gothic style. However, Upjohn, an eclectic, also built in the Romanesque mode, such as his Church of the Pilgrims in Brooklyn of 1844–1846; in the Italianate mode, such as his Utica, New York, City Hall of 1853; and in the Stick Style.

During the 18th and 19th centuries, the Gothic Revival was used in a nonarcheological way for its picturesque and romantic qualities. In contrast with this, during the last years of the 1830s and through the 1850s, the Gothic style was also used to fulfill theological ends. The religiously conservative Cambridge Camden Society, founded in England in 1839, professed that the Gothic style, applied only in the historically accurate way, was the one style appropriate for Christian architecture. The society also contended that the solely acceptable approach to construction was the "honest" expression of structure and materials. These ideas, based on the writing of A. W. N. Pugin (1812–1852), were disseminated through the society's journal, *The Ecclesiologist* (first issued in 1841). In general, the Gothic Revival in America drew on the historical Gothic as a source for details, plans, and elevations, but often combined these in a nonarcheological manner. Upjohn, however, whose attitudes toward construction were influenced by Pugin as well as by the major American exponent of such construction principles, Andrew Jackson Downing (1815–1852), based his Gothic Revival buildings on historical precedents. He was one of the few architects acceptable to the American equivalent of the Camden Society, the New York Ecclesiological Society, which published in 1848 the first American journal devoted solely to architecture, *The New York Ecclesiologist*.

Upjohn's most far-reaching contribution to the Gothic Revival in America was his book, *Rural Architecture*, of 1852, which provided plans for carpenters (or "mechanics," as Upjohn called them) to construct Gothic churches in wood at low cost. Upjohn's book is directly connected in spirit to the 18th- and early 19th-century builders' guides, such as those by Asher Benjamin (page 74). Upjohn's brief introduction explains only the content of the book and describes the audience to whom it is directed; it is not concerned with esthetic or theological issues.

The plans for the St. Mark's Episcopal Church (44) of 1852 in Palatka, Florida, are extremely close to those in Upjohn's book. The simple basilican plan, plastered on the interior, was constructed in the wood-framing technique in which the joints of the boards are covered by vertical battens. The invention of this technique is attributed to Andrew Jackson Davis (page 100) in the late 1830s. Davis's designs were published by Andrew Jackson Downing, one of the most influential apologists for the picturesque in America, in his *Cottage Residences* of 1842 and *The Architecture of Country Houses* in 1850. Downing approved of the technique, which, he felt, was a true expression of the real structure of the vertical supports of the house.

Downing's attitude toward reality in building and his apology for the picturesque provided the theoretical background for the "Stick Style," which flourished in the United States between the 1850s and the late 1870s. Upjohn's Hamilton Hoppin House (45) in Middletown, Rhode Island, of 1856–1857 is a prime example of this style. In the Stick Style, the external framing of vertical, horizontal, and diagonal wooden members, or sticks, reflects in a pronounced way the concept of the internal structural skeleton. In the Hoppin House, the sticks take the form of double Ys. The image presented, as with all Stick Style buildings, is of lightness, paralleling the lightweight construction technique of the building.

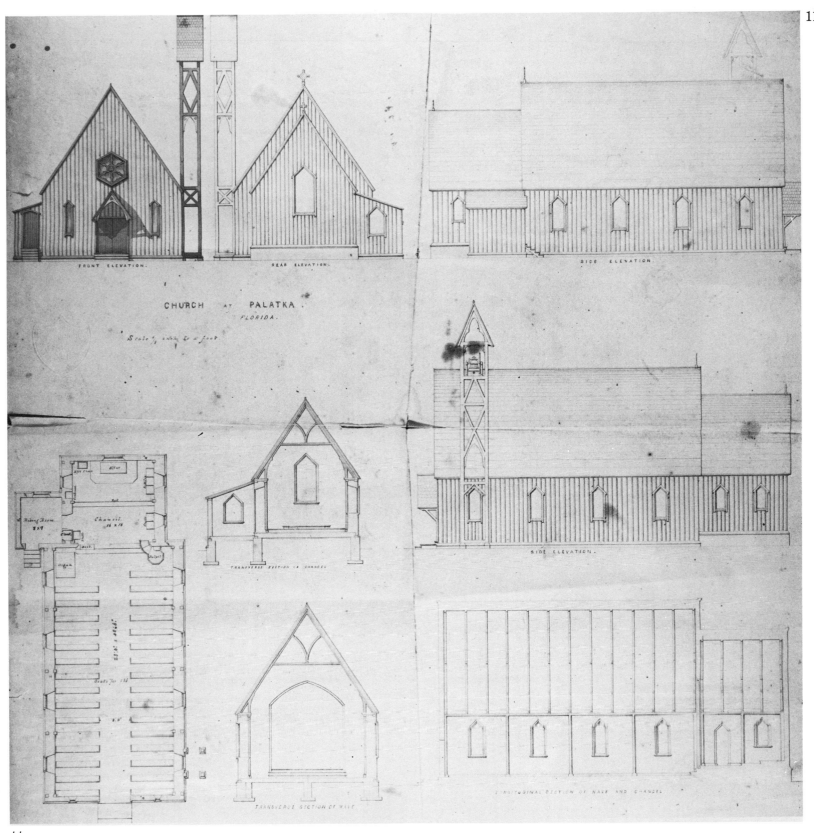

FRONT ELEVATION. REAR ELEVATION. SIDE ELEVATION.

CHURCH AT PALATKA.
FLORIDA.

SIDE ELEVATION.

44

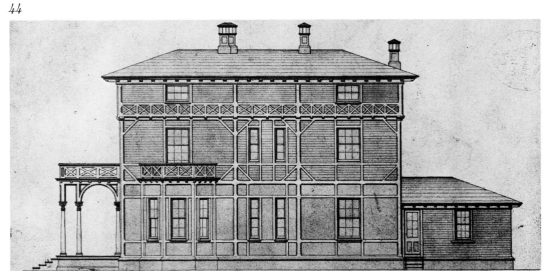

45

The Englishman Calvert Vaux was asked to come to America in 1850 by the leading American theorist and landscape architect of the picturesque movement, Andrew Jackson Downing, who, until his death in 1852, was Vaux's partner. Vaux made contributions to the American environment in several related but distinct areas. In 1857 he published *Villas and Cottages*, in which he put forth the idea that through inexpensive books such as his own and through a well-informed popular press, the public's taste could be improved. He collaborated between 1857 and 1872 with Frederick Law Olmsted (1822–1903) on the design of sylvan landscapes such as Central, Prospect, and Morningside parks in New York and on the Riverside, Illinois, suburb between 1865 and 1870. He designed outstanding High Victorian buildings, like the home of the Hudson River School painter Frederich Church, "Olana," in Hudson, New York, begun in 1870 and completed by 1889, with landscaping by Olmsted; the original Metropolitan Museum of Art in 1880 in collaboration with Jacob Wrey Mould (1825–1884); and the Jefferson Market Courthouse in Greenwich Village of 1876 with Frederick Withers. Between 1888 and 1895 Vaux was the landscape architect for the New York City parks. In all these ventures Vaux believed, as had Downing, that architectural form had to be considered jointly with the site and that the landscape had to be ordered in a picturesque manner to give the effect of a natural setting. Vaux and Downing believed that the most appropriate form for domestic building was an asymmetrical plan combined with a picturesque elevation, either Gothic or Italian in inspiration. The irregularities of the massing were held to parallel those of the natural landscape.

Vaux's villa, Ammadelle (46), of 1859 was built for a railroad magnate, Thomas Pegues, and was published by Vaux in the first edition of his *Villas and Cottages*. It is in the Italianate villa style, which by the mid-1840s was, with the Gothic, the most popular mode of picturesque design. Typical of the style are the building's projecting bays, loggias, round-headed windows, classical detailing, brackets, balustrades, and asymmetrical planning. Downing particularly favored this style because its very practicality enhanced its naturalness. The plan could be extended as needed while adding to the asymmetry and therefore the picturesqueness of the whole.

46

46 *House for Thomas Peques, Oxford, Mississippi*
Now known as "Ammadelle"
East elevation, c. 1859
Ink and wash, 15½ x 22½" (39.4 x 57.2 cm)
Collection of Mrs. John Tatum
Oxford, Mississippi

EAST-ELEVATION

C VAUX Architect. NY 1857

Thomas Ustick Walter (1804–1882)

Thomas U. Walter was trained in Philadelphia by William Strickland (page 114), who had apprenticed under the Philadelphian Benjamin Latrobe (page 82). All three men made contributions to American engineering. One of Walter's most distinguished works is the alteration of the United States Capitol in 1855–1865, which included the design of the present dome. The dome, a monumental work in cast iron, is a spectacular visual focus to the city of Washington, and has become an important American symbol. (For discussion of the first capitol designs see pages 82 and 88.) His most important works were in the Greek Revival style: the facade of Nicholas Biddle's estate, Andalusia, in 1836; Hibernian Hall in Charleston of 1835; and the Philadelphia Savings Fund Society of 1837–1840. Walter associated specific stylistic vocabularies with symbolic meaning. The Greek was appropriate for the home of a Grecophile such as Biddle, a bank, or a government building. When Walter designed a prison, such as his Debtor's Prison of 1831, he, as other architects before and after him, reverted to the Egyptian style, associated with solidity, power, darkness, and mystery.

Walter took over the design and construction of the Jayne Building in Philadelphia of 1849–1852 from William J. Johnston. Though the Jayne Building is of traditional wood and masonry construction with only two lines of interior iron columns, it rose ten stories, a height remarkable for the time. Most important was the verticality of the facade design produced by the uninterrupted piers of the Venetian Gothic facade of Quincy granite. The verticality of this brings to mind both Louis Sullivan's (page 185) definition of the skyscraper as in a word "loftiness" and his Bayard Building of 1898 on Bleecker Street in New York City. The office of Frank Furness where Sullivan held his first job was located directly across the street from the Jayne Building, and it is likely that it was a key influence in the formulation of his ideas.

In 1832 Walter won the competition for Philadelphia's Girard College for Orphans (47, 48) over his mentor Strickland, who placed second; the distinguished architect from Boston, Isaiah Rogers, who placed third; the firm of Town & Davis (page 100) of New York; and John Haviland (page 106). The competition and construction for Girard College was initiated in 1831 by the bequest of Stephen Girard, one of the first American multimillionaire philanthropists. The isolation of the main building from the others is typical of the Greek Revival and related, as is the temple form and the orders, to Greek prototypes. After the competition was announced, Nicholas Biddle, who had been to Greece in 1806, was appointed head of the board of trustees, and through his intervention the facade colonnade was changed to a marble Corinthian peristyle.

The interior was ingeniously structured by Walter. According to Girard's will there were to be four rooms to each story. This was carried out through Walter's three stories, which were vaulted entirely in brick, the weight of the vaults being concentrated on thick corner piers. The upper story is vaulted with pendentive domes with skylights. This imaginative device brings natural light to the rooms that are directly behind the solid entablature.

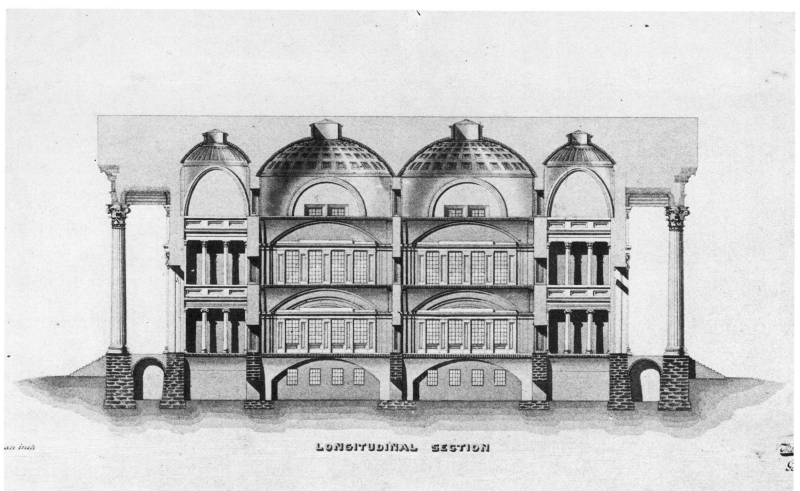

an inch   LONGITUDINAL SECTION

47

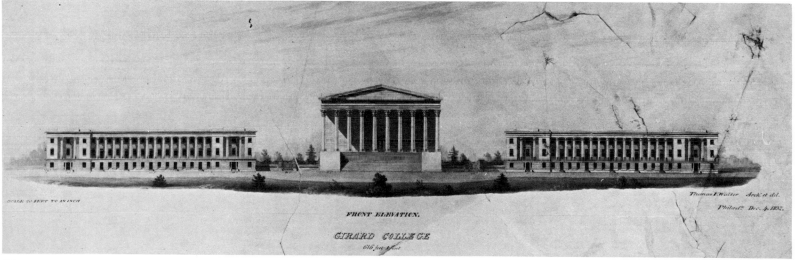

FRONT ELEVATION.

GIRARD COLLEGE

48

47   Girard College, Philadelphia
Longitudinal section, 1834
Ink and wash, 16½ x 26½" (41.9 x 67.3 cm)
The Historical Society of Pennsylvania
Philadelphia, Pennsylvania

48   Girard College, Philadelphia
Front elevation, December 4, 1832
Ink and wash, 12⅓ x 26½" (31.3 x 67.3 cm)
Historical Society of Pennsylvania
Philadelphia, Pennsylvania

1862/1889

The architect Claude Bragdon rather romantically described Harvey Ellis as the "gifted but irresponsible genius . . . , poet-architect, whose pencil death stopped ere it had traveled more than a few soft lines of his dream of beauty." Ellis produced some of the most innovative designs of the last two decades of the 19th century while he was responsible for some of the best work of many Midwestern architectural firms. Throughout his career he decorated his buildings with beautiful, highly inventive ornamentation executed in stone, mosaics, and paint in forms derivative from many periods including Byzantine, Romanesque, American Indian, and early Art Nouveau. Yet he led a shiftless personal and professional life, constantly changing jobs, living in boarding houses, drinking excessively, and at one point assuming the alias Albert Levering. Part of Ellis's contribution lies in his famous drawing technique, in which more than any other architect of that time he was able to master a range of tones in pen and ink almost equal to those of a photograph. Architectural draftsmen copied his style as they became familiar with it through periodicals.

Harvey Ellis was the son of a Rochester, New York, politician. He attended West Point for a year in 1871 and in 1875 worked in New York for Arthur Gilman, a conservative and eclectic architect. In the same year he met Henry Hobson Richardson (page 137), then at work on the New York State Capitol. Richardson's simple massive forms and Romanesque sources would profoundly influence Ellis. Ellis formed a partnership with his brother Charles in 1879 in Rochester, where until 1885 the firm produced churches and commercial, residential, and institutional buildings, including the Federal Building of 1884–1889. Harvey Ellis was the designer, his brother the businessperson.

During Ellis's years in the Midwest, 1886–1894 (after which he returned to Rochester), he produced his most original and inventive designs. He was employed during his Midwest period by a series of firms, including that of Leroy Buffington in Minneapolis; Mould & McNichol in St. Paul; and Eckel & Mann in St. Louis. As he moved among these firms, he worked as a designer delineator. The historian Eileen Michaels has been able to attribute many buildings built by these firms to the designs of Ellis.

Of the projects produced at Buffington's office attributed to Ellis, two are especially important and influential contributions to American architecture. The first, the 1891 project for the Security Bank in Minneapolis, revolutionized bank design. The bank is a rectangular block of masonry surmounted by a dome, which some critics have described as a jewel box or a vault. A frieze of human figures is placed below the roof line; intricate ornament decorates the entrance. The bank is a departure from the traditional temple form or Renaissance palazzo used for banks in the 19th century. In form it is a precursor of Sullivan's banks and tombs and is one of the earliest instances of what has become known as the Prairie School style, which flourished in the Midwest from 1900 to World War I. Many of the qualities characteristic of the school are present in Ellis's bank: rejection of historical styles; compact cubical massing; emphasis on the horizontal in most aspects of form; low, long hipped or gable roofs; precise clear, angular detailing.

The second particularly outstanding design produced while in Buffington's employ—an 1886 project for a 28-story skyscraper (50)—was surrounded by controversy. Buffington tried to obtain a patent for the invention of the steel frame skyscraper in 1887, claiming that he originated the idea in 1882. Later he confessed that Ellis had designed it. Buffington was not granted the patent because in 1884 William Le Baron Jenny had used a similar system in his Home Life Insurance Company in Chicago. Ellis's design, however, is the first to conceive of a skyscraper as one continuous vertical form. This prefigures Sullivan's work along these lines and his definition of the skyscraper's essence as "loftiness." In Ellis's design piers rise uninterrupted to the conical pointed roof, emphasizing the vertical. The piers at the corners are strongly reminiscent of those at Richardson's Allegheny County Courthouse in Pittsburgh of 1884–1888.

In 1889 Ellis designed a steel cable tent (49) to house all the exhibitions at the 1893 World's Columbian Exposition in Chicago —an amazing conception for the period, especially in light of the academic Beaux-Arts plan that was built. The tent is entered through Romanesque gateways. At its center is an auditorium,

49

50

with seating for 120,000 people. Around the outer ring are placed the expositions; an electric road circles the perimeter of the tent's exterior and leads to the globe. Later Buffington changed the lettering and submitted it as his proposal for the Century of Progress Exhibition slated for 1933 in Chicago.

49   Steel Tent, project for the World's Columbian Exposition
Chicago, 1893
Perspective, c. 1888
Pen and ink, 17¼ x 32" (43.8 x 81.3 cm)
Northwest Architectural Archives
University of Minnesota Libraries
Minneapolis, Minnesota

50   Twenty-eight-story skyscraper, project
Plan and elevation, c. 1887 or 1888
Pen and ink, 33½ x 22" (85.1 x 55.9 cm)
Northwest Architectural Archives
University of Minnesota Libraries
Minneapolis, Minnesota

51 Unidentified house
Side and front elevation, 1890
Ink and colored wash, 13⅜ x 21¼" (34 x 54 cm)
The Historic New Orleans Collection
New Orleans, Louisiana

52 Small cottage, New Orleans, Louisiana
Plan, side and front elevation, undated
Ink and colored wash, 17 x 16⅜" (43.2 x 41.6 cm)
The Historic New Orleans Collection
New Orleans, Louisiana

Richard Fourchy (dates unknown)

Almost nothing is recorded about the career of Richard Fourchy except that he was a member of the New Orleans chapter of the AIA; in the 1890s he set up the partnership of Fourchy & Fourchy, Civil and Marine Engineers, with André Fourchy, presumably his brother; and during the same period he was United States Inspector of Public Buildings. The firm disbanded sometime between 1894 and 1909. It can be surmised from the extant Fourchy drawings and the New Orleans City building records that Fourchy's architectural work involved modest domestic buildings typical in form to the vernacular architecture of New Orleans.

Fourchy's plan for a small cottage (52) of the 1890s is similar to the Creole cottages of New Orleans developed in the 1820s and 1830s. Attributes of Fourchy's cottage that are similar to the vernacular cottages preceding it are French doors; centralized chimney; simple plan; roof overhanging to provide shade, called "abat-vent"; brick piers; board and batten side framing; and horizontal weather boarding on the front elevation, presumably over vertical planks called "madriers deboutz."

The unidentified wood frame house (51) of the same era as the cottage is similar to many examples of late Victorian architecture in New Orleans and throughout America. Elements of the design that are particularly common in New Orleans are the second floor open porch and the double story projecting polygonal bay.

51

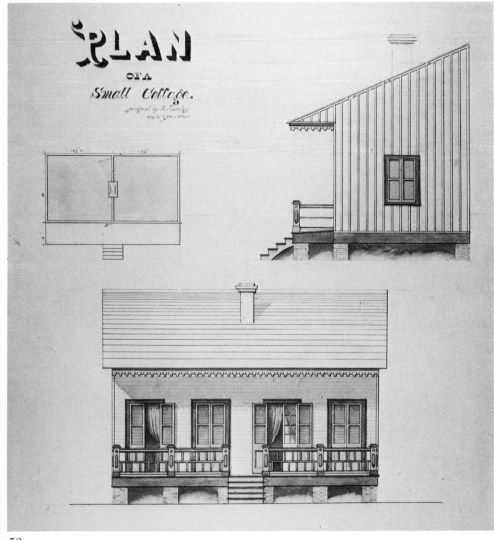

52

ELEVATION : ON : BROAD : STREET :

Except for an uninspired obituary in the *Philadelphia Real Estate Record and Builder's Guide*, the professional architectural press did not acknowledge the death of Frank Furness, whose work is among the most individualized and complex in the history of 19th-century American architecture. His obituaries in the Philadelphia press recognized his kinship with an intellectual, liberal Philadelphia family (his father was an important Unitarian minister, a friend of Ralph Waldo Emerson, and an outspoken abolitionist; one brother was a Shakespearean scholar) and emphasized his bravery in the Civil War, while saying little about his contribution to Philadelphia's cityscape and the suburban Main Line, where, with few exceptions, all his work was built.

From the 1890s until the late 1950s, Furness's work has been rarely praised and most often ignored or criticized for its aggressive forms and unusual scale, its freewheeling eclecticism and its polychromy; ironically, it is just these attributes for which his work is admired by many today. Such admiration has been given impetus by the writings of the architectural historian Vincent Scully and by the architect Robert Venturi (page 291), whose *Complexity and Contradiction in Architecture* of 1966 provides a theoretical basis for the acceptance of high style, as well as vernacular architectural precedent, into the design process. This is in contrast with International Style buildings and theory, which philosophically rejected the use of history as a source and which Venturi's book sought to supplant. The culmination of the reevaluation of Furness was the exhibition of his work at the Philadelphia Museum of Art and the catalog for that exhibition, with an introduction by James O'Gorman.

Furness trained in Richard Morris Hunt's (page 134) atelier in New York between 1859 and 1861; these years provided the stimulus for Furness's mature and idiosyncratic work. Hunt's office attracted some of the brightest young architects of the period, and it was filled with books and *objets d'art*, which O'Gorman has called a *"Kunst und Wunderkammer."* In this milieu, Furness would have been surrounded by discussion of the important architectural ideas of the period: the theories of John Ruskin (1819–1900) and Viollet-le-Duc (1814–1879) as well as attitudes toward form and symbol that Hunt absorbed at the École des Beaux-Arts. New York provided Furness with buildings by Leopold Eidlitz (page 102) and Jacob Wrey Mould (1825–1886) to stimulate his imagination.

Furness integrated the ideas of Ruskin, who believed that beautiful architecture was essentially derived from surface effects and decoration, and Viollet-le-Duc, who believed that architecture was essentially concerned with structure. For Ruskin, the most beautiful architecture, and that to be emulated, was the Italian Gothic, with its rich surfaces and polychromy. Among the criteria for architecture Ruskin discusses in his *Seven Lamps of Architecture* of 1849 that were of prime importance to Furness are boldness and irregularity in massing, truth to materials (not representing one material with another), and the use of nature as a source for ornament. Of importance to Viollet-le-Duc, like Ruskin, was the truthful or realistic use of materials. However, Viollet-le-Duc advocated a rational and direct expression of structure; his frank use of new materials, particularly exposed iron, is of great importance in understanding Furness's work and the buildings of High Victorian Gothic architects.

The Pennsylvania Academy of Fine Arts in 1872–1876 is Furness's first masterpiece. Its facade drawing (53) of 1873 reflects a great deal of what Furness absorbed in New York and reveals qualities in his work that would be further developed in the following years. Eclectic in its stylistic sources, drawing on

53   Pennsylvania Academy of the Fine Arts, Philadelphia Elevation on Broad Street, c. 1873
Ink and wash, 25½ x 34½" (64.8 x 87.6 cm)
Pennsylvania Academy of the Fine Arts
Philadelphia, Pennsylvania

54

both Italian and French architecture, the academy's facade is constructed of a rich variety of materials that would have pleased Ruskin. Furness used dressed sandstone, rusticated brownstone, polished granite, painted glass, and red and black brick. The elevation is organized as a tripartite composition, with the central section more prominent than the others. This becomes typical of many of Furness's later works. The central portion is based on Leopold Eidlitz's Temple Emanu-El in New York of 1866–1868 and Hunt's design for the Pavilion de la Bibliothèque at the Louvre of 1852–1855 in Paris, which he designed while working for Hector Lefuel. It is the unusual scale contrasts of certain passages of the elevation and the distinctive ornamentation that make the building so compelling. For example, Furness places short, stubby columns in the section of the facade over the entry next to much thinner, taller ones. Consistent with Ruskin's philosophy, Furness relied on nature as a source for ornamentation, yet his abstraction of these forms relates to the ideas of the Englishman Owen Jones (1809–1874), who stated in his *Grammar of Ornament* in 1856 that "all ornament should be based upon a geometrical construction." Furness would have been aware of Owen Jones through his education at Hunt's office and his friendship with Jacob Wrey Mould, who had worked for Jones.

In the facade of the First Troop Armory (55) built in 1874, Furness again used a rich variety of materials, including iron. The medieval fortress was, of course, a common image for an armory. A sketch for a bank from Furness's notebook (54) again reveals Furness's inclination to use a tripartite scheme for the facade with a dominant central section, giving the building, in Ruskin's terms, a sense of power and force. During the 1870s, Furness produced several magnificent banks in Philadelphia that reveal this attitude, such as the Centennial National Bank (now the First Pennsylvania Bank) of 1876 and the Provident Life and Trust Company of 1879 (now demolished).

Built on a small lot, the Provident was one of Furness's most outstanding works. In this building exaggerated scale contrasts combined with huge ornamental details are deftly manipulated to create a dramatic facade, pressurized and tense in feeling. These sensations were appreciated by the Philadelphia press at the time of the building's construction. The building called attention to itself. In this regard James O'Gorman has written: "What our advertising experts do now with neon tubing, Furness achieved through caricature, putting fully developed architectural details onto a stunted field—just as he drew in one of his sketchbooks a caricature with a fully developed head on a miniature body."

54   *Unidentified bank*
Facade study, sketchbook, undated
Pencil, 9½ x 8" (24.1 x 20.3 cm)
Collection of George Wood Furness
Nether Providence, Pennsylvania

55   *First Troop Armory, Philadelphia*
Front elevation, 1874
Ink, 23 x 25½" (58.4 x 64.8 cm)
First Troop Philadelphia City Cavalry
Philadelphia, Pennsylvania

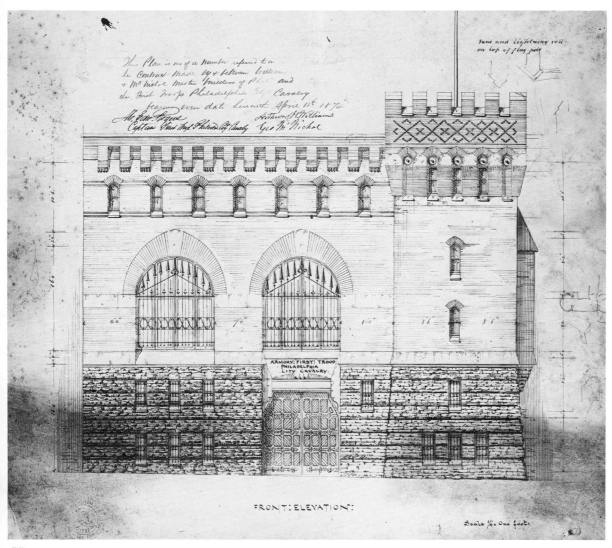

55

134 56 *Pedestal for the Statue of Liberty, New York City*
  Elevation, 1886
  Pencil, 16½ x 23" (41.9 x 58.4 cm)
  American Institute of Architects
  Washington, D.C.

57 *J. N. A. Griswold House, Newport, Rhode Island*
  Main elevation, 1862–1863
  Ink and wash, 8½ x 11½" (21.6 x 29.2 cm)
  American Institute of Architects
  Washington, D.C.

58 *J. N. A. Griswold House, Newport, Rhode Island*
  Plan, 1862–1863
  Ink and wash, 10 x 13½" (25.4 x 34.3 cm)
  American Institute of Architects
  Washington, D.C.

56

Richard Morris Hunt (1828–1895)

The first American graduate of the École des Beaux-Arts in Paris, Richard Morris Hunt (Harvard College, class of 1845), made important contributions through his influence on the emerging architectural profession and with the powerful, eclectic buildings he designed during the more than 40 years of his professional career. Hunt returned to America from France in 1855, and in 1857 he established an atelier in New York where he taught architecture after the principles of the École des Beaux-Arts. It was at Hunt's studio that such eminent architects received architectural training as Frank Furness, Charles Gambrill (who was Henry Hobson Richardson's partner from 1867 to his death in 1878), George Post, William Ware (the first professor of architecture at MIT, where in 1865 the first American professional school of architecture was established), and Henry van Brunt (Ware's partner).

Hunt is primarily associated with the design of lavish mansions for the very rich, such as the Vanderbilt Mansion on Fifth Avenue of 1879, "The Breakers" of 1892–1895 in Newport and "Biltmore" of 1890–1895 in Asheville, North Carolina—both also executed for the Vanderbilts. He is also known for elegant, often monumental public buildings, such as the Administration Building at the 1893 World's Columbian Exposition in Chicago. All these buildings call on European stylistic models for their formal imagery. However, the picture of Hunt would be incomplete without referring to his outstanding buildings designed in a more informal mode, indigenous to America, named by its historian, Vincent Scully, the "Stick Style." The J. N. A. Griswold House (57, 58) in Newport Rhode Island, of 1862–1863 is a typical example of this style. The drawings illustrated here are similar to but not exactly like the building, which is now the Newport Art Association. In the Stick Style, the external framing of vertical, horizontal, and diagonal wooden members or sticks reflects the internal construction of the building.

The side and front elevations of the Griswold House, built in a traditional wood frame technique, indicate the placement of the sticks symbolic of the interior structure. The front elevation, with its many gables at different heights and its tower, gives the house its picturesque effect evocative of a rural environment appropriate for a home in a resort town. The bedroom and drawing and dining rooms are organized as a series of wings off a core of parlor, hall, and vestibule, with wide porches surrounding much of the house. This organization orients the public rooms to a great variety of views. The porches, treated as transitional spaces, mediate between the interior of the house and the landscape.

It is fitting that the base for the Statue of Liberty (56), sculpted by Frederic Auguste Bartholdi as a monument to American-French friendship, was designed in 1883 by Hunt, the outstanding symbol of the 19th-century American architect developed by and imbued with the French system. In one of the only contemporary discussions of this monumental work of Hunt's, the critic Montgomery Schuyler points out that Hunt had to find a form that would be at once visually powerful enough to harmonize with the statue and yet not be competitive with it, while incorporating important sections of Gustav Eiffel's iron and steel armature needed to support the 225-ton weight of the colossal statue. Hunt's base is an elegant symbol of strength. The roughly dressed granite of the four-sided pedestal, wider at the base, with dark recessed openings, is suitable to the scale of the statue and is almost fortresslike in its imagery. The medallions around the base are inscribed with the emblems of the states, and the two flanking the entry are inscribed "U.S.A." and "R.F." (République Française). They were never carved as intended. The Doric order traditionally regarded as the simplest and strongest of the classical orders is used for the columns framing the windows in an elegant allusion to the academic and classical sources for the statue; the choice of the Doric further enhances the image of power that Hunt regarded as essential.

-SOUTH EAST VIEW-

57

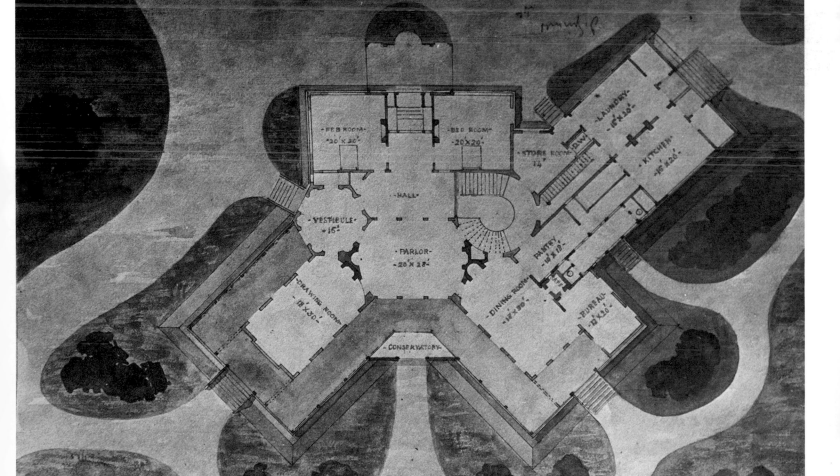

58

59

59 *Marshall Field Wholesale Store, Chicago*
Perspective study, on verso; pencil sketch of a group
of standing figures, 1885–1887
Pencil, black crayon, red wash heightened with white on buff
paper, 11⅜ x 19⅞" (28.9 x 50.5 cm)
Gift of Henry Richardson Shepley
Houghton Library
Harvard University
Cambridge, Massachusetts

60 *Trinity Church, Boston*
Plan study, c. June 1872
Pencil, blue pencil, brown ink on watercolor paper,
3¾ x 6" (9.5 x 15.2 cm)
Gift of Henry Richardson Shepley
Houghton Library
Harvard University
Cambridge, Massachusetts

60

Not only are Henry Hobson Richardson's buildings some of the most compelling structures of the 19th century, but they also had an immediate as well as long-range impact on American architects, including such outstanding figures as Louis Sullivan (page 185) and Frank Lloyd Wright (page 234). Richardson was one of the first architects in America to design important, large-scale structures for a broad variety of building types that emerged in the 19th century as a result of industrialization, concomitant urbanization, and social reform. These included commissions for public libraries (the Winn Memorial Library, Woburn, Massachusetts, 1877–1878, and the Ames Memorial Library, North Easton, Massachusetts, 1877–1879); railroad stations (primarily for the Boston and Albany Railroad); large governmental buildings (the New York State Capitol, Albany, with Leopold Eidlitz, Albany City Hall, 1880–1882; the Allegheny County Courthouse and Prison, Pittsburgh, 1884–1888; Cincinnati's Chamber of Commerce Building, 1886–1888); large commercial buildings (the Cheney Block, Hartford, 1875–1876; the Ames Building, Boston, 1882–1883; the Marshall Field store, Chicago, 1885); and hospitals (the Administration Building of the State Hospital, Buffalo, 1872–1878). Richardson's work is dominated by the concern for spatial continuity expressed both in the interior planning and in the exterior scuptural massing of his buildings. This approach is Richardson's most important legacy to Louis Sullivan (page 184) and Frank Lloyd Wright (page 234), and it is this conception that is America's greatest contribution to the beginnings of Modern architecture. Richardson's second most important contribution was the direct and often highly expressive use of materials. These attitudes were often clothed in a vocabulary derived from Romanesque architecture but manipulated in a manner that is purely "Richardsonian." Richardson played a crucial role in freeing American architecture from its dependence on European developments by establishing a powerful, individualistic idiom in the realm of both residential and public buildings.

Around 1880, Richardson and William Ralph Emerson were among the most important initiators of a new domestic idiom now called the "Shingle Style," which involved a new attitude to space as well as to imagery. The Shingle Style house contained a large stair–living hall, surrounded by suites of rooms through which space flowed freely. Their shingled exteriors were largely free from direct references to historical styles, except for general references to 17th-century colonial buildings, although the interior ornamentation of these houses sometimes relied on classical and medieval sources (see also page 142). Among the best examples of Richardson's Shingle Style houses are the Bryant House in Cohasset, Massachusetts, of 1880 and the Stoughton House in Cambridge of 1882–1883. In both his public and private commissions, Richardson consistently used materials in a manner that underlined their inherent physical properties; in the most exaggerated example of this, the Ames Gate Lodge of 1880–1881 in North Easton, Massachusetts, huge undressed boulders form the walls.

Richardson graduated from Harvard College in 1859 and continued his education at the École des Beaux-Arts in Paris from 1859 to 1862, as the second American, following Richard Morris Hunt (page 134), to study there He settled in Brookline, Massachusetts, after winning the Trinity Church competition in 1872. It was through Richardson's Cambridge education and the social milieu of which he became a part in Boston and Brookline that he developed some of his richest and most distinguished private and institutional clients, including Henry Adams, the Ames family, and Harvard University, for which he built Sever

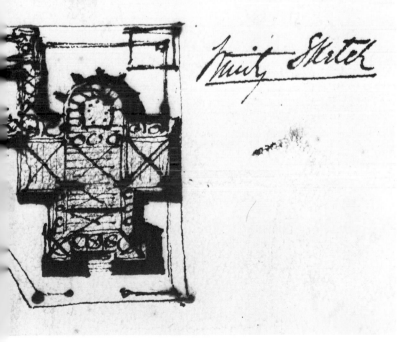

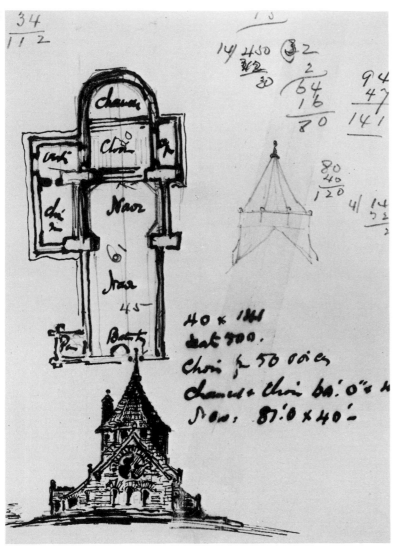

61

61 *Unidentified church*
Plan, elevation, and tower study, sketchbook, leaf 62r,
sketchbook dated 1869–1876
Brown ink over pencil, 12 x 19¾" (30.5 x 50.2 cm)
Gift of Henry Richardson Shepley
Houghton Library
Harvard University
Cambridge, Massachusetts

62 *Young Men's Association Library Competition*
Buffalo, New York
Plan study, May 7, 1884
India ink and pencil on stiff white paper
17¾ x 11¾" (45.1 x 29.8 cm)
Gift of Henry Richardson Shepley
Houghton Library
Harvard University
Cambridge, Massachusetts

Hall in 1878–1880 and Austin Hall in 1881–1883. His Brookline office employed men who would later be important architects, such as Charles Coolidge, John Shepley, and Stanford White.

Richardson's experience at the École des Beaux-Arts, where he studied at the Atelier André (André was the architect for the Jardin des Plantes), and his employment that followed with Théodore Labrouste (brother of Henri, the architect of the brilliant Bibliothèque Ste. Geneviève of 1843–1850), implanted in his mind the most esssential and important aspects of French Beaux-Arts theory and formed a vital part of his approach to design.

Almost every drawing for Richardson's buildings known to be by his own hand is a conceptual sketch. It is through these seminal sketches that he established on paper the essence of a particular building; they communicated the conceptualization of his design to his staff, who carried out the more formal and technical drawings. Richardson, however, often developed many of the most important details of a building on site. The use of the conceptual sketch to determine the essence of the design probably came from habits developed at the École des Beaux-Arts, where the student was asked to do a quick *esquisse*, or a conceptual sketch that fixed all the major design elements and laid the foundation for the more specifically developed scheme.

For Richardson, as for any architect thoroughly imbued in the École's system, the plan indicating both the configuration of rooms and a sense of the superstructure was usually the dominant factor in the initial conceptualization of a building. The forms and organization of the archetypal Beaux-Arts plan, dependent on functional and symbolic requirements of the program, are composed of defined units of space arranged *en suite* around symmetrical axes.

Richardson's conceptual sketch (62) of 1884 for the Young Men's Association Library in Buffalo, prepared for a competition that he lost to C. L. W. Eidlitz, shows a continuity of spaces to serve the complex building program, housing a library, Fine Arts Academy, Society of Natural Sciences, and the Buffalo Historical Society under one roof, and reveals a general Beaux-Arts influence. Separate spaces are articulated within a spatial continuity by vaulting and by changes in plan. In the area of the plan designed for public use, a cross axis is created. One axis extends from the general room to the conference room, while another intersects this and runs from the general and newspaper room through the alcove. Although Richardson does not consistently orient his buildings around strict cross axes, several of his most distinguished plans are organized around two different axes of movement, and all his plans have a strong and clearly articulated spatial direction.

Interior spatial unity and coherence were matched by external continuity of surface and unity of composition, as in the Marshall Field Warehouse (59) of 1885–1887 in Chicago, where several of the seven stories of this building are grouped under massive stone arches. There was almost no ornament on the building; the decoration was in the use of the stone itself. Large rough stones form the bottom section, conveying a sense of support, while small square blocks are used in the spandrels. This elevation recalls the configuration of Italian Renaissance palazzi. The sketch, which may well be by Richardson, suggests the *parti* of the final design, although it may only be a study for a scheme to have been built in brick.

The sketch for the plan for Boston's Trinity Church (60) of 1872 is typical of Richardson's drawing style. Richardson usually first drew in pencil and then drew over this with ink. This was not the design that won the 1872 competition, but Richardson's second scheme, prepared when the original rectangular site was changed to the triangular one on which the present building was constructed in 1878. The sketch shows in broad outline the configuration of the building on the site, the basic details of the plan, and a general scheme for the vaulting. Thus, it is a typical Beaux-Arts drawing in which the plan can be used to describe the entire *parti* of the building.

The study for an unidentified church (61) from a sketchbook dated 1869–1876 shows again his approach to drawing, which in broad outline describes the plan of a building. In the elevation of this Romanesque Revival building, we see how Richardson also thought of an elevation, as he did the plan, as a composition of large elemental forms. It is the outline of the large mass, not the detailing, that gives the drawing its power.

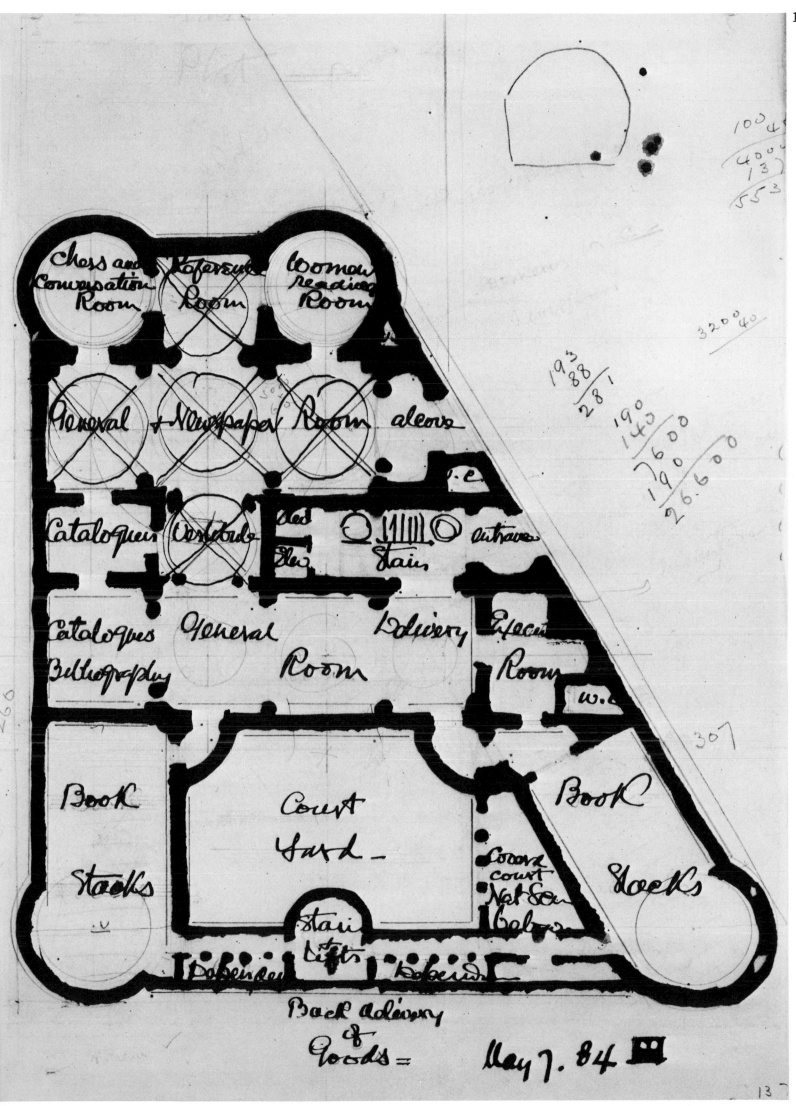

63   John Goddard Stearns
House for W. (William) S. (Sumner) Appleton
Newton, Massachusetts
Side elevation and details of windows, 1875
Ink and colored wash on linen, 29 x 35" (73.7 x 88.9 cm)
Society for the Preservation of New England Antiquities
Boston, Massachusetts

64   John Goddard Stearns
House for W. (William) S. (Sumner) Appleton
Newton, Massachusetts
Main floor plan and elevation of interior wall, 1875
Ink and colored wash on linen, 29 x 35" (73.7 x 88.9 cm)
Society for the Preservation of New England Antiquities
Boston, Massachusetts

John Goddard Stearns (1843–1917)
Robert Swain Peabody (1845–1917)

John Stearns began his preparation for the practice of architecture before the Civil War at the Lawrence Scientific School, from which he graduated in 1863. After 1865 he apprenticed with the architectural firm of Ware & Van Brunt in Boston. In 1870 he joined in partnership with Robert Peabody, who had studied at Harvard College and the École des Beaux-Arts. In the 1940s Karl Putnam of Smith College called the firm "the most important arbiters of building taste after H. H. Richardson" (page 137). Stearns was primarily concerned with getting the buildings built and supervising their drawings. Stearns encouraged his draftsmen to "Sketch! Sketch! And if you can't find anything to sketch, sketch your boots!" Between 1873 and 1915 he published three sketchbooks of his own. Peabody took the initiative for the firm in design matters and wrote articles defending the validity of eclectic architecture, biographical and travel notes, and articles about the profession. The firm, one of the largest of the era, once had branches in New York, St. Louis, Colorado Springs, and Pittsburgh and continued until 1917, the year its founders died. Peabody and Stearns were responsible for domestic, institutional, and commercial structures built in a variety of styles following the most advanced mode of the particular decade. Their clients were often very rich and socially prominent. Up to 1890 Peabody and Stearns employed the Victorian Gothic, French Academic styles, the neo-Romanesque, the Queen Anne, and the Stick Style. In their domestic work of the 1880s they substituted for these modes the Shingle Style, the prevailing form for advanced domestic design of that decade. In the nineties and after, much of their work is either Georgian, as epitomized by their Massachusetts Building at the World's Columbian Exposition of 1893 in Chicago, or Beaux-Arts as their Machinery Hall also at the 1893 Fair.

The Appleton House (63, 64) of 1875 in Newton, Massachusetts, is a combination of essentially a Stick Style massing and approach to materials, with certain aspects of the Queen Anne in planning and motifs. The Stick Style, dominating American domestic design between the 1850s and mid-1870s, was an architecture of wood in which the nature of that building material and its use in construction were emphasized. This took the form of large exposed brackets under projecting eaves; the use of the wooden sticks placed on the facade to refer to the light-weight framing technique of the construction; and diagonal wooden bracing, board and batten, or horizontal clapboards overlaid by other boards. Deep porches and irregular massing, giving the building a picturesque effect, also characterized the style. This realistic approach to structure and picturesque effect was supported by the ideas of the influential landscape architect, Andrew Jackson Downing (1815–1851), who published *Cottage Residences* in 1842 and the *Architecture of Country Houses* in 1850. The roots of Downing's philosophy are in English Gothic revival and romantic theory of the late 18th and first decades of the 19th century. Downing insisted on truthfulness to materials and program as well as the integration of building and site.

Several prominent gables with large brackets seem to sprout from the mass of the Appleton House. This, with the octagonal projecting room and polygonal bays—favorite devices of the firm—creates a picturesque asymmetrical mass. The trefoil and quatrefoil detailing of the windows, gables, and chimneys, combined with the leaded windows, recall the late Medieval English vernacular sources of the Queen Anne style, elements of which are contained in the plan of the house as well. One of the major contributions of the Queen Anne style to American architecture was the introduction of the large living hall, with other rooms arranged around it; this became the dominant element in the Shingle Style. In the Appleton House a large hall extends through the house from veranda to veranda. The hall works as the primary organizing element in the plan; its termination at both ends by porches and ultimately the landscape work to create a close relationship between building and nature.

FRENCH WINDOW

Portion of 1st Story Kitchen Wing, which is hidden
on Elevation by Billiard Room.

WINDOW IN STUDY

63

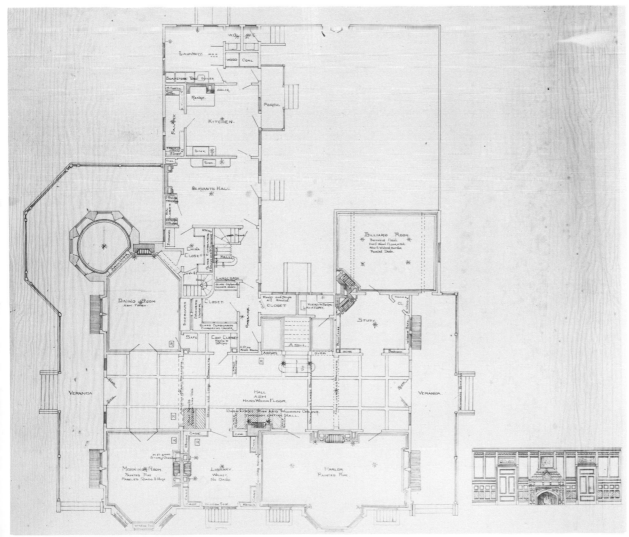

64

142 65 *Classical School, project, Waterville, Maine*
Perspective before 1884
Pencil, 15⅛ x 18¾" (38.4 x 47.6 cm)
Avery Library
Columbia University
New York, New York

66 *Cottage for Lewis Chase, Esq., Squirrel Island, Maine*
Perspective, 1886
Pencil on tan paper, 13½ x 22½ " (34.3 x 55.2 cm)
Avery Library
Columbia University
New York, New York

John Calvin Stevens (1855–1940)

John Calvin Stevens, whose practice included largely domestic and institutional buildings in Maine, was one of the outstanding practitioners of the Shingle Style, which flourished in the 1880s. Stevens, with his partner Albert W. Cobb, published *Examples of American Domestic Architecture* in 1889. The book, primarily illustrated by their work, is one of the few documents of the period by architects to discuss the theoretical premises on which the Shingle Style was based. Stevens apprenticed in architecture in 1873 with F. H. Fassett of Portland and was later in charge of Fassett's Boston office. He was a partner in the firm Fassett and Stevens from 1880 to 1884, and between 1885 and 1891 he was associated with A. W. Cobb. In 1906 Stevens was joined in practice by his son.

The Shingle Style, initiated by William Ralph Emerson and Henry Hobson Richardson (page 137) by 1880, was primarily a domestic idiom, although it was also adapted for clubs, small-scale churches, and institutional buildings. The shingled exteriors of these buildings were largely free from direct references to past styles, except for a general reference to American 17th-century colonial architecture. The image evoked by Shingle Style buildings was of a truly American architecture, which through its use of "natural" materials, sensitive integration of the plan of the house to the site, orientation of rooms to dramatic views, and large porches giving direct access from interior to exterior, directly connected the building to the landscape. The open interior planning of the style, organized around a large living hall with fireplace, stairs, and sometimes built-in seating, is an important development in American domestic design. The uniform shingle sheathing and often the use of large overhanging roofs integrate the masses and produce a contained, unified building.

Stevens' and Cobb's book is a plea for reform in American domestic architecture, whose end is the provision of comfortable, simple buildings for all, as they state, "released from the influence of extravagant ideality, and directed instead by rational righteous ideals." The authors have the highest praise for the informality of planning, integration of building with site, and use of natural materials of William Ralph Emerson's buildings, which they write are "lovely because there is instilled into it the power of a chivalrous, joyous nature, revering everything pure and brave and holy in his fellow creatures, while scorning all that is extravagant, meretricious." The authors imply a connection between Emerson's buildings and his cousin Ralph Waldo Emerson's philosophy. The historian Vincent Scully writes in his book *The Shingle Style* that the "very looseness, naturalness, and informality of its organization can remind one of the older Emerson who renounced rule, embraced nature, and had a vision of free society based upon love and the acceptance of life." In "The Cottage for Lewis Chase, Esq." (66) at Squirrel Island, Maine, of 1886, the large continuous porch connected to the terrace by the steps extends the building into the landscape. The gambrel roof of this Shingle Style house extends fully over the porch containing it within the building itself. The image is of simplicity, order, and harmony with nature.

The Classical School for Waterville, Maine (65), probably of the early 1880s, is designed in the Queen Anne Style, a mode typical of the 1870s and early 1880s and derived from developments in English architecture of the preceding decade. Characteristic of the style is the picturesque massing and the detailing derived from English late-medieval architecture.

Sketch for Classical School:
Waterville: Me.
Fassett & Stevens: Archts: Portland:

65

Cottage for Lewis Chase. Esq:
Squirrel Island.

66

67

67   Brooklyn Mercantile Library, Brooklyn, New York
Column detail, c. 1867
Opaque watercolor, 17⅞ x 8 5/6" (45.4 x 22.4 cm)
The Burnham Library
The Art Institute of Chicago
Chicago, Illinois

68   Brooklyn Mercantile Library, Brooklyn, New York
Perspective study for main facade, c. 1867
Watercolor, 10⅛ x 7½" (25.7 x 19.1 cm)
The Burnham Library
The Art Institute of Chicago
Chicago, Illinois

Peter Bonnet Wight (1838–1925)

Peter Bonnet Wight was born and educated in New York City and studied architecture in the office of Thomas R. Jackson. Wight's involvement with architecture ranged from the design and construction of some of the first High Victorian Gothic structures in America during the 1860s to the construction of commercial buildings in Chicago in the 1870s and early 1880s. In the eighties he virtually stopped designing except for his participation in the 1893 World's Columbian Exposition in Chicago, where he supervised the construction of some of the foreign pavilions and built several smaller buildings of his own. From the eighties through the first decade of the 20th century Wight was essentially involved with writing architectural criticism. His most important articles reported on the development of Midwestern architecture, particularly commercial structures, and new construction techniques, especially ones related to problems of fireproofing, which had become critically important after the Chicago fire of 1871. Wight was also interested in the development of the skyscraper city, which had to incorporate automobile traffic, and he reported on this development as it affected Chicago.

Based on the Doges' Palace in Venice, Wight's National Academy of Design in 1862–1865 (the facade of which is now reconstructed at 467 West 147th Street in Manhattan) is credited as the first High Victorian Gothic building in the United States. The High Victorian Gothic was initiated in England with William Butterfield's All Saint's Margaret Street of 1849 in London. The style is distinguished from the earlier phase of the Gothic Revival in both England and America by its dependence on Italian and German stylistic sources as opposed to English and French ones. More important, however, is a new approach to form. High Victorian Gothic buildings are polychromed, a change from the subdued coloration of buildings of the earlier phase; their detailing is heavier; and often there are large-scale changes among the parts of the buildings. The materials of these buildings are used in a realistic manner— they do not represent one material with another. John Ruskin (1819–1900) is the style's major theorist. In *The Seven Lamps of Architecture* of 1849, Ruskin advocates the truthful expression of materials, nature as a source for ornament, and powerful irregular massing that would be expressive of strength and power. Wight was sympathetic to these ideals and also espoused Ruskin's philosophy that the worker must truly collaborate with the architect, be committed to craft and be integrally involved with the process of construction, all in order to produce a work of architecture that adds to the happiness of society. To "give the worker the opportunity to think" as well as to develop the connection between nature and architecture, Wight would bring real flowers and foliage for the workers to use as models for the building's decoration.

The Mercantile Library (68) built in 1867 in Brooklyn is Wight's second venture into the High Victorian Gothic and is like his first based on Venetian models. Typical of the style are the banding of the windows in two colors of stone, the horizontal strips of stone contrasting with the dark wall, and the bay window projecting to one side on the facade. The polychromed columns (67) of the library are decorated with naturalistic flower ornament, coupled with Gothic trefoils and quatrefoils.

1890/1919

69

Albert Bendernagel (1876–1952)

Simultaneous with Louis Sullivan's (page 184) later works, Frank Lloyd Wright's (page 234) Prairie Houses, and the rethinking of architectural values at the beginning of the 20th century was the continuation of the eclectic tradition, which was a hallmark of 19th-century architecture. This tradition continued into the first decades of the 20th century with Ralph Adams Cram (page 156) and Bertram Grosvenor Goodhue (page 166) among its 20th-century masters. Architects such as Albert Bendernagel made important contributions to this stream of American architecture in the design of structures of note throughout the country.

Bendernagel, Thomas Sully, Paul Andry, and Samuel Stone were among those architects whose buildings at the turn of the century made an appreciable contribution in the business district of New Orleans. One of Bendernagel's earliest works, the Tilton Memorial Library of 1900 at Tulane University in New Orleans, was inspired by the Richardsonian Romanesque and was designed to harmonize with the earlier Gibson Hall at Tulane. Bendernagel also designed buildings in an academic Beaux-Arts mode, such as his New Orleans Stock Exchange of 1906, and in the Gothic style, especially for ecclesiastical structures such as his Ursaline Convent in New Orleans of 1909. Like many of the American architects who made significant, although not innovative contributions to American architecture, Bendernagel's career is yet to be fully documented. He spent one year at Columbia University's School of Architecture and then returned to New Orleans where he had been born. He was associated with the architect Hayward Burton and during another period with Paul Andry. During these partnerships and at the end of his career he also worked independently. The exact dates of his partnerships are yet to be clarified.

Bendernagel is responsible for many churches throughout Louisiana. The undated projects for Gothic cathedrals (69, 70) illustrate only one mode in which he designed. Extant drawings indicate that he would conceive of a project in several modes before making a final stylistic choice.

70

69   Unidentified Gothic cathedral
Perspective and elevation study of principal facade, undated
Unidentified lighthouse
Perspective study of elevation and entrance, undated
Pencil and colored pencil on tracing paper,
23 x 18" (58.4 x 45.7 cm)
Collection of Edmund J. Bendernagel, Jr.
New Orleans, Louisiana

70   Unidentified cathedral
Elevation, undated
Pencil and colored pencil on tracing paper
13 x 16" (33 x 40.6 cm)
Collection of Edmund J. Bendernagel, Jr.
New Orleans, Louisiana

Arnold W. Brunner (1857–1925)

Arnold Brunner, who spent both his early life and his professional one in New York City, was educated in a Beaux-Arts manner at MIT's School of Architecture from which he graduated in 1879. The work of his mature period, beginning in the mid-1890s, is monumental in scale and uses a classical or Renaissance-derived vocabulary. His New York City commissions, executed primarily for governmental or institutional clients, included Mt. Sinai Hospital, 1898; the 1906 Public Baths at Asher Levy Place; Montefiore Hospital, 1913; Lewisohn Stadium at City College, 1915; and Barnard Hall at Barnard College, 1917. Brunner was also active as a city planner in major projects for the cities of Albany, Rochester, Baltimore, and Cleveland. Today he is usually remembered for his generous monetary endowments to the American Institute of Architects and the National Institute of Arts and Letters.

Brunner was a major figure in the City Beautiful movement in America, which grew out of the 1893 World's Columbian Exposition in Chicago and developed under the leadership of Daniel Burnham (1846–1912). Burnham's famous statement, "Make no little plans—they have not the magic, they have not the power to stir one's soul," expresses the general mood of the fair and of the City Beautiful movement. The "White City," as the fair was appropriately called, as well as the City Beautiful movement to which it gave birth, can be characterized by long, symmetrical axes, often punctuated by statuary or fountains, ending in a dramatic vista, and by the use of monumental buildings, uniform in their neoclassical styling. [The only American building not using the traditional neoclassical vocabulary at the fair was Louis Sullivan's (page 185) Transportation Building.] The dream city created in Chicago in the summer of 1893, which to the 20th-century eye looks like a movie set, was seen by millions who carried its powerful visual image with them during the economic depression years of the mid-1890s. When prosperity returned and building was again possible, city governments desired schemes related to the image of the fair.

A perfect exemplification of the City Beautiful movement is the Cleveland Plan of 1902–1903. The plan's commissioners, Arnold Brunner, Daniel Burnham, and John Carrère (1858–1911), planned a civic center composed of Beaux-Arts buildings, of classic detailing, uniform scale, and material situated around symmetrical axes. The Cleveland officials who hired the commissioners saw them as comprehensive planners who would supervise and control "the location of all public, municipal, and county buildings to be erected upon ground acquired within the limits of said city, and . . . have control of the size, height, style and general appearance of all such buildings. . . ." It is in connection with this plan that Brunner built his Federal Building in Cleveland of 1910.

The perspective of a project for an art complex in New York (71) in 1915 and that for a bridge at Queens Boulevard (72) c. 1920 exemplify Brunner's attitudes toward planning and architectural design. The notion of building centralized cultural complexes in America dates from the last decade of the 19th century. It was a period in which Americans began to sense and use their power in an international arena and in which they wanted to be associated with intellectual power as well. The monumental City Beautiful approach suited this *zeitgeist*. The buildings in Brunner's art complex are uniform in scale, classical in inspiration, and planned around symmetrical axes. As outlined above, this was his typical approach to planning and design.

In a 1911 report that Brunner prepared for the improvement of the city of Rochester, he wrote that "next to buildings, the bridges of a city are perhaps the most telling elements in its general appearances." He went on to say that these bridges should combine the "dignity and utility" with the "simplicity" of the "world's great viaducts." The major design element of his 1920 bridge is the construction itself, which has not been overlaid by classical columns or other decorative devices. Its form and image recall the viaducts to which Brunner refers in his 1911 report.

71

72

71 Art complex, project, New York City
Perspective, c. 1915
Pastel and pencil on brown paper, 18⅞ x 27¼" (47.9 x 69.2 cm)
Cooper-Hewitt Museum of Decorative Arts and Design
Smithsonian Institution
New York, New York

72 Railroad Connecting Bridge, Queens Boulevard
Queens, New York
Perspective c. 1920
Charcoal, 19¾ x 22⅞ " (50.2 x 58.1 cm)
Cooper-Hewitt Museum of Decorative Arts and Design
Smithsonian Institution
New York, New York

Beginning in the 1870s Galveston grew to become the financial capital of Texas, the state's major port, and a sophisticated Southern city. From 1874 when he settled in Galveston to the mid-1890s, Nicholas Clayton designed many of the city's most important ecclesiastical, commercial, civic, and private buildings. Clayton built 11 buildings in the four blocks of the Strand, the commercial center of downtown Galveston, most of Galveston's public schools of the 1880s and 1890s, the two large hospitals, and all but two of the residences in the elegant "Castle District." Building in other parts of Texas and in Louisiana, Alabama, Florida, and Georgia, he became one of the South's most outstanding architects. Nonetheless, only one of his buildings was ever published in the professional press, the Sylvain Blum House in Galveston, in the May, 1893, issue of the *Southern Architect*. However, Clayton's work is mentioned in discussions of Galveston in 1895 in *Harper's Weekly* and in 1896 in *Frank Leslie's Illustrated Newspaper*.

Clayton's work in Galveston encompassed several Victorian modes: the Neo-Greek; the Second Empire style, such as St. Mary's Infirmary of 1874; the Stick Style, exemplified by houses and small churches built for the Diocese of Galveston and by the 1880 Galveston Pavilion in which this domestic mode was blown up to a large public scale; the Romanesque Revival, as in the Galveston News Building of 1883–1884; the High Victorian Gothic of the Ursuline Convent of 1891–1894. At times this eclecticism produced an amalgamation of historical details so heady, as in the Gresham Mansion in Galveston of 1884-1893, that they transcend ready stylistic categorization.

Perhaps the most outstanding example of Clayton's Romanesque mode is the University of Texas Medical Branch Building in Galveston of 1888–1891. The polychrome building of brick and artificial red sandstone (actually concrete) with blue and green tile roofs is composed of a central block with flanking and rear apsidal-ended dependencies on a high basement. A series of large and small arcades and the entry porch recall the work of Henry Hobson Richardson (page 137). Clayton uses opus spicatum, the laying of bricks diagonally, each row overlapping the voids of the row beneath, and horizontal bands of artificial red sandstone to create a richly patterned facade. The column capital for the front entrance, dated 1890 (73), is composed of lush vegetal forms and a Lone Star, all carved with deep undercutting. The conception of this capital is yet another element in the creation of rich surface effects.

The small unidentified church (74) is one of several prototypes Clayton developed for the mission activities of the Galveston Diocese. None of these small wooden structures is known to exist today, as they were intended to be temporary structures used only until the parish became established and could construct a more substantial church. The board and batten construction and decorative woodwork are typical of Clayton's work of the 1880s. The plan of this church was a simple rectangular box.

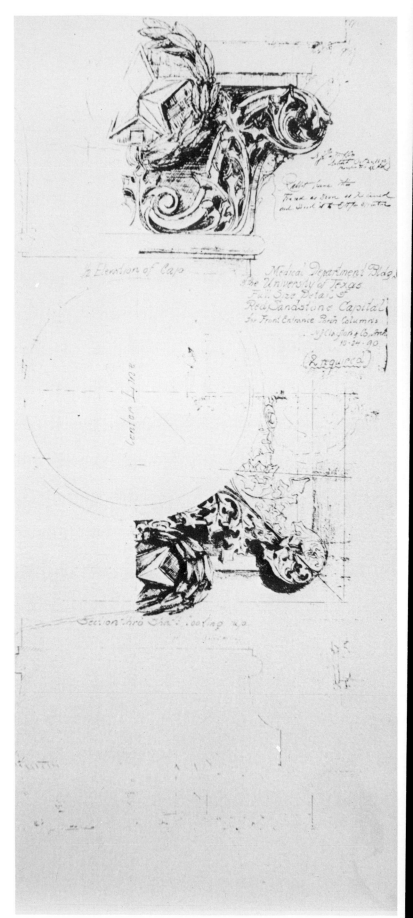

73

REAR ELEVATION.

74

73 Detail of capital, University of Texas Medical School
Austin, Texas
Front entry, 1888–1890
Medium and size unknown
School of Architecture
University of Texas
Austin, Texas

74 Unidentified church, Texas
Elevation, 1890
Pencil and ink, 12 x 19" (30.4 x 48.3 cm)
Rehm College
The Rosenberg Library
Galveston, Texas

154 75 *Unidentified house*
Perspective, sketchbook, c. 1897
Pencil, 6 x 4⅝" (15.2 x 11.7 cm)
Collection of John Beach
Berkeley, California

76 *Public building, California*
Perspective, 1900
Pencil on tracing paper, 20 x 27¼" (50.8 x 69.2 cm)
Collection of John Beach
Berkeley, California

Ernest Coxhead (1863–1933)

Ernest Coxhead, born and educated in England, settled in San Francisco in 1890 at a time when there was tremendous growth in that city and architectural patrons required buildings presenting an image of permanence, elegance, and connection to past culture. Yet these patrons did not require an exact adaptation of a particular historical mode, thus giving the architects of the First Bay Area tradition, such as Coxhead, John Galen Howard (1864–1934), Bernard Maybeck (page 177), Julia Morgan (page 181), Willis Polk (1867–1924), to name a few, wide latitude to draw on many vocabularies and to combine these with unusual spatial configurations and abrupt changes in scale, creating what David Gebhard has called its "Alice in Wonderland" quality. In Coxhead's work ornament derived from Baroque, Renaissance, Classical, Georgian architecture, to name only a few sources, was applied to wooden houses, often shingled and in massing reminiscent of Shingle Style or Medieval vernacular architecture. Coxhead introduced the long gallery of English country houses as a spine into many of his domestic structures, making this the center of experience in the building. At other times he used the stair as the major spatial element of a building, and in some instances the stairs become the building itself by widening landings and forming rooms from them. The sketchbook study (75) c. 1897 for a house presents the irregular massing, dormers, and leaded windows that in their totality create a romantic image common to Coxhead's buildings.

In London Coxhead apprenticed with George Wallis and then worked for Frederic Chancellor. Just preceding his departure for America, Coxhead was awarded the Royal Institute of British Architects' Silver Medal for drawing (1884–1885). In partnership with his brother Almeric in Coxhead and Coxhead, he built many domestic structures, ecclesiastical and public buildings, including the Telephone Company Building, San Francisco, 1909; the Oakland Gas Company Building, 1894; St. John's Episcopal Church, Monterey, 1891; St. John's Episcopal Church, San Francisco, 1890. Ernest Coxhead seems to have been the chief designer in the firm.

Coxhead surrounds the exterior of his project for a commercial building (76), probably a bank, of 1900 with a huge Corinthian colonnade and an overscaled entablature capped by a row of stars; this entablature forms almost a third of the height of the building. The expected continuity of the entablature is broken at the corners, revealing the building behind it. All this is combined with a huge arched entrance, flanked by tall square-headed doors. This idiosyncratic use of classical and Renaissance forms might be called "Bay Area Hellenistic."

75

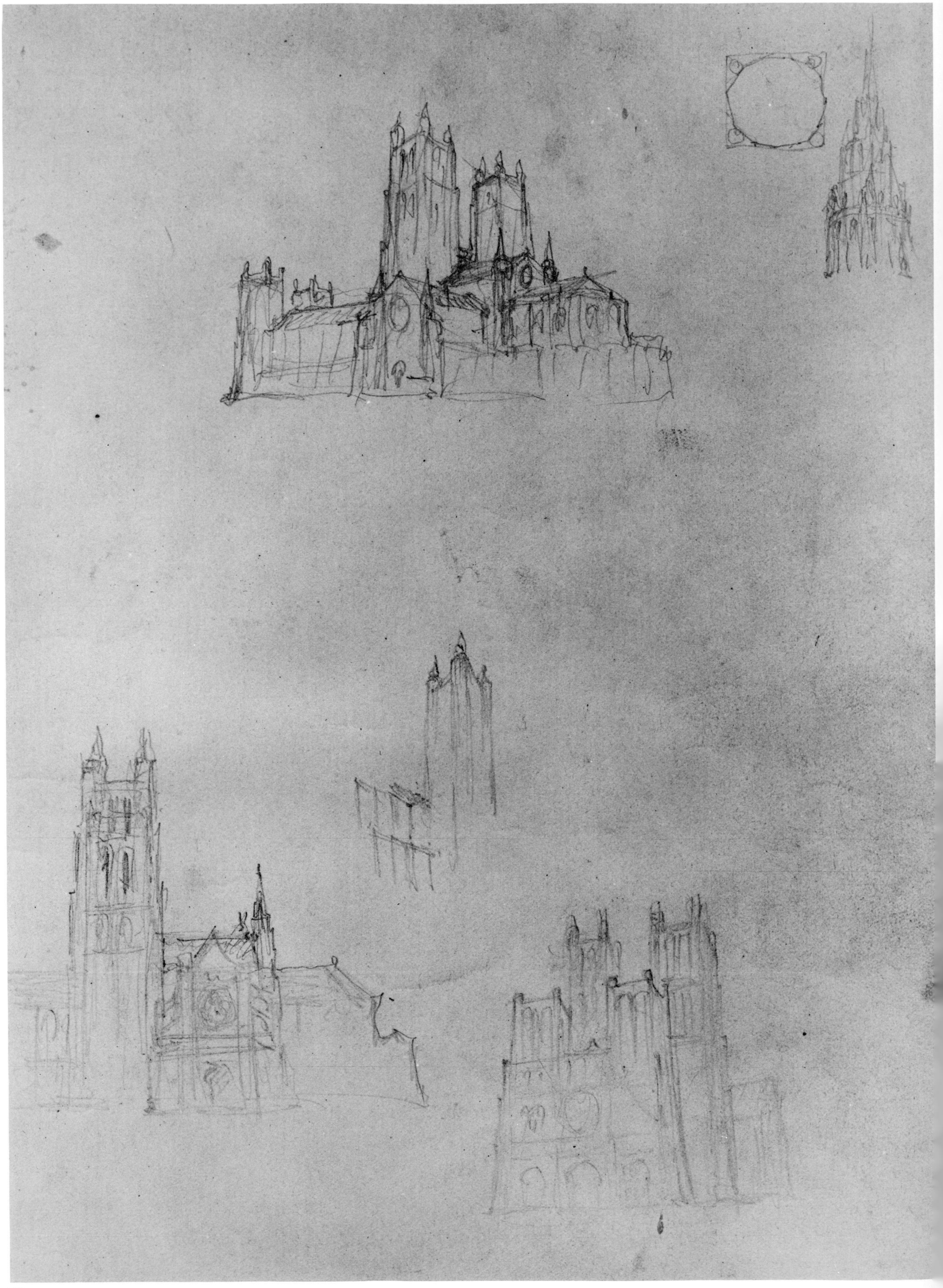

77

Ralph Adams Cram (1863–1942)

Ralph Adams Cram was the leading figure of the Gothic Revival in its late archeological phase. All Soul's Church in Ashmont, Massachusetts, of 1894, designed in collaboration with his partner Charles Wentworth and a young architect associated with the firm, Bertram Goodhue (page 166), stands as the first important early monument of this style. Cram advocated the return to the Gothic, which, he believed, went into decline in the 16th century as a result of the synchronization of the development of Renaissance architecture and the Protestant Reformation. Cram vehemently opposed copying former Gothic glories, since for him the Gothic "organism" consisted of basic principles rather than decorative details or forms. A devout Catholic, Cram's involvement with the Gothic style extended beyond esthetic concerns to deep personal involvement. In his book *The Gothic Quest* of 1907 he wrote, "It [the Gothic] has stood for life palpitating with action, for emotional richness and complexity, for the ideals of honor, duty, courage, adventure, heroism, chivalry. Above all for a dominating and controlling religious sense and for the supremacy of an individual church and all that it signified."

Cram had a highly successful career building over seventy cathedrals and churches among many other important structures. His position as supervising architect at Princeton University and Bryn Mawr, Mount Holyoke, and Wellesley Colleges reinforced the Gothic Revival as the appropriate style for colleges. Cram's Graduate College of 1913 and Chapel of 1929 at Princeton are outstanding examples of his academic Gothic. Cram was in control of a varied eclecticism and built in the Colonial, Georgian, as well as Byzantine style. He was prolific as an author as well as an architect. Indicative of his broad interests are his 24 books that deal with religion, philosophy, architectural and art history and his autobiography, *My Life in Architecture*, of 1936.

Cram was born in Hampton Falls, New Hampshire, in 1863, the son of a Unitarian clergyman. After studying at Phillips Exeter Academy and touring Europe, he wrote art criticism for the *Boston Transcript*, and between 1881 and 1885 he apprenticed with the Boston architectural firm of Arthur Rotch and George Tilden. After ranking as a finalist in the Boston Court House competition of 1886 and second in the Massachusetts State House competition of the same year, Cram left for a European study tour. In 1890 he opened his own Boston architectural practice in partnership with Charles Wentworth. The firm's first projects consisted of remodelings, a tenement design, and a few houses. Cram's extensive lecture tours throughout the country on ecclesiastical, art, and architectural subjects promoted his name and attracted his early church commissions. Bertram G. Goodhue entered the firm in 1891 and became a partner in 1897; Frank Ferguson joined the firm in 1899 and became the business partner. Cram, Goodhue, & Ferguson won the competition to rebuild the United States Military Academy at West Point, New York, in 1903. After winning the competition for St. Thomas Church in New York City in 1906 and after completion of West Point's Cadet Chapel in 1910, the firm received national recognition.

Cram's role in his firm's design process can be characterized as the overall planner and initiator of the *parti*. In the initial design phase Cram executed a rapid series of rough pencil sketches primarily in perspective, blocking out the mass, proportion, composition, and articulation of the project. Next, the appropriate stylistic idiom was selected. While Cram often admitted his lack of interest in decorative details, this domain remained Bertram Goodhue's forte. In the early years of their partnership Cram and Goodhue benefited from their complementary strengths. Yet there was always considerable rivalry over the control of the design, particularly as Goodhue's skill as a designer developed. Even while they were partners, they often resorted to preparing separate schemes. In the St. Thomas Church competition both men submitted widely divergent schemes to the church's building committee, which chose Cram's design. This was the last building on which they collaborated. Goodhue opened a New York branch of the firm and after further difference with Cram ended the partnership in 1914.

In 1889 four finalists were selected in the Cathedral of St. John the Divine competition in New York City from among sixty entries. Cram originally submitted a Romanesque design, while Goodhue proposed a quasi-Byzantine scheme. Heins & LaFarge were awarded the commission in July 1891 based upon their Romanesque-Byzantine scheme. They executed the Romanesque choir, the two apsidal chapels, and the main structural elements of the crossing. With Heins's death in 1907, Heins & LaFarge's contract was legally terminated. La Farge's tenure as supervising architect continued until April 1911 when Cram received the appointment. Cram and Ferguson continued work on the cathedral until 1942 when Cram died. The enormous cathedral (77) was designed by Cram in a very personal French Gothic idiom. Its nave is said by Douglass Shand Tucci, Cram's most recent biographer, to rise double the height of any medieval cathedral. The aisles rising to the full height of the nave vault add to the soaring feeling of the interior. This great height and openness were achieved by buttressing the building primarily from within its own structure. Steel trusses help support the roof as do exterior buttresses. Cram also introduced the lightweight Guastavino vaulting technique for the dome of the crossing. His innovations on Gothic structure were all part of what Cram called "creative scholarship."

77 Cathedral of St. John the Divine, New York City
Sketchbook, 1911
Pencil, 9 x 11" (22.9 x 27.9 cm)
Collection of Hoyle, Doran and Berry
Boston, Massachusetts

SMALL HOUSE MINNEAPOLIS 1914 PURCELL & ELMSLIE ARCH.

1914

78

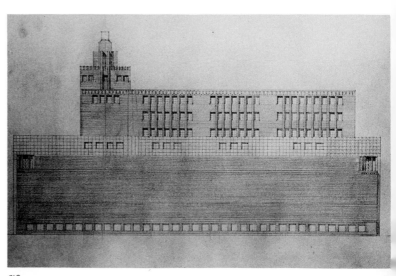

79

George Grant Elmslie (1871–1953)
William Gray Purcell (1880–1965)

The firms of Purcell, Feick, & Elmslie (1909–1913) and its successor Purcell & Elmslie (1913–1922) were the most prolific among the Prairie School architects. They were primarily concerned with the design of small, moderately priced houses and banks, although they did build several residences for wealthy clients, such as the Bradley Bungalow of 1911–1912 on the Crane Estate at Woods Hole, Massachusetts, as well as a number of churches, commercial and industrial buildings, and the one major civic building to be constructed by any of the Prairie School architects, the Woodbury County Court House in Sioux City, Iowa, of 1915–1917.

The most productive and significant period for the Prairie School was between 1909 and the beginning of the First World War, although its beginnings as a movement date from 1900 and its roots are in part in the Shingle Style of the late 19th century (page 137). Both Louis Sullivan and Frank Lloyd Wright (pages 185 and 234) provided formal and philosophical inspiration for the Prairie School architects, although Wright's work was perhaps more influential than Sullivan's. Among the architects associated with the school were William Drummond (1876-1946), Barry Byrne (page 198), and Walter Burley and Marion Mahony Griffin (page 173). In the work of these architects emphasis was often placed on the horizontal in massing and elements of design. Vertical elements, mullions and piers, may counterpoint the primacy of the horizontal. The Prairie School architects rejected open historical revivalism and relied on the interplay of forms and materials for their imagery. In the early 20th century, periodicals were important vehicles, as they are today, for the dissemination of a style. Elmslie and Purcell's work, as that of other Prairie School architects, was published in *The Western Architect*. Three special issues of the magazine were devoted to their work in 1913 and 1915.

George Grant Elmslie was born in Scotland and was brought to the United States by his parents in 1884. In 1887 he was employed by J. L. Silsbee in Chicago. In 1889 he began his 20-year employment with Louis Sullivan, becoming Sullivan's chief draftsman and translating Sullivan's ideas into visual form. In 1909 he left Sullivan to collaborate with William Purcell and George Feick, Jr. (1881–1945). Elmslie's method of working in the firm of Purcell & Elmslie was related to his experience with Sullivan: Elmslie relied on drawing as the initial means to develop an idea; Purcell conceived of the design as an abstract idea, expressed first through language and then realized in drawing. Purcell described this difference as follows: "mine must pass through the word laboratory, his passes through the graphic meadows. . . ."

Purcell received an American version of a Beaux-Arts education at Cornell University, graduating with a Bachelor of Architecture in 1903. After graduation he obtained work for five months with Louis Sullivan where Elmslie was employed. He left Sullivan and worked in San Francisco for a year and a half for John Galen Howard (1864–1931). In 1906 he traveled extensively with Feick in Europe and Asia Minor; and he contacted many architects, including the Dutch architect, H. P. Berlage, for whom he arranged a United States lecture tour in 1911.

Purcell & Elmslie's most active period was between 1910 and 1915. During this time they were particularly concerned with the design of moderately priced houses, such as the Palmer-Cantini project (78) of 1914 in Minneapolis, Minnesota. These houses were inspired by Frank Lloyd Wright's "A Fireproof House for $5,000," published in *The Ladies' Home Journal* of April 1906 and delineated by Marion Mahony (page 173). Purcell & Elmslie's compact, characteristically cubelike houses, such as the Palmer-Cantini project, were either hip roofed or gabled with rows of casement windows close to the wall plane. The wall is stressed as surface by the windows and the use of huge areas of plaster, often in combination with brick or wood. Their most spatially exciting and carefully planned house in this genre is that for William Gray Purcell of 1913 in Minneapolis.

During the first two decades of the 20th century, the building type given most prominent siting in the Midwestern town, after those serving democratic institutions such as courthouses, was the bank, called by Frank Lloyd Wright, the "Temple to the God of money as modern temples go." The firm of Purcell &

78 *George Grant Elmslie*
Palmer-Cantini House, project, Minneapolis, Minnesota
Elevation, 1914
Pencil and colored pencil, 9¼ x 9½" (23.5 x 24.1 cm)
Anonymous Lender

79 *George Grant Elmslie*
Humboldt Park Distribution Station, project, Chicago
Elevation, 1924
Pencil, 12½ x 21¼" (31.8 x 54 cm)
Anonymous lender

80

Elmslie built more banks than Sullivan and Wright combined. It was, however, Wright's 1901 project, "A Village Bank" published in *The Brick Builder*, and his project for the First National Bank and offices of Frank L. Smith in Dwight, Illinois, of 1904, as well as Harvey Ellis's (page 126) Security Bank in Minneapolis of 1891 that were the first examples of the boxlike Prairie School bank. Its first great built example was Louis Sullivan's Owatonna Bank in Minnesota of 1906–1908 on which Elmslie worked. The projected First National Bank of Mankota, Minnesota (80), in 1911 was designed in the same year as their most outstanding bank, the Merchant's Bank of Winona, Minnesota. The Mankota Bank combines the huge arched entry, characteristic of Sullivan, with the large recessed piers placed in front of windows or a glass wall derived from Wright. In the brick Winona Bank enlarged piers frame a recessed glass wall and support a wide lintel. Ornament is used in the Mankota Bank to accent the entrance, the piers, and the angle where the horizontal cornice of the facade meets the edge of the entrance facade. This use of ornament to make the relationship of parts more precise relies to some extent on Sullivan's approach (page 185).

The firm of Purcell & Elmslie officially dissolved in 1922, although effectively it had done so by 1918. Elmslie designed several banks, churches, and private residences. He prepared a campus plan for Yankton College in Yankton, South Dakota, in 1927 and subsequently built a science building, Forbes Hall of Science, in 1929 and a dormitory, Look Hall, of 1931 there. During the Depression he worked briefly with William S. Hutton, after which he retired. Elmslie's Humboldt Park Distribution Station (79) of 1924 reflects the interest seen in the firm's last banks of the late 1910s in the International Style. The lower wall section of the building is a solid, sheer plane; the upper wall pierced by windows and divided by piers appears as a screen. The stepped massing of the tower is not unlike the work of Art Deco or Moderne architecture.

During the First World War Purcell moved to Philadelphia and worked as advertising manager for Alexander Brothers; in 1920 he moved to Portland, Oregon, and subsequently retired to Pasadena, California. During the 1930s while in Portland he designed a number of houses in Minnesota, including a projected house (81) in Rochester in 1928. Like his former partner, Purcell's work during the twenties was an outgrowth of the firm's last works, which began to treat the wall as a flat plane. The flat roof, smooth wall, window banks, and large glass wall section off the patio relies on the International Style idiom of the twenties. However, recalling Purcell's Prairie School roots is the ornament of the round windows, the vertical paning of the strip of second story windows, and the change in materials between the first and second stories.

81

80   William Gray Purcell
First National Bank, project, Mankota, Minnesota
Perspective, 1911
Pencil, 13¾ x 25¼" (34.9 x 64.1 cm)
Anonymous lender

81   William Gray Purcell
House, project, Rochester, Minnesota
Perspective, 1928
Pencil, ink, and watercolor, 15½ x 24½" (39.4 x 62.2 cm)
Anonymous lender

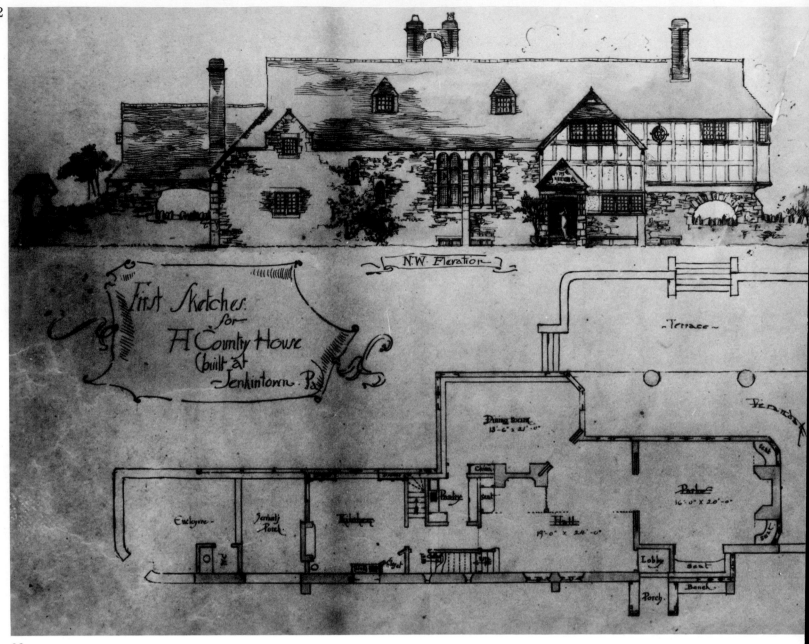

82

Wilson Eyre, Jr. (1858–1944)

Directly following his graduation in 1878 from the School of
Architecture at MIT, Wilson Eyre entered the Philadelphia
office of James P. Sims. Philadelphia and its suburbs would be
the center for Eyre's architectural activity. Inheriting Sims'
office in 1881, Eyre began his independent practice and
developed a clientele wealthy enough to commission large
suburban dwellings, townhouses, and commercial and
institutional buildings of importance. Among the most
outstanding of his works are the Archaeological Museum at the
University of Pennsylvania, designed with Cope & Stewardson
and Frank Miles Day, begun in 1893 and completed in 1926; the
Borie Building of 1908; and the Richard Ashurst House in
Overbrook, Pennsylvania, c. 1885.

Eyre's suburban houses were variations on what has become
known as the Shingle Style. This style was initiated by William
Ralph Emerson (1833–1917) and Henry Hobson Richardson
(page 137) in the context of suburban and resort architecture in
Maine and Massachusetts during the early 1880s; it was
subsequently adapted by architects throughout the country. In
the prototypical Shingle Style dwelling, rooms are loosely
organized around a large living hall in a manner often
determined by the site in order to provide dramatic views of
nature. The exterior sheathing of shingles—the material that
gives its name to the style—unifies the massing and stresses
the horizontal. These buildings do not rely on direct historical
allusions for their imagery, although they are inspired by past
architecture such as that of the American colonial era.

Eyre's very personal manipulation of the style deviates from the
norm in three ways: many of his buildings rely on the Queen
Anne style for much of their vocabulary; entirely shingled

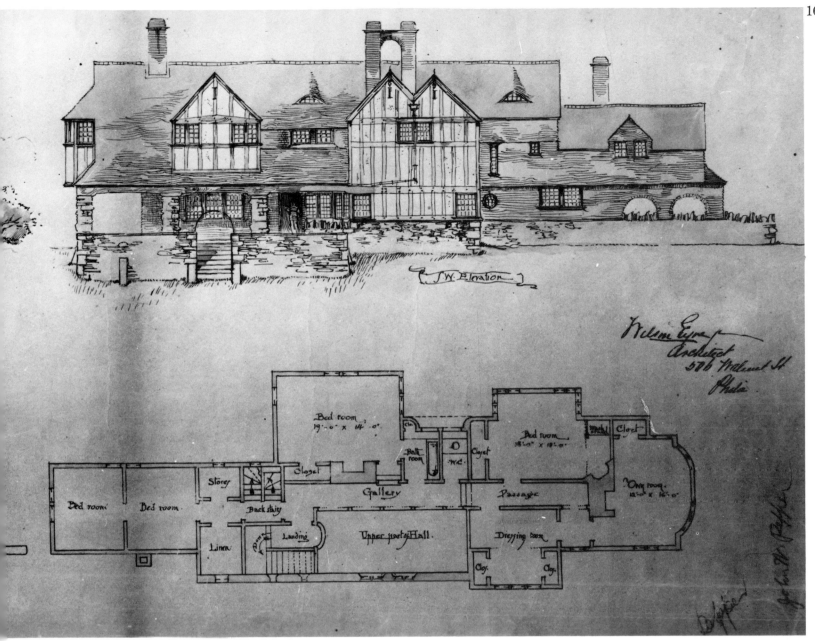

buildings are rare; and in certain of his most innovative houses, such as the Ashurst Residence c. 1885 in Overbrook, he orients the hall and adjacent rooms along a long axis in contrast with the more common clustering of spaces of other Shingle Style architects. This spatial arrangement is an important precedent for the stress on a horizontal continuity of space in Frank Lloyd Wright's Prairie Houses (page 234).

The wood framing with plaster infill and the leaded windows of the J. S. Pepper House (82) of 1886 in Jenkintown recall the medievalizing Queen Anne mode of the 1870s, a style that Eyre often referred to. However, Eyre uses the style for image only. He handles it in a manner different from the often abrupt massing of Queen Anne buildings. Instead he maintains one consistent wall plane, thus unifying the mass. The house is extended along a long axis. Its interior is disposed around a double story living hall.

82 J. S. Pepper House, Jenkintown, Pennsylvania
Southwest and northwest elevation, 2 floor plans, 1886
Ink and wash on thin bristol board, 13 x 34" (33 x 86.4 cm)
Rare Books Room
Furness Art Library
University of Pennsylvania
Philadelphia, Pennsylvania

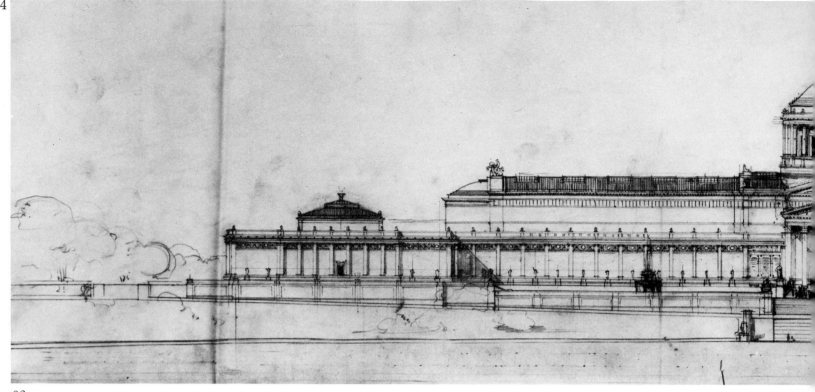

83

84

Cass Gilbert (1859–1934)

Some of the most outstanding Beaux-Arts buildings for public use, built between the last decade of the 19th century and the mid-1930s in both the Midwest and New York City, were designed by Cass Gilbert. He studied architecture at MIT, whose educational system was Beaux-Arts in its orientation, and between 1880 and 1882 he was a personal assistant to Stanford White, a partner in one of the most influential firms in the United States—McKim, Mead,& White.

The late 1890s and the first part of the 20th century before the First World War was a period of tremendous financial growth in the United States, accompanied by the expansion in size and power of cultural institutions, corporations, and certain government agencies—all of which required more physical space and a grand image. Most of these institutions, when they acted as architectural patrons, chose a Beaux-Arts design, and several chose Gilbert as their architect. His buildings of this era in the Beaux-Arts mode include: the Minnesota State Capitol in St. Paul, designed in 1893; the United States Custom House in New York, commissioned in 1899 and completed in 1907; the Allen Memorial Art Museum of 1917 (page 292) at Oberlin College; the United States Supreme Court Building of 1933–1935, completed posthumously; and the Federal Court House in New York's Foley Square of 1934, completed posthumously. In 1911 Gilbert designed the spectacular, Gothic-inspired Woolworth Building in New York.

The Louisiana Purchase Exposition of 1904 on a 657-acre site in St. Louis, for which Gilbert built the Art Building, was designed in the tradition started by the 1893 World's Columbian Exposition in Chicago. The buildings at both fairs were primarily sited along symmetrical axes and for the most part designed with a uniform cornice line (at St. Louis, 65 feet/198 meters above grade) within a Beaux-Arts mode based on Renaissance and classical styles. The 1893 fair was called a "White City." This epithet would describe the St. Louis fair as well.

Gilbert's fair building of light-colored stone, now used as the St. Louis Art Museum (see also page 264), was the only permanent structure constructed for the fair. Two small buildings of buff brick on either side of the present museum were also built, but were later demolished. Gilbert's study for the Art Building (83) differs from the completed structure in that in the finished building a high room with a large large semicircular window and pitched roof is placed behind the colonnaded entrance, whereas in the study a temple front, like that of the Pantheon, is combined with a dome. In the study a colonnade runs along the entire front, whereas there is no colonnade in the finished building. There are also many other less outstanding differences

between the two conceptions. Both, however, present an image of power and high art, basing their symbolism on the classical architecture of the past. The symmetrical organization of the plan, around a sculpture garden, is also typical of the Beaux-Arts mode.

Gilbert, however, did not always produce Beaux-Arts buildings clothed in classical detailing, planned around symmetrical axis, and built of luxurious materials. Beginning in 1882 he started his independent practice in St. Paul (he moved his practice to New York after winning the commission for the United States Custom House). Between 1882–1892 he was associated with his MIT classmate James Knox Taylor, later architect of the United States Treasury Building in Washington.

During the earlier part of the St. Paul period Gilbert's work, often asymmetrical in planning, is picturesque and recalls both the Shingle Style and the Queen Anne modes. Richardson was also an important source for Gilbert at this time. In the nineties Gilbert's work becomes more formalized in planning and draws on the Colonial Revival, Chateauesque, and academic Beaux-Arts styles. The elevation study (84) of 1897 for the Crawford Livingston House in St. Paul, Minnesota, to be built of stone and brick is a mixture of certain Queen Anne detailing and materials, such as that of the second story gable over the window to be executed in plaster and wood and a Chateauesque massing.

83   Art Building, Louisiana Purchase Exposition
(now the St. Louis Art Museum)
Principal facade, elevation study, c. 1904
Pencil on tracing paper, 7 x 28½" (17.8 x 72.4 cm)
The New-York Historical Society
New York, New York

84   Crawford Livingston House, project, St. Paul, Minnesota
Elevation and detail studies, 1897
Ink on stationery, 7½ x 9¾" (19.1 x 24.8 cm)
Division of Archives and Manuscripts
The Minnesota Historical Society
St. Paul, Minnesota

85

86

Bertram Grosvenor Goodhue (1869–1924)

Beginning with his Gothic Revival work with Ralph Adams Cram (page 156), Bertram Goodhue's career is marked by innovative eclecticism. As supervising architect for the Panama-California Exposition of 1915 in San Diego, he was a prime force in the fashionable resurgence of the Spanish Colonial Revival in America and especially in California. After his exasperation with the Gothic, Goodhue pursued a diverse, historicist path, whose goals were an embellished classicism with modernist overtones. These buildings were presented by the hand that, some have said, "drew like an angel."

Bertram Goodhue was born on April 28, 1869, in Pomfret, Connecticut. He completed his early education at Edwin Russell's Collegiate and Commercial Institute in New Haven. Goodhue began his career with the New York architectural firm of Renwick, Aspinwall, & Russell when he was 15 and within 2 years became the firm's head draftsman. During that period James Renwick, the renowned Gothic Revival architect, trained Goodhue. After winning first prize in a competition for the Cathedral of Dallas, Goodhue brought the commission in 1891 to the Boston firm of Cram & Wentworth. His long association with Ralph Cram dates from that point. In 1897 Goodhue became a partner in the firm, renamed Cram, Goodhue, & Wentworth. In 1899 the firm became Cram, Goodhue, & Ferguson, with Frank Ferguson the business partner. In the early years of Cram and Goodhue's collaboration, Cram was generally responsible for the overall planning of the projects, while Goodhue focused on the decorative detail. By the mid-1890s Goodhue had developed into one of the best American draftsman. An intense rivalry developed between Cram and Goodhue, while Goodhue's design capabilities became strengthened. When the firm won the commission to build West Point in 1903, Goodhue returned to New York City to open a branch office. Goodhue's West Point Chapel of 1910 foretells his later modernist work in its expanses of blank wall and lack of moldings. As Cram and Goodhue drifted further apart, the New York and Boston offices became relatively independent. St. Thomas Church in New York City of 1909–1914 was Cram and Goodhue's last collaborative design. In 1914 Goodhue formally severed his connections with Cram.

Goodhue's dissatisfaction with the Gothic led to exploratory designs in a style simultaneously modernist and classicist. His Nebraska State Capitol in Lincoln of 1916–1928, one of his most important later works, was a manifestation of this tendency. Goodhue won the 1920 competition, a mandate for "a practical working home for the machinery of state" as well as "an inspiring monument." Fiske Kimball, among others, criticized the resulting building for its ununified form amid a plethora of detail. Its plan is derived from a Greek cross inscribed within a square. A 400-foot high square tower of stone on a steel framework ascended from the central crossing. Henry-Russell Hitchcock states that the Nebraska State Capitol is "an eclectic sort of semimodernism" that was "vaguely Byzantinesque, yet towered instead of being domed in what had been the tradition for state capitols ever since Bulfinch's in Boston." Eliel Saarinen's (page 222) 1908 Finnish Parliament House in Helsinki influenced the stark form, the organizational clarity, and the increased verticality of Goodhue's 1920 design. This building firmly established a classicized modernism as the stylistic paradigm for government buildings. Goodhue's other important late works are the Los Angeles Public Library and the National Academy of Sciences in Washington, D.C., both completed posthumously. The page of small sketches (86) reveals Goodhue's capacity to handle a variety of eclectic styles: Gothic, Spanish Colonial, Beaux-Arts, Byzantine, and Indian. Intricate detail, of which Goodhue was a master at both conceptualizing and communicating on paper, adorns the Gothic cathedral for the Diocese of Los Angeles and the bookcover for the German Emperor. Notes on the sketches suggest the sensuosity of Goodhue's conceptions achieved with lavish and varied materials. The baldachino over the throne would have been constructed of oak, stone, and ebony inlaid with copper, ivory, and silver gilt; the throne would have been constructed in teak and redwood inlaid with ebony.

Goodhue used the Gothic for residential as well as ecclesiastical buildings. The force of his design for an undated Gothic house (85) in Westchester County, New York, lies in the blank walls accented only by the Gothic detailing and form of the windows, occasional protrusions in the form of bays or small towers, and

its siting. A comparison of this house project with the Spanish Colonial house for Santa Barbara on the page of sketches (86) reveals a consistent approach to massing a building on a hilly site. In both schemes the house is locked into the hill by extending the mass of the building down the side of the slope, giving the impression that it is almost hewn from that rise. In both studies a long wall defines the edge of the plateau of the hill and terminates in a small tower or pavilion. Goodhue's buildings take control of their sites; this gives them their powerful visual impact.

85   *House, project, New York*
Perspective, 1915
Pencil, 2½ x 37½" (62.2 x 95.3)
Collection of John Rivers
Houston, Texas

86   *Miscellaneous studies*
Sketchbook leaf, undated
Pencil, 17⅜ x 13½" (44.1 x 34.3)
Collection of John Rivers
Houston, Texas

87 Henry Mather Greene
Pratt House, Ojai Valley, California
Three elevations, 1909
Ink on linen, 24⅛ x 38" (61.3 x 96.5 cm)
Greene and Greene Library
The Gamble House
Pasadena, California

Charles Sumner Greene (1868–1957)
Henry Mather Greene (1870–1954)

Charles and Henry Greene were born in Cincinnati and then moved to St. Louis, where they attended the Manual Training High School under the auspices of Washington University. Manual Training was a pioneering school at which instruction in the manual arts of woodworking, metal working, and machine tool design was given equal weight with academic training. Completing their education at MIT, where they received a Beaux-Arts architectural training, they were graduated in 1891, after which they worked in Boston until 1893, when they moved to Pasadena. Their first houses in California were Colonial Revival or Queen Anne in style, but in the brief period between 1907 and 1909, they helped forge a new domestic idiom in Pasadena and environs, which would immediately provide inspiration for two decades of California building and which continues to be admired as a major development in American architecture. The four most outstanding houses of the period were built for rich patrons: David B. Gamble in 1907–1909, Robert R. Blacker of 1907–1909, Charles M. Pratt in 1908–1909, and William R. Thorsen of 1908.

These houses, nonrevivalistic in terms of historical high styles, were built in an era when many of Greene and Greene's peers were producing buildings whose imagery was based on Renaissance and Classical architecture. The major figures, however, who parallel the Greenes' search for a nonrevivalistic architecture are the architects of the Prairie School, such as Frank Lloyd Wright (page 234) and Walter Burley and Marion Mahony Griffin (page 173). The form of the Greenes' houses was determined by a primary concern for relating the building to the site, a response to environmental conditions, and an interest in making dramatic and explicit the illusion of the wood and shingle construction technique. The only historical styles that inspired their work at this point were Japanese architecture and the American Stick and Shingle styles, modes that employed indigenous natural materials in a truthful way in which a close relationship was established among nature, site, and building.

The plans of Greene and Greene's buildings of their innovative period are variations on the themes of either a loose agglomeration of rectangular units, sometimes around a court, or a grouping of large spaces that flow into each other as in the best examples of the Shingle Style. The houses are always surrounded by patios and gardens, which directly relate the structures to their sites. Large roof overhangs and sleeping porches provide relief from the hot climate and visually extend the buildings' volumes into the surroundings.

The variety of woods used—redwood, teak, maple, cedar, mahogany—for the walls and rafters, and the exterior shingles, boulders, and clinker bricks (overfired bricks that become irregular in shape) further associate the building with the environment. The effect, however, was not of crudity but of extreme refinement. All the woods were hand-rubbed and sanded, and beam ends were rounded. A relative of one of the Greenes' patrons described the surfaces as looking like "fresh butter, so soft are the surfaces and the corners." Further refinement and visual richness came from the multiplicity of wood-joining techniques: mortise and tenon, dovetail, scarf, among others. Some of these joints were structural, others

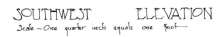

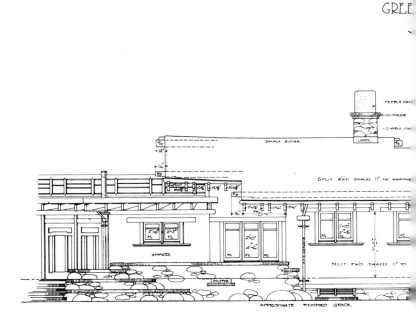

SOUTHWEST ELEVATION
Scale – One quarter inch equals one foot

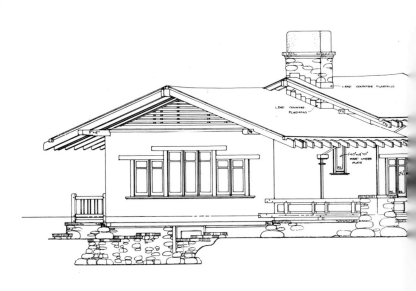

or CHARLES M. PRATT, ESQ., IN THE OJAI VALLEY, CAL

REENE, ARCHTS, 215-31 BOSTON BLD'G., PASADENA, CAL

19 5

MARCH 18, 1909

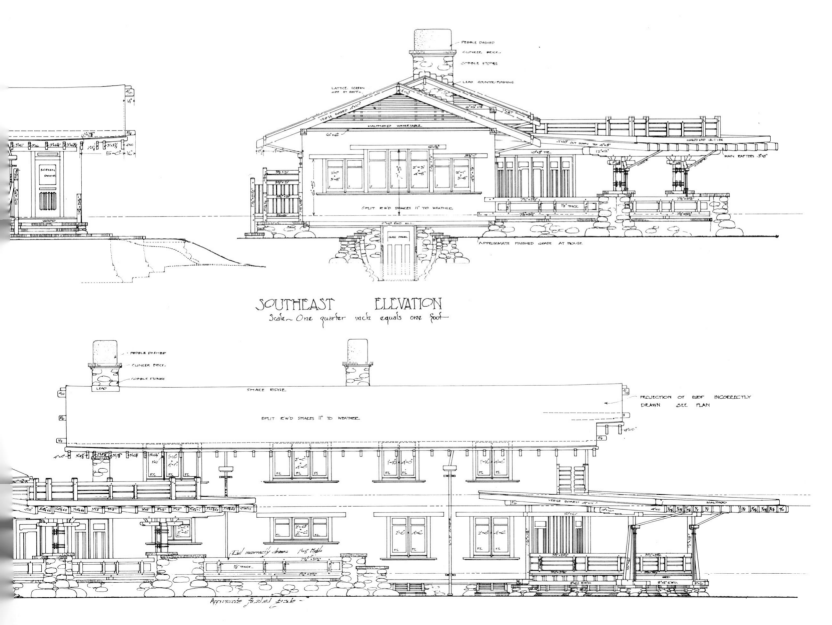

SOUTHEAST ELEVATION
Scale— One quarter inch equals one foot

EAST ELEVATION
Scale— One quarter inch equals one foot

88

decorative. These interlockings were secured by metal clasps, wooden pegs, and wedges. The level of detail is that of the fine cabinetmaker. The larger structural elements such as beams, rafters, and other linear structural members are designed to emphasize the separate identity of each: window sills and lintels are pulled out beyond the window frame, rafters extend beyond the roof line, beams reach beyond the posts of the sleeping porches.

In the situations where patrons could afford it, Charles Greene designed all the stained glass (executed by the Judson Studio in Los Angeles), all the furniture (executed by Peter Hall in Pasadena), and the lamps. Sometimes the flowers depicted in the stained glass were the same as those used in the garden. This comprehensive approach to design was related to the American Craftsman's movement of the first two decades of the 20th century. Gustav Stickley published the Greenes' work in his magazine *The Craftsman*, which spread the ideas of the movement. Stickley's idea of fine craftsmanship as a measure of the good life derived from the philosophy of the English designer William Morris (1834–1896) and the theorist John Ruskin (1819–1900), to whom the first two issues of *The Craftsman* were dedicated.

The shingled Adelaide Tichenor House (88) of 1906, overlooking the ocean at Long Beach, California, is one of the most Japanese conceptions of the Greenes. The green-tiled roof, Japanese garden, pool with bridge, and tea house all contributed to the Oriental flavor of the house and its grounds. The house's sleeping porches, deep verandas, and inspired use of wood are elements that characterize their work of the first decade of the century. The house was planned as a two-story wing on the oceanside, with one-story wings around a courtyard. This drawing is by Charles Greene, who was responsible for most of the design work; Henry Greene was involved with the administration of projects and working drawings.

The Pratt House (87) of 1908–1909 in Ojai is one room deep (except for the bedroom area that is double storied) and bends around its hilly site, making six turns while appearing to grow out of it. However, given the California climate, the terraces and sleeping porches almost double the effective living area of the structure. The projecting rafters and beams, lintels extending beyond the window frames, the boulders and the extensive terraces make this one of the more typical houses of the Greenes' mature period. Henry Greene is responsible for the working drawings for this house.

88   *Charles Sumner Greene*
Adelaide Tichenor House, Long Beach, California
Perspective, 1906
Watercolor, 10⅝ x 15¾" (27 x 40 cm)
Greene and Greene Library
The Gamble House
Pasadena, California

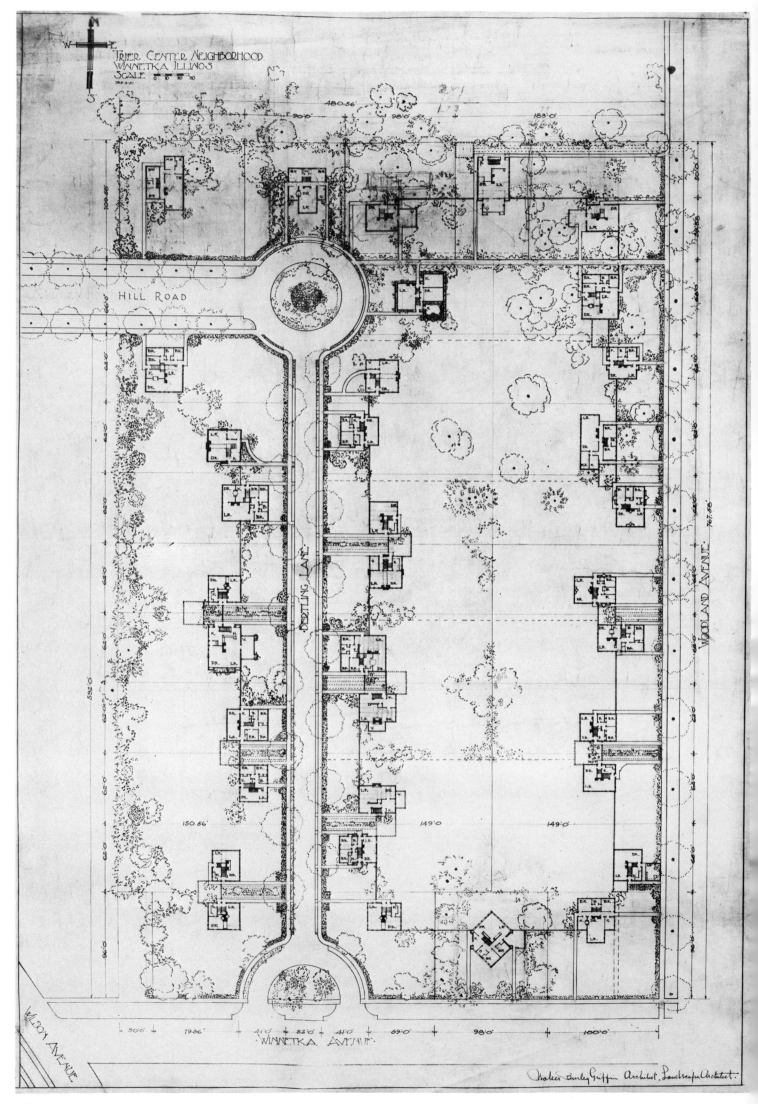

TRIER CENTER NEIGHBORHOOD
WINNETKA ILLINOIS
SCALE

HILL ROAD

SEETLING LANE

WOODLAND AVENUE

WILSON AVENUE

WINNETKA AVENUE

Walter Burley Griffin Architect. Landscape Architect.

Marion Mahony Griffin (1871–1962)
Walter Burley Griffin (1876–1937)

The partnership of Walter Burley and Marion Mahony Griffin began essentially with their marriage in 1911, after both architects had made their own individual contributions to the Prairie School (see also pages 158, 198, 234). They were a major force in the planning of the Rock Crest–Rock Glen Development begun in 1912, the most important planning scheme of the Prairie School; and they produced some of the most distinctive domestic dwellings of the movement. In 1912 Walter Burley Griffin won the competition to plan the new capital of Australia, Canberra. His scheme combined the long vistas and avenues of the City Beautiful movement (page 150) with the zoning concepts of Ebenezer Howard and the Garden City movement. His plan also involved an extremely sensitive and imaginative approach to landscaping. But much of the scheme was not built. Because of this large commission, the Griffins moved to Australia, introducing to that region a modern architectural idiom. Among their most outstanding buildings there are Newman College of 1916; the Capital Theater in Melbourne of 1922; and the planned community of Castelcrag begun in 1919. In 1936 the couple moved to India where they received large private, institutional, and commercial commissions, including that for Lucknow University. The following year he died, and Marion Mahony Griffin returned to America in 1940.

The Prairie School movement of the first two decades of the 20th century had its center in Chicago, but its architects built throughout the Midwest. It was a movement for stylistic reform in architecture, and it sought to make little or no reference to high styles of the past. It was in reaction to and in direct contrast with the Roman and Renaissance Revivalism of the 1890s epitomized by the World's Columbian Exposition of 1893 in Chicago—the city that nurtured the Prairie School's principal architects. Many of the Prairie School's practitioners worked for Frank Lloyd Wright, including both of the Griffins; and many of them shared offices in Chicago's Steinway Hall. Most of the Prairie School architects participated in the Chicago Architectural Club, the Architectural League of America, the Chicago Arts and Crafts Society. These shared professional activities provided an environment for the fruitful interchange of political and architectural ideas. For many of the Prairie School architects their interest in stylistic reform was paralleled by an interest in the social reform of the era as exemplified by the careers of Robert La Follette, Governor of Wisconsin, and Henry George, who advocated the economic philosophy of the single tax. Many of the architects around Wright were also interested in the ideas of Herbert Spencer. In contrast with the clients of Beaux-Arts architects who were often very rich, the patrons of Prairie School architects were of more modest means.

In 1894 Marion Mahony graduated from the School of Architecture at MIT. She was among the first women to complete the full 4-year course. In 1895 she joined Frank Lloyd Wright in his Oak Park studio and produced some of his finest renderings; her artistry was unsurpassed among the Prairie School architects. She also had an important design input into several of Wright's houses, like the David Amberg House of 1909–1910 in Grand Rapids, Michigan, and worked on Wright's designs for furniture, glass, lighting fixtures, and mosaics. In 1909 Hermann Von Holst and James Fyfe took over Frank Lloyd Wright's office while he was in Europe, and Marion Mahony designed several houses for them, such as the Adolph Mueller House in Decatur, Illinois, in 1910. Mahony's buildings are characterized by the disposition of space along a lengthy major axis with a change in floor level, but not ceiling height. Against the major mass of the building subsidiary forms are generally set at right angles forming a pinwheel shape.

In 1911 Mahony and Griffin were married. In the partnership that followed she was an important design critic and contributed especially to detailing and selection of materials as well as producing spectacular renderings; but the general conception of their work was Walter Burley Griffin's. When Marion Mahony Griffin returned to America from India after her husband's death, she continued to design and produced a 12-volume unpublished autobiography, *The Magic of America*. Marion Mahony Griffin's work and attitude towards life has won her an important place in the Women's Movement. In her autobiography she wrote that work "is the one great satisfaction for human beings which means that those women who have not

89 *Walter Burley Griffin*
Trier Center Neighborhood, project, Winnetka, Illinois
Plan, 1912–1913
Ink on linen, 21 x 31" (53.3 x 78.7 cm)
The Burnham Library
The Art Institute of Chicago
Chicago, Illinois

90

90   Marion Mahony Griffin
Rock Crest–Rock Glen, Mason City, Iowa
Perspective of site and buildings, 1912
Polychrome gouache on beige sateen, 23 x 79" (58.4 x 200.7 cm)
The Burnham Library
The Art Institute of Chicago
Chicago, Illinois

grown up to take life's work seriously as our men do are being deprived of life's great continuous satisfaction."

Walter Burley Griffin studied architecture with N. Clifford Ricker at the University of Illinois, graduating in 1899. Ricker's ideas were in harmony with those of the École des Beaux-Arts, but he was also interested in the work of his avant-garde contemporaries in Europe, such as that of the Viennese architect Otto Wagner (1841–1918). Between 1899 and 1901 Griffin worked in the famous drafting rooms of Steinway Hall in Chicago and from 1901 to 1905 worked for Frank Lloyd Wright as a job captain and supervisor. It was there that he met Marion Mahony. During 1905 Wright was in Japan and Griffin was in charge of the office in Oak Park; Wright was displeased with Griffin's handling of the office during his absence and dismissed Griffin, paying him in Japanese prints. The work of Griffin's maturity began about 1911 with the B. J. Ricker House of 1911 in Grinnell, Iowa, and especially "Solid Rock" of 1911 in Kenilworth, Illinois. The houses of his early maturity are generally based on square or rectangular plans with low hipped or gabled roofs. The contained massing is bounded by heavy corner piers. Where Frank Lloyd Wright achieved spatial complexity in the horizontal plane, Griffin was a master at the manipulation of space in the vertical. The houses at the Rock Crest–Rock Glen and Trier Center Neighborhood belong to this mature period, and it was this building form that he brought with him to Australia.

Throughout their careers both Griffins were interested in community planning and development; six community developments of their design were published in 1913 in the *Western Architect*. Their major American work was the 18-acre Rock Crest–Rock Glen subdivision (90) at Mason City, Iowa, begun in 1912. The presentation drawings were by Marion Mahony Griffin. The site, divided by Willow Creek, sloped up from one side of the water's edge, called Rock Glen; the opposite slope, Rock Crest, was a limestone bluff. The houses looked onto a park that was communally owned. The building history of the development site is complex; it involved first Frank Lloyd Wright, then the Griffins and Purcell and Elmslie (page 158), and later Barry Byrne (page 198), who took over the

Griffins' practice when they went to Australia. Griffin designed and built four houses at Rock Crest–Rock Glen before leaving for Australia and designed four others; two were redesigned and built by Byrne, and two were never built. The Melson House by Griffin in 1912 was built on a limestone cliff that dropped sharply to the water. Griffin wedded the form of the structure into the cliff and utilized roughly cut stone to further harmonize with the site. The Blythe House of 1913 was entirely constructed of reinforced concrete. His interest in the material continued, and in 1917 he developed a "knit lock" system of concrete blocks either before or contemporaneously with Frank Lloyd Wright's block system of the 1920s. The drawing of the subdivision shows 16 houses; only 8 were built. Griffin, intensely interested in landscape architecture, signed his name in the period 1906 to 1911 "Walter Burley Griffin Landscape Architect and Architect." His highly developed landscaping program for Rock Crest–Rock Glen, as for all his developments, combined an informal scheme, using local flora and fauna with more geometrized elements. Much of the landscaping indicated for the Rock Crest–Rock Glen subdivision, however, was never built.

The 9-acre Trier Center Neighborhood (89) in Winnetka, Illinois, of 1912-1913 is among the best of his subdivision schemes. It was there that the Griffins proposed to build their own house. Griffin paired the 30 houses around shared, walled service yards and low garages. The houses were oriented to take advantage of the landscape and preserve as rural an environment as possible; he projected planting 10,000 shrubs and plants. There was no through traffic to intrude upon this idealized environment. This scheme was never executed.

91

In 1889 Bernard Maybeck settled in San Francisco, the center of his professional career—a career that included a large number of residences in San Francisco, Oakland, Berkeley, and Marin County as well as several important institutional buildings in that region. Maybeck came to California from an Eastern background and a European education at the École des Beaux-Arts in Paris, from which he graduated in 1886. His father, a woodcarver, immigrated from Germany to New York City where he was a foreman in a shop of carvers that produced ornament for furniture. It is from his father that Maybeck's craftsmanlike treatment of materials and direct expression of structure, so important in his work, must have come. His European experience provided Maybeck with an appreciation for historical architecture and Beaux-Arts principles. On his return from Europe, Maybeck worked for 2 years in New York City with the highly successful and important firm of Carrère & Hastings, the architects of the New York Public Library. After a brief partnership with James Russell in Kansas City, he settled in California, where he worked for A. Page Brown and eventually established his own firm. In 1894 he met Phoebe Apherson Hearst, who would become one of his important patrons.

The two streams in Maybeck's background—the craftsman and the Beaux-Arts—produced a highly varied and complex body of work. Maybeck is as noted for his 1915 Palace of Fine Arts at the Panama-Pacific Exposition in San Francisco, derived from Renaissance and classical sources and evoking a High Art image, as for his important position in the first phase of the Bay Area tradition, which evokes an informal, anti-urban image. The outstanding monument of this phase of Maybeck's work is the First Church of Christ, Scientist in Berkeley, California, of 1909–1911.

Buildings of the Bay Area tradition are "woodsy," domestic in feeling, and intimately related to their site. Played against their vernacular image in which the natural, physical properties of materials were exploited was detailing often derived from many historic sources. All this was combined with a complex, sophisticated, and sometimes eccentric manipulation of space. In some instances, Maybeck's axial layout of spaces leads to more complex and mysterious arrangements where stairs and landings are at times expanded to roomlike proportions. Maybeck included medieval, Byzantine, Japanese, and Swiss detailing and influences in his architecture. He created a folk- and craftsmanlike feeling through carved and painted decoration and elaboration of beams, thus placing him closer than others of the Bay Area tradition to the American Craftsmen's movement. Finally, Maybeck is distinguished from other architects of the Bay Area tradition by an innovative use of materials. In Hearst Hall of 1899 at the University of California at Berkeley, huge laminated wood arches span the medievally inspired hall. In the First Church of Christ, Scientist in Berkeley of 1909–1911 asbestos siding is employed as well as industrial windows, which Maybeck filled with rose-colored rippled glass to effect a romantic and spiritual mood.

Maybeck's career also encompasses more formal buildings inspired by medieval architecture and the Spanish Colonial mode in the 1920s. The various modes within his career,

91   San Francisco City Hall Competition
Elevation, c. 1910
Pencil, 8 x 12" (20.3 x 30.5 cm)
Documents Collection, College of Environmental Design
The University of California at Berkeley
Berkeley, California

92   Earle C. Anthony House, Los Angeles
North elevation of bedroom and dining room wing and section through stair passage toward tower, 1927
Ink on tracing paper, 20½ x 62" (52 x 157.5 cm)
Documents Collection, College of Environmental Design
The University of California at Berkeley
Berkeley, California

93   *Pennell Residence, Berkeley, California*
Perspective, elevation, and plan studies, 1932
Pencil on tracing paper, 14 x 13" (35.6 x 33 cm)
Documents Collection, College of Environmental Design
The University of California at Berkeley
Berkeley, California

however, are linked by Maybeck's attitude toward architecture. For him the essence of architecture was beauty and mood. The use of building vocabularies of the past and manipulation of materials and siting were all means to achieve this end. In a pamphlet written for his widely acclaimed circular Palace of Fine Arts situated in a lagoon at the San Francisco Exposition, Maybeck stated that architecture is the "conveyor of ideas or sentiments" and that the architect should "examine historic form to see whether the effect it produced on your mind matches the feeling you are to portray." For Maybeck "physical form reflects a mental condition."

The three drawings illustrated represent the three important phases of Maybeck's career. The Pennell Residence (93) in Berkeley of 1932 set on a hilly lot exemplifies Maybeck's attitude that buildings constructed on such locations should work with the irregular configurations. This attitude was described by him in a pamphlet, "Programme for the Development of a Hillside Community," which he prepared with his wife and published in 1906–1907. The picturesque massing and the huge arched window are typical of Maybeck, as are the variety of spatial experiences that would exist within the house, as implied by the sketches.

The lavish Earle C. Anthony House (92) of 1927 in Los Angeles was designed in a formal medieval mode. Materials from Europe, including $35,000 worth of stone from Caen, France, and tiles from Barcelona, Spain, were imported for the house. Maybeck draws diverse materials and detailing into a "Maybeckian" whole. Most distinctive of Maybeck's touch are the dramatic spatial changes encompassing 21 different levels.

In 1910 Maybeck entered the competition for the San Francisco City Hall (91). The City Hall was one of the five buildings in the San Francisco Civic Center complex planned by John Galen Howard, Frederick Meyer, and John Reid, Jr. The City Hall, built between 1913 and 1916 by Bakewell & Brown of San Francisco, is a classical, Beaux-Arts scheme, as is Maybeck's competition entry. The Bay Area style was appropriate for architecture at a domestic scale only. When faced with a large civic commission Maybeck here, as in his 1915 Exposition building, turned to his academic past for inspiration.

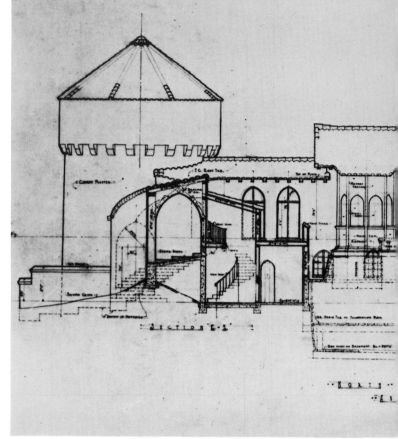

92

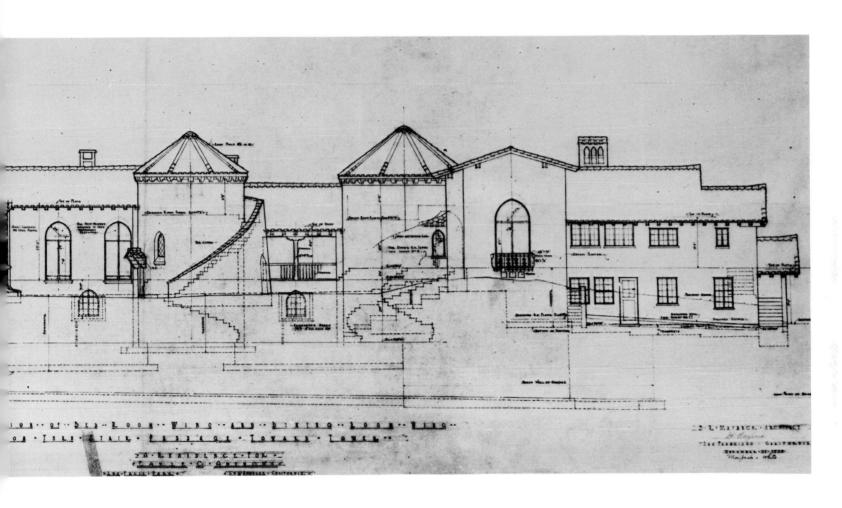

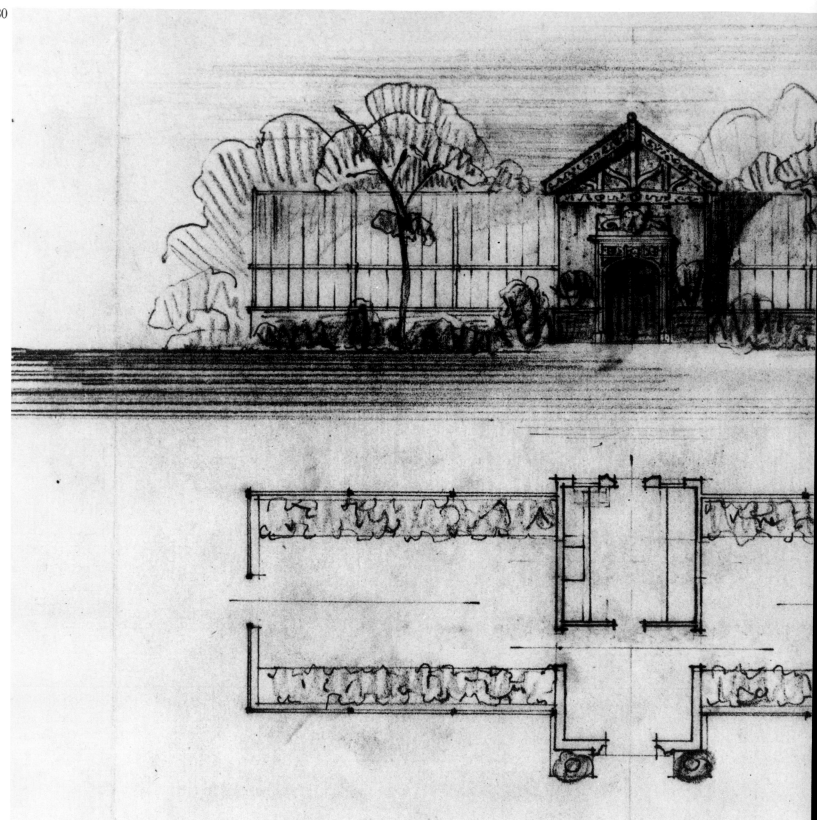

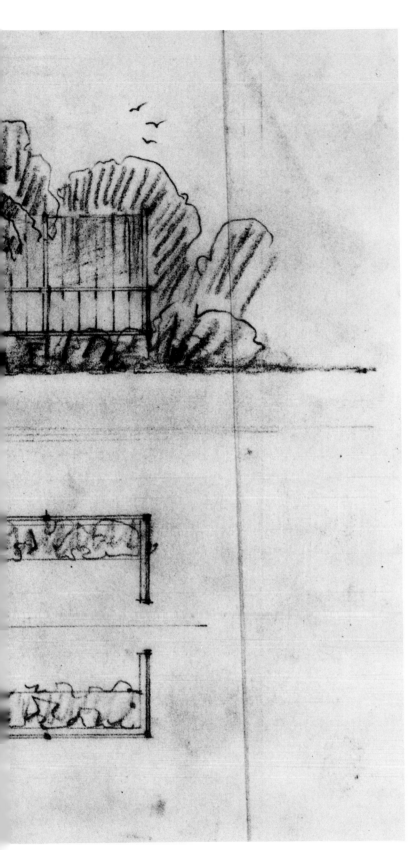

Julia Morgan (1872–1957)

That Julia Morgan designed and built more than 800 buildings, including William Randolph Hearst's San Simeon, in the forty-odd years of her independent practice in California stands as a powerful testament to her professional competence. The quality, practicality, and economic feasibility of her designs are a strong statement for her commitment to the art of building. The fact that in 1902 she became the first woman to attend and graduate from the École des Beaux-Arts in Paris is witness to her ability and independent spirit.

"J.M.," as her office staff was to call her, graduated from the University of California at Berkeley in 1894 with a degree in engineering—her first "first"; she was the only woman there. She attended classes in architecture at the Berkeley home of Bernard Maybeck (page 177), who taught descriptive geometry at the university, and after graduation she worked with him for a year. Through Maybeck she made contact with Phoebe Apherson Hearst, who became one of her most important patrons. With Maybeck's encouragement and that of her New York cousins, the architects Napoleon and Pierre Le Brun, Morgan left Berkeley in 1895 for Paris and the École des Beaux-Arts with no assurance that a woman would be admitted. Following two years at the Atelier Marcel de Monclos in preparation for the École's difficult entrance examinations, she ranked 13 among an examination group of more than 390. With support from William Aldrich of the American Academy in Rome and the American ambassador in Paris, Morgan was duly admitted. Morgan studied at the Atelier Chaussemiche and graduated from the École in 1902. After graduation she worked briefly for Chaussemiche. She returned to Berkeley in 1902 and worked for John Galen Howard, a Beaux-Arts graduate, who was directing the campus plan for the University of California at Berkeley. She is said to have contributed to the design of the Greek Theater there while working for Howard. Howard's assessment of his employee was that he possessed "the best and most talented designer whom I have to pay almost nothing as it is a woman."

From 1904 to the mid-1940s Morgan headed her own firm and took complete control of every building. She began a design by making studies with a T square, straight edge, and triangle; these were then developed by the staff in close collaboration with J.M. During the construction phase of a project she received highly detailed and frequent progress reports. At the busiest period of her practice she had from 18 to 30 employees and three branch offices. The clientele who supported this office included both extremely wealthy patrons and those of more moderate means, who commissioned a great number of residences in Northern California especially around San Francisco; and institutions such as Mills College, the YWCA, and other women's clubs and churches. Through her entire career Morgan maintained a stonewall attitude toward publicity. Her first interview in 1906 was also her last, and until 10 years ago her work was little known outside the Bay Area. In 1952 she officially closed her office and in the process destroyed many drawings and papers. She consciously sought to prevent popular recognition of her place as the first professionally successful woman architect. Her credo was "the buildings speak; I do not speak."

94 *Greenhouse for Marion Davies, project*
Beverly Hills, California
Elevation and plan, c. 1930
Pencil and colored pencil, 14¾ x 15" (37.5 x 38.1 cm)
Documents Collection, College of Environmental Design
The University of California at Berkeley
Berkeley, California

182

95   Bell Tower, Mills College, Oakland, California
Three elevations, 1904
Pencil on tracing paper, 37¾ x 24½" (95.9 x 62.3 cm)
Documents Collection, College of Environmental Design
The University of California at Berkeley
Berkeley, California

Her remarks during the interview given at the site of her reconstruction of the Fairmont Hotel in San Francisco after the 1906 earthquake and fire are a key to her attitude to design. The interview revolves around a tour of the site. The interviewer commenting on how good it is to have a woman architect since the color of wallpaper is so important is met with Morgan's reply that on the contrary her work is structural. "Structural," exclaims the interviewer; he had always thought that women had "no more serious problem in life than the construction of an Easter bonnet."

Morgan's buildings were well planned and well constructed and their costs were suited to her clients' assets. Structure in many of her best works, as in the shingled St. John's Presbyterian Church in Berkeley of 1910, is clearly revealed and functions as the prime object of esthetic interest. Although Morgan was trained at the École where the plan was the initial and primary focus in design development, resulting in plans whose complexity often reflects compositions dramatic in cross section, her plans were practical, but not of outstanding invention. What she derived from the École's system was a rational approach to design and an eclectic esthetic philosophy. Her pragmatism was clothed in two ways: through facades derived from various historic sources, but particularly Medieval and Renaissance styles, and the inversion of this approach in facades derived from vernacular wood architecture in which decorative ornament is largely suppressed. The houses of the latter type are usually considered part of the Bay Area tradition. Her choice of mode was directly connected to her client's desires and often received inspiration from the volumes in her large architectural library.

The illustrated drawings reveal two sides of this eclecticism. One of Morgan's first important clients was Mills College for Women in Oakland, California. This association began in 1904 with the commission for the campus bell tower (95). Morgan designed this in the Mission Revival style with tiled roofs and round arches and constructed it in reinforced concrete. The bell tower withstood the 1906 earthquake, and this fact resulted in publicity and commissions including the reconstruction of the Fairmont Hotel.

Julia Morgan had already built a house for Marion Davies when she designed the project for a greenhouse for the actress c. 1930 (94). The greenhouse is a simple glass box with a medievalizing entrance embellished with half timbering and medieval detailing. The facade is similar to a design solution Morgan often used for domestic commissions combining brick, stucco, half timbering, leaded windows in geometric patterns, and decorative carving derived from Gothic sources.

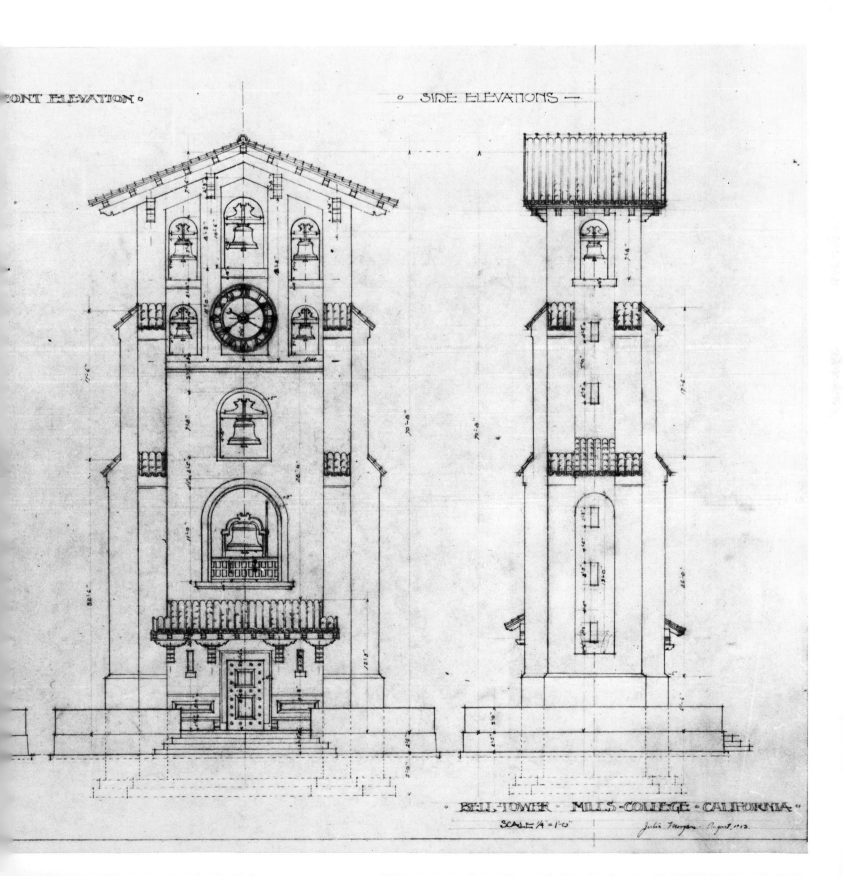

FRONT ELEVATION·

· SIDE ELEVATIONS —

· BELL·TOWER · MILLS·COLLEGE · CALIFORNIA ·

SCALE ¼" = 1'-0"   Julia Morgan · August 1903

Louis Sullivan is the pivotal link between such important figures of American Victorian architecture as Henry Hobson Richardson (page 137) and Frank Furness (page 131) and the hero of American Modernism, Frank Lloyd Wright (page 234). Sullivan worked for Furness and was influenced by his use of ornament; he was profoundly impressed by Richardson's work, especially his Marhsall Field Building of 1885 in Chicago; and he was Frank Lloyd Wright's employer and mentor. Sullivan's influence on American architectural theory, architectural ornament, and the form of the skyscraper was profound.

Sullivan came to Chicago in 1876 after spending 1873 at MIT, a few months with Furness in Philadelphia, and 6 months at the École des Beaux-Arts in 1874. In 1876 he settled in Chicago and by 1881 had become Dankmar Adler's (1844–1900) partner in Adler and Sullivan. The firm lasted to 1895, with Sullivan acting as the principal designer for the firm and Adler assuming responsibility for most of the technical and business aspects of the partnership. It was both during the years of this collaboration and in the following decade that Sullivan's outstanding tall buildings were built, among them: the Wainwright Building, St. Louis, 1890–1891; the Guaranty Building, Buffalo, 1894–1895; the Bayard Building, New York, 1897–1898; the Gage Building, Chicago, 1898–1899; the Carson, Pirie and Scott Store, Chicago, 1899–1904. After the turn of the 20th century Sullivan built a series of small Midwestern banks, such as the National Farmers Bank, Owatonna, Minnesota, 1907–1908, whose cubic massing, monumental form, and approach to ornament had an important effect on the architects of the Prairie School, including George Grant Elmslie, Walter Burley and Marion Mahony Griffin, and William Gray Purcell. Finally, it is not only his buildings but also his books—*Kindergarten Chats* of 1901, *The Autobiography of an Idea* of 1922–1923, and *A System of Architectural Ornament* of 1924—presenting his philosophy of architecture that are his important legacy to the 20th century.

Sullivan's now famous dictum, "form follows function," has been misunderstood by many. This misinterpretation derives from an erroneous idea that Sullivan equated function with utilitarian and technological components of design. For Sullivan, a building's function had to fulfill social and emotional or expressive ends as well as utilitarian and technological ones, and its form had to be expressive of all these functional components. This attitude he called his "organic approach" to building. It was so named because he believed in the existence of an analogy between the determination of style in architecture and the determination of style or form in nature. For Sullivan style in building and in nature were both determined by environment. The famous example he gave of style, or form in nature, was of the pine tree, whose tapered trunk, particular configuration of branches, coloration, seeds, cones, and sap reflect its particular climatic milieu. Many of these ideas grew out of Sullivan's contact with such important 19th-century theorists as: Viollet-le-Duc (1814–1879), the French author and architect who advocated a rational approach to architecture whereby each structural element of a building has a purpose and who also contended that architecture should serve expressive and emotional ends; the evolutionist Charles Darwin (1809–1882); and Gottfried Semper (1803–1879), the German architect and author, who advocated that materials and program be the prime generators of form and whose writing was translated in 1889–1890 in Chicago by the architect John Root and published in *The Inland Architect*.

96 St. Nicholas Hotel, St. Louis, Missouri
Elevation study for fireplace (notes by Frank Lloyd Wright)
1893–1894
Pencil, 13 x 20" (33 x 50.8 cm)
Avery Library
Columbia University
New York, New York

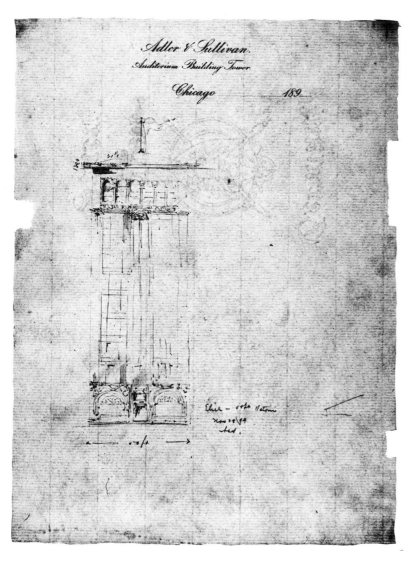

97

In 1896 Sullivan outlined his notion of the ideal form of the skyscraper in an essay entitled "The Tall Office Building Artistically Considered." This ideal type, having three major divisions, was exemplified by his own buildings of the mid-eighties and nineties. The Eliel Building (97) of 1894, a project for which no records remain, may have been designed for Gustav Eliel for whom Sullivan built a house in Chicago in 1886. The building conceived along the outlines of Sullivan's ideal type has three major divisions: a lower section with large windows and portals, which Sullivan explained in his essay were appropriate for stores or banks, providing easy access into the building; a middle section, composed of an unspecified number of floors of identical configuration, expressive of the uniform office spaces behind the facade; an attic story, which according to Sullivan would visually terminate the building. This organization was formally manipulated by Sullivan to vividly convey that sense of "tallness or loftiness" that for him was the essence of the skyscraper. In this sketch as in many of his built works, Sullivan favors thinly proportioned piers rising uninterrupted to the attic story to sweep the eye and the imagination upwards. In executed works such as the Guaranty Building terra-cotta or cast iron ornament subtly underlines this impression of tallness and carries much of the expressive power of design.

By comparing the Eliel sketch with the studies for the capital of the Guaranty Building (98) of 1894–1895 in Buffalo, New York, and the fireplace of the St. Nicholas Hotel (96) of 1893–1894 in St. Louis, Missouri, we have a good understanding of Sullivan's use of ornament. By keeping the composition of a particular design pattern discrete and complete within each building element, Sullivan emphasizes the individual parts of a building. This is in contrast with much contemporary Art Nouveau ornament that flows over one building element to another, thereby creating a lack of distinction among them. Sullivan's ornament is a unique synthesis of motifs drawn from his 19th-century contemporaries as well as the past: Asa Gray's *Gray's School and Field Botany*; Irish medieval, Romanesque, Islamic ornament; and Owen Jones' *Grammar of Ornament* of 1856, also important to Frank Furness.

The purpose of Sullivan's ornament is to enhance the perception of the building's structure. As Vincent Scully observed, Sullivan's use of ornament is empathetic in its intentions, encouraging the viewer to better understand the structure and purpose of a building. Again formal manipulations and meaning are integral for Sullivan. By keeping the building elements visually separate from one another, he is able to emphasize their role in the total physical organization of the building. The vines of the Guaranty capital are discrete from the bands of the pier, underlining their different structural and formal roles. As the vines swirl upward, they make a visual connection between the pier and the building above, keeping the eye moving upward and helping to create a sense of tallness. The pier's decoration encircles it in horizontal bands emphasizing its solidity and volume and its power to support. The thin spears of ornament of the St. Nicholas Hotel fireplace underline the radial forces of the voussoirs that form the arch. The lush vines organized in a circular composition emphasize the wholeness of the stone it decorates and through the centralization of the pattern make reference to the physical importance of the keystone above its center, essential to maintaining the structural integrity of the arch.

97 *Eliel Building, project, Chicago*
Elevation study, November 28, 1894
Pencil on stationery, 11½ x 8" (29.2 x 20.3 cm)
Avery Library
Columbia University
New York, New York

98 *Guaranty Building, Buffalo, New York*
First floor terra-cotta capital, perspective study
August 23, 1895
Pencil, 8½ x 11½" (21.6 x 29.2 cm)
Avery Library
Columbia University
New York, New York

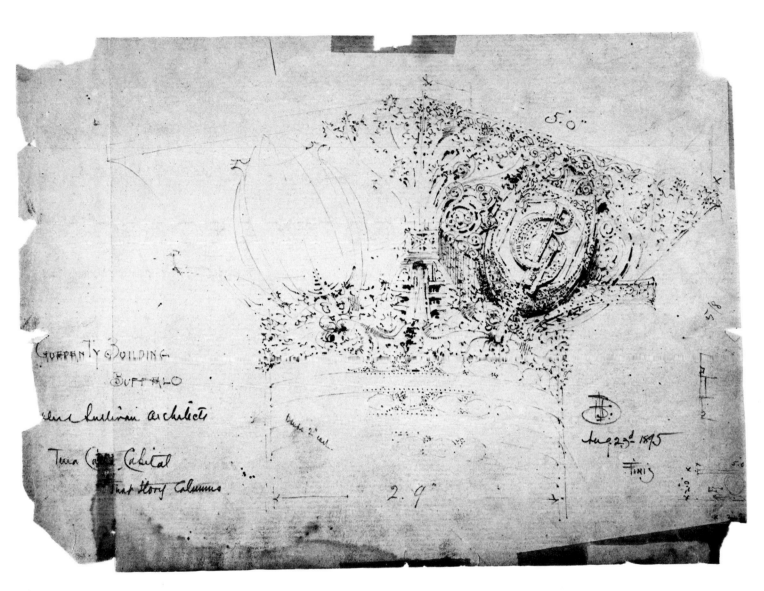

98

99

Whitney Warren (1864-1943)

Whitney Warren was a New York architect whose patrons were wealthy New Yorkers and large corporations. Like so many of his peers who built for this clientele, he was educated at the École des Beaux-Arts, and in the process he became a Francophile. He attended Columbia College for one year in 1883 and then left for Paris where he remained for a decade. In 1896 he persuaded one of his clients, the lawyer Charles Wetmore, that his real talents lay in architecture, and the firm Warren & Wetmore was formed. The firm first came to national attention when they won the competition for the New York Yacht Club in 1899. The Yacht Club is distinguished by its prow-shaped bay window along the street, ornamented with stone sculpted to represent sea water. It is a remarkably lucid example of the idea of "architecture parlante"—architecture whose function is literally articulated by its shape or decoration; it has in its sensuous form overtones of the Art Nouveau. Between 1903 and 1913 Warren & Wetmore, in collaboration with the firm Reed and Stem, produced one of the greatest American buildings— Grand Central Station. The firm's other work includes commercial buildings like the Hecksher Building of 1921 and a number of large city residences for the rich, such as that for Mrs. Marshall Orme Wilson of 1903, now the New India House. The firm also designed a number of fine hotels including: the Commodore of 1915 and the Vanderbilt of 1912, both in Manhattan, and the Broadmoor of 1915 in Colorado Springs.

Whitney Warren devoted himself to establishing the Beaux-Arts system of architectural education in America and encouraged contact with the École des Beaux-Arts in Paris and its graduates in the United States. On his return from France in 1894 he became instrumental in organizing the Beaux-Arts Society of Architects, which was incorporated as the Society of Beaux-Arts Architects in 1895 with 72 members; it became the Beaux-Arts Institute of Design in 1911. Warren writes of its goals: "Not only did we want to keep the old crowd together with all its joyous memories; we wished also to continue our teachings and traditions, to keep the flame alive. And to hand on the torch to those who were to come after us in our own

99　New York Public Library competition entry
Fifth Avenue elevation, 1897
Ink, pencil, gray, white, and black wash on brown cardboard
9¼ x 24⅝" (23.5 x 62.5 cm)
Cooper-Hewitt Museum of Decorative Arts and Design
Smithsonian Institution
New York, New York

100   Grand Central Terminal, New York City
Elevation study, 1910
Ink on paper, 10⅛ x 12⅞" (25.7 x 32.7 cm)
Cooper-Hewitt Museum of Decorative Arts and Design
Smithsonian Institution
New York, New York

country." An atelier system under the auspices of the Society's Committee on Education was created in which practicing architects would train young people in their studios after work and organize and judge competitions among the ateliers. The first atelier was organized under the auspices of the Architectural League of New York, which had been formed in 1881 by many of the same men who formed the Beaux-Arts Society. In 1913 Warren organized the annual Beaux-Arts Ball to raise scholarship money for students to attend the École. This was an annual event for 24 years.

Between 1903 and 1913 Grand Central Terminal was built by Warren & Wetmore with Reed & Stem. Controversy exists over the role of each firm in the design. It is now generally believed that Reed & Stem handled the large-scale planning and technical questions of the complex, as they had already built large railroad stations at Troy, New York, and Tacoma, Washington. Warren is believed to be responsible for the architectural conception or *parti* and all the elegant detailing. The building is one of the most inventive as well as beautiful Beaux-Arts buildings in America. Of essential importance to Beaux-Arts theory was rationalized planning clearly expressive of the building program in both a pragmatic and symbolic sense. Behind Grand Central's Beaux-Arts façade, which is derived from Renaissance, Baroque, and Classical sources, was a workable plan. Louis Sullivan, who only spent 6 months at the École des Beaux-Arts, said, "It was at the school that I first grasped the concrete value of logical thinking."

The design of Grand Central Station—by underlining the hierarchical relationship of the parts of the building to one another through the manipulation of space and materials— makes the experience of travel, gathering, and social concourse dramatic and perceptually exciting to even a casual observer. The main concourse space is elegantly detailed, and its huge height is crowned by vaults, painted to suggest the firmament, with a gallery from which to watch the activity below. Circulation spaces or tunnels tangent to the concourse and leading to it are constructed in less rich materials than the central space to accent their less ceremonial function. The 1910 sketch for the façade of the station (100) essentially contains all the elements of the station as built, including the placement of the sculpture by Jules Coutan. It is typical of the grand image that we expect for Beaux-Arts buildings and reflects the grandeur with which corporations at the turn of the century viewed themselves.

In 1897 an open competition for the New York Public Library was held from which were selected 12 architects, including Warren, to compete in a second competition. The commission was awarded to the prolific New York firm of Carrère and Hastings. Warren's entry (99) is close in image and scale to other submissions, all Beaux-Arts schemes inspired by Classical and Renaissance sources. At least two of the designs incorporated the dome of the Pantheon in Rome with an elevation derived from a Renaissance palazzo.

The original sketch for the facade
of the Grand Central Terminal New York
Whitney Warren
1910

1890/1919

Gregory Ain (b. 1908)

In the thirties Los Angeles was the one area where there was a small clientele that was ready to accept a variety of modern architecural styles. The most popular mode in Los Angeles for larger commercial development was the streamlined Moderne. However, in the Los Angeles area Gregory Ain, Richard J. Neutra (page 218) for whom Ain worked between 1932 and 1935, R. M. Schindler (page 226), and others produced some of the first Modern buildings in the U.S. The rationale presented in Henry-Russell Hitchcock's and Philip Johnson's *The International Style* of 1932 for this approach to design, consisting of flat, unornamented, planar walls, strip windows, large walls of glass, and flat roofs was that these stylistic devices were reflective of the non-load-bearing walls dependent on a structure of steel and concrete whose primary function was closure, not support. Ain and others employed the formal and special aspects of the style using traditional wood frame construction sheathed in a thin skin of stucco.

Ain began his own independent practice in Los Angeles in 1935 where he designed small commercial and domestic structures. He had a continuing interest in economical housing, and his buildings are similar to those of commercial builders in that they employed traditional low-cost construction utilizing available materials and methods of construction. In 1940 Ain was awarded a Guggenheim Foundation grant to study low-cost housing. In 1949 he built a 100-unit subdivision that provided a scheme in which interior planning and siting could be adjusted to suit individual family needs. This was an early example of the tract housing of the post–World War II era constructed all over America in which a few basic plans are alterable to suit particular purchaser requirements. In 1950 Ain designed a prototype house for a subdivision, sponsored by The Museum of Modern Art and the *Woman's Home Companion* magazine, which was economical to build and provided interior flexibility by using sliding doors and walls. This was erected in the museum's garden.

Ain's often illustrated Dunsmuir Apartments (101) of 1937 in Los Angeles exemplify his practical and imaginative approach to site planning. Ain stepped back the four units so that each enjoyed its own private garden on the 49-foot/147-meter lot. All bedrooms open onto a deck and have windows on three sides for cross ventilation. Privacy was maintained on the entrance side by windows that were placed at a clerestory height to allow light to enter but prevent visibility into the house. The construction method used of two-story wooden posts notched to continuous lintels provides a rigid earthquake-resistant structure.

Characteristic of his post–World War II dwellings was the house for Mr. and Mrs. I. Becker (102) of 1938 built on a steep narrow site overlooking Silver Lake. In spite of the difficult site, the clients required a great deal of outdoor living space. Ain's solution was to provide a 42-foot/127-meter roof deck serviced by a dumbwaiter connected to the kitchen and an 18-foot/53-meter balcony off the living room also served by the dumbwaiter. All the major windows faced toward the lake while clerestory windows introduced light and maintained privacy at the same time.

101

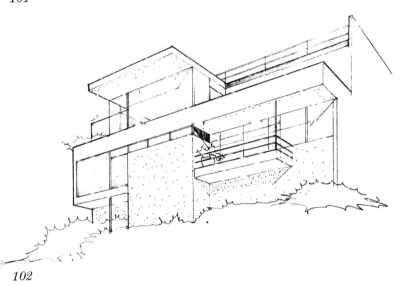

102

101 *Dunsmuir Apartments, Los Angeles*
Perspective, 1937
Pencil on tracing paper, 14¾ x 22½" (37.5 x 57.2 cm)
Collection of Gregory Ain
Los Angeles, California

102 *Becker House, Los Angeles*
Perspective, 1938
Pencil on tracing paper, 11¾ x 13" (29.8 x 33 cm)
Collection of Gregory Ain
Los Angeles, California

103 Edla Muir
House, project, Bel Air, Los Angeles, California
Perspective, 1938
Pencil and colored pencil on paper, 7½ x 11¾" (19.1 x 29.9 cm)
The University Art Galleries
University of California at Santa Barbara
Santa Barbara, California

104   Edla Muir
Wanger House, Brentwood, Los Angeles, California
Perspective, 1936
Pencil and colored pencil on paper, 8½ x 13½" (21.6 x 34.3 cm)
The University Art Galleries
University of California at Santa Barbara
Santa Barbara, California

John Byers (1875–1966)
Edla Muir (1906–1971)

The years 1920 through the early 1930s provided one of the few periods where a conscious effort was made to establish a regional style in America. By 1932 all the major cities and towns of Southern California had adopted the Spanish Colonial Revival as *the* style for America's own "Mediterranean" coast. Two of the principal contributors to the emergence of this unified style were the Santa Monica architects John Byers and Edla Muir.

Though both Byers and Muir became highly respected practitioners, neither had formal training in architecture. Byers, who was born in Grand Rapids, Michigan, graduated in electrical engineering from the University of Michigan, and then went on to do advanced studies in the sciences at Harvard. Until he was 44 years old, Byers taught languages in private schools in Uruguay and San Raphael, California, and in the public school system in Santa Monica, California. In 1919 he abandoned his career as a teacher and became a designer and builder of adobe houses (forming the "John Byers Mexican Handmade Tile Co."). In 1926 he took the examinations and became a registered architect in California.

Edla Muir was born in San Francisco and later moved with her family to Santa Monica. While finishing high school, she began to work as a parttime draftsperson for Byers, and in 1923 she became a fulltime designer-draftsman in his office. With her facility as a delineator and as a designer, Muir's talents perfectly complemented those of Byers. In 1934, when she received her license to practice architecture, she became a partner with Byers.

Byers' and Muir's Spanish Colonial Revival designs of the 1920s were strongly puritanical and relied heavily on provincial Andalusian examples from Spain. By the mid-1920s they abandoned the almost exclusive use of adobe for construction and turned to the convenient stucco-covered wood frame. Though most of their designs of the 1920s were Spanish, their vocabulary began to broaden to include the Monterey Spanish, and by the 1930s they were producing designs of half-timber/Norman, American Colonial, French Provincial, and "Bermudan." An example of the Monterey Spanish is the Wanger House (104) of 1936 in the Brentwood area of Los Angeles, and the project for a house (103) built in the Bel Air section of Los Angeles illustrates the Colonial Revival style. Their period of greatest activity was during the Depression years of the 1930s. Their clients during those years included J. Paul Getty, George Temple (Shirley Temple's father), Joel McCrea, Irving Cobb, and others associated with the Hollywood film industry.

All the presentation drawings of the firm were by Edla Muir, while the initial conceptual sketches were developed by both of them. Muir's characteristic presentation drawings were highly pictorial in intent—their buildings were depicted in what appears to be an untrampled rural environment. Shadow lines, suggestions of varied texture, coupled with enveloping vegetation, were meant to suggest the close "natural" unity of the building to its site. Like the perspective presentation drawings of the Queen Anne/Shingle Style of the 1880s, Muir's drawings place the viewer at a considerable distance from the building, and usually the view is from a low point looking up at the building. These techniques enhanced the pictorial intent of the designers—an intent fully and convincingly carried out in their built buildings.

103

104

CONCRETE & GLASS.
105
STUDIO APARTMENTS: 610 CHURCH ST.
1926
Barry Byrne Arch't.

Francis Barry Byrne (1883–1967)

Frank Lloyd Wright's (page 234) Oak Park studio-office was an environment where young devotees of the master could learn the craft of architecture from Wright's mature staff and absorb his design philosophy. It was in this office that many of the architects of the Midwestern Prairie School, whose work was inspired by the early work of Wright and Louis Sullivan (page 185), received their first introduction to architecture. Barry Byrne, who had lived in Chicago since birth, saw an exhibition of Wright's work at the Chicago Architectural Club in 1902, which inspired him to seek an interview with the architect. From 1902 to 1908 Byrne worked for Wright and not only acquired the skills needed for professional practice but also made contact with Walter Burley and Marion Mahony Griffin (page 172), whose practice he would take over in 1914 when the Griffins left for Australia to implement the design for the plan of the new capital, Canberra. Byrne worked closely with Marion Mahony Griffin, who was one of the outstanding delineators of the period. Among the buildings Byrne worked on at Wright's were the important Unity Temple of 1906 in Oak Park, Illinois, and Coonley House of 1908 in Riverside, Illinois.

Byrne's independent work, built in Illinois, Indiana, and Iowa in the teens when he took over the Griffins' practice, was largely domestic. As H. Allen Brooks in *The Prairie School* of 1972 points out, Byrne's work was ultimately more influenced by Louis Sullivan's (page 185) buildings than by Wright's. Brooks writes that the preference for Sullivan's form was "reinforced by his contact with Irving Gill, the architecture of the Southwest, and his association with the Griffins. Severe, space-enclosing cubic shapes, rather than space-defining intersecting verticals and horizontals, typified his [Byrne's] work." Important works of this period were the J. B. Franke House in Fort Wayne, Indiana, of 1914 and the J. F. Clarke House, Fairfield, Iowa, in 1916. It was at this point that he began a life-long collaboration with the sculptor Alfonso Iannelli (1888–1965), who had worked with Wright on Midway Gardens in Chicago in 1914.

A turning point in Byrne's career came in 1922 when he designed the Church of St. Thomas Apostle in Chicago. From then on he seldom did domestic work. His churches through the twenties were some of the first, with those of the Frenchman Auguste Perret (1874–1954), to be designed in a modern style. St. Thomas Apostle Church has the simple massing derived from Sullivan, and its roof is accented by rich ornament outlined against the sky. Since Byrne was actively involved with liturgical reform within the church—he felt that the Eucharist should be the focus of the service and that the congregation should participate more fully in the ritual—his church plans, beginning in 1922, physically integrate nave and sanctuary. He did not try to evoke an aura of mystery created by dramatic light but instead flooded his churches with natural light.

In 1925 Byrne traveled in Europe where he was able to see firsthand the contemporary work of architects in Holland, Germany, and France. He was especially impressed by German and Dutch "Expressionists," which resulted in a shifting of emphasis in his work toward a more dramatic and personal massing. Two churches of 1926–1927 reflect this directly—the Church of Christ the King in Tulsa and the Church of Christ the King in Cork, Ireland. At Cork the massing becomes gradually higher toward the entrance, with a proportionately high, powerfully simple entry tower. A sculpture of Christ spans the entry. In 1948 Byrne built St. Francis Xavier in Kansas City, Missouri, which again employs the simple massing and exaggerated tower of his earlier work. The plan is in the shape of a fish, a symbol of Christ.

The formalistic turn that Byrne took after his European experience is apparent in the illustrated drawings. The stepped massing of the Studio Apartments (105) of 1926 emphasizes the building's verticality and recalls the almost completely unornamented walls and stress on height of his churches of the post-1925 era. The project for Chicago's DePaul University (106) of 1926 is forward looking in American architecture for the time. Its design takes its form purely from the structure, probably concrete and steel framing with glass infill. The joints of the supporting structure are the only ornament in this architecture of skin and structure.

106

105   Studio Apartments, project
Perspective, 1926
Black ink and white gouache, 31½ x 14½" (80.6 x 36.8 cm)
Avery Library
Columbia University
New York, New York

106   De Paul University, project, Chicago
Perspective, 1926
Ink on tracing paper, 16⅛ x 10¼" (41 x 26 cm)
[18¼ x 12½" on board (46.4 x 31.8 cm)]
Avery Library
Columbia University
New York, New York

107

108

Paul Philippe Cret (1876–1945)

Paul Cret, born in Lyon and educated at the École des Beaux-Arts in Paris, came to Philadelphia in 1903. During the next 40 years he produced some of the most distinguished Beaux-Arts buildings in the United States and helped to solidify the Beaux-Arts system within American architectural education. Many of his buildings were collaborative efforts including: the Pan American Union in Washington, 1907–1910, done with Albert Kelsey; the Central Public Library at Indianapolis, 1913–1916, and the Detroit Institute of Art, 1922, with the firm of Zantzinger, Borie, and Medardy; the Folger Shakespeare Library of 1932 with Alexander Trowbridge in Washington, D.C.; and the Rodin Museum in Philadelphia, 1929, with Jacques Gréber. In these projects he was certainly the active designer. Working on his own, he is responsible for many outstanding structures, including the Federal Reserve Board Building of 1935–1937. These are eminently functional buildings whose spaces are organized around defined axes and whose exteriors are clothed in unique and sometimes highly personal interpretations of classical forms.

Cret was a devoted teacher and from 1903 to 1937 was a professor at the University of Pennsylvania. He also helped run the atelier at the T Square Club in Philadelphia, giving criticism to students in the evening. Although much Beaux-Arts work is associated with the sort of buildings Cret designed—that is, revivalistic in spirit and monumental in scale—these values did not control his educational philosophy. In fact, Cret stressed that it was almost the official duty of the architect to "run the chance of failure in experiment, rather than follow established precedent." His greatest student, Louis Kahn (page 269), absorbed from Cret the essential attitudes of the Beaux-Arts that lay beneath its classical monumentality and produced forms unrelated to revivalistic styles. Cret's own work developed from the beautiful, traditional mode of his 1912 Valley Forge Memorial Arch (107) at Valley Forge, Pennsylvania, for which he studied various schemes as perceived in varying conditions of daylight, to the stunning Art Deco forms of his 1933 Hall of Science at the Chicago Exposition.

In 1928 Cret was appointed to the commission to plan the 1933 Century of Progress Exposition on 1,300 acres of Chicago's lake front. His colleagues on the commission were Edward Bennett, Arthur Brown, Jr., Daniel Burnham, Harvey Wiley Corbett, John Holabird, Raymond Hood, and Ralph T. Walker. The buildings built in what is now described as the Art Deco mode were designed by such outstanding architects as Edward Bennett, with Arthur Brown, Jr., Cret, the firm of Hood and Fouilhoux, Albert Kahn, and Ely Jacques Kahn. The commission decided that the narrow site (2 miles long and ½ mile wide) was to be divided by a central axis around which the exhibition buildings would be situated. Quays were to be built along the lake front that would be used for restaurants and amusements. Cret acknowledges in documents preserved at the University of Pennsylvania that the guidelines set for the plan were primarily determined by Hood. Cret's studies for the fair (108) are but two of many that exist in which he worked to bring the Beaux-Arts concepts of the commission's scheme to reality. In both studies huge pylons mark off plazas and accent vistas. The lower scheme on the page extends the site further into the water through the use of a causeway than does the upper scheme. In the completed design two large irregularly shaped lagoons are integrated into the fairground.

In 1938 Cret was asked to design a monument in Balboa, Panama, to General George W. Goethals, engineer of the Panama Canal. None of the many schemes he sketched were carried out. His more traditional schemes included a statue of Goethals seated in the manner of the statue of Lincoln in the Lincoln Memorial in Washington, D.C.; Goethals standing, looking out to the harbor; variations on the American eagle; variations on a ship's prow inscribed "Goethals." One of Cret's more unique ideas was for a lock of the canal made of stone inscribed with Goethals' name (109). Another was in the form of the side of a Roman ship (110). In both cases Cret has monumentalized a subject directly connected to the everyday workings of the canal and created an architecture parlante—literally "talking architecture," a phrase first used to describe the work of certain French 18th-century architects, such as Claude-Nicholas Ledoux (1736–1806) and Étienne-Louis Boullée (1728–1799). What is meant by this term is that a built object takes its form directly and literally from its program.

109

110

107 Valley Forge Memorial Arch, Valley Forge, Pennsylvania
Perspectives (board containing small sketches), 1912
Pencil and colored pencil, I: 9⅜ x 12¼" (23.8 x 31.1 cm)
II: 9½ x 12" (24.1 x 30.5 cm)
III: 10 x 12¼" (25.4 x 31.1 cm)
The Van Pelt Library
University of Pennsylvania
Philadelphia, Pennsylvania

108 1933 Century of Progress Exposition, Chicago
Site plan, 1930
Bird's-eye view, 7½ x 6½" (19.1 x 16.5 cm)
The Van Pelt Library
University of Pennsylvania
Philadelphia, Pennsylvania

109 Monument to General George W. Goethals, project
Balboa, Panama
Perspectives, 1938
Pencil and colored pencil, 5 x 8½" (12.7 x 21.6 cm)
The Van Pelt Library
University of Pennsylvania
Philadelphia, Pennsylvania

110 Monument to General George W. Goethals, project
Balboa, Panama
Perspectives, 1938
Pencil, 6¾ x 9¼" (17.2 x 23.5 cm)
The Van Pelt Library
University of Pennsylvania
Philadelphia, Pennsylvania

202 *111 Grape leaves and floor plan*
    Sketchbook, 1933
    Pencil, 6⅞ x 9" (17.5 x 22.9 cm)
    Collection of Alden Ball Dow
    Midland, Michigan

112 Alden Ball Dow House and Studio, Midland, Michigan
Three elevations, c. 1932
Pencil and colored pencil, 20¼ x 19" (51.4 x 48.3 cm)
Collection of Alden Ball Dow
Midland, Michigan

113 Alden Ball Dow House and Studio, Midland, Michigan
Perspective, c. 1932
Pencil and colored pencil, 12 x 26" (30.5 x 66 cm)
Collection of Alden Ball Dow
Midland, Michigan

Alden Ball Dow (b. 1904)

Alden Dow received his architectural training at Columbia University, graduating with a Bachelor of Architecture in 1931. In 1933 he studied with Frank Lloyd Wright at Taliesin in Spring Green, Wisconsin. This was one of the most influential experiences in Dow's architectural development and had a marked influence on both his philosophy and his attitude toward form. In 1937 Dow received the Gold Medal for Domestic Design at the Paris Exposition. He has built structures of all types, mainly in Michigan and the Far West, including the design and construction of the town of Lake Jackson, Texas, in 1943. Many of the public buildings and outstanding houses of Midland, Michigan, home of the Dow Chemical Corporation founded by Dow's father, are designed by Alden Dow. In 1970 Alden Dow published *Reflections*, documenting his work and outlining his philosophy, which he calls his "way of life." This philosophy places primacy on the free expression of individual imagination, tempered by what Dow calls "humility and honesty," or the compatibility of the individual creative expression with the constraints posed by the environment and society.

One of Dow's outstanding works is the house and studio he built for himself (112, 113) in Midland, Michigan, of 1935. The house is constructed of uniformly sized cinderblocks specially designed by Dow; the same material is used in the garden walls and walks. The roof is sheathed with copper and wood battens. Dow's intent in this building and others of the same period was to harmonize the building as closely as possible with nature. To this end the building's mass is organized so that it appears to be growing out of the landscape; pools of water are brought to the edge of the house. The plan is disposed so that the house winds around the site and seems to grow out of it. Dow's interest in the correspondence of nature and architecture fills many of his notebook studies, which are equations between natural forms and forms in architecture. In one sheet (111) the plan of a grape leaf is used as the inspiration for that of a house. On another page in the sketchbook Dow derives the form of a bird house from that of an orchid plant.

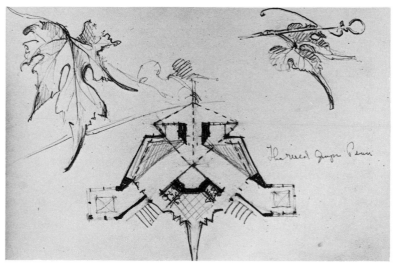

111

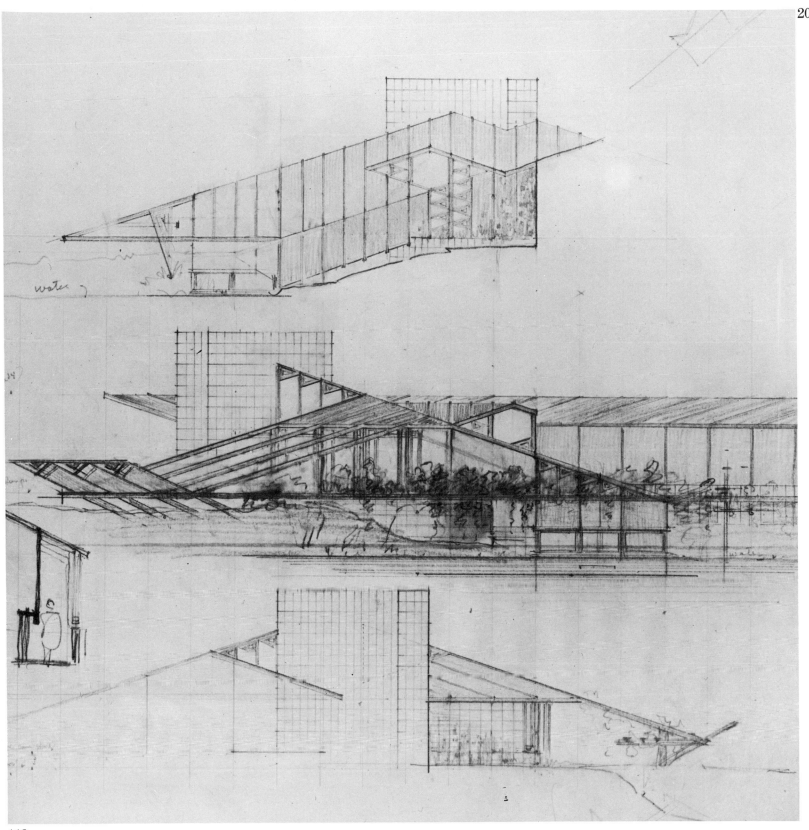

112

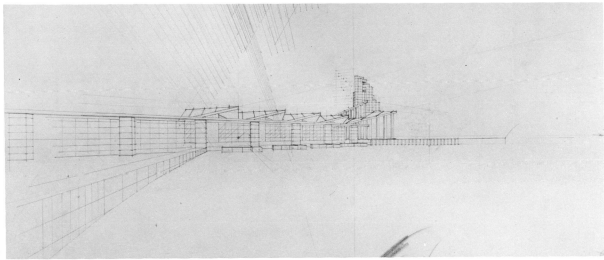

113

204 114 *John Entenza House, Santa Monica Canyon*
Los Angeles, California
Perspective, 1937
Pencil on tracing paper, 7½ x 7½" (19.1 x 19.1 cm)
Collection of Harwell Hamilton Harris
Raleigh, North Carolina

115 *Lowe House, Altadena, California*
Perspective, 1933–1934
Ink on linen, 7½ x 10" (19.1 x 25.4 cm)
Collection of Harwell Hamilton Harris
Raleigh, North Carolina

Harwell Hamilton Harris (b. 1903)

It was during the 7 years from 1935 through 1941 that a strong, coherent Modern Movement came to the fore in Los Angeles. The father figures of the movement were R. M. Schindler (page 226) and Richard J. Neutra (page 218); the younger exponents were Gregory Ain (page 194), Raphael Soriano, and Harwell Hamilton Harris. All three of the younger designers looked with admiration at Schindler, and they had all worked in Neutra's office in the early 1930s. By 1941 each of these Los Angeles architects had evolved a strong, recognizable personal style.

The older by a few years of the younger contingent was Harris, who was born west of Los Angeles at Redlands, California. He attended Pomona College and then studied design at the Otis Art Institute and at the Frank Wiggin's Trade School, both in Los Angeles. From 1929 through 1933 he worked in Neutra's office, devoting much of his time to that architect's ideal city of the future, Rush City Reformed. In 1934 he began his independent architectural practice. Harris almost immediately established a national reputation with his often illustrated Lowe House (115) of 1933–1934 in Altadena, California, which he designed with Carl Anderson. The Lowe House was characterized in the Museum of Modern Art exhibition, "Built in USA, 1932–1944," as "one of the earliest and most inventive" of the courtyard houses of the thirties. The design of this dwelling impressively brought together the modern ideals of open and flowing space and a close spatial relationship between indoors and outdoors through fixed and sliding glass doors and enclosed patios, courtyard, and terraces. The imagery of the house was loosely Modern, but in its extensive use of wood and in its emphasis on out-of-door space, the design looked back to the turn-of-the-century houses of Charles and Henry Greene (page 168) and to traditional Japanese architecture.

While the woodsy imagery of the bungalow and of the Japanese house dominated Harris's work, he designed a number of projects, such as the Entenza House (114) in Santa Monica, California, of 1937, which utilized either the International Style or the Streamline Moderne. Harris also absorbed many design elements from the then-current work of Frank Lloyd Wright (page 234), especially from Wright's wood Usonian house of the late 1930s.

In the mid-1950s Harris moved to Texas to teach at the University of Texas, and later he went to Raleigh to teach at the University of North Carolina. His later designs in Texas and North Carolina are more openly classical, more reserved and controlled. One of his most significant designs was his sensitive and skillful remodeling in 1958 of Louis H. Sullivan and George Grant Elmslie's 1907–1908 National Farmers Bank in Owatonna, Minnesota.

Few of Harris's sketches or formal presentation drawings have been published. He relied, as did others, on photographs and simple plans to reveal his intent. Surprisingly, his perspective presentation drawings are classically Modern in style, and they do not reveal his romantic pictorial intent. The precise hard edge of the drafting board and the uniform stippling of surfaces forcibly convey a Modern machine quality, which is only marginally present in his buildings. His typical drawing presented his modular plan superimposed on a grid, while his perspective drawings tend to view the building from above—with the building and other manufactured elements dominating the site.

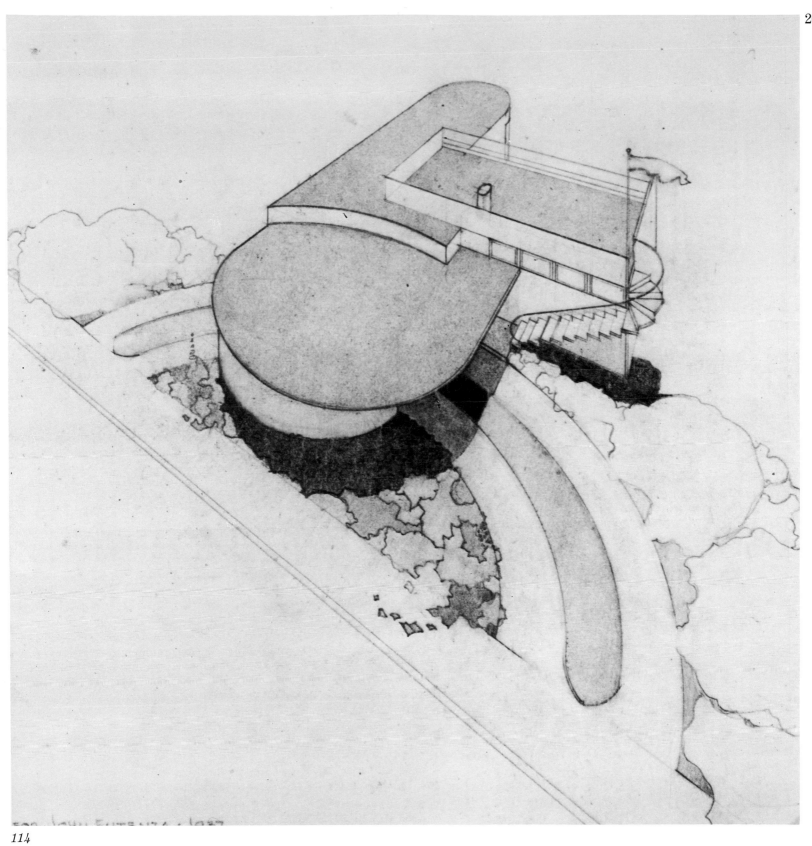

114

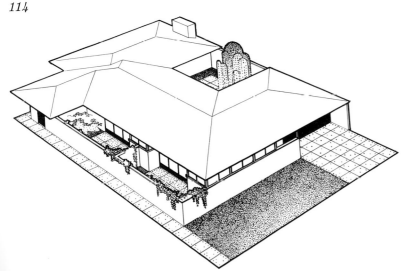

115

116 *New York City skyscraper, project*
Perspective, 1930
Pencil on tan paper, 22 x 13½" (55.9 x 34.3 cm)
Cooper-Hewitt Museum of Decorative Arts and Design
Smithsonian Institution
New York, New York

Ely Jacques Kahn (1884–1972)

New York has long been distinguished by the tallest and most formally inventive skyscrapers in the world, and the Art Deco mode of the late 1920s and early 1930s, typified by the Chrysler Building of 1930 or the Empire State Building of 1931, provides some of the most memorable images of this aspect of the city's character. Ely Jacques Kahn in the firm of Buchman & Kahn (1918–1930) designed some of the best and earliest examples of the style in the United States, beginning with his 2 Park Avenue building of 1927. Of it the critic Lewis Mumford wrote, "One swallow may not make a summer, but one building like this, which faces the entire problem of design and has a clean, unflinching answer for each question, may well serve to crystallize all the fumbling and uncertain elements in present-day architecture." Kahn was extremely productive in the late twenties, building over thirty commercial structures before 1931. The outstanding examples in New York include the Film Center Building, 1929; the Squibb Building, 1930; and the Casino Building, 1410 Broadway, 1931. In 1940 Kahn formed a partnership with Robert Jacobs. Kahn & Jacobs produced largely commercial buildings in the corporate International Style idiom such as the American Airlines Building of 1960 at John F. Kennedy International Airport.

Many of the outstanding architects who helped establish the Art Deco style in New York attended the École des Beaux-Arts. These included Kahn, who studied there between 1907 and 1911, after receiving his Bachelor of Architecture from Columbia University; Raymond Hood; and William Van Alen. It would be difficult for these men to relinquish a predilection for massive solid walls and defined, particularized spaces fostered by the École for the transparent glass walls of the International Style, which characterize Park Avenue's commercial buildings of the fifties and sixties. Perhaps as a result of this background Art Deco buildings appear to be constructed of massive solid walls, when in reality these walls are generally non-load bearing. Another aspect of Art Deco is elaborate stylized ornament of a variety of materials and color derived from many historical sources as well as plant and animal life. Mumford said of the lobby decorated with berries and vines in the first Art Deco building in New York, the Barclay-Vesey of 1927 designed by McKenzie, Voorhees, and Gemelin, that it was "as gaily . . . decorated as a village street in a strawberry festival." Decoration was applied to entrances, lobbies, and the tops of buildings to delight the public. A critic, Forrest F. Lisle, wrote in 1933 that "basic to the development and acceptance of the Moderne (Art Deco) was the existence of, and regard for, democratic, egalitarian, middle-class, commercial, free enterprise, popular cultural values and comprehensions."

Kahn wrote several illuminating articles about his attitude toward decoration that underline the importance of the observer's ability to relate to and appreciate a building. Kahn believed that the color and form of decoration should be determined by its placement on the building so that, for example, ornament at the top of the building could be seen from the street or a nearby building. Kahn writes: "The dream of a colored city . . . may be less of a vision if the enterprising city developer suspects the result. There is evident economy of effort in the application of color, in lieu of carved decoration that cannot be seen and the novelty of structure that can be distinguished from its nondescript neighbors, has a practical value that must appeal without question to the designer and his public."

The massing of the Art Deco skyscraper as exemplified by Kahn's project (116) of 1930 often emphasized its verticality. This was due in part to the 1916 New York City zoning ordinance requiring set-backs in a tall building's massing at a level determined by a complex formula related to the width of the street and the width of the building, but permitting the incorporation of a tower of unlimited height. This law had an obvious influence on Kahn's project. Verticality is stressed in this design by the dramatic contrast between the blocky forms of the lower stepped massing and the huge soaring tower, rarely interrupted by a horizontal element and culminating in a domed termination.

BUCHMAN III KASH ARC'TS

117

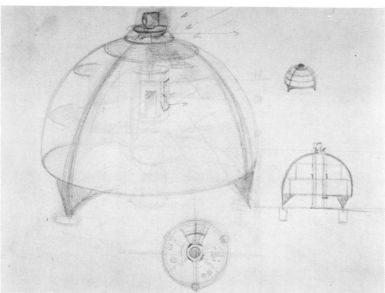

118

George Fred Keck (b. 1895)

George Fred Keck began his own practice in Chicago in 1926 and has continued throughout his career to build distinctive and often innovative buildings, mainly in Illinois and Wisconsin, the greatest number of which are residential. Also an educator, Keck headed the Department of Architecture at the Institute of Design in Chicago from 1938 to 1944. In 1937 he joined in partnership with his brother William (b. 1908). George Fred Keck's buildings executed alone and with his brother are predominantly variations on the International Style. Among the best of these are his 1937 apartment house in Chicago, a designated landmark, and his 1936 Morehouse Residence in Madison, Wisconsin. There a reentrant exterior corner detail articulates the joining of two wall panels in a manner that anticipates the famous corner detailing that Mies van der Rohe (page 215) developed in the steel and brick Chemical Engineering and Metallurgy Building at the Illinois Institute of Technology 9 years later in 1945. George Fred Keck has continually been involved with the application of mass-produced materials to residential building to lower construction and maintenance costs and provide greater functional flexibility. Many of his more radical ideas were implemented in his "House of Tomorrow" at the 1933 Century of Progress Exposition in Chicago and in his 1934 Crystal House built for the fair in its second season.

The 1933 polygonal House of Tomorrow replete with airplane hangar as well as garage is enclosed on its two main levels with glass. The steel frame is fabricated in the shop and bolted together on site; the floors are supported by a central core, which houses utilities (like Buckminster Fuller's Dymaxion House of 1927–1930), while the perimeter is supported by steel lally columns just inside the transparent walls. The house could be erected within 30 to 60 days, with only 48 work hours required on site for frame assembly. This was the realization not only of the use of mass-produced, prefabricated elements in house design but also of the spatial and economic efficiency of a minimum perimeter house. Keck traces his interest in this form to the mid-19th-century octagon houses of Orson Fowler, one of which was built in Watertown, Wisconsin, where he was raised.

The circular house project (118) c. 1932 is similar in plan to the 1933 House of Tomorrow. Here, however, Keck is experimenting with a pure circle lifted off the ground by three supports. This may be an early scheme for the 1933 house, and he may have intended that it be constructed primarily of glass.

The totally glass, totally air conditioned Crystal House (119) of 1934, which could be visited for 10 cents, was designed to test the economics and feasibility of the prefabricated house and, in Keck's words, "to provide a scientifically healthful, light, cheerful residence which capitalizes Nature's fickle moods to man's incessant advantage, night and day—bringing the life-giving sunshine indoors, and excluding alike dry, hot, humid air in summer and damp, raw, cold, biting winds in winter." The house could be built for $3,500 or less if 10,000 were produced and for $2,900 if 50,000 were produced. The glass walls were supported by a steel framework of welded trussed columns and open webbed roof trusses. Clear plate glass and two types of textured translucent glass were used. The building is one of the earliest constructed domestic buildings of glass. In the forties Keck did an about-face in terms of the use of technological control of the environment and developed his buildings so that the building materials themselves attract solar heat in winter and reduce its effects in summer. In these houses large glass walls with projecting eaves face south. In the Bennett House of 1944 in Barrington, Illinois, the flat roof is designed to carry a sheet of water to reduce summer heat. Interior and exterior walls and floors are built of stone to further control climate.

The Holzworth House (117) built in 1930 in Wilmette, Illinois, is typical of Keck's domestic work of the early thirties. It combines the flat planar walls of the International Style with the simple linear ornament of moldings at the entrance more typical of the Moderne or Art Deco mode.

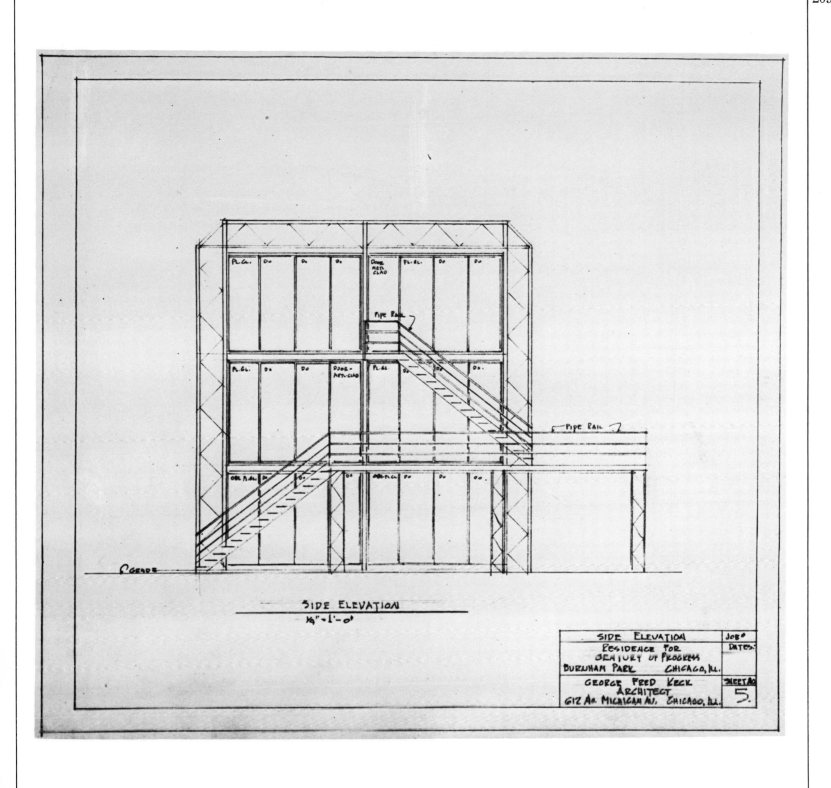

SIDE ELEVATION
1/4" = 1'-0"

SIDE ELEVATION
RESIDENCE FOR
CENTURY OF PROGRESS
BURNHAM PARK   CHICAGO, ILL.
GEORGE FRED KECK
ARCHITECT
612 No. MICHIGAN AV. CHICAGO, ILL.
JOB°
DATES:
SHEET N°
5.

119

117   Holzworth House, Wilmette, Illinois
Principal door elevation, c. 1930
Watercolor, 11⅝ x 9⅝" (29.5 x 24.4 cm)
State Historical Society of Wisconsin
Madison, Wisconsin

118   Circular House, project
Elevation, section, plan, two perspectives, c. 1932
Conté crayon on off-white paper, 8½ x 11" (21.6 x 27.9 cm)
State Historical Society of Wisconsin
Madison, Wisconsin

119   Crystal House, for the 1933 Century of Progress
Exposition, Chicago
Elevation study, 1934
Ink on paper, 21 x 17⅜" (53.3 x 44.1 cm)
State Historical Society of Wisconsin
Madison, Wisconsin

120

120   *Arthur Peck House, project, Paoli, Pennsylvania*
Perspective, 1931
Pencil and white chalk, 19 x 30" (48.3 x 76.2 cm)
Avery Library
Columbia University
New York, New York

121   *House of 2089, project*
Perspective, 1928
Pencil and colored crayons, 24 x 37½" (61 x 95.3 cm)
Avery Library
Columbia University
New York, New York

William Lescaze (1896–1969)

One of the earliest and most important International Style buildings constructed in the United States—the Philadelphia Savings Fund Society Building, or PSFS, of 1929–1932—was designed by William Lescaze in collaboration with George Howe (1886–1955). Lescaze, born in Geneva, graduated in 1919 from the Technische Hochschule where he studied with Karl Moser (1860–1936), who was one of the first people to give instruction, based on Modern principles, in a formal academic setting. Between 1919 and 1920 Lescaze worked for Henri Sauvage (1873–1932), architect of the 1911 apartments in Paris at 26 Rue Vavin, notable for their extraordinary set-back composition and the use of white and blue ceramic tile on the facade. In 1920 Lescaze came to the United States and worked first for the architecturally conservative Cleveland firm of Hubbell & Benes. On his own in the twenties in New York he designed primarily interiors and furniture in a Moderne style. He did, however, complete the Capital Bus Terminal of 1927, which was destroyed in the thirties, and the Edgewood School of 1925 in Greenwich, Connecticut, in Collegiate Gothic. He also opened a store, Lescord, which sold his own furniture and that of other modern designers. From 1929 to 1935 Lescaze was in partnership with Howe; he was primarily concerned with design and Howe with gaining new clients and business. The partnership's production included two of the first International Style schools—the Oak Lane Country Day School of 1929 in Philadelphia and the Hessian Hills School of 1931–1932 in Croton-on-Hudson, New York—as well as several innovative schemes of 1930–1931 for the first Museum of Modern Art building. Lescaze also designed his own New York townhouse of 1934, which was the first International Style building in New York. After 1935 he continued to produce International Style buildings, including the Aviation Building and Swiss Pavilion at the 1939 World's Fair, 711 Third Avenue in New York of 1956, and 22 Water Street of 1969.

George Howe had been the architect for several branches of the PSFS before he received the commission in 1929 for the Market Street skyscraper. There has been discussion about the

121

authorship of the building's design: Lescaze claimed credit for the entire design; Howe was willing to give Lescaze credit for all the design work of the partnership except for that of PSFS and its garage. William Jordy and Robert Stern, the historians of the building, credit Howe with the building's theoretical and structural conception based on his Beaux-Arts background and Lescaze with its International Style skin, detailing, and furniture. What distinguishes this building from European examples of the International Style is its basis in the rationalism of Beaux-Arts theory—that is, the explicit expression of program through form and the direct expression, not revelation, of structure. According to Julien Guadet, the author of the treatise on Beaux-Arts theory, *Elements et Theories de l'Architecture* of 1902, the program was the prime generator of a building's character.

The program for PSFS, as set by its president James M. Willcox, was that it should be "ultra practical"; this meant it would function physically and help make money. The banking room is set on the second floor to free the ground floor for shops, while above the banking section is an office tower with rentable units. This program is accented by form and material. The stores and banking area are set within a curved facade of polished charcoal granite and glass. The office tower, cantilevered over the base to express its different function, has columns of sand-colored limestone and spandrels of gray matte brick. The elevator wing is made explicit from the office slab by setting it at right angles to the slab and sheathing it in black glazed and unglazed brick. Finally, the vertical structure of the tower is expressed by pulling the piers out from the mass of the building. This was the second fully air-conditioned skyscraper in the United States (the first was the Milam Building in San Antonio, Texas, of 1928).

The Arthur Peck House (120), a project of 1929, is typical in form to much of Howe & Lescaze's work, although larger in size and more expensive (estimated cost $147,000) than any of their constructed domestic designs. The house's glass walls, flat roofs, and planar unornamented walls mark it as International Style. The projecting roof with rounded form is an element also used in Moderne streamlined buildings of the late twenties and early thirties.

The House of 2089 (121) designed in 1928 is similar in program and form to Lescaze's House for 1938 published in the 1928 *Architectural Record*. Both the *Record* house and this scheme incorporate an airplane runway on the roof and a two-car garage, as does George Fred Keck's 1933 House of Tomorrow at the Century of Progress Exposition in Chicago (page 208). Lescaze was concerned with creating a futuristic, technological environment that would provide a healthy, functional light-filled home. In the building published in 1928, foil faces the interior walls to reflect light; the bathrooms are skylighted; floors are cork, sponge rubber, or cement; walls are movable for functional flexibility. The house includes an exercise room, pool, meterological instruments, and elevator.

Arthur Meigs, descended from a wealthy Philadelphia family, received a B.A. from Princeton University in 1904, but had no formal training in architecture. He was a partner in the firm of Mellor & Meigs (1906–1916) with Walter Mellor and Mellor, Meigs, & Howe (1916–1928), in which he was chiefly responsible, with George Howe, for the design of some of the most influential residential buildings of the period in America. Most of these were constructed in the wealthy suburbs of Philadelphia and established a romantic image of informal living termed by Howe "Wall Street Pastorale." These structures were based on many historic domestic styles, but particularly French and English rural vernacular architecture, the buildings of the 19th-century progressive architect C. F. A. Voysey, and the work of the firm's older Philadelphia colleague, Wilson Eyre (page 162). In later years after Howe had broken with his partners and established himself as a leading modernist and educator, he defended this image and somewhat apologetically wrote that the rural nature of these estates was intended to produce a "symbol of the fruitful soil as opposed to the hundred-acre suburban lot with its dreary monotony of lawn and landscaping. . . ." When the firm's Arthur Newbold Estate received the coveted Architectural League of New York Gold Medal in 1925, Lewis Mumford took issue with the designation on sociological grounds and wrote that "the critical weakness of the romantic architect is that he is employed in creating an environment into which people may escape from a sordid workaday world whereas the real problem of architecture is to remake the workaday world so that people will not wish to escape from it."

Robert Stern who has presented an important analysis of the firm in his book, *George Howe*, of 1976 has written that "they [Mellor, Meigs, & Howe] were imagists but they were builders as well." The firm's work was as concerned with creating a mood by stirring the imagination as it was with functional planning and with the clear expression of the nature and process of construction and craftsmanship. Materials and methods consistent with the rural sources and images of the designs were employed in the buildings, and more emphasis was placed on simple volumetric relationships than surface effects and ornamentation. These attitudes toward materials and structure were akin to those fostered by the École des Beaux-Arts where Howe studied and by schools in America that supported similar ideas, such as the University of Pennsylvania's School of Architecture from which Mellor graduated in 1904.

The house for W. Curtis Bok (122) of 1929 and the Charles J. McManus House (123) of 1924 are typical of the firm's work before and after Howe's involvement. The Bok House, composed of several wings that intersect and form interior spaces on many levels, is related in a formal way to the landscape by terraces that lead off the different wings and walls that are incorporated into the flow of the land. The gable roofs, large chimneys, and gatehouse all establish a rural mood far from the financial world, which usually engrossed the firm's male clients on weekdays.

The McManus House is close to a photograph of a French farm, which Howe took in 1921. It relies on simple massing and materials for its image rather than ornamentation. The mood these houses create is not unlike that presented by architects and builders to clients less wealthy than Mellor, Meigs, & Howe's in many American suburbs of the era.

122

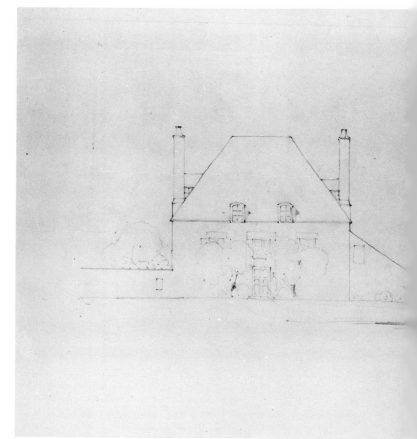

123

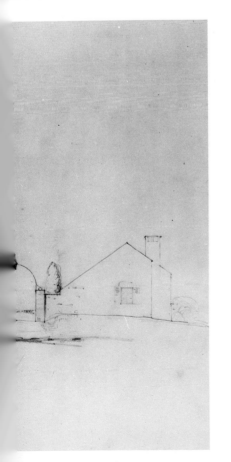

122   *W. Curtis Bok House, Conshocken, Pennsylvania*
Perspective, 1929
Pencil on tracing paper, 12½ x 23" (31.8 x 58.4 cm)
Rare Books Room
Furness Art Library
University of Pennsylvania
Philadelphia, Pennsylvania

123   *Charles J. McManus House, Germantown, Pennsylvania*
Elevation, 1924
Pencil on tracing paper, 17½ x 23" (44.4 x 58.4 cm)
Rare Books Room
Furness Art Library
University of Pennsylvania
Philadelphia, Pennsylvania

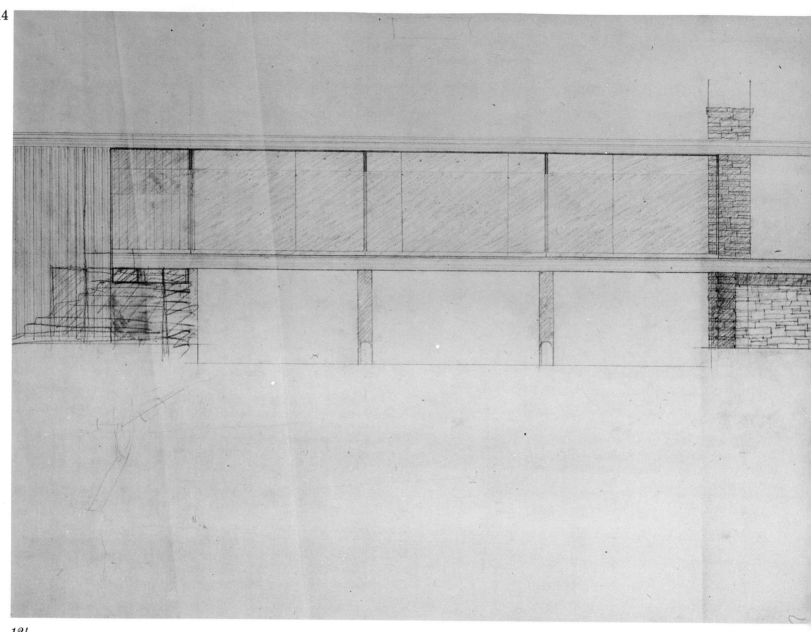

124

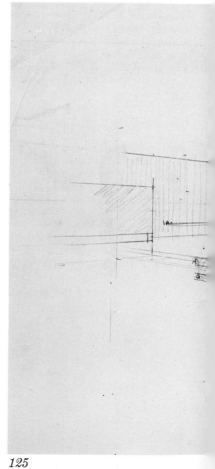

124   *Resor House, project, Jackson Hole, Wyoming*
Studio drawing with additions by Mies van der Rohe
Perspective of living room, 1937–1938
Pencil on tracing paper, 12 x 18" (30.5 x 45.7 cm)
Mies van der Rohe Archive
The Museum of Modern Art
New York, New York

125   *Resor House, project, Jackson Hole, Wyoming*
North elevation, 1937–1938
Pencil on tracing paper, 20 x 42" (50.8 x 106.7 cm)
Mies van der Rohe Archive
The Museum of Modern Art
New York, New York

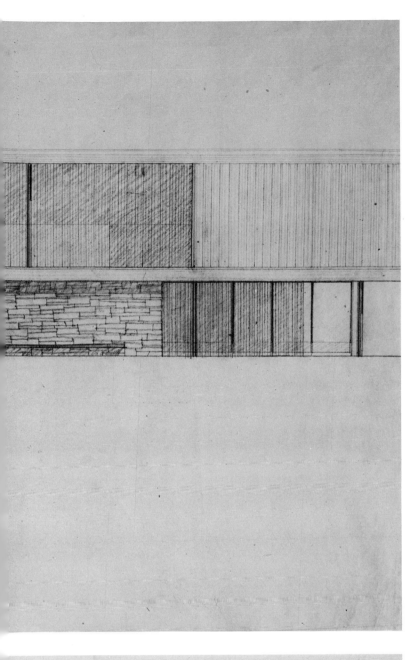

Ludwig Mies van der Rohe, who with Le Corbusier has been the most influential form-giver for post–World War II American and European architects, came to the United States from his native Germany in 1937 with only one client, the Resor family, and no knowledge of the English language. However, by 1938 he was made director of architecture at the Armour Institute in Chicago, which in 1940 became the Illinois Institute of Technology and for which he later designed the master plan and a number of buildings. Only at the close of World War II was he finally given the opportunity to build on a large scale.

In the 1920s in Germany, Mies made his ideas public through his involvement with the Bauhaus, of which he was director from 1930 until 1933, when it was closed under Nazi pressure; with the German Werkbund, of which he was made vice-president in 1926; and with progressive art organizations. In 1918, he helped found the Novembergruppe, serving between 1921 and 1925 as director of its architecture committee. In this capacity, he organized four major exhibitions, which included his own work. It was in these exhibits that he showed his important projects for the "all-glass" skyscraper and "concrete and glass" skyscraper; this was the first time that the use of glass was proposed as a total sheathing for a nonengineering or nonexposition building. Mies labeled this minimalist attitude toward enclosure "skin and bones" architecture, which remained unrealized as a form until the late forties. In 1923 and 1924, Mies underwrote the cost of a magazine, *G* (which stood for "Gestaltung"), to deal with contemporary esthetic problems. In 1925, he founded the organization, The Ring, to offset official prejudice against the Modern Movement in Germany. Under the sponsorship of the Werkbund, he organized and planned the Weissenhof Seidlung (a housing estate) near Stuttgart, one of the first planned communities in the International Style. It included a building by Mies and others by such outstanding European architects as Walter Gropius, Le Corbusier, J. J. P. Oud, Hans Scharoun, and Mart Stamm.

In 1929, Mies designed the German Pavilion at the International Exposition at Barcelona, which provided a powerful image of a new approach to form and space, and would serve as a model for post–World War II building as well as a prototype for much of Mies' subsequent work. In the Barcelona Pavilion, built of steel, glass, marble, and travertine, the interior space is only defined by partitions placed asymmetrically in the whole and by walls of glass. The thin roof slab is supported by regularly spaced, slender cruciform steel columns sheathed in chromium. This creates a free-flowing yet ordered space that has a visual continuation with the exterior. It is an architecture of immateriality dependent on 20th-century technology and materials.

In America, Mies reached the height of his development. With roots in his prewar projects, he developed two primary building types: the glass-walled skyscraper modulated by evenly spaced mullions and piers, often with the entry floor set behind the wall of the tower; and the one-story glass-walled rectangular pavilion. In both the tower and the pavilion, Mies expresses the structure on the exterior of the building by pulling extensions from the supporting piers out from the glass wall. These are not actually the supporting piers themselves, but extensions welded onto them, which in effect make them analogous to moldings, except that they also act as wind bracers. Often, the corner piers are highly articulated, recalling the corner detailing of the German neoclassical architect Karl Friedrich Schinkel (1781–1841), whose work Mies admired.

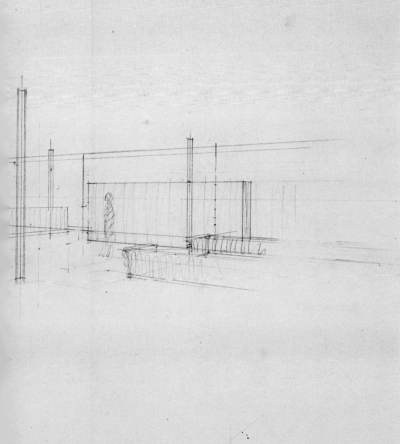

216 In the rectangular pavilion, space is divided as little as possible. Mies wanted to create a universal architectural form appropriate for a multiplicity of functions, with only the essentials fixed. It was his intention that this form language not be principally determined by program. Mies said, "For me novelty has no interest, none whatsoever." This is in distinction with the French architect Le Corbusier, whose work varies from almost sculptural forms, such as the chapel at Ronchamp, to his pure International Style buildings of the twenties, to his brutalist buildings, which appear throughout his *oeuvre* from the thirties to his death. Among the most outstanding examples of the two building types he developed in America are the one-story house for Dr. Farnsworth in Plano, Illinois, 1950; the Lake Shore Drive Apartments in Chicago, 1951; and the Seagram Building in New York City, 1958.

The house in Jackson Hole, Wyoming, for Mr. and Mrs. Stanley Resor, president and vice-president of the J. Walter Thompson Advertising Company, was commissioned in 1937, the year the Resors played an influential role in bringing Mies to the United States. The Resors had originally hired Philip Goodwin, a trustee of The Museum of Modern Art and architect of the first Museum of Modern Art in 1939, to build the house. (Mrs. Resor was a trustee of The Museum of Modern Art.) But the patrons and architect parted after only a service wing was constructed. The site for the house was at a mill race, with the Goodwin structure on one side. Mies' project (124, 125, 126) is a cage of steel enclosed in part by cypress planking, but glassed for three-fifths of the length of the structure at a point over the mill race. This opened the living room, which was behind the glass, to a view of the water on both sides; the living room bridge, supported by piers, connects the service wing, which Mies altered, to his own new structure on the other bank. The design is a radical departure from most of his last European domestic projects, which were based on a court or patio *parti* and physically tied to the ground. There is, however, a 1934 sketch by Mies for a hillside house, which, like the Resor House, is conceived as a bridge. The Resor project would have had the free-flowing spatial configuration in its interior as developed in the Barcelona Pavilion. The house progressed to the stage of working drawings and bids went out for construction in 1938, but the estimates were too high and changes had to be made. The spring floods of 1943 destroyed the service wing and bridge that were on the site, and the house was never built.

Mies often presented the conceptualization of a scheme through the use of a collage and drawing technique. Three collages of the Resor House were made by Mies in collaboration with students at the Armour Institute. In two of the three, one of which is illustrated here (126), the structure of the living room section of the house is superimposed on a photograph of the site. In the third of the series, a photograph of a painting by Paul Klee, which the Resors owned, is collaged with the structural grid. A model of the house was shown in 1947 at the first retrospective of Mies' work at The Museum of Modern Art, which now houses a repository of Mies' drawings and papers.

126

126 Resor House, project, Jackson Hole, Wyoming
View from north wall of house to site, collage, 1938
Pencil and photograph on illustration board
30 x 40" (76.2 x 101.6 cm)
Mies Van der Rohe Archive
The Museum of Modern Art
New York, New York

127

127   Rubens Residence, Santa Monica, California
Perspective, 1936
Pencil and crayon on brown paper, 15 x 20" (38.1 x 50.8 cm)
University of California at Los Angeles
Los Angeles, California

128   Rush City Reformed Transportation Center, *project*
Los Angeles
Perspective, c. 1931
Pencil on linen, 13 x 18" (33 x 45.7 cm)
University of California at Los Angeles
Los Angeles, California

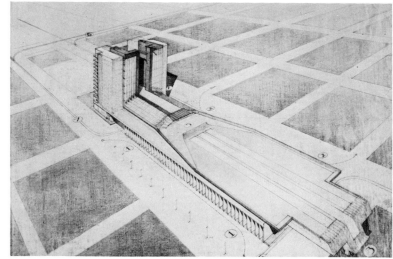

128

Richard J. Neutra (1892–1970)

A major factor in the establishment of the Modern Movement in America was the immigration of a group of European architects who had been involved through their own contributions or through their educational experience with the European architectural avant-garde of the first two decades of the 20th century. This group included Richard J. Neutra, R. M. Schindler (page 226), Eric Mendelsohn, Walter Gropius, Mies van der Rohe (page 215), and Marcel Breuer, the last three having been key figures at the Bauhaus.

Neutra was born in Vienna and graduated from the Technische Hochschule. In 1910 Neutra met the Viennese architect and theorist Adolf Loos (1870–1933) whose Steiner House of 1910 was a milestone in the development of the International Style, embodying an esthetic of pure cubic forms, lack of ornament, and the treatment of the facade as a continuous, flat surface. Loos's esthetics and his advocacy of an architecture free of ornament were to influence Neutra as well as other important leaders of the Modern Movement, notably Le Corbusier (1887–1965). Neutra's interest in American architecture was spurred by Loos whose admiration for American building developed while working at odd jobs in the United States between 1893 and 1896. In 1923 Neutra came to America and worked first for Holabird & Roche in Chicago and then for a few months with Frank Lloyd Wright at Taliesin in Spring Green, Wisconsin. Neutra's impressions of American architecture and technology were published in 1927 in *Wie Baut Amerika*. From 1925 to 1930 he shared studio space with R. M. Schindler in Los Angeles, and it was in California that his greatest architectural successes were achieved. Together with Schindler in 1927 he entered the League of Nations competition. Neutra, Schindler, together with Carol Arnovici worked on several planning projects and architectural schemes under the title Architectural Group for Industry and Commerce (AGIC).

Most histories of modern architecture include two elegant buildings by Neutra, the Lovell House in Los Angeles of 1927–1929 and the Kaufmann House in Palm Springs, California, of 1946–1947. They represent the two formalistic periods of his development. The Lovell House, set on a hillside, is one of, if not the most important early monument of the International Style idiom in America. Its counterpart for a commercial building type is the PSFS Building in Philadelphia of 1928–1931 by Howe and Lescaze (page 210). The Lovell House is a structure of thin transparent glass and concrete walls with balconies hung from the roof by steel cables. Much of the steel frame was welded in the shop and then erected in only 40 hours on the site. The concrete was sprayed from a hose onto metal panels covered with insulation. This construction presents a machine age esthetic and signifies Neutra's interest in using experimental building materials as well as traditional ones in new ways.

The Rubens Residence (127) in Los Angeles of 1936 exemplifies Neutra's machine esthetic of sheer wall planes, flat roofs, and rectangular massing. The garage is situated symbolically like the front door, acknowledging the dependence of the Los Angeles environment on the automobile.

Neutra's Nesbitt House of 1942 in Brentwood, California, of glass, redwood board and batten, and brick marks a change in his esthetic that leads to the Kaufmann House. In this later house Neutra moves away from the rectangular plan and spreads the building out horizontally into the flat desert terrain.

Many discussions of Neutra generally overlook the philosophy central to his thinking: that design must evolve from psychological, biological, and sociological factors and not from a priori formalistic considerations. This attitude is the thesis for his book *Survival through Design* of 1954. Neutra was interested throughout his career in the development of low-cost, easy-to-build, and socially responsible housing. Among his projects are the Channel Heights Housing Project in San Pedro, California, of 1941–1942, in which the site was treated as a common park. Neutra also built schools and health centers, several of which are in Puerto Rico. In his open air Corona Avenue School in Bell, California, of 1952 almost all the floor space is devoted to movable classroom seating and large glass walls, some of which open to the exterior. This continues a California tradition of combining indoor and outdoor space in school buildings.

In 1949 Robert Alexander joined Neutra and together they produced general large-scale planning projects, including a 10-year master plan for Guam. Many of Neutra's ideas for large-scale planning were first worked through in his studies for an ideal city of one million called "Rush City Reformed." Collaborating with him on the project were Gregory Ain (page 194) and Harwell Hamilton Harris (page 204). In this conception high-rise housing would have the ground floor open to through traffic, with parking and speed traffic lanes depressed below ground. Pedestrians would reach pedestrian walks on the second and third levels of the building via elevators from the street. Low-rise housing would face parkland with property lines as Neutra said "treated like legal fiction." One of the most important notions for this city was that transportation systems should be integrated. A subway and automobile route, for example, would be joined in one terminal at an airport. It can be assumed that the transportation center study (128) connected several types of transportation systems.

COMMERCIAL BUILDING - Nọs 189·191 BROADWAY · NEW YORK CITY·
OCEANIC INVESTING CORPORATION, OWNER ▣ C.F. ROSBORG, ARCHT.- Nọ 141 EAST 40ᵀᴴ STREET - NEW YORK CITY

129

Christian Francis Rosborg (1875–1953)

Little is known about the career and life of C. F. Rosborg, as he
signed his drawings. He was a pupil of Ernest Flagg (1857–
1947) and also apprenticed with Haydel and Shepard in New
York. His first works—such as his submission for a new State
Department Building of 1911, the drawings for which exist
at the Cooper-Hewitt Museum of Decorative Arts and
Design—are Beaux-Arts projects similar to those produced by
Flagg.

By the mid-1930s Rosborg's work could be categorized as
Moderne, as in his studies for the Oceanic Investing
Corporation (130) of 1933. Rosborg's John David Building (129)
of 1940, which still stands, illustrates how he carried the
Modern Style into a version of the International Style. This
change from Beaux-Arts to Moderne to International Style was
a progression not uncommon to many American architects
trained just after the turn of the century under a Beaux-Arts
master or at the École des Beaux-Arts itself.

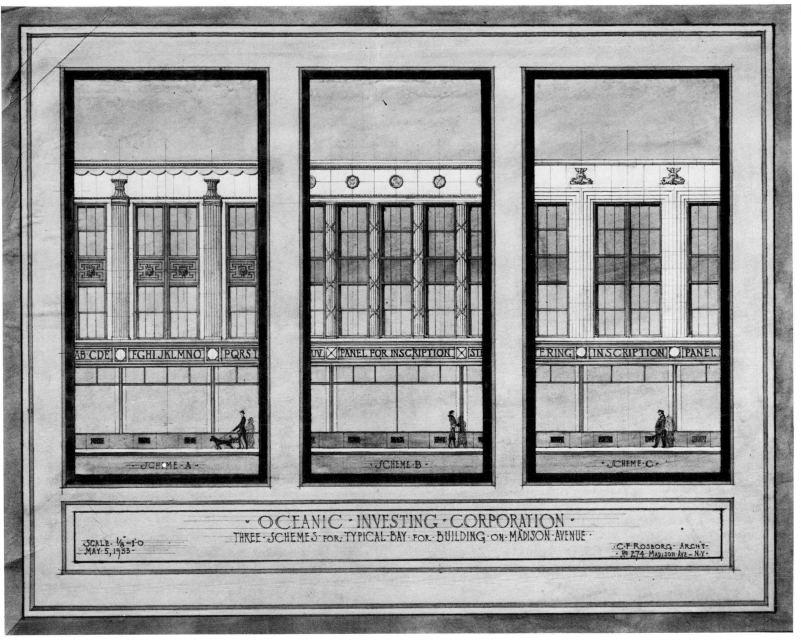

130

129   *John David Building, 189–191 Broadway, New York City*
Perspective, April 4, 1940
Ink, pencil, gold and silver tempera, watercolor
13¾ x 12⅜" (34.9 x 31.4 cm)
Cooper-Hewitt Museum of Decorative Arts and Design
Smithsonian Institution
New York, New York

130   *Oceanic Investing Corporation, project, New York City*
Three schemes for a typical bay for
building on Madison Avenue
Elevation, May 5, 1933
Pencil and watercolor, 13½ x 16½" (34.3 x 41.9 cm)
Cooper-Hewitt Museum of Decorative Arts and Design
Smithsonian Institution
New York, New York

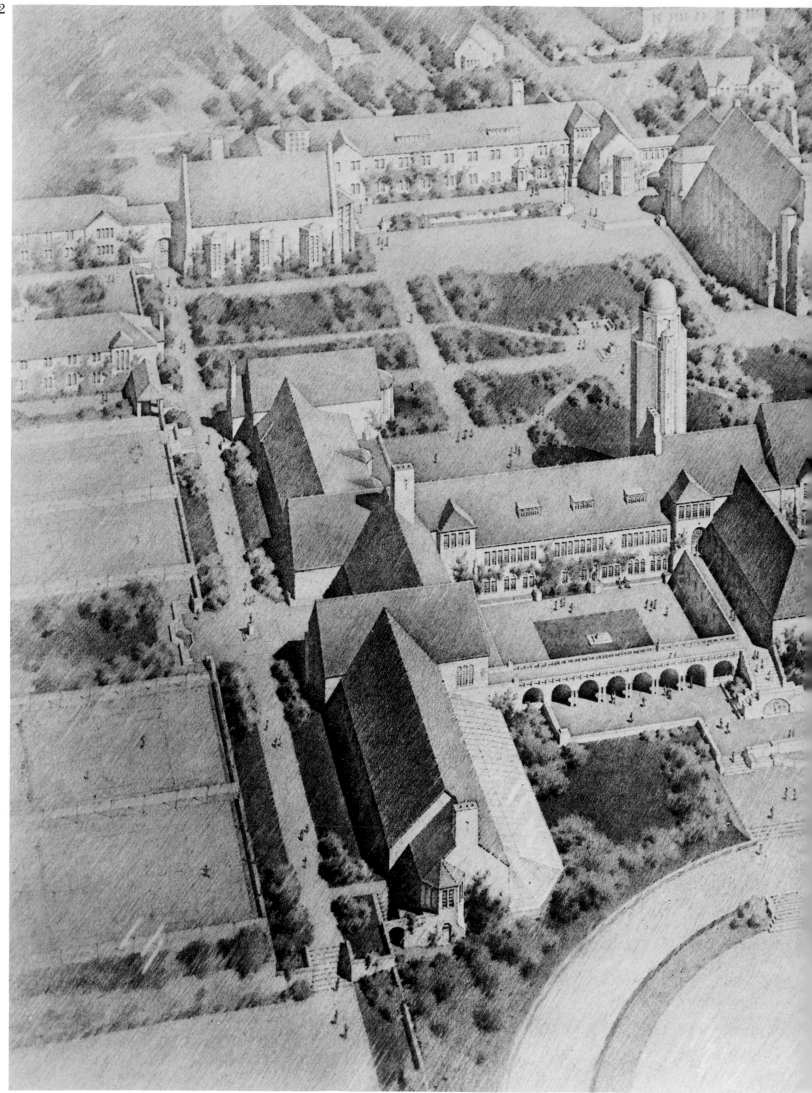

When Eliel Saarinen came to the United States from Finland in 1923 to accept second prize in the Chicago Tribune Tower Competition, he was the most respected contemporary architect in Finland. He had built, in collaboration with his partners Herman Gesellius and Armas Lindgren, the monumental and romantic Helsinki Railroad Station, designed in 1904 and built in 1910–1914, as well as the Finnish Pavilion at the 1900 Paris Exposition—a most unusual building based in part on traditional Finnish structures and called by one critic "the simplest building there." Saarinen chose to remain in America with his family, and from 1926 through the early forties he designed the buildings and interiors of the Cranbrook Academy of Art, the Cranbrook Schools, and the Cranbrook Institute of Science in Bloomfield Hills, Michigan, whose benefactor and founder was George Booth. This important complex of buildings was completed with the participation of his wife, Loja, his daughter, Pipsan, and his son, Eero (page 284), who himself would become an important American architect in the post–World War II era, and with the Finnish sculptor, Carl Milles. From 1937, when Saarinen joined in partnership with his son, to his death, he designed some of the most distinguished buildings of his career in a modern idiom: the Kleinhans Music Hall, Buffalo, 1938; the Tanglewood Music Shed, 1938, and Opera House, 1944, in Lenox, Massachusetts; Christ Lutheran Church, Minneapolis, 1949–1950; the first project for the General Motors Technical Center, designed in 1945 and completed in a somewhat different form by his son; and the Tabernacle Church, in Columbus, Indiana, 1940–1942.

Saarinen, like Frank Lloyd Wright, received his architectural training in the late 19th century and took with him to the 20th century the belief—based on a general influence from Viollet-le-Duc—that the nature of materials should be a major force in the production of form. Saarinen habitually used a building material in a manner that is consistent with and emphasizes its physical properties. This is expressively manifest in his house at Hvittrask near Helsinki of 1902 where in the main living room logs are used as columns in the fashion of vernacular architecture and are cut simply to retain the suggestion of the trees from which they came. The furniture, weavings, tile, and other forms of decoration that richly cover the surfaces of Hvittrask reflect influences from several sources: Finnish craft tradition, English arts and crafts, the geometrized natural forms of the Viennese Sezession, and the Scottish Art Nouveau of the firm of Charles Rennie Mackintosh. This total approach to the design of an environment is an important precedent for Cranbrook as is the notion of community at Hvittrask, which was originally created by Saarinen and his partners as a place to live and work and in which European intellectuals might gather.

The idea for the Cranbrook community of institutions was developed by George Booth with Eliel Saarinen. The philosophy of Cranbrook's Art Academy was that it should be a place where mature artists could work and where students could come to study with them. Saarinen and Booth believed, as did the masters of the German Bauhaus, that both the fine arts and the crafts had to be integrated into the technological society of the 20th century. It was their intention that the fine arts and crafts should be practiced in an environment in which there could be an interchange between the two. Among those artists who have worked at Cranbrook were the sculptor Harry Bertoia, the architect and furniture designer Charles Eames (page 245), the ceramicist Maija Grotell, and the painter Zoltan Sepeshy. The first complex of buildings that Saarinen designed in Bloomfield Hills was the Boys School (131) of 1925 that had to conform to already existing farm buildings. The buildings are arranged around a courtyard. Covered walkways, gabled roofs, figurative decoration together with the site plan produce a medieval and romantic ensemble.

Yet Saarinen's design is developed from an abstraction of medieval forms with a minimum of nostalgic pretension. In the colonnade elevation (132) and in the tower rising above the complex in the bird's eye view the wall and piers are stripped of intricate detailing and reduced to almost pure geometric forms retaining in their massing a reference to medieval architecture. This reductionism of historical forms is characteristic of one aspect of Art Deco architecture with which Saarinen's work has been associated.

224 In contrast with the furniture of such International Style architects of the twenties as Marcel Breuer, Le Corbusier, or Mies van der Rohe, Saarinen's dining room chairs for Cranbrook (133) c. 1928 recall traditional furniture design. However, the chairs' striking beauty results not from copyism, but from the subtle manipulation of the fluted back and the elegant combination of blond wood with black detailing, a coloration typical of Art Deco furniture. These chairs also rely for formal inspiration on the furniture produced in the first decade of the 20th century by the Vienna Sezession and particularly the work of Josef Hoffmann.

132

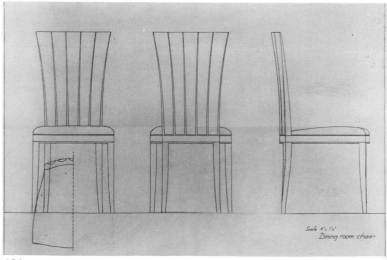

133

131   Cranbrook Academy, Bloomfield Hills, Michigan
Aerial perspective, 1926
Pencil and ink, 28½ x 38½" (72.4 x 97.2 cm)
Cranbrook Academy of Art Museum
Bloomfiled Hills. Michigan

132   *Cranbrook Academy*
Bloomfield Hills, Michigan
Two elevations and detail of floor pattern, 1927
Pencil, 25½ x 38" (64.8 x 96.5 cm)
Cranbrook Academy of Art Museum
Bloomfield Hills, Michigan

133   *Cranbrook Academy, Bloomfield Hills, Michigan*
Dining room chair for Saarinen House, three elevations,
and plan of back, c. 1928
Ink, 18¼ x 26½" (46.4 x 67.3 cm)
Cranbrook Academy of Art Museum
Bloomfield Hills, Michigan

134

Rudolph M. Schindler (1887–1953)

From the late 1930s to the early 1960s R. M. Schindler's work was undervalued by critics, although his Lovell House in Newport Beach, California, of 1922–1926 is as important an example of the modern esthetic of the 1920s as are Le Corbusier's Villa Savoye of 1927–1929 and Mies van der Rohe's (page 214) Barcelona Pavilion of 1929. Schindler's houses and commercial buildings, built during the thirty-odd years of his independent practice in California, show a continuous inventiveness and an unwillingness to settle for formulas. Why then was Schindler largely ignored? In part the answer lies in the fact that unlike other heroes of modernism such as Le Corbusier or Frank Lloyd Wright, Schindler was not a forceful propagandist. Perhaps a more complex reason is related to his particular formal manipulation of the modern idiom; it is unlike that of the orthodox modernist and difficult for critics to totally accept. In a 1940 article, "An Eastern Critic Looks at Western Architecture," Henry-Russell Hitchcock wrote: "The case of Schindler I do not profess to understand. There is certainly immense vitality perhaps somewhat lacking among many of the best architects of the Pacific Coast. But this vitality seems in general to lead to arbitrary and brutal effects."

Schindler's buildings from the late twenties on were essentially organized as a system of projecting and interpenetrating volumes related to de Stijl esthetics, although he never employed their use of primary colors. Schindler's mature works at times built of concrete but more commonly of wood frame and stucco construction had smooth machinelike surfaces. However, unlike the work of his Modern contemporaries in America and Europe, they were not regular volumes sheathed by taut, continuous surfaces. The essence of his work was the dramatic manipulation of space in the vertical dimension. To this end he would sometimes (especially from the late 1930s on) use gabled or hipped roofs and in several instances curved roofs in order to attain these complex interior spatial changes.

As David Gebhard has observed, ambiguity is another aspect of Schindler's art. It is that kind of ambiguity outlined by Robert Venturi, who writes in his *Complexity and Contradiction in Architecture* of 1966 that "A valid architecture evokes many levels of meaning and combinations of forms: its space and its elements become readable and workable in several ways at once." Aspects of the Lovell House relate to this context. In this house five huge concrete frames, major supports of the building, are not visually related to the building's volumes. These frames at once dominate and are denied in the composition. On the primary elevation the frames project out from the volume and thus heighten the awareness of these forms as major structural elements. At the same time, ramped stairs penetrate the frames, creating a tension between these two visually dominant elements and diminishing the supportive symbolism. Yet, in contrast with this facade, the frames are suppressed on other elevations.

Schindler was born and educated in Vienna. In 1911 he graduated from the Imperial Institute of Engineering and in 1913 from the Vienna Academy of Arts then under the direction of Otto Wagner (1841–1918). Between 1911 and 1914 he worked in Vienna for Mayr & Mayer. In Vienna he was part of the art world, which included the painters Egon Schiele and Gustav Klimt and the architect and theorist Adolph Loos (1870–1933). It was Loos's preference for interior spaces organized as a series of vertically related platforms that had the profoundest effect on Schindler's work. In 1914 Schindler left for Chicago and was employed by the conservative firm of Ottenheimer, Stern, & Reichert. Between 1917 and 1921 he worked for Frank Lloyd Wright (page 234) and was particularly involved with the design of Wright's Imperial Hotel in Tokyo and the Olive Hill Development for Aline Barnsdall of 1913–1921 in Los Angeles (pages 234-235). Schindler had first come in contact with Wright's work in Vienna through the 1910 Wasmuth portfolio that presented his early work and through this was influenced by Wright's flowing interior space. In direct contact with Wright in America, Schindler was impressed with Wright's almost obsessive attention to each detail in the building process and continued this approach in his own career.

The work of the late teens and early twenties showed influence from Vienna as well as from Wright. In 1921 Schindler opened his own practice in the double house he built for himself and his wife and Mr. and Mrs. Clyde Chase on Kings Road in Los Angeles. The house was arranged as a set of pavilions around

135

courtyard gardens and was constructed on a concrete slab floor with walls of tilt slab concrete construction, wood, or canvas and a wooden roof. From 1925 to 1931 Richard Neutra shared studio space with Schindler, and together they entered the League of Nations competition in 1927 with a clearly formulated design in which the separateness of the different administrative components of the organization was visually emphasized. With Neutra and the urban planner Carol Arnovici, the Architectural Group for Industry and Commerce was founded, which prepared designs for planning and housing projects, few of which were built. It was perhaps through this close association with Neutra that Schindler's work took on a more machinelike esthetic. The skyscraper project (134) for the Playmart in Los Angeles of 1921 is a loose combination of constructivism de Stijl and Moderne. The facade is stepped toward the central focus of the building; a detached, glazed elevator tower is connected to the building at each floor by bridges. The building's clearly expressed steel frame is clad in alternating black glass and aluminum materials favored by the Moderne Style, which Schindler would use but once again in the 1924 project for the Peoples Bank in Los Angeles.

During the late 1930s and early 1940s, though Schindler continued to design within a vocabulary influenced by de Stijl and the machine esthetic of the International Style, he also designed a group of houses more romantic in character, such as the A. Timme House project (135) in Los Angeles of 1938. In many of these houses stone walls and wooden roofs were introduced side by side with flat, stuccoed walls, but in all of them a rectilinear massing was combined with shed or gabled roofs in order to create ever more dramatic interior space. These houses are in some ways related to the contemporaneous California work of William W. Wurster, Lloyd Wright (page 238), and Harwell H. Harris (page 204). In the Timme House, Schindler covers one wing with a shed roof and the other with gabled roofs of two different slopes. The roofs are separated from the side walls by glass and are thereby read as separate elements imposed on rectangular volumes. In a characteristically "Schindleresque" manner the strict geometry of the house is echoed in the highly structured arrangement of garden walls and hedges.

134   *Skyscraper in Black Glass and Aluminum, project*
Los Angeles
Perspective, 1921–1923
Pencil, ink, gouache, and watercolor
20½ x 9⅛" (52.1 x 23.2 cm)
R. M. Schindler Collection
The University Art Galleries
University of California at Santa Barbara
Santa Barbara, California

135   *Dr. A. Timme House, project, Los Angeles*
Perspective, 1938
Pencil, 21 x 34" (53.3 x 86.4 cm)
R. M. Schindler Collection
The University Art Galleries
University of California at Santa Barbara
Santa Barbara, California

George Washington Smith (1874–1930)
Lutah Maria Riggs (b. 1896)

George Washington Smith is best known for domestic buildings although he was a designer of a number of clubs and commercial structures. Smith's work represents some of the finest built in California in the Spanish Colonial idiom during the late 1910s and 1920s. He began his practice in Santa Barbara in 1916 and in 1921 was joined by Lutah Maria Riggs, who was of vital importance in the creation of consistently high-quality buildings produced by his office. Smith studied architecture at Harvard University and then spent 2 years in Paris from 1912 to 1914 painting. This period, not primarily concerned with architecture, brought him into direct contact with the paintings of Cézanne, which, he related, taught him to see all the arts with "the consciousness of simplicity." It was this attitude toward form and an intellectual approach to design that created outstandingly original buildings derived, however, from historic styles.

Lutah Maria Riggs graduated in architecture from the University of California at Berkeley in 1919 and worked for Ralph D. Taylor in Susanville, California, for 3 months before joining Smith. Since Smith's death in 1930, she has continued to practice and has been actively involved in planning and historic preservation in Santa Barbara.

The widespread acceptance of the Mission Revival of the 1890s in California set the stage for the acceptance of the Spanish Colonial Revival of the late teens and twenties of this century. The first major monument to the Mission style, borrowing the round arches, undecorated stucco walls, and arched loggias from California missions, was A. Page Brown's (1859–1896) California Building at the 1893 World's Columbian Exposition in Chicago. At the same time Charles Fletcher Lummis, founder of the California Landmarks Club in 1894, provided intellectual support for the style in his magazine *Land of Sunshine*. By 1915 taste had changed, and Bertram G. Goodhue (page 166) inaugurated the Spanish Colonial Revival with his California Building at the Panama–California Exposition of 1915 in San Diego. This had been preceded by Cram and Goodhue's Gillespie House in Montecito of 1902, which was both Spanish and Classical, and Myron Hunt's Churriqueresque First Congregation Church at Riverside, California, of 1912–1913.

The 20th-century California version of the Spanish Colonial was really a Mediterranean Revival, drawing on the Plateresque and Churriqueresque of Spain, the Moorish of North Africa and Spain, the vernacular adobe of Mexico and New Mexico, and Italian Renaissance and Baroque architecture. The California revivalist architect intended not to reproduce any of these styles either whole or in part but rather to use them as reference points.

Typical of Smith's work, alone and with Riggs, such as the Montecito project "Residence for Mrs. Richard Heimann" (136) of 1928–1929, was a concern with the interrelationship of cubelike masses organized in L plans or less characteristically H or U plans and adjoined by formal gardens laid out in strict geometric patterns. Smith and Riggs never presented materials as something other than what they were, yet they endeavored to create an image through the manipulation of materials. For example, to effect thick walls they would construct two wooden walls spaced apart and then stucco the whole. What was important were image and form. Smith's interest in this unadorned interpretation of the Spanish Colonial or Mediterranean style must have been nourished by the vernacular rural architecture of France and Spain, which Smith observed and which was so admired by Cézanne for its simplicity and purity of form.

As a member of the Community Arts Association of Santa Barbara, Smith presented plans for the redesign of De la Guerra Plaza (137) in Santa Barbara in 1922 and for a new City Hall. The plaza, which was finally built, followed certain of the ideas contained in Smith's perspective. He intended to unite the stores around the plaza by an arcaded loggia. The plaza itself would be organized by a series of paths around a central fountain. Although his scheme for the City Hall was never realized, he did build the Daily News Building at the south end of the plaza in 1922.

136

137

136 *Lutah Maria Riggs*
Heimann House, Santa Barbara, California
Perspective, 1928–1929
Pencil and charcoal, 19 x 32" (48.3 x 81.3 cm)
Collection of Lutah Maria Riggs
Santa Barbara, California

137 *Lutah Maria Riggs*
De la Guerra Plaza, project, Santa Barbara, California
Perspective, 1922
Pencil and charcoal, 16 x 33½" (40.6 x 85.1 cm)
Collection of Lutah Maria Riggs
Santa Barbara, California

138 Chicago Tribune Tower Competition
Perspective, 1922
Pencil on tracing paper, 28 x 14" (71.1 x 35.6 cm)
Avery Library
Columbia University
New York, New York

139 Chicago Tribune Tower Competition
Perspective, 1922
Pencil on tracing paper, 28 x 18¾" (71.1 x 47.6 cm)
Avery Library
Columbia University
New York, New York

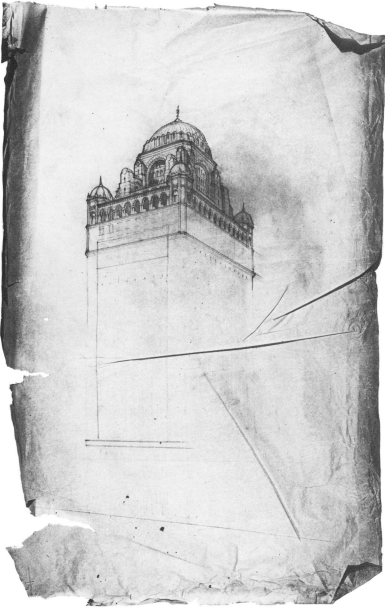

138

Isaac Newton Phelps Stokes (1867–1944)

Isaac Newton Phelps Stokes, member of a wealthy New York family, was educated at Harvard College, class of 1891; Columbia University School of Architecture, 1892–1895; and the École des Beaux-Arts, 1896–1897. A "gentleman architect" in the best sense of the term, his career was divided between professional practice and civic responsibilities. In 1900, he was appointed to the New York State Tenement House Commission, and his interest in low-cost housing was one that continued throughout his life. From 1911 through 1930, he served as Secretary of the Phelps Stokes Fund for Housing and Education. Between 1915 and 1928, he published the monumental six-volume *Iconography of Manhattan Island*, which documents social, political, and cultural aspects of the city's history from the early 16th century to the first decade of the 20th century.

Stokes, in partnership between 1897 and 1917 with John Mead Howells, designed buildings in several historical styles. The choice of style usually carried with it symbolic associations particularly meaningful to the individual or institutional client. For example, Howells' and Stokes' house for Mark Twain in Redding, Connecticut, c. 1906 was based on Italian Renaissance villas. Twain lived in a villa called "La Quercia" in Fiesole near Florence, and a critic of the period remarked on the similarity between Twain's Italian house and his Connecticut one. The firm designed the Music Building of 1916 at Harvard University, which is Colonial in style, recalling the earliest buildings in Harvard Yard. The firm's civic buildings for urban locations, such as the American Geographical Society Building in New York of 1902, no longer extant, and the Baltimore Stock Exchange of 1905, are typical products of American Beaux-Arts–trained architects. They relied on classical sources, as well as those of French 17th- and 18th-century architecture, and are of a scale and formality appropriate for prestigious turn-of-the-century institutions.

Perhaps their finest building is St. Paul's Chapel at Columbia University of 1904–1906, a gift to Columbia by Stokes' relatives, Olivia Eggleston Phelps Stokes and her sister, Caroline Phelps Stokes, in memory of their parents, James and Caroline Phelps Stokes. The general source for this brick and limestone building was Donato Bramante's (1444–1514) Ste. Maria degli Grazie in Milan begun in 1492. The details of the dome and apse are very closely related to McKim, Mead, & White's Earl Hall, directly across the campus from the chapel. The building was clearly made to harmonize with McKim, Mead, & White's work at Columbia; and although Howells and Stokes often relied on Renaissance models, in no example of their work before or after St. Paul's is a similar massing used.

The chapel is vaulted in the lightweight, easy-to-build method of Guastavino vaulting (also used in Grand Central Terminal). The building is outstanding for its integration of structure and decoration. The decorative pattern formed by the brickwork of the walls and that of the vault serves as an important element in the interior decorative scheme. The frieze of crosses, squares, and circles around the exterior of the chapel is a component of the load-bearing wall and is not superimposed on it.

In 1922, *The Chicago Tribune* sponsored a competition for its new building. The object of the competition, as stated by *The Tribune* in the announcement of its program, was to celebrate the 75th anniversary of the newspaper, "secure for Chicago the most beautiful office building in the world," and provide "inspiration" for both its workers and other newspapers. The winning design by the firm of Howells and Hood (the same Howells who had been Stokes' partner) was a Gothic-inspired tower replete with flying buttresses. Eliel Saarinen (page 223) took second place. Stokes' entry (138, 139) is a tower with a set-back top section, based on the elevation of the Hagia Sophia in Istanbul. This use of a form derived from a building type unrelated to the skyscraper was typical of most of the entries. The few outstanding entries that were done in the contemporary idiom of the International Style were submitted by Europeans; some of the best among these were by the German architect Walter Gropius, head of the Bauhaus, and by the Dutch firm of Duiker & Bijvöet.

232 Horace Trumbauer (1869–1938)
Julien F. Abele (1880–1950)

Horace Trumbauer produced eclectic buildings, often of lavish materials, that were expressive of the self-importance with which many of his wealthy clients viewed themselves. In 1892 he opened his own office in Philadelphia where his firm built residences and commercial buildings for powerful families such as the Wideners and institutional buildings such as the Public Library designed in 1908 and built between 1917 and 1927 and the Philadelphia Museum of Art of 1928 executed in collaboration with Zantzinger, Borie, & Medary. By the first decade of the 20th century Trumbauer was successful beyond the limits of his hometown, and he built in New York (the James Duke House of 1912, now the New York University Institute of Fine Arts; and Wildenstein & Company of 1932) and in Newport (the Elms of 1901 and Miramar of 1914).

Trumbauer's chief associate for many years was the black architect Julien Abele. Abele graduated from the University of Pennsylvania's School of Architecture in 1902 and spent his entire career with Horace Trumbauer Associates. He was the firm's chief designer and is responsible for the design of the Philadelphia Museum of Art, the Philadelphia Free Library, as well as the elaborate houses the firm produced.

Trumbauer received his professional training as a draftsman in the office of G. W. and W. D. Hewitt in Philadelphia, the city in which he spent his entire life. He most frequently turned to French 17th- and 18th-century architecture for inspiration, but he also designed in the Gothic, Georgian, Classical, and Elizabethan styles. In the mid-twenties and early thirties he even produced a few buildings which could be described as Art Deco or Moderne, such as the Evening Post Building of 1926 in New York. There was, however, no clear chronological development in his use of styles. Years after the Evening Post Building, he built Wildenstein & Company and Rose Terrace in Grosse Point, Michigan, of 1933, both of which rely on French 18th-century architecture for their models. Trumbauer's choice of style was determined by the client's needs and the associations that might be established between a style and a given program. Trumbauer's position on the use of styles and his method of design is summed up in the 1904 *Architectural Record* article "A New Influence in the Architecture of Philadelphia" by an anonymous author. The author comments on the fact that because Trumbauer had a large practice he often relied on carefully chosen, previously employed design solutions. The author writes, "standardization is almost as necessary here [in architecture] under modern conditions as it is in other departments of production where the output is perforce large and the pressure for time necessarily high." The author concludes the essay with: "The note of any leaning or predilection is almost wholly absent from the mass of the work we [the magazine] present. It is extremely difficult in it [Trumbauer's work] to catch the designer, so to speak, 'at' any of his preferences."

The Duke University Campus of 1927–1930 in Durham, North Carolina, in which Julien Abele had an active role in the design, exemplifies the "associationism" connected to Trumbauer's formalistic choices. For the Chapel, Medical School, and Men's College (140), Trumbauer, who had been selected by James Duke, chose an English Gothic mode. Buildings are arranged around courtyards, which add to the medieval feeling. This stylistic mode had been used for colleges from the beginning of the 19th century as in Town & Davis's New York University; it is meant to recall the campuses of Oxford and Cambridge. The Women's College, however, is executed in a Classical Revival style on the model of Thomas Jefferson's University of Virginia. Buildings are arranged along two sides of a long lawn with a Pantheon-like building at its head that serves as an auditorium.

140

140   Julien F. Abele
Duke University, Durham, North Carolina
Campus plan, aerial perspective, c. 1925
Pencil, 27 x 53" (68.6 x 134.6 cm)
Duke University Library
Durham, North Carolina

Frank Lloyd Wright (1867–1959)

Frank Lloyd Wright is perhaps the only architect whose name is a household word in America. The genius of his work is the foundation for his unquestioned position; but it was his unconventional life-style, his writings, and the media that created his almost movie-star reknown within American culture. Although his concerns were much broader and escape easy formulas, two architectural concepts have become associated with his work: continuous space and organic architecture.

Of primary concern to Wright was the creation of an abstract interior space whose form was derived from the nature of the human action it was to serve and from the desire to create, in Wright's words, "space the continual becoming. . . ." Wright's spaces are flowing, continuous, and expressed on the exterior through a sculptural massing of the whole. In *The Natural House* of 1954 Wright explained that in the first decade of the 20th century he made his first protest "against the building coming up at you from the outside as an enclosure." He went on to explain that he discovered the parallel to this idea in oriental thinking and quotes Okakura Kakurzo's *The Book of Tea*, "The reality of a room was to be found in the space enclosed by the roof and walls, not in the roof and walls themselves."

The ideal for Wright was the integration of structure with his sculptural form. This was not always achievable, but when space and structure were integrated, it produced what he called an "organic" architecture. Wright's organic architecture has been defined by Vincent Scully: "He [Wright] clearly believed that, when a building built by men to serve a specifically human purpose not only celebrated that purpose in its visible forms but became an integrated structure as well, it then took on the character of an organism which existed according to its own complete and balanced laws. In this way, it dignified by its wholeness and integrity the purely human intellect and the hand which had created it."

Wright's first great architectural innovation, where his approach to architecture came to maturity, was the development of the Prairie Houses. These houses, expressive of the flat Midwestern land where they were built, received their name from the publication of one of the earliest examples of the type in *The Ladies' Home Journal* of 1901 in an article entitled "A Home in a Prairie Town." The centrifugal space of these houses, stressing horizontal extension, radiates from a stable core of hearth and chimney. Hovering roofs, long bands of windows, terraces, and porches extend the horizontality of the interior to the exterior in an ordered composition. Existing within this house are elements of tradition, as in the hearth, and of modernity, the Wrightian space symbolizing, as Vincent Scully has said, the essence of modern life—flux and change. Scully also sees these houses as particularly American creations and compares them with the crossroads in the prairie and with the long rafts floating under continuous skies in the 19th-century paintings of George Caleb Bingham. Gertrude Stein, who came to maturity in the same years as Wright, wrote in "The Gradual Making of the Making of Americans" that "it is something strictly American to conceive a space that is filled with moving, a space of time that is filled always filled with moving. . . ."

Contemporary with the Prairie Houses, the Larkin Building of 1904 in Buffalo was one of the most important early examples of a high degree of integration among structure, program, and form. The Larkin Building, now demolished, was conceived of as a glass-roofed core of space extending the entire height of the building around which were disposed the office floors. Encased in vertical hollow piers, stairways are grouped in the four corners of the building. The brick fabric of the structure is at once wall, space definer and space container.

The roots of Wright's approach can be found in his first 30 years. As a child he played with the educational reformer Friedrich Froebel's toys—blocks, sticks, and weaving materials —purchased by his mother at the 1876 Centennial Exposition in Philadelphia. The child was supposed to create from these elements structures and objects having a disciplined compositional order. The sense of order, integration of form and structure, and even some of the actual forms in Wright's architecture may be derived from these early experiences. He wrote in his 1932 autobiography that these patterns are "in my fingers to this day."

141

141 *Olive Hill Development, Los Angeles*
Studies for site, c. 1917
Pencil on brown wrapping paper, 15½ x 14" (39.4 x 35.6 cm)
Art Department
The City of Los Angeles
Los Angeles, California

142 *Hollyhock House, Barnsdall Park, Los Angeles*
Perspective, c. 1917
Pencil on tracing paper, 18 x 21" (45.7 x 53.3 cm)
Art Department
The City of Los Angeles
Los Angeles, California

143   *Yahara Boat Club, project, Madison, Wisconsin*
Perspective, 1902
Sepia ink, 6⅔ x 22″ (17 x 56 cm)
The Royal Institute of British Architects
London, England
144   *All Steel House, project, Los Angeles*
Perspective, 1937
Pencil, 15 x 18″ (38 x 46.5 cm)
The Royal Institute of British Architects
London, England

Wright studied engineering at the University of Wisconsin for 2 years and at this time read the work of Eugène Viollet-le-Duc (1814–1879) and John Ruskin (1819–1900). Ruskin's insistence on the realistic expression of materials and nature as inspiration for architecture impressed him, as did Viollet-le-Duc's advocacy of the direct expression of structure. Beginning his professional career in 1887 in Chicago, he was employed by James Lyman Silsbee. Silsbee designed within the Shingle Style idiom (see page 136) of the 1880s, and that style's open interior planning around a central hall with a fireplace and use of "natural materials" have great importance for Wright's Prairie Houses. After a short time Wright left to work for Louis Sullivan (page 184), or as Wright called him, "Lieber Meister." He remained with Sullivan until 1893. Sullivan was important for Wright in a variety of ways. Sullivan's unconventional background and independence of approach gave Wright confidence in his own ideals. Sullivan's own concept of organic architecture and sense of ordered, disciplined design that he had been imbued with during his 6-month study at the École des Beaux-Arts in Paris played a suggestive role in Wright's philosophy and thinking.

The first period in Wright's career, symbolized by the Prairie Houses and the formation of the ideals that characterize his entire development, ended in 1914. Due to difficulties in his personal life, World War I, and the Depression, Wright was less prolific in terms of built work from 1914 to the end of the thirties than in the preceding period. This was for him, however, a time of expansion and experimentation that included many unexecuted projects. During this period he tested out new construction methods. He pursued a new massiveness. He experimented with circles, spirals, and 30° and 60° angles. He designed large-scale developments, such as the San Marcos in the Desert project of 1927 for Chandler, Arizona, and he conceptualized schemes for skyscrapers, such as the St. Marks in the Bowery project of 1929 for New York City. In 1935 he published and exhibited his utopian Broadacre City, a vision of a decentralized suburban world laid out along the highway in which a plot of land was provided for every person. In general, then, these years show a widening of Wright's scope in terms of program, structure, and form as well as a desire to have a more comprehensive impact on society.

A new, productive period of Wright's career begins with one of his outstanding masterpieces, the Edgar Kaufmann, Sr. House of 1936–1937, Fallingwater, in Bear Run, Pennsylvania. Here the developments of the previous decades are amalgamated with his unique approach to architecture first formulated in the Prairie Houses. Important monuments of this period—such as Fallingwater, the Johnson Wax Administration Building of 1936–1939 and Laboratory of 1950 in Racine, Wisconsin, and the Solomon R. Guggenheim Museum, in New York City, first designed in 1943–1945 and built between 1956 and 1959—also reveal a consciousness of International Style developments in Europe. During this period Wright also developed his Usonian House, his answer to the problem of the low-budget dwelling.

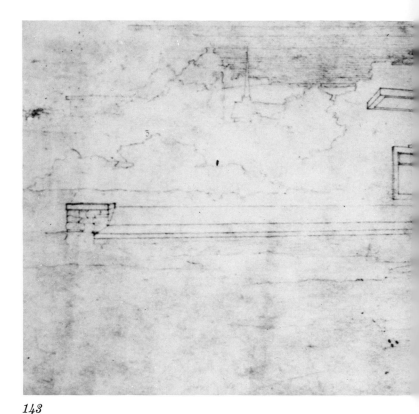

143

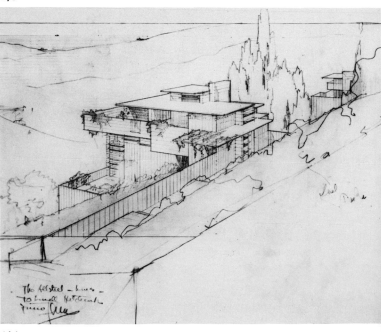

144

The Jacobs House of 1937 near Madison, Wisconsin, is the first Usonian he constructed. These houses were designed on a rectangular module with concrete floor slabs, wood sandwich walls, and a central fireplace. Their horizontal spatial extension and stabilizing hearth establish their continuity with his Prairie Houses.

The Yahara Boat Club project (143) of 1902 in Madison, Wisconsin, is one of the first designs where the gable or hip roof of Wright's earlier houses is abandoned. This results in greater emphasis on the horizontal, so powerfully developed in his Robie House of 1909. The project was published in Germany by Ernst Wasmuth in the 1910 *Ausgeführte Bauten und Entwürfe von Frank Lloyd Wright*, also known as the Wasmuth portfolio. It reached a wide audience and had an important influence on European architects, particularly the Dutch de Stijl group.

As early as 1913 Wright prepared plans for the Olive Hill Development in Los Angeles commissioned by Aline Barnsdall. The project (141), to be a cultural center and residential area for artists, included the house for Barnsdall, called the "Hollyhock House," two other individual houses, studio apartments, a theater, and stores. The project, executed in collaboration with Wright's son Lloyd (page 238) and R. M. Schindler (page 226), was carried out while Wright was involved with the Imperial Hotel and therefore spending most of his time in Japan. Schindler had an important role in the Hollyhock House and is responsible for the other two houses, the only structures realized. Lloyd Wright did the landscaping. The Hollyhock House (142) was completed by 1920 and is so named for the abstract hollyhocks that decorate the structure. The building recalls Mayan architecture in its massing. Wright could have been familiar with Mayan monuments through either published drawings or models displayed at the 1893 Chicago Columbian World's Exposition. In accordance with the requirements of the commission, the building of poured concrete is a massive form more public than domestic in scale.

In 1937 Wright designed his All Steel House (144) for a development of 100 houses. Prefabricated and with a structural steel skeleton, the house is related to the contemporary Usonian House in its use of panels and its concern with low cost, while it also recalls the Kaufmann House in its massing.

145

Lloyd Wright (b. 1890)

In 1916 Lloyd Wright, the eldest son of Frank Lloyd Wright (page 234), opened his own office as a landscape architect and architect in Los Angeles. His first constructed work was the W. J. Weber House in Los Angeles of 1921, which was formally dependent on his father's Prairie Houses of more than a decade earlier. He received no academic training in architecture, but instead learned about the profession from his father. After two years (1907–1909) at the University of Wisconsin, he joined Wright in Fiesole, Italy, and helped prepare the drawings for the famous 1910 Wasmuth portfolio, a publication of Wright's work. His professional life before the Weber House was primarily concerned with landscape architecture. He worked first for Olmstead & Olmstead in Boston and California and then began independent practice, working closely with the architect William J. Dodd in Los Angeles. Between 1916 and 1917 he was the head of the Design and Drafting Department of Paramount Studios. Both of these experiences had important consequences on his later architectural work: landscape architecture would continually be an integral part of his career, both in connection with his architectural projects and as an independent activity; his involvement with the movie industry contributed to the exceptional drama of certain designs of the 1920s and 1930s. The majority of Lloyd Wright's built work is residential, including both his independent work and collaboration on his father's commissions in California from the 1920s to the 1940s as landscape architect and construction supervisor. However, he has received highest acclaim for his Swedenborgian Memorial Chapel at Palos Verdes, California, of 1946–1971. The structure, overlooking the ocean, is conceived integrally with the redwood trees that surround it.

Throughout Lloyd Wright's career, his work has been dependent on his father's formal imagery. However, he has made forays into the Moderne and Spanish Colonial Revival of the 1920s and 1930s, the Colonial Revival of the late 1930s, and the post-war California ranch house. The distinction between buildings by Lloyd Wright, reliant on the elder Wright's vocabulary, and their models could be called one of tone. Wright molds his father's forms into structures more romantic and more dramatic than those which originally inspired them. "Romantic" is meant as the dictionary defines it: "escape from the realities of life; fanciful, fabulous and with implications of unrestrained sensuousness." The intimate integration of lush landscaping and architecture is one expression of the romance that marks his career. During the 1920s and 1930s he somewhat romantically sought to establish a connection between his work and the indigenous architecture of the Americas, particularly that of the American Indian and the Mayans. This was accomplished in part through the use of patterned and textured concrete block or stucco. The interiors of these buildings are often mysterious and cavelike.

Pauline (Schindler) Gibling perceptively discussed Wright's intentions in a 1932 issue of *Creative Arts*: "The garden is not a continuation outward of the house, but a frame or setting or else he (Lloyd Wright) draws it within the house which thereupon surrounds it as a double wall, secluding it still more deeply and mysteriously. He has a gift for monumental majesty which he however occasionally counteracts by an abundance, a richness of applied ornament which any pure functionalist—who will naturally reject all applied decoration—would find burdensome." Although Lloyd Wright was theatrical and dramatic, he was not impractical, and he was interested in developing new building materials and methods. His Hollywood Bowl Shells of 1925 and 1928 were highly successful acoustically. From the late 1950s on, Lloyd Wright produced continuously dramatic and theatrical images, drawing on, as David Gebhard has written, "the sparkling and tinsely world of Wilshire Boulevard."

The most dramatic of Lloyd Wright's houses was the Sowden House (145) of 1926 in Los Angeles. The exterior of the house was a combination of solid planar walls and pyramidal agglomerations of sculptural concrete block whose forms have been likened to soft ice cream. One enters through an opening under one of the agglomerations to the house situated around a courtyard with rows of piers and pyramidal entrances of concrete block.

Lloyd Wright assisted his father and Rudolph Schindler (page 226) during the design and construction of the Olive Hill

146

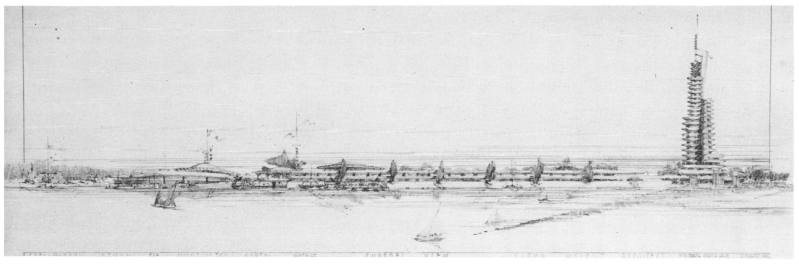

147

Development (pages 234–235) in Los Angeles for Aline Barnsdall. In 1931, subsequent to this collaboration, Lloyd Wright designed a project for a children's outdoor theater (146) at Olive Hill. In play here are the two elements that continually inform his work: integration with the landscape and reliance on his father's vocabulary. Lloyd Wright's use of the circle against the rectangle and the sharp angle recall the interests of the elder Wright.

In 1962 Lloyd Wright developed the Huntington Portal scheme (147) for a four-mile coastal strip originating at Santa Monica. Characteristic of Wright's work and of current California attitude is the intention to remake the landscape while pulling the freeway out to the ocean. The sharp geometries of the structure are characteristic of the drama of his 1960s imagery.

145   *John Sowden House, Los Angeles*
Elevation detail of column, 1926
Pencil and colored pencil, on tracing paper,
21 x 15½" (53.3 x 39.4 cm)
Collection of Lloyd Wright
Los Angeles, California

146   *Olive Hill Development, Los Angeles*
Children's Outdoor Theater, project
Perspective, 1931
Tempera on gray matte board, 16 x 34¼" (40.6 x 87 cm)
Collection of Lloyd Wright
Los Angeles, California

147   *Huntington Portal, Surfside, California*
Perspective, 1962
Blue-line print redrawn with pencil and hand colored, 28 x 49"
(71.1 x 12.4 cm)
Collection of Lloyd Wright
Los Angeles, California

1945/1976

242　148　*Guest House, Wellfleet, Massachusetts*
Site plan, section, and elevation studies, 1953–1954
Colored crayon, black ink, and pencil on buff paper
11⅝ x 17½" (29.5 x 44.4 cm)
Cooper-Hewitt Museum of Decorative Arts and Design
Smithsonian Institution
New York, New York

149　*Serge Chermayeff's Studio, Wellfleet, Massachusetts*
Elevations and perspectives, 1953–1954
Colored crayon, ink on buff paper, 13¾ x 16¾" (34.9 x 42.5 cm)
Cooper-Hewitt Museum of Decorative Arts and Design
Smithsonian Institution
New York, New York

Serge Chermayeff (b. 1900)

Born in Russia in 1900, Serge Chermayeff emigrated to England in 1910, where he studied architecture between 1922 and 1925. His work in England gave that country some of its first International Style buildings and included collaboration with Erich Mendelsohn (1887–1953) between 1933 and 1936, most notably on the De La Warr Pavilion at Bexhill of 1935. In 1942, he emigrated with his family to America, where he continued architectural practice and for the next 27 years made an outstanding contribution to American architectural education, teaching at Brooklyn College, 1942–1946; the Institute of Design in Chicago, of which he was president and director, 1947–1951; Harvard University, 1953–1962; and Yale University, 1963–1969.

In *Community and Privacy* of 1963, which he wrote with Christopher Alexander, the authors develop criteria for urban housing that respond to problems of high-density living, with primary importance placed on balancing individual privacy with possibilities for communal interaction, both in the family unit and on an urban scale. Chermayeff built his own house in New Haven in 1963 as a prototypical model of the book's conclusions. The house is arranged as a grouping of one-story pavilions around courts, making a physical separation between communal functions and private ones. This prototype courtyard house can be arranged in several configurations to fit within an urban block structure. This book and the prototype made an important contribution to the acceptance of low-rise housing as a solution for the high-density urban situations.

Chermayeff's and Alexander Tzonis' *The Shape of Community* of 1971 is an attempt to provide a theoretical model for future and contemporary urban design. A basic premise of the book is that the community requires public gathering places for communal interaction and that because movement and communication networks are the most dominant features in contemporary urban life, these should be so designed as to foster social interactions.

Chermayeff's built work in the United States is largely for domestic programs. Functional planning, response to special environmental conditions, and use of simple materials characterize the houses. His own studio (149) and guest house (148) of 1953, both built on Cape Cod at Wellfleet, are according to Chermayeff, related in principle to vernacular Cape Cod houses. His houses, like those of the New England vernacular, are made of simple, easily available materials: stock siding, lumber, fiberboard, windows, and doors. The houses are divided into 8-foot/24.5-meter bays; "bow-tie" trusses of 2- by 10-foot/6- by 31-meter wooden members support the roof. Exterior walls are glazed, enclosed with fiberboard panels, painted in primary colors, or are left open. Wind bracing of 1- by 4-foot/3- by 12-meter members is clearly exposed. This use of clearly articulated repetitive members reveals an attitude toward building that Chermayeff admired in his writing on the work of Mies van der Rohe and Konrad Wachsman.

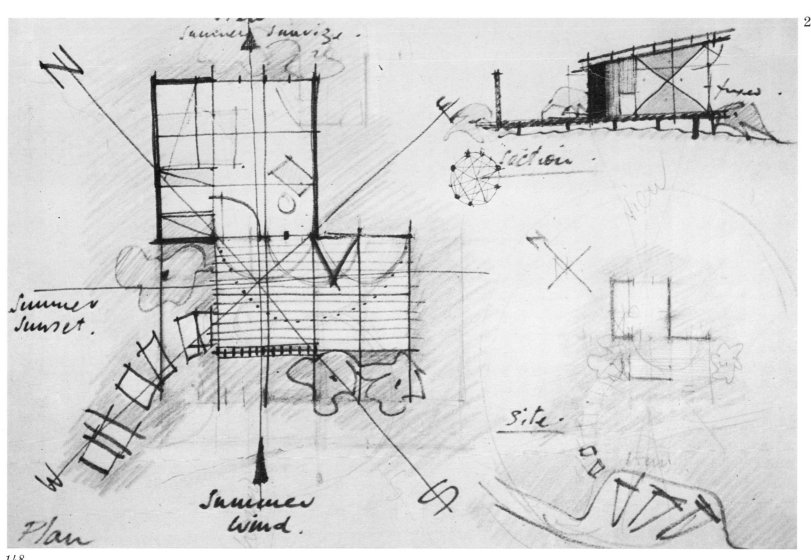

Summer sunrise.

N

Summer
Sunset.

Summer
Wind.

Plan

section.

site.

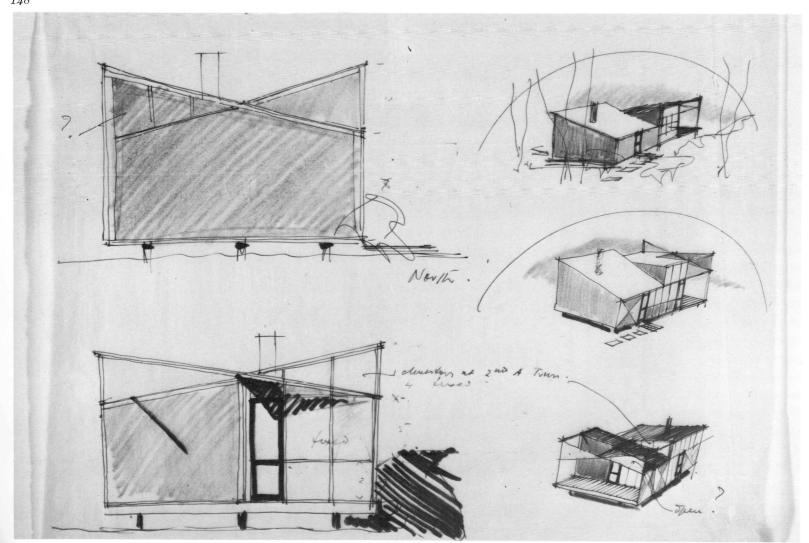

North.

elevators at 2nd & Turn.
4 lines

150

151

Charles Eames (b. 1907)

Through his technically innovative furniture designs constructed of molded wood or plastic in combination with rubber and metal produced by the Herman Miller Company; his work in prefabrication; as well as the exhibition designs and films he has made in association with his wife, Ray, Charles Eames has made an extremely important contribution to American architecture and design. Eames studied architecture at the University of Washington in St. Louis for 18 months between 1924 and 1926. Until 1937 he lived in St. Louis and was a partner in Gray & Eames from 1930 to 1935 and Eames & Walsh from 1935 to 1937. These partnerships produced primarily domestic buildings and churches. In 1937 he was made head of the Department of Experimental Design at the Cranbrook Academy of Art and began a long association with Eero Saarinen. He assisted both Eero and Eliel Saarinen (pages 284, 223) in the design of the Kleinhans Music Hall in Buffalo of 1938 and the Crow Island School at Winnetka, Illinois, in 1939.

In 1940 The Museum of Modern Art awarded Eames and Eero Saarinen first prize in the competition for the design of "Organic Furniture." The Eames/Saarinen submission was a design for a chair in which molded wood was bonded with metal. In 1942, after settling in California, the Eameses established a design studio with Gregory Ain (page 194), John Entenza, Margaret Harris, and Griswold Raetze and continued to experiment with the low-cost production of metal and laminated wood furniture. Eames also established a company with Entenza to produce plywood furniture and war supplies.

In 1945 John Entenza, the influential and creative editor of *Arts and Architecture*, initiated the Case Study House Program whose main goal was "good environment." The houses, open to the public, were conceived as low-cost prototypical dwellings with open plans for servantless families; they generally had two bedrooms and baths. Unfortunately, many of the houses were not economical due to the rising price of materials. The first six houses to be constructed, including buildings by J. R. Davidson, Richard Neutra (page 218), and William Wurster, received 368,554 visitors. Among the designers who later built Case Study Houses were Craig Ellwood (page 248), Pierre Koenig, Ralph Rapson, and Raphael Soriano. Many of the sites were landscaped by Garret Eckbo.

Case Study House 8 (150) for the Eameses and Case Study House 9 (151), both designed in 1945, are situated on adjacent lots. They were programmatic exceptions to the Case Study type. Case Study House 8 and its adjoining studio building were conceived for a married couple who worked together. The illustrated drawing represents the first scheme designed to be built off the side of a hill with a concrete retaining wall that also acted as a support for the house. The house would have been constructed of two trusses with the floor and ceiling as stiffeners, forming a box-beam, prevented from collapse by the end walls. The house as built in 1949 is a steel and glass cage, flat on the ground, with the studio separated from it by a courtyard. Most of the materials employed in the structure— the steel trusses and roofing infill panels—were not normally used in domestic design at that time but were mass-produced parts generally used in industrial buildings. Eames underlined the industrial character and separateness of the parts by painting the metal sash, flashing, and steel members gray and the stucco panels white, blue, and black. The use of prefabricated parts in house construction has precedents in American architecture of the West Coast, particularly in the use of factory windows and asbestos board in Bernard Maybeck's (page 177) First Church of Christ, Scientist of 1910–1912 in Berkeley and in a vacation cabin by Maybeck, featuring factory windows and corrugated metal roofing at Lake Tahoe. However, in both instances the industrial nature of these materials was not expressively articulated.

Case Study House 9 for John Entenza was designed in collaboration with Eero Saarinen; it was constructed in 1950 largely as first designed. Again, industrialized components were used; the structural system consisted of four steel columns in the center of the structure and others along the edge; and fiberboard steel decking forms the roof independent of walls and partitions. Structure, however, except for one column, is not expressed here as it is in the Eameses' own house. Walls are plastered, and ceilings are covered in wood.

150　*Case Study House 8, Pacific Palisades, California*
Perspective, 1945
Pen on vellum, 9 x 11¼" (22.9 x 28.6 cm)
Collection of Charles Eames
Venice, California

151　*Case Study House 9, Pacific Palisades, California*
Perspective, 1945
Pen on vellum, 9 x 11¼" (22.9 x 28.6 cm)
Collection of Charles Eames
Venice, California

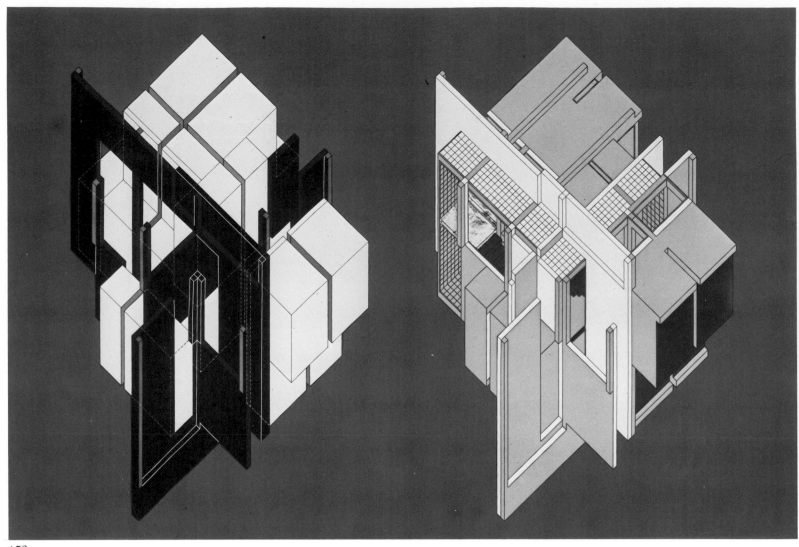

152

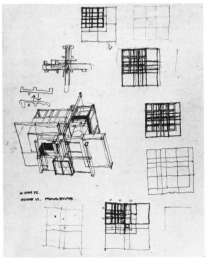

154

Peter Eisenman (b. 1932)

In Peter Eisenman's professional activity, architectural criticism and theory have been integral with the production of built form. In the 1960s he developed a theory of architecture antithetical to most modernist theory. Initially published in a cohesive manner in *Five Architects* of 1972, Eisenman's writing and polemical buildings have placed him in the forefront of the architectural dialogue of the last decade.

Eisenman has developed an architectural theory that divorces the building and its conceptualization from traditional cultural and pragmatic concerns. He is interested in exploring the inherent nature of architecture divorced from the specificity of program. The nature of plane, line or column, and volume is of primary concern as is the relationship among these elements. This relationship is organized by a rule system, which Eisenman, to borrow an analog from linguistic theory, has called "deep structure." Eisenman, profoundly influenced by linguistic theory, has vigorously maintained that architecture is a language whose surface variations, as those in language, are dominated by an underlying structure.

Eisenman's explorations are dependent on 20th-century technology, in which non-load-bearing walls free the architect from formal limitations imposed by physical requirements. He has explained this and his consistent use of a structural grid: ". . . modern technology provided architecture with a new means for conceiving space . . . in a sense, space was no longer necessarily limited or defined by structure, and this was especially true with respect to the use of the load-bearing wall; the column became both the primary structural and the primary formal element. With a diminishing of these structural constants, it was possible to examine the column and the wall in a capacity other than in the solution of pragmatic problems . . Le Corbusier's Maison Domino was paradigmatic in this respect."

To concentrate attention on his formal investigations, Eisenman has adapted a revision of the International Style that he calls "cardboard architecture." The modernist work of the 1920s and

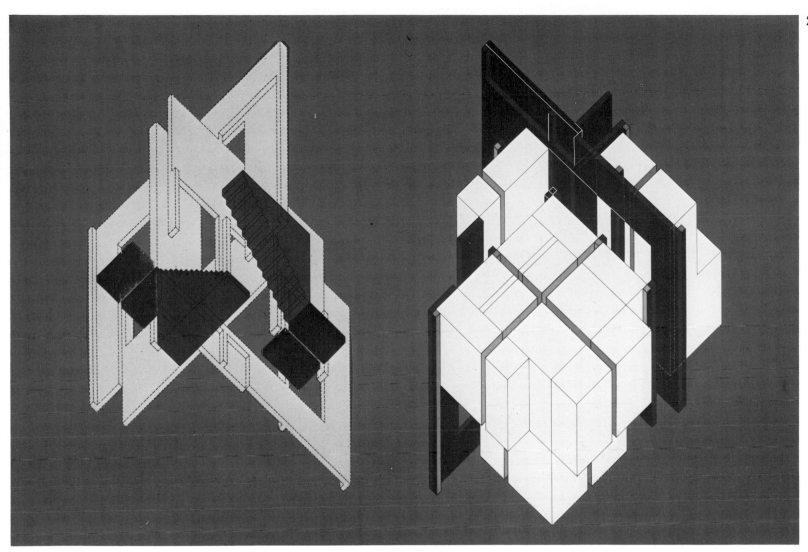

153

1930s of Le Corbusier (1887–1965) and Giuseppe Terragni (1904–1942) have been inspirational in the development of Eisenman's formal vocabulary. His buildings, white or white and gray with the addition of a limited use of primary colors more recently, have the feeling of cardboard models. This results not only from their color but more importantly from the visual suppression of all structural detailing, the uniform texture of the walls, and the shallow interior space. Eisenman has written that "cardboard is connotative of less mass, less texture, less color, and ultimately less concern for these. It is closest to the abstract idea of plane." It is Eisenman's intention that the "deep structure," although not explicitly apparent, would be apprehended by the viewer, thereby intensifying the viewer's understanding of architectural space.

Peter Eisenman is Director of the Institute for Architecture and Urban Studies (IAUS) in New York City. In 1973 the first issue of the journal *Oppositions* was published by the IAUS with Peter Eisenman, Kenneth Frampton, and Mario Gandelsonas as its editors. Both the IAUS and *Oppositions* have played a crucial role in maintaining a high level of theoretical and critical dialogue in this country. Eisenman has taught at Princeton University and Cooper Union and has collaborated on several important urban design projects, including a 3-year study of the urban street commissioned by the U.S. Department of Housing and Urban Development and the development of a low-rise/high-density housing prototype for the New York State Urban Development Corporation. The results of the latter study were exhibited at the Museum of Modern Art in 1973 and were published as *Another Chance for Housing: Low Rise Alternatives*.

Peter Eisenman's houses are numbered consecutively to eliminate cultural associations and stress the abstract concerns of the architect. The Frank House (152, 153, 154), built for an architectural historian and her husband in Cornwall, Connecticut, is House VI and was completed in 1976. Of essential importance to Eisenman is the process by which the final form of the house is arrived at. The building, or final design, is but a by-product of a conceptualization that is developed in conjunction with writing and a large number of complicated drawings. His means of representation, other than the small study sketch, is the axonometric perspective. The four axonometrics illustrated here are part of a 15-unit sequence that explicates the generative ideas of the house. The form of the house is organized around two grids of unequal size formulated by a module. They are locked together by a double cruciform defined by cross planes. The arms of the cross are shifted from their normal configuration, resulting in the phenomenon of "sheer." Terms such as "sheer" or "compression" and "tension," also important in Eisenman's work, are used by him as abstract conceptualizations of statics. An overriding concern that informs the structure is that of dialectic. The dialectic is established between such notions as inside and outside or up and down. The latter is most explicitly stated by the stairway situated beneath an upside-down stairway. To emphasize this dialectic the upside-down stairway is painted the primary color red, while the real stairway is painted its complement, green.

152　*Frank House, Cornwall, Connecticut*
Two axonometrics, 1973
Tape, ink, and Zipatone, 20 x 24" (50.8 x 61 cm)
Collection of Suzanne and Richard Frank
New York, New York

153　*Frank House, Cornwall, Connecticut*
Two axonometrics, 1973
Tape, ink and Zipatone, 20 x 24" (50.8 x 61 cm)
Collection of Suzanne and Richard Frank
New York, New York

154　*Frank House, Cornwall, Connecticut*
Studies, 1972
Ink, 10 x 8" (25.4 x 20.3 cm)
Collection of Peter Eisenman
New York, New York

155

155 Art Center School, Pasadena, California
Perspective, 1975
Black ink on tracing paper, 13¼ x 18" (33.7 x 45.7 cm)
Collection of Craig Ellwood
Los Angeles, California

156 Security Pacific National Bank, Los Angeles, California
Aerial view, 1973
Ink, 18 x 22½ (45.7 x 57.2)
Collection of Craig Ellwood
Los Angeles, California

Craig Ellwood (b. 1922)

Craig Ellwood forged a new and elegant approach to
architecture in California in the decade after World War II. It
was dependent on industrialized elements available in catalogs
—the boards and battens of American 20th-century industrial
building. Yet the elements he employed had not been used
extensively by other architects. Ellwood's work was in direct
contrast with the prevailing woodsy, West Coast style.
Ellwood's mature work combines a sophisticated use of
industrialized materials with modular planning and strict
geometries. The industrialized elements are manipulated to
create an architecture based on the opposition between clearly
expressed steel structural cage and panel infill of various
materials. This esthetic is consistent with Ellwood's statement
that "great architecture is primarily technique." Ellwood's work
is not, however, coldly technological; a richness exists that is
derived from varieties of texture and color. By constructing
walls of a variety of translucent and transparent materials, they
function as manipulators of light, allowing a somewhat romantic
mechanization to take command. Ellwood's approach,
particularly from the late 1950s on, has been especially
influenced by Mies van der Rohe (page 214). Yet, as Esther
McCoy has written, "Mies van der Rohe's Barcelona Pavilion of
1929 and later his Farnsworth House of 1950 were the most
honored precedents, but the catalogs were the law givers."

Born in Clarendon, Texas, in 1922, Craig Ellwood charted his
own education outside traditional architectural institutions.
After a tour of duty in the U.S. Air Force, his fascination with
advances in building technology led him to work as a cost
estimator, draftsman, and construction supervisor in the office
of an outstanding Los Angeles contractor. Here he was involved
with the buildings of Charles Eames (page 244), Harwell
Hamilton Harris (page 204), Richard J. Neutra (page 218), and
Eero Saarinen (page 284). From 1946 to 1949 Ellwood
codesigned two houses and three apartment buildings with
the contractor. After opening his own office in 1948, he
supplemented his work experience by studying structural
engineering at night at UCLA for five years.

Ellwood's sophisticated comprehension of steel technology enabled him to construct his first steel-framed house at the age of 29. Begun in 1949, the Hale House contained all the structural trademarks of Ellwood's early work. Exposed H-columns contrasted with wood beams, while doors and windows are expressed at full ceiling height. The finely detailed steel framework emphasized Ellwood's structural discipline. The nonstructural infill panels clearly contrasted with the expressed structure. His 8-foot module suggested a scale more industrial than residential.

Ellwood became the first architect under 30 years old to participate in the Case Study program sponsored by the magazine *Arts and Architecture* (see page 244). His first Case Study House, #16, of 1951–1952 continued the differentiation between infill panels (in wood or brick) and interior planes from the structural frame (2½-inch square tubes). Ellwood's two other Case Study Houses, #17 of 1955 and #18 of 1957, employed all prefabricated components. Case Study House #18 demonstrated a closer knowledge of Mies, whom Ellwood discovered as late as 1956. The Rosen House of 1963 in West Los Angeles followed the Miesian spirit, yet innovated in perfected details (such as the introduction of web stiffeners at the intersection of the roof beams and wide-flange columns). The plan formulated on a square grid with a central square as an atrium is dependent on Andrea Palladio's Villa Rotonda begun c. 1550 as much as on Mies's 1951 Fifty by Fifty project. Like Mies, landscape and structure are separated and not integrated in a romantic fashion.

Large-scale projects enabled Ellwood to activate the full power of steel. His first use of a steel truss in his courtyard apartments of 1953 in Hollywood garnered him a first prize at the International Exhibition of Architecture at São Paulo (with Alvar Aalto, Le Corbusier, Walter Gropius, and José Luis Sert among the jurors). Ellwood's preoccupation with simplification as well as low-construction costs continued in his larger projects. His first major commercial structure, the South Bay Bank of 1957 at Manhattan Beach, California, was innovative in its introduction of aluminum grilles as sun screens and incorporated concrete block as infill panels and wireglass on the roof canopy. In the Security Pacific National Bank (156) in Hollywood of 1973 Ellwood explores the triangular plan, a form in harmony with the structural system of the roof. Ellwood's large commercial projects also include the Scientific Data Systems complex of 1966 (where the frame and walls were constructed simultaneously, since the trusses rest on columns outside the perimeter walls) and the Acme-Arcadia Building project of 1960–1961 (where the frame was to be composed entirely of aluminum parts).

The Pasadena Art Center College of Design (155) completed in 1976 on a steeply folded hillside is conceived as a long spine that includes a 192-foot bridge over a ravine housing the library and administrative offices. The minimalist Miesian esthetic is formed from an exposed steel truss with opaque gray insulated panels and glass panels set into the frame. The building as bridge over a canyon was earlier developed by Ellwood in a 1963 scheme for a weekend house, which was also designed as an exposed truss.

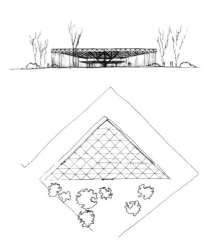

157 *Residence, Tuolumne River, California*
Elevation, 1976
Magic marker on tracing paper, 14 x 38" (35.6 x 96.5 cm)
Collection of Joseph Esherick
San Francisco, California

158 *Demonstration House, Sea Ranch, California*
Section, c. 1963
Ink, 12 x 18" (30.5 x 45.7 cm)
Collection of Joseph Esherick
San Francisco, California

Joseph Esherick (b. 1914)

During the last 25 years Joseph Esherick has played an important role in strengthening and continuing what has become known as the "Bay Area tradition" of San Francisco. This tradition, with its beginnings in the late 19th century, includes the work of such architects as Ernest Coxhead (page 154), Bernard Maybeck (page 176), and Julia Morgan (page 180). It depends on the use of wood and other natural materials and a massing reminiscent of vernacular architecture to suggest an anti-urban image. Esherick's interpretation of this tradition includes sculpturally expressive wood detailing, sensitive manipulation of space in the vertical dimension, and a highly sophisticated approach to the modulation of light. Esherick's approach to design development has been distinguished by particularly close and thorough consultation with his client.

Esherick was born in Philadelphia, the son of an engineer. His uncle, Wharton Esherick, a sculptor, cabinetmaker, and friend and occasional collaborator of George Howe (page 210) and Louis Kahn (page 268), was a major influence in Joseph Esherick's development. Wharton Esherick encouraged his nephew to draw and construct furniture from the time he was 12, and the uncle's direct and natural handcrafted solutions to design problems affected Esherick deeply. In 1937 Esherick graduated from the University of Pennsylvania School of Architecture, an institution deeply entrenched with Beaux-Arts values. At Pennsylvania he studied with Paul Cret (page 200) among others. After graduation Esherick spent 6 months in Europe and on his return worked briefly for George Howe in Philadelphia and then for Walter T. Steilberg in San Francisco. Steilberg, a structural engineer and Julia Morgan's former head draftsman, introduced him to the woodsy-crafted traditions of the Bay Area. Rural, vernacular architecture, specifically barns, became an abiding interest for Esherick from this point on. Following his employment with Steilberg, he worked for Gardner A. Dailey in San Francisco and was especially involved with the design of the Owens House and the Coyote Point Training School of 1942–1943, which emphasized modular wood frame construction. Esherick's experience in the Dailey office confirmed his belief in the validity and clarity of repeated, modular construction and prefabrication. After duty in the Navy he opened his own office in 1945 in San Francisco.

His early houses reflected Dailey's influence in their insistent verticality, coupled with elongated window punctures. In his own house at Ross of 1946, Esherick explored the problem of "packing the box," a theme that continued to preoccupy him, along with the challenge of "packing the triangle." He compressed a hierarchically ranked series of interpenetrating single- and double-height spaces into the tight rectangle. By virtue of its double height the living room attained the greatest volume. Esherick set windows flush with room corners and juxtaposed large glass panes to activate an interplay of light and shadow. Designed with Rebecca Woods Esherick in 1950, his second home in Kentfield was inspired by the rural, vernacular image of the California barn. A 1957 house in Kentwoodlands was derived more from the East Coast Shingle Style of McKim, Mead, & White than the West Coast craftsman legacy. In the Cary House of 1960 in Mill Valley, Esherick masterfully exploits light in its esthetic dimension, and by the placement of windows each responds to the specific nature of the view beyond it. Esherick has also executed outstanding townhouses in San Francisco.

In some instances in more recent years Esherick's domestic work has taken on the image of the California ranch house, as in the residence (157) of 1976 at Tuolumne River, California. Esherick has also been involved with MLTW Associates (page 274) and the landscape architect, Lawrence Halprin, in the design of the Sea Ranch development at Sea Ranch, California. Here Esherick designed individual houses whereas MLTW was responsible for condominium units as well as several individual houses and an athletic club. Esherick's designs at Sea Ranch (158), including the Hedgerow House c. 1963, have shed roofs to deflect the winds and are sheathed in redwood. Like MLTW's solution, Esherick creates an image of the vernacular 19th-century and early 20th-century architecture that existed in this region.

While Esherick's office has been extremely influential in the area of residential design, his practice became diversified in the late 1950s. His university commissions included the Adlai

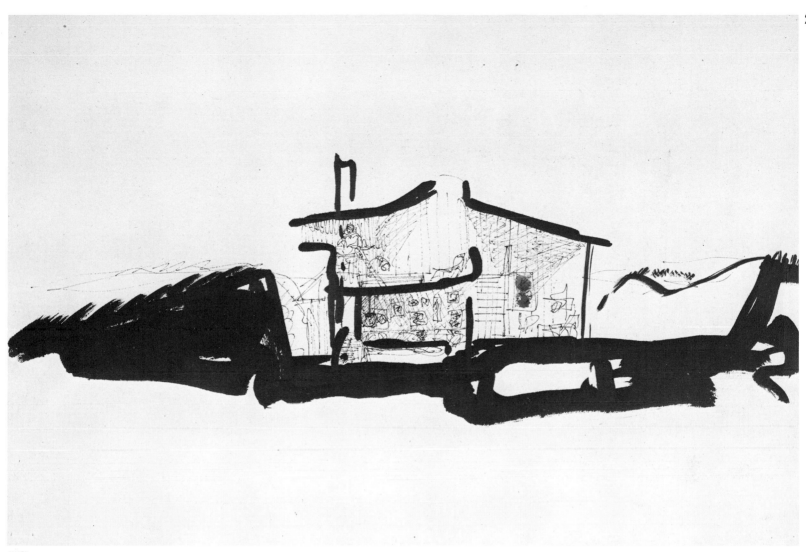

157

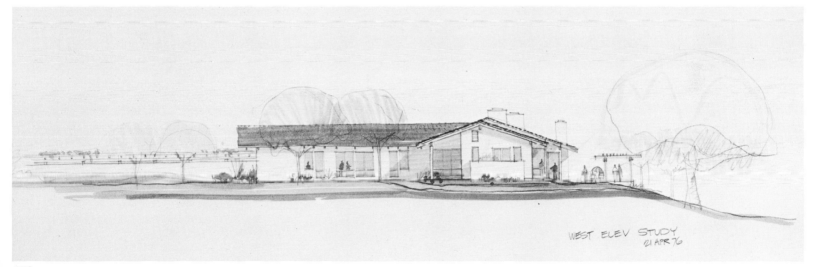

WEST ELEV STUDY
21 APR 76

158

Stevenson College of the University of California at Santa Cruz
of 1966, where the unit plans varied from floor to floor, and
Wurster Hall at the University of California at Berkeley in
1964, with modular concrete construction and exposed services.
Another of his well-known works is The Cannery, a vertical
shopping center in San Francisco of 1968 that was converted
from a cannery. Since 1972 Esherick's firm has been called
Esherick, Homsey, Dodge, & Davis. Having taught at the
University of California at Berkeley since 1952, he has been
active as a full professor there since 1958.

159 *Jungian Institute, Los Angeles*
Study, 1976
Pen, 14 x 8½" (35.6 x 21.6 cm)
Collection of Frank O. Gehry
Santa Monica, California

160 *Ron Davis Residence, Malibu, California*
Perspective, 1975
Graphite, 24 x 45" (61 x 114.3 cm)
Collection of Frank O. Gehry
Santa Monica, California

161 *Gemini Lithography Workshop, Los Angeles, California*
Elevation, 1975
Graphite, 24 x 45" (61 x 114.3 cm)
Collection of Frank O. Gehry
Santa Monica, California

159

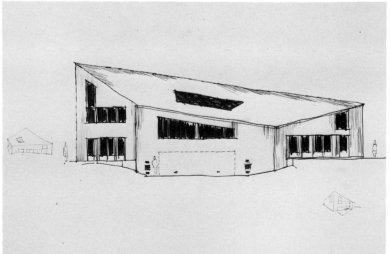

160

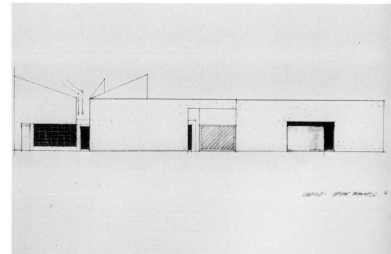

161

Frank O. Gehry (b. 1929)

Of enduring interest to architects since the beginning of the Modern Movement has been the use of prefabricated stock building components to create an industrialized esthetic. In America it was only after World War II that this interest was actualized in High Art buildings. During the 1950s in California Charles Eames (page 244) employed "off-the-shelf" elements to create an elegant Miesian esthetic within a residential program. During the 1960s and into the 1970s stock industrial materials have been of continuing interest. The esthetic appeal, however, is through the exaggeration of the industrialized nature of the materials to create a pop image. In the United States this has characterized some of the work of Hardy Holzman & Pfeiffer Associates (page 264) and in Europe that of the English group Archigram.

Frank Gehry, who also employs stock industrialized materials in much of his best work, is not concerned with the symbolic content derived from the formalistic exploitation of the industrialized materials, but rather with the intellectual concept of creating an architecture that employs materials used by the society at large and that is inexpensive and unpretentious. He has called this "cheapskate architecture." His highly publicized, durable, cardboard furniture designed in the late 1960s is consistent with these attitudes. In spite of sophisticated formal manipulations that inform some of his best work—such as the house for the graphic designer Louis Danziger in Los Angeles of 1966, the Gemini Studios of 1975 in Los Angeles, and the Ron Davis House of 1972–1976 in Malibu, California—Gehry's building seems a part of the vernacular contractor-built architecture of southern California. This is the result of not only the massing and siting but the materials used: in the Davis house metal paneling and in the other two structures stuccoed facades. One could broadly term Gehry's work of this ilk an ecological approach to architecture. It is materialistically ecological in that it utilizes materials already produced by society; it is visually ecological in that it is in visual harmony with its environment.

The Ron Davis House (160) of 1972–1976 is a large—as big as four typical California tract houses—trapezoidal space, set on a 3¼-acre site in the Malibu hills. The building is constructed of corrugated, galvanized, unpainted metal paneling. Its sloping roof changes from a 30- to a 15-foot elevation from the ground. Of primary concern to Gehry here and in much of his work is that of functional flexibility. As first constructed, the building contains several living platforms and a spine in its center with bathrooms and storage space. During two successive stages in the building's development, additional platforms and a bridge connecting them were constructed to respond to the artist's changing needs. The second determinant of the design is its relationship to Ron Davis's paintings, which are particularly concerned with studying perspective and trompe l'oeil spatial effects. The interior trapezoidal shape creates a feeling of forced perspective and an illusion that the form is a rectangle. The parallelogram windows and skylight create interesting interior geometric patterns and frame striking views of the exterior.

Illusion plays a role in the relationship of the building to the landscape. The site is on a curving street. As one drives toward the house, one has a view of the building as a very thin form. As one continues toward the building, the roof and the building are revealed as the complex form it is. From one location, as studied in the illustrated drawing, all three sides are visible at once.

In 1975 Gehry remodeled the Gemini Lithography Workshop (161) in Los Angeles after a fire. Gehry's major task was to create a unifying facade connecting the older and newer sections that were separated by a courtyard. By constructing a noncontinuous facade Gehry made obvious the nature of the building as a grouping of several structures. The facade is a layer in front of the building and is symbolically related to the false fronts of the strip architecture present throughout the Los Angeles area. Illusion is also an element in this design. Set on a curved street, the facade's angled roof creates the illusion as one approaches the site from the left that the building curves with the block. Finally, Gehry incorporated into the conception of the facade the "street architecture" of a billboard, its support, and telephone wires. The building makes a strong statement, but does not compete with its environment.

In collaboration with the painter Sam Francis, Gehry prepared plans for a Jungian Institute (159) on a site in an industrial area of Los Angeles. The Institute is composed of five different groups that function independently of one another. In response to this Gehry created five different buildings to underline the structure of the organization and enclosed the complex with an 11-foot wall. This enclosure is intended to create a very direct relationship between the sky and the person within the complex. The space between the buildings was intended to be blacktopped and covered with a thin sheet of water in order to reflect the building and serve as a metaphor for the subconscious as symbolized by water in Jungian philosophy. The drawing itself is close in feeling to a child's conception of a building. It is almost as if Gehry were seeking to express archetypal structures, paralleling the Jungian concern with archetypal images.

In addition to residential structures Frank Gehry's work includes: planning projects; the design of several art exhibitions; corporate headquarters, such as the Rouse and Company Building in Columbia, Maryland, 1974; and public facilities for the arts, such as the Merriweather-Post Pavilion of Music for the Washington National Symphony, Columbia, Maryland, 1967.

Romaldo Giurgola, chief design partner with Ehrman Mitchell in Mitchell/Giurgola Architects, has had a prolific practice that has produced a number of the most distinguished buildings in America built during the last 15 years. Giurgola regards the individual building as a fragment of the environment and not as a discrete object. He has written that "As in life, complexity is a characteristic factor in architecture, the solution comes from exploration of various successive degrees of complexities thus making the environment more and more understandable." This philosophy has produced an *oeuvre* of highly complex buildings. Especially in the urban context, Giurgola's buildings respond to the various site conditions of a particular location through variation in elevations, use of materials, and section. In the clearest and most recent examples of this—the Pennsylvania Mutual Life Insurance Building in Philadelphia of 1975 and the Insurance Company of North America Building in Philadelphia of 1976—close reading of the various elevations illuminates the particularized urban context in which these buildings exist. Although Giurgola's attitudes grow out of the thinking and forms of Louis Kahn (page 269), his work and philosophy is closer to his contemporary, Robert Venturi (page 291). Mitchell/Giurgola and Venturi & Rauch are outstanding figures in what has at times been labeled the "Philadelphia School."

Giurgola, born and educated in Italy, began his practice in Philadelphia and now has offices there and in New York. Mitchell/Giurgola has been distinguished for outstanding corporate building, primarily in Philadelphia, university and institutional buildings, as well as domestic structures. In the Bicentennial year, Giurgola created a new pavilion for the Liberty Bell and a Museum of Living History, both in Philadelphia. Besides an influential practice, Giurgola's contribution extends to architectural education. Between 1954 and 1966 he taught at the University of Pennsylvania and then at Columbia University where he was chairman of the Department of Architecture.

The design of the 22-story Pennsylvania Mutual Life Insurance Company Building (162) of 1976, located adjacent to the company's original structure and facing a square behind Independence Hall, had to respond to complex parameters. The new building had to be physically connected to the preexisting building and had to respond to the low scale of old Philadelphia to the east and the tall scale of new Philadelphia to the west, situated as it is at the juncture of the two. Furthermore the new building complies with the old city lot line dimensions, 5 feet/1.5 meters closer to the street than those of today. Giurgola has kept the scale of the old city by reassembling the Egyptian Revival facade (by John Haviland and added to by Theophilus Chandler in 1902) on its original site as a false front to the first floor of the building at the old city lot line. The 22 floors of the new structure match the height of the old building, while its setbacks and cutouts respond to the elevation of the old building. A domed exhibit and observation area at the top of the building is set back from the glass facade facing the square to "announce" its existence to the public. A free-standing elevator

162   Pennsylvania Mutual Life Insurance Company Building
Philadelphia
Perspective of main elevation, 1972
Pencil, 36 x 39½" (91.4 x 100.3 cm)
Collection of Romaldo Giurgola
New York, New York

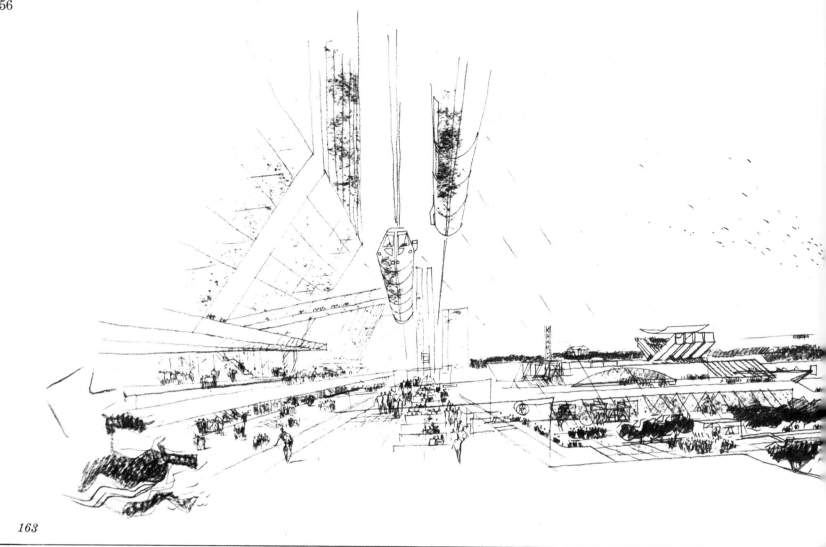

163

163   Bicentennial Exposition, project, Philadelphia
Perspective, 1971
Pencil, charcoal, and ink, 42 x 89¼" (106.7 x 226.7 cm)
Collection of Romaldo Giurgola
New York, New York

shaft that connects to this top level enhances the sense of accessibility. The building responds not only to the context of its particular site but also to the history of the tall building in Philadelphia. The precise articulation of its functional parts in response to urbanistic and programmatic considerations relates it to the Beaux-Arts rationalism and International Style constructivism of Howe & Lescaze's (page 210) Philadelphia Savings Fund Society Building of 1929–1931.

Giurgola's project for the Bicentennial Exposition grounds (163) in Philadelphia of 1971 was executed in collaboration with the planners, David Crane Associates, and was projected to be built over the railroad tracks of the Broad Street Station. The exposition site at the edge of the Schuylkill River and in direct view of the Philadelphia Museum of Art would have been connected to the rest of the city by a monorail, indicated on the left of the drawing. The terminal for the monorail is situated to the side of a large office building constructed over a garage. The site itself is terraced to the river. Temporary exhibition buildings were projected for the site and would be replaced by low-rise commercial building at the close of the exposition. The projected development of the area, adjacent to a section of Philadelphia known as Mantua, includes low-rise housing, a response to the prevailing physical context.

164

165

Bruce Goff (b. 1904)

In the 55 years since Bruce Goff built his first house in 1919, he has constructed more than 100 structures and designed almost 400 projects. Nearly half of this output is of a domestic nature and nearly every client has been, like himself, a Midwesterner. His professional training was acquired through work in architectural offices, beginning with employment with a Tulsa firm at age 12. He graduated in 1922 from Tulsa High School, which was his last contact with formal education until he began to teach at the University of Oklahoma at Norman, 1947–1955.

His professional career has been peripatetic: in 1929 he was a partner in Rush, Endicott, and Goff; in 1934 he worked with Alfonso Ianelli, the sculptor (1888–1965), who worked with Barry Byrne, Frank Lloyd Wright, and other Prairie School architects; between 1935 and 1937 he was independently employed in Chicago and also worked for the Libby-Owens Ford Company; between 1942 and 1945 he served in the Navy and after his discharge opened an office in Berkeley; between 1947 and 1955 he taught at the University of Oklahoma; from 1956 to 1964 he had an office in Frank Lloyd Wright's Price Tower in Bartlesville, Oklahoma; from 1964 to 1970 he worked in Kansas City; and in 1970 he moved to Tyler, Texas, where he continues to practice.

Goff has stated that the essential quality of modern life is change and his own work, difficult to qualify, is modeled after this. His work combines distinct geometrical units, intricate sections, involved perimeters, and mysterious effects caused by unusual uses of materials and light. The Bavinger House (166) of 1950 near Norman, Oklahoma, was Goff's strongest statement to that time of mystery and surprise—two of the most essential aspects of architecture for Goff. These qualities are discussed at length in Goff's published and unpublished writings. The house was built for a couple who partook of its construction. They required that the structure be integrated into their wooded site along a ravine and that it have an unrestrictive open plan that would provide ample space for Mr. Bavinger's horticultural hobby. The house's enclosing wall of rough masonry imbedded with glass fragments is a logarithmic spiral 96 feet/301 meters long with a height of 50 feet/150 meters at its center. An interior garden of plants with irregular pools creates the effect of a natural landscape. Soft light from roof skylights pervades the house. Sleeping areas, carpeted in gold and enclosed with fishnet, are suspended within the open space of the house by steel hooks welded to the mast at the center of the spiral. The unconventional arrangement of continuous space and complex form Goff calls an architecture of "continuous present," which he relates to Gertrude Stein's writing and Debussy's music.

The Giacomo Motor Lodge project (164) in McAlester, Oklahoma, the Viva Hotel project in Las Vegas (165), and the Black Bear Motor Lodge project in Jackson Hole, Wyoming, were all commissioned in 1961. They all succeed in providing a romantic, sensuous architecture, each particularly suited to their locale.

The Giacomo Motor Lodge in plan is a composition of regular circular units situated around the perimeter of a rectangular site. One room occupies an entire floor of each of the circles. Balconies divided by irregularly shaped stone fins divide the units and obscure the regularized plan. Goff is no structural rationalist and wrote of his attitude in 1957: "The human skeleton is a beautiful structure, but who wants to shake hands with it." Fins like those on the balconies are combined with lights and pools to create a mysterious landscape in the courtyard.

The 16-story Viva Hotel, with two levels below grade and four stories of duplexes at the top, would have been built of reinforced white concrete with quartz aggregate. It is organized around a court with a free-standing enclosed elevator shaft in its center connected to the main hotel by bridges to balconies outlined in white neon. Each typical floor is triangular with concave sides and exterior balconies with scalloped parapets. The image created is of spectacular, glamorous Vegas. Ada Louise Huxtable wrote in 1970 that this hotel is "in a style that might be called space-camp, would have raised Vegas to a creative level that its humdrum hotel caricatures have always lacked."

166

164   *Giacomo Motor Lodge, project, McAlester, Oklahoma*
Perspective, 1961
Colored pencil and pastel, 30 x 40" (76.2 x 101.6 cm)
Collection of Bruce Goff
Tyler, Texas

165   *Viva Hotel, project, Las Vegas, Nevada*
Perspective, 1961
Pencil, 40 x 40" (101.6 x 101.6 cm)
Collection of Bruce Goff
Tyler, Texas

166   *Bavinger House, Norman, Oklahoma*
Perspective, c. 1950
Colored pencil, 18 x 24" (45.7 x 61 cm)
Collection of Bruce Goff
Tyler, Texas

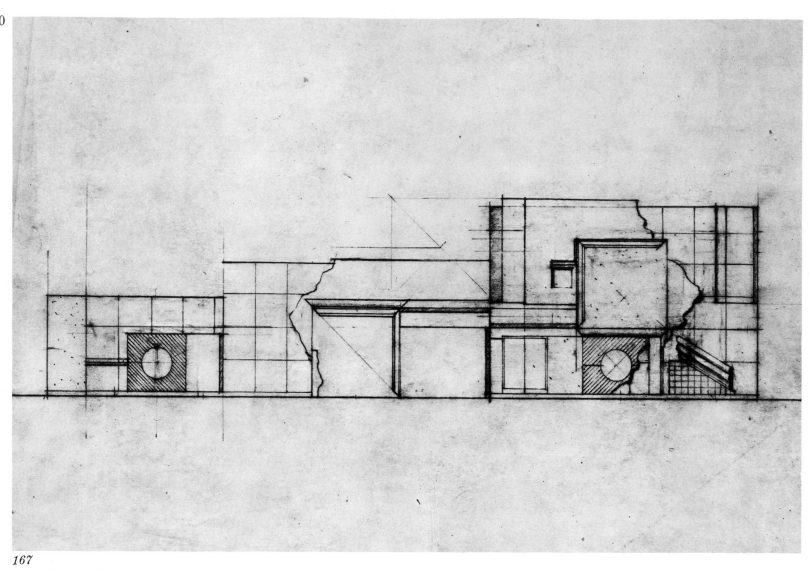

167

167 *Crooks House, Fort Wayne, Indiana*
Elevation, 1976
Pencil on tracing paper, 12 x 19" (30.5 x 48.3 cm)
Collection of Michael Graves
Princeton, New Jersey

168 *Crooks House, Fort Wayne, Indiana*
Elevation and projection studies, sketchbook, 1976
Colored pencil and ink, 8 3/16 x 5 3/4" (20.8 x 14.6 cm)
Collection of Michael Graves
Princeton, New Jersey

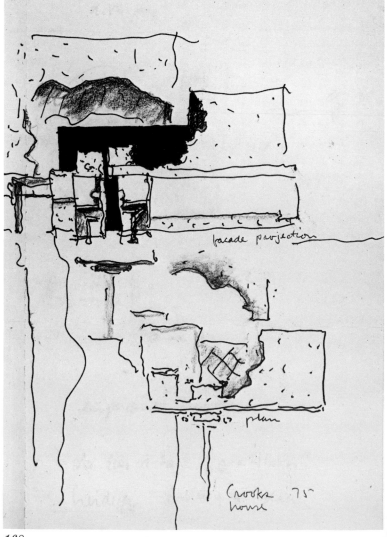

168

Michael Graves is among a group of architects who since the mid-1960s have explored the issue of an architectonic presentation of meaning, thus departing from the theoretical and formal foundations of the International Style. This reevaluation of content and form in architecture is reflected in two books on theory: Robert Venturi's *Complexity and Contradiction in Architecture* of 1966 and Christian Norberg-Schulz's *Intentions in Architecture* of 1965. The architects who, with Graves, are committed to this reevaluation differ substantially from one another both in their formal vocabularies and in the aspects of the symbolic and cultural meanings of architecture that concern them. Among these architects are Mitchell/Giurgola (page 254), Peter Eisenman (page 246), Hardy Holzman & Pfeiffer (page 264), MLTW Associates (page 274), Venturi & Rauch (page 290), and John Hejduk (page 266).

Michael Graves is particularly concerned with architecture as a language of elements—doors, windows, molding, rustication, walls, and so on—that while performing their obvious structural functions also carry symbolic meaning with which our culture has imbued them. This architectural language is seen by Graves as referring inevitably to its own past history; that is, its meaning is self-referential. Graves aims to heighten the conceptual awareness of both this architectural language and of experience in architecture. This experience consists of those ritualistic events intrinsic in one's involvement with all architecture—for example, the acts of procession, entry, and arrival. Graves physically defines these ritualistic ideas through the creation of oppositions or dialogues: the transition from public to private realms, from disorder to order; the perception of the elements of nature and the elements of building, and their transmutations from one into the other; and the idealization of the horizontal or ground plane in contrast with the more particularized vertical or wall plane. To further define the symbolic elements, Graves—who is also a painter—employs a palette of colors that suggests the elements of nature, such as sky, earth, and foliage. He also uses rustication and molding to mark the base and successive levels of a building or a space.

Graves has explored these symbolical and metaphorical notions in his built—largely residential—work and in larger projects yet to be constructed. The latter include additions and renovations to the Newark (New Jersey) Museum and the Fargo-Moorhead Cultural Center Bridge connecting North Dakota and Minnesota.

Graves' sketchbook studies for the Crooks House (168) under construction in 1976 in Fort Wayne, Indiana, present his earliest ideas for this suburban house. The program includes a courtyard, a garage connected to the house, and a well-defined garden space. In its initial form, the plan and garden elevation of the house were to be irregular in configuration, much like the edge of a torn piece of paper or of a ruin. This configuration reflects the meandering outline of the arbor vitae hedges that enclose the garden. Thus the perimeters of the house and of the garden through their interrelationship create an intimate connection between landscape and architecture. In the later stages of the design development, the plan of the house was regularized and the arbor vitae were treated as wedges of growth enclosing the exterior space. The Crooks House elevation study (167) shows the courtyard or entry wall standing between the garage on the left and the house itself on the right. A primary focus is the ritual of entry, and the facade, with its central opening, emphasizes the place and moment of entry, as well as the fact that the winding path of the driveway becomes axial and frontal at this moment. The blind window on the right is at once the physical center of the wall of the house proper and the right-hand side of a "facade within the facade"—its limits defined by the "torn" edges applied to the house and courtyard portions of this elevation. The center of this secondary facade is the corner of the house marking the plane through which one enters the house from the courtyard. The fragment of molding placed in projection on the right side of the elevation guides our attention again toward the center.

A sense of connection among the pieces of this facade is achieved by several means. The great square of the blind window is replicated in the actual opening of the courtyard entrance. Both are framed by molding at the top and one side. This framing is reversed in each element so that one completes

169   *Graves House renovation, Princeton, New Jersey*
Courtyard elevation studies, 1976
Pencil and colored pencil on tracing paper
18 x 32½" (45.7 x 83.1 cm)
Collection of Michael Graves
Princeton, New Jersey

the other. The motif of the circle in the latticed square appears on both sides of the facade. Experiments with an architectonic language are seen in the juxtapositions of elements and surfaces: the large blind window adjacent to the small actual window; the planarity of the blind window in contrast with its three-dimensional molding; the solid mass of the house against the torn edge applied to it.

Similar themes are explored in the elevation study (169) of a warehouse that Graves renovated as his own residence. The study shows three elevations of the courtyard through which one enters the house. To the existing pink stucco walls is applied metal, plywood, stucco, and tile. The windows are either clear glass or glass block. The "torn" fragment that frames one side of the entry elevation is an ideograph of the notion that the building is made of fragments: a fragment of the original structure added to new fragments of disparate materials. In the elevation on the right side, stone rustication is simulated by scored stucco and is stepped like the stairway that exists behind the wall.

This composition of collaged elements visually and symbolically emphasizes the principal entrance in the center elevation. This emphasis is accomplished in part by placing a bent plywood marquee over the doorway. At the same time, a small window at the upper corner of each of the two side elevations is placed adjacent to a double set of larger windows, establishing a focus again toward the central door. Although this focus suggests that the door is in the middle of the elevation, tension is created by the actual asymmetrical position of the door. The real center is marked by the division of the double windows that contain an ambiguity, being read as one element or two. Unity is achieved within this collage of elements through the use of color and the marking of the interior floor levels, which are uniform on the three sides.

Michael Graves received his education in architecture at the University of Cincinnati and Harvard University and spent two years in residence at the American Academy in Rome. Since 1962 he has taught at Princeton University.

169

264 Hugh Hardy (b. 1932)
Malcolm Holzman (b. 1940)
Norman Pfeiffer (b. 1940)

American, realist, pop, collage all describe the work of the firm
of Hugh Hardy, Malcolm Holzman, & Norman Pfeiffer
Associates (HHPA). The firm has made it policy that all
partners are involved in the design process. HHPA's intention
is to create an architecture expressive of both the cultural and
technological environment of the American present and of our
architectural heritage of the last 200 years. The form of their
work relies heavily on metal and plastic industrialized building
parts, the vernacular architecture of our time, in combination
with more traditional building materials.

The firm, and critics such as Stuart Cohen, term the association
of industrialized vernacular building elements with more
traditional elements and the combination of intellectual
references to present and past culture a "collage" approach.
Such an approach is realist in intent in that it is representative
of and drawn from all levels of the present. The very manner in
which HHPA's diverse forms are assembled is like that of a
collage. Buildings are generally in massing like irregular boxes.
Within this are placed smaller containers of space, with rooms,
stairs, mechanical elements clearly expressed; the space
between these elements, the residual space, becomes the public
space.

An example of this formal and intellectual collage is the Mt.
Healthy Elementary School in Columbus, Indiana, of 1972. This
open plan team-teaching school is formed of three multilevel
clusters supported by a structural grid and enclosed by two long
brick masonry walls that meet at right angles. The "rooms" are
enclosed volumes within the larger volume and are constructed
from common inexpensive industrialized materials. The two
walls that enclose the school and front the street approach are
in scale with the highway; they are over 200 feet/600 meters
long and extended beyond the limits of the angled volume they
surround. Small, square limestone-framed windows punctuate
this wall, recalling the traditional public school architecture
of America. This building is realist in that it refers to the
industrialized and material world and the highway of the 20th
century as well as to the archetypal image of "school," which
although past as a reality is still retained as part of our cultural
heritage.

HHPA have designed institutional buildings, including most
recently the Brooklyn Children's Museum of 1977, and
influential houses, such as the Hadley House of 1968 on
Martha's Vineyard, inspired by Shingle Style architecture of the
19th century. They have gained particular admiration for their
theaters, such as the Orchestra Hall of Minneapolis in 1974 and
the Robert G. Olmstead Theater at Adelphi University on Long
Island also in 1974. Their most recent work is the renovation of
the Carnegie Mansion in Manhattan for the Cooper-Hewitt
Museum of Decorative Arts and Design.

The "collaged" drawing for HHPA's addition (170) of 1976 to
Cass Gilbert's (page 164) St. Louis Art Museum is composed of
newsprint, photographs, rubber stamps, tape, and printed
transfer sheets. This technique parallels their intellectual and
formal attitude toward buildings. The Beaux-Arts building was
originally constructed for the 1904 St. Louis exposition. The
program for the addition included more permanent gallery
space, space for changing exhibitions, administrative offices, an
auditorium, cafeteria, and library. HHPA's solution was to
attach a complex of distinct interconnected volumes to one end
of the Beaux-Arts building. The new volume that is the most
public and direct connection to the old museum encloses a row of
six columns and is lit from above by skylights. A fountain is
placed in the center of this new volume, and it is appropriately
called "fountain court," making an intellectual reference to the
large courtyard, plazalike interior spaces of Beaux-Arts public
buildings.

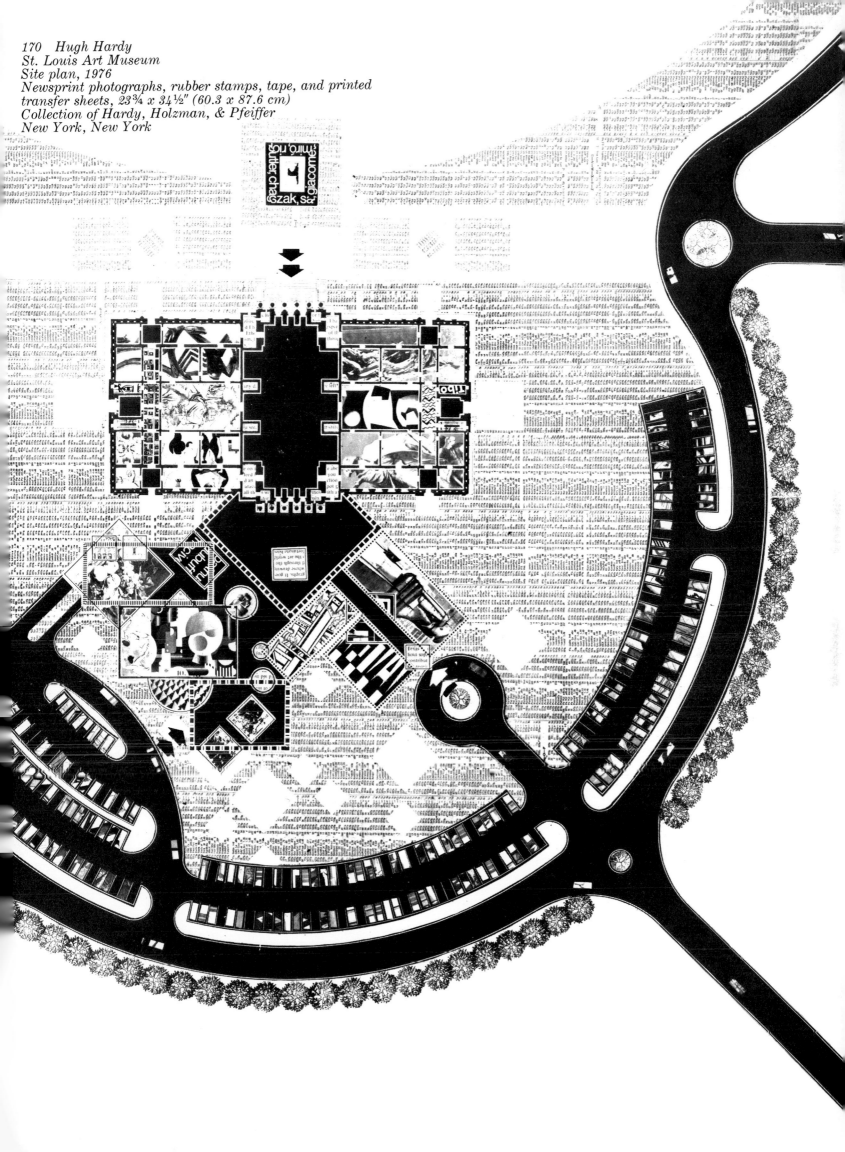

170 *Hugh Hardy*
St. Louis Art Museum
Site plan, 1976
Newsprint photographs, rubber stamps, tape, and printed
transfer sheets, 23¾ x 34½" (60.3 x 87.6 cm)
Collection of Hardy, Holzman, & Pfeiffer
New York, New York

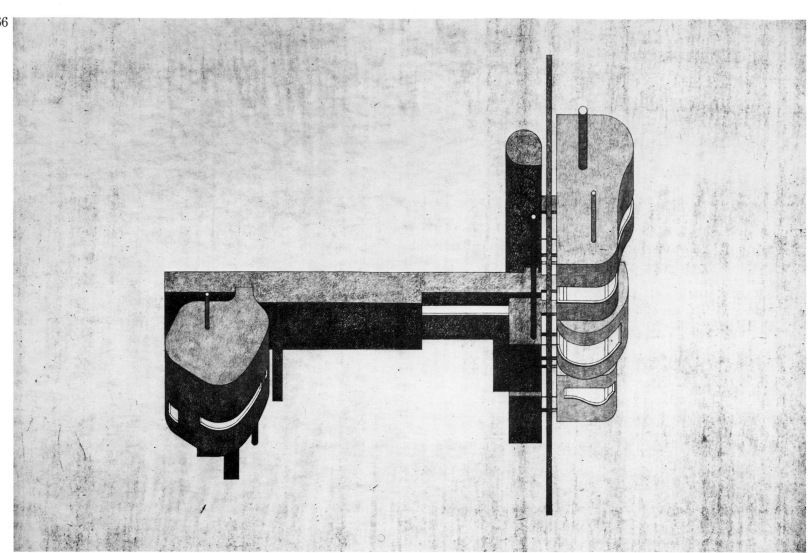

171

171　*A. E. Bye House, Ridgefield, Connecticut*
Projection, 1971
Colored pencil, 30 x 40" (76.2 x 101.6 cm)
Collection of John Hejduk
New York, New York

172　*A. E. Bye House, Ridgefield, Connecticut*
Projection, 1971
Colored pencil, 35½ x 42" (90.2 x 104.1 cm)
Collection of Ulrich Franzen
New York, New York

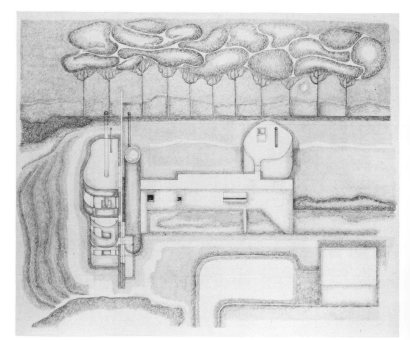

172

John Hejduk (b. 1929)

John Hejduk's highly theoretical and at times lyrical investigations into the nature of architecture have been realized largely on paper. Hejduk's most important completed project, done in collaboration with the engineer Peter Bruder, is the highly acclaimed renovation of the Foundation Building at Cooper Union built in the Italianate style in 1853 by Fred E. Peterson. Hejduk retained only the four facades of the building and the Great Hall, inserting into this envelope a columnar structural grid, to suggest a series of loftlike spaces that serve as classrooms, studios, a library, and an exhibition area. This solution executed in pristine whiteness creates a powerful dialogue between the old and the new.

Hejduk, dean of the School of Architecture at Cooper Union, has for the past twenty-odd years, dating from the time he taught at the University of Texas at Austin, continued a search for what he and others have called "first principles" in architecture. This has been a formal investigation not directly concerned with social or environmental issues. These concerns were elaborated in the catalog introduction for an exhibition of his work at the Fondation Le Corbusier in Paris in 1972. Hejduk writes: "The problems of point-line-plane-volume, the facts of square-circle-triangle, the mysteries of central-peripheral-frontal-oblique-concavity-convexity of right angle, perpendicular, perspective, the comprehension of sphere-cylinder-pyramid, the questions of structure-construction-organization, the questions of scale, position, the interest in post-lintel, wall slab, vertical-horizontal, the arguments of two dimensional-three dimensional space, the extent of a limited field, of an unlimited field, the meaning of plan, of section, of spatial expansion-spatial contraction-spatial compression-spatial tension, the direction of regulating hues of grids, the meaning of implied extension, the relationships of figure to ground, of number to proportion, of measurement to scale, of symmetry to asymmetry, of diamond to diagonal, the hidden forces, the ideas on configuration, the static with the dynamic, all these begin to take on the form of a vocabulary."

These issues have been studied by Hejduk in the context of a series of house types each linked to a specific concern of the architectural vocabulary. These concerns are easily identified by the catalog section headings from the Paris exhibition: "Column-Pier-Wall House/the relationship between form and structure; Diamond House/the edge as conflict in architectural action; Wall House and Element House/the wall as original architectural means."

The first of these investigations took form as a "nine square" problem inspired by the Palladian villas. The Renaissance prototype is itself derived from a nine-square format that is manipulated in various ways. Later this nine-square problem became an essential aspect of the pedagogical program at Cooper Union. With the diamond house series begun in 1962 a direct relationship was established between his work and cubist and de Stijl esthetics. The structure of the diamond-shaped house is formed by a square grid of columns interrupted by the perimeters of the plan. The diamond house derives from the diamond-shaped canvases of Piet Mondrian. In these paintings Mondrian created 90° relationships between the lines on the canvas, while tipping the square of the canvas 45° to the viewer's space, thus forming the diamond. Hejduk has written of this in *Three Projects*; "The formal ramifications of this action [Mondrian's tipping of the canvas] were shattering, the peripheric tensions of the edge and contours were heightened and the extension of the field was implied beyond the canvas. The ideas in this point of view were not experimented with as far as the spatial implications in architecture were concerned."

Hejduk's presentation of his interpolation of Mondrian's attitudes was his first development of a system of isometric projection related to the cubist shallow space. In this system [used from then on, as in the A. E. Bye House (171, 172)] the plan is projected upwards by means of lines parallel to the side of the plan, not at the more traditional 60° or 40° angle. The resulting form presents a stronger two-dimensional than three dimensional reading in which the building tips forward. This system is akin to the space and form of analytic cubism in that depth is suppressed and frontality is stressed.

In the middle sixties Hejduk began the wall house series. The so-called second wall house, the A. E. Bye House of 1971, will be constructed on a wooded site in Ridgefield, Connecticut. In the wall house series the traditional concept of a building as a series of rooms within an enclosed volume is altered, and rooms and circulation systems are extracted from the enclosed volume and stand as isolated objects interconnected by means of a similarly isolated circulation system. Large walls that do not enclose space but mark off location in space are major components of this system. It is mandatory to pass through these walls to gain access to the circulation system. Hejduk isolates the wall to intensify its meaning. "Life," Hejduk has written, "has to do with walls; we are continuously going in and out back and forth and through them."

In the Bye House, bedroom, kitchen, and dining area are stacked above one another. Access among them is achieved by passing through the wall that rises above these volumes and then by descending or ascending via the stairs housed in the circular, pipelike form. A long corridor, like a hollow wall, separates these spaces from the ameboid shape of the study. Each of these spaces is painted in a muted color that is symbolic of its function. The kitchen is yellow, signifying energy, the dining area green for nourishment, the bedroom black for night, the living room brown for earth, the study gray to signify the twilight one enters between reality and nonreality while in the process of reading and thought. Hejduk's *parti* constantly underlines for the occupant some of the elemental experiences in architecture. Franz Oswald writes of this in the Fondation Le Corbusier catalog: "Architecture belongs to the spheres of contemplation and action. Conflicting situations in the unstructured conditions of our environment are topics of contemplation. They contain the material for architectural dramas which are enacted within defined locations in space. Space and building are objects of architectural action."

173

173   John Olin Library, Washington University
St. Louis, Missouri
Perspective, 1956
Ink on tracing paper mounted on board
18 x 18" (45.7 x 45.7 cm)
Washington University
St. Louis, Missouri

174   John Olin Library, Washington University
St. Louis, Missouri
Plan, 1956
Ink, tracing paper on board, 20 x 30" (50.8 x 76.2 cm)
Washington University
St. Louis, Missouri

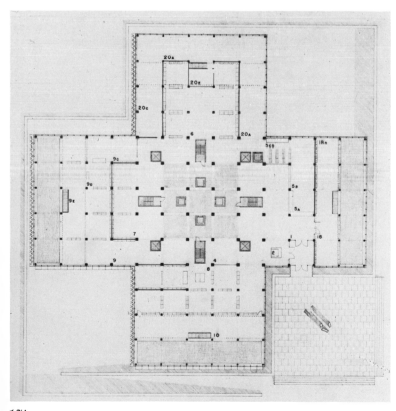

174

Louis Kahn, one of the unquestioned masters of 20th-century architecture, did not build his first important building—the Yale University Art Gallery of 1951–1953—until he was over fifty. During the two and a half decades between his graduation from the University of Pennsylvania School of Architecture with a Bachelor of Architecture in 1924 and the construction of the Yale Gallery, Kahn devoted his efforts primarily to low-cost housing, urban planning, and after 1947 teaching, first at Yale, where he remained until 1952, and then at the University of Pennsylvania, where he taught until the end of his life.

Kahn's influence as a teacher is of great importance, but it is his architecture that secured his reputation. Vincent Scully, author of the first and still the most comprehensive volume on Kahn, writes that in the late fifties he did what each artistic genius does, "he broke the pre-existing model of reality within which most of us were thinking." At this time, Kahn began to design buildings constructed of massive brick and concrete walls in which service and mechanical functions were given expression in form and in which space was made particulate by the program and physically defined by the structure. In his mature work his plans are most often composed of spaces based on a variety of pure geometric forms juxtaposed to create "enfilades," or series of interconnected but discrete rooms, often symmetrically arranged, producing a highly formalized and controlled circulation pattern. This was in contrast with the prevailing mode of International Style buildings of glass walls, hidden mechanical systems, and interior space either organized around a free or open plan or composed of closed rectangular units.

Kahn's spaces are categorized according to function to create what he called "servant and served spaces." For example, in the Trenton Bath House of 1956 mechanical services are contained within large piers that mark off space and support the roof. These are the "servant" elements, and they are juxtaposed to the public areas, the "served" spaces. Thus, Kahn establishes a hierarchical organization of space articulated by form. Other important early examples of this conception in Kahn's work are the Richards Medical Laboratories at the University of Pennsylvania of 1957–1961 and the project for the Trenton Jewish Community Center of 1954–1959.

"Parlance," as Vincent Scully describes the literal inclusion of image and symbol in architecture, does not concern Kahn's esthetics; what is of primary interest are the basic elements of building: light, walls, structure, circulation patterns, and space. This approach to architecture is similar to that of Mies van der Rohe (page 215), who was also essentially involved with a formalism derived from pure structure and the basic elements of building. Mies' mature architecture develops around two building types: the steel and glass skyscraper and the rectangular glass pavilion, which are formed by steel, transparent glass walls, and interior space with as few permanent divisions as possible, creating what Mies calls a "universal" form and space applicable to most building programs. However, in contrast with Mies, Kahn individualizes each separate building program, through the manipulation of plan and structure. This approach is directly related to his notion of servant and served spaces and is similar to that espoused by such Beaux-Arts theorists as Julien Guadet, author of *Eléments et Theories de l'Architecture* of 1902. In fact, Kahn acknowledged his debt to Beaux-Arts thinking as a source for his notion of servant and served spaces.

Kahn's connection to Beaux-Arts principles came through the Beaux-Arts approach to architectural education at the University of Pennsylvania, where he was taught by the French architect Paul Cret (page 201). Kahn was also influenced by the drawings in Auguste Choisy's *Histoire de l'Architecture* of 1899. Choisy defined materials and construction technique as the prime generator of architectural form and illustrated his ideas with isometric drawings of buildings in which detailing is suppressed. These images (Kahn did not read French) influenced not only Kahn's thinking and use of isometric projection but may also have inspired the almost scaleless, unornamented elevations of his buildings at Dacca in Bangladesh and Ahmedabad, India.

Kahn begins his design process by finding what he calls the "form" of a building, which however is without physical shape

175

175   *Penn Center Planning Project, Center City, Philadelphia*
Aerial perspective, 1956–1957
Ink on tissue, 11 x 14" (27.9 x 35.6 cm)
The Museum of Modern Art
New York, New York

176   *Second Capital of Pakistan, Dacca, East Pakistan*
Hostels, perspective, 1963
Charcoal and colored pencils on tracing paper
18 x 20" (45.1 x 50.8 cm)
The Museum of Modern Art
New York, New York

and actually is formless. Form is for Kahn "that which characterizes one existence from another." Finding the form is finding the essential character of a building. Finding the form for a specific building type such as a church would be for Kahn redefining the "essence of church." Kahn writes, "Form has nothing to do with circumstantial conditions." He explains, "The realization of what particularizes the domain of spaces good for school would lead an institution of learning to challenge the architect to awareness of what School *wants to be*, which is the same as saying what is the form, School." Once Kahn has found the form, it determines "what it (the building) wants to be" and thereby its design and physical configuration.

This method of finding form and then proceeding to the design of the actual physical form and structure is related to the notion of *parti* in the Beaux-Arts system under which Kahn was trained. The first step in the Beaux-Arts design process was the development of the *parti*, which means to take a stand or a position. It meant to find through intuition and experience the salient characteristic of a building. The *parti* is not directly connected to the specifics of construction and design. It is the dominant idea of a building.

In 1963 Kahn was commissioned to design a national assembly, supreme court, hotels, hostels for diplomats, courts, markets, and living section for Dacca, the capital of Bangladesh, on 1,000 acres of land. The drawing for the hostels (176) indicates several schemes for the elevations of these brick buildings. By creating a double wall with a space of several feet between them and cutting large openings of simple geometric shapes in the wall, Kahn said that he was attempting to let light but not glare into the buildings. These buildings are typical of Kahn's architecture of pure elemental forms, massive walls, and clearly defined space. They recall the monumental fragments of brick walls, stripped of their original facing, defining volumes and voids, of the ruins at Hadrian's Villa in Tivoli, which greatly impressed Kahn.

In 1956–1957 Kahn produced a plan for the reorganization of downtown Philadelphia, which he revised and updated in 1961–1962 under a grant from the Graham Foundation for Advanced

Studies in the Fine Arts. Kahn believed that the city should be treated at the same level of detail as a building, an idea promoted by other American Beaux-Arts trained architects such as Arnold Brunner (page 150). In Kahn's plan, Philadelphia would be "walled" or ringed by an expressway creating a rectangle around the city. Four types of traffic corridors would be established: "go" streets, with through traffic for automobiles only and without parking; "stop" streets for the staccato traffic of local buses, service vehicles, and parking; pedestrian ways for shopping areas where all traffic other than local buses is prohibited; "dock" streets only for delivery and service vehicles. Large "docks" or monumental parking garages are placed on the outer edges of the center city. The sketch for the new center city (175) indicates the large circular parking structures, which were closed on the lower level for parking, but open midway up for a shopping center to be ringed by offices and perhaps apartments. Kahn suggested a new government tower, indicated to the left of the drawing, based on his City Hall project of 1952–1953.

The entry for the John Olin Library Competition at the University of Washington (173, 174) in St. Louis of 1956, which Kahn did not win, is a building formed of discrete one-story 17-feet 4-inch/52-meter bays, each defined by the structure itself, whose stepped massing can be added to vertically if needed. The project is essentially concerned with form derived purely from structure and function. Writing about another project, Kahn could have been describing his competition entry: "If we were to train ourselves to draw as we build from the bottom up, when we do, stopping our pencil to make a mark at the joints of pouring or erecting, ornament would grow out of our love for the expressive method."

176

Richard Meier has produced a large volume of work notable for its dramatic spatial effects and great elegance. He has been associated with a group of architects, the "New York Five," which includes Peter Eisenman (page 246), Michael Graves (page 261), John Hejduk (page 266), and Charles Gwathmey. The title of this group derives from a book that they published, *Five Architects* of 1975, that discusses and illustrates their work. Richard Meier has been prolific in the area of domestic architecture and has been involved in less numerous but important institutional and corporate commissions. These include Westbeth Artists' Housing, New York City, 1970; the Olivetti Corporation Branch Office prototype design, 1970; Twin Parks North East Housing, Bronx, New York, 1969–1974; The Atheneum, New Harmony, Indiana, under construction in 1976.

Both in his domestic work, such as the Smith House, Darien, Connecticut, 1965–1967; the Shamberg Pavilion, Chappaqua, New York, 1972–1974; and the Douglas House, Harbor Springs, Michigan, 1971–1973, as well as in his institutional work, such as the Cornell University Housing, designed in 1974, Meier is concerned with the duality of private and public space. The greatest number of Meier's constructed works are residential and provide a model for his approach to this duality. In these buildings Meier characterizes these two types of space through the differentiation of materials and construction method: solid material for closure of private space and a columnar grid and glass as material for closure of public space. The primary public space in these houses is always more than one story. As a function of this Meier most often groups the smaller and closed private spaces of bedrooms, bathrooms, and related areas through a vertical layer of space adjacent to but distinct from the two-story open space. These clearly articulated polarities create a visual tension resolved by circulation spaces linking the two realms. Many of these houses command spectacular views, which Meier acknowledges by placing the public, glazed realm and often the circulation elements in a manner that takes best advantage of the site.

The concerns important to Meier in domestic work influence his public buildings, such as the Bronx Developmental Center of 1970–1976, a school for 384 retarded and mentally ill children run by the New York State Department of Mental Hygiene. The triangular site for the school is bounded by the Hutchinson River Parkway on the east and railroad tracks on the west. Because no pleasant views exist here, Meier oriented the complex containing quarters for teaching, living, and therapy around a double courtyard. The building is in part clad with natural-colored anodized aluminum and glass panels with

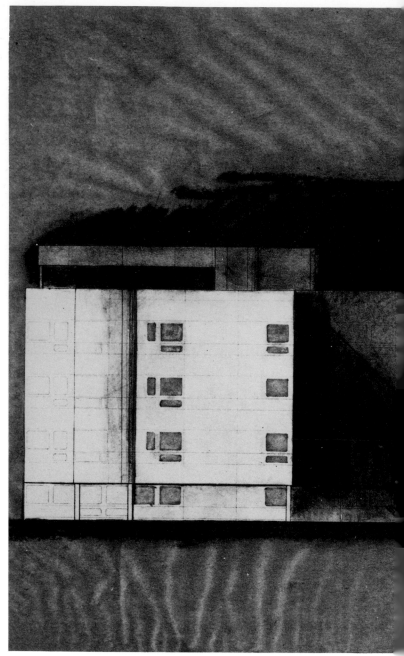

177

windows and vents punched out at the factory. This prefabricated paneling is combined with other types of fenestration and materials designed for specialized conditions and a palette of primary pastel and muted colors that include 45 hues. Meier uses three-dimensional form here like letters of a braille alphabet to provide information about the location of each of the different functions and public and private realms contained in the complex. Four L-shaped residential units— each floor contains three suites for eight people—are disposed together along one side of the courtyard (177). Small windows indicate private spaces, with larger windows indicating living rooms. Opposite this wing support facilities are placed in a slablike building. The two courtyards are filled as if with sculpture by ramps, projections from the slabs, and a small building. A plan similar in concept to the Bronx Developmental Center was used by Meier at the Monroe Developmental Center in Rochester, New York, of 1969–1974. In the earlier structure the one-story complex was oriented around three courtyards. Precedents in Meier's work for the use of prefabricated exterior paneling are in the Olivetti Corporation prototype studies and the Fredonia Health and Physical Education Building, the State University of New York at Fredonia, New York, designed in 1968.

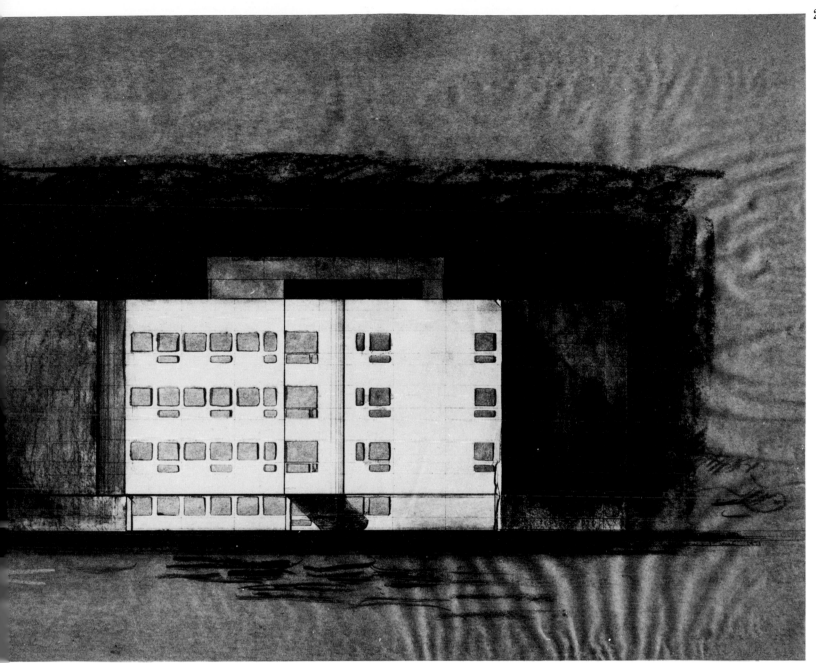

177 Bronx Developmental Center, Bronx, New York
Elevation study, 1971
Pastel on brown paper, 18 x 36" (45.7 x 91.4 cm)
Collection of Richard Meier
New York, New York

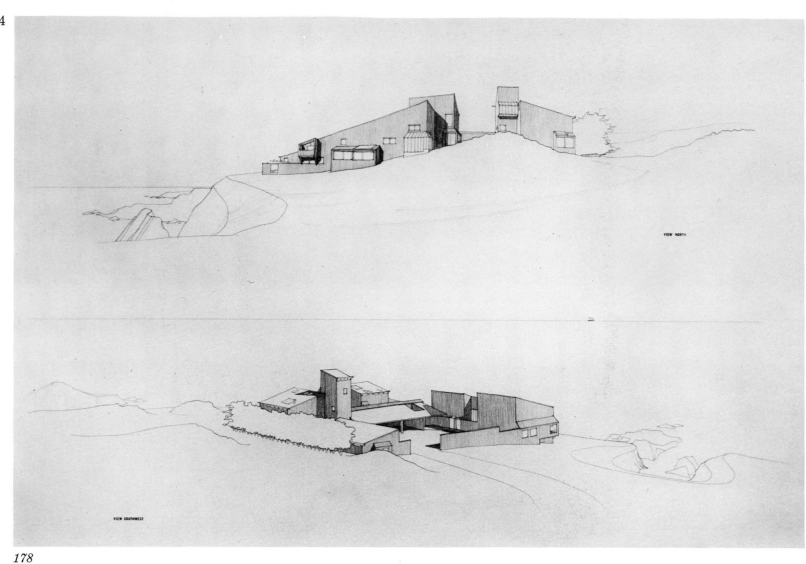

178

178   William Turnbull
Condominium, Sea Ranch, California
Two perspectives, 1964
Pencil, 30 x 42" (76.2 x 106.7 cm)
Collection of Moore, Lyndon, Turnbull, Whitaker Archives
San Francisco, California

179   William Turnbull
Talbert House, Oakland, California
Axonometric, 1962
Ink, 21½ x 26" (54.6 x 66 cm)
Collection of Moore, Lyndon, Turnbull, Whitaker Archives
San Francisco, California

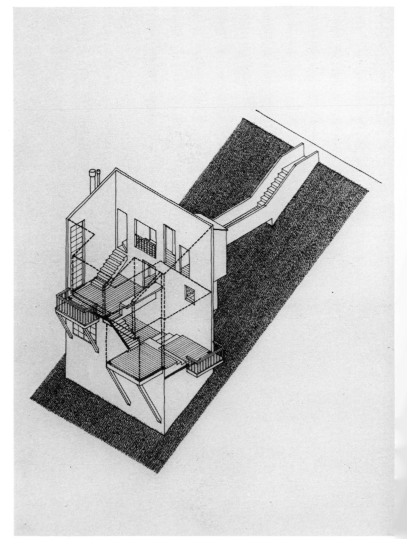

Charles W. Moore (b. 1925)
William Turnbull (b. 1935)

The partnership of Charles Moore, Donlyn Lyndon, William Turnbull, & Richard Whitaker (MLTW), formed in 1962, was centered on the West Coast. Later Moore opened an office in Connecticut, and today his principal office is in Los Angeles. In 1970 the firm became Charles Moore Associates and in 1975 Moore/Grover/Harper. MLTW work has largely been known for its domestic and university clients. The firm's work is very much a product of group design, with Turnbull and Moore executing the illustrated drawings. Moore, like Lyndon and Turnbull, studied at Princeton University where they came under the lasting influence of the strong personalities of Louis Kahn (page 269), Jean Labatut, and Enrico Peressutti. Moore received a Ph.D. in architecture at Princeton in 1957 where he wrote about the use of water in architecture. Since that period he has continued to write important articles presenting his attitude toward architecture and published *The Place of Houses* in 1974 with Gerald Allen and Donlyn Lyndon. From the early sixties Moore has been involved in architectural education, first as chairman of the Department of Architecture at the University of California at Berkeley from 1962 to 1965; and then at Yale University as chairman of the Department of Architecture from 1965 to 1969, dean of the School of Architecture from 1969 to 1971, and a professor from 1971 to 1975. He is presently a professor at UCLA and a visiting professor at Yale.

Moore has written that architecture is "territoriality" and that it is the architect's responsibility to create a sense of place "in space, time and the order of things." Of his work and that of his partners, he states: "We do not reject games, postures or the apparently arbitrary fancies and associations of those for whom we build, but rather seek to fashion from these a sensible order that will extend our own, and our users' ability to perceive and assimilate the delights and complexities of an untheoretical world." This attitude resulted in MLTW's acceptance of a broad variety of intellectual and formal sources of inspiration for their work, including high style and vernacular examples from the history of architecture as well as principles and forms of Louis Kahn. This often leads to forms or decoration, sometimes picturesque or "pop" in quality, that jar the eye while stimulating the mind.

In the last few years Turnbull and others in the firm have executed works independently from MLTW, with Turnbull designing several outstanding houses. Among them is the innovative Zimmerman House in Fairfax County, Virginia, of 1974–1975, which is surrounded by porches and ground-to-roof lattices. It is Turnbull's attitude that the architect's role is to satisfy the functional needs of a program as well as the less pragmatic desires and aspirations of the client. Turnbull's conception of this house is of "house as porch." Here the lattice provides modulated light in the house, satisfying the desires of one of the Zimmermans for a light-filled environment. The large porches respond to the other Zimmerman's reminescences of a childhood spent in a rambling house on the Maine coast.

In MLTW's large-scale planning, such as their controversial Church Street South Housing in New Haven of 1969 or their highly successful Sea Ranch in California begun in 1964, the forms of individual units are subordinated to the whole to create a sense of place for the total community. Yet the uniqueness of individual units is asserted through variations in form or the use of supergraphics that are hallmarks of much of the firm's work. Louis Kahn's sense of creating spatial order, his search for archetypal forms—"what a building wants to be" and the notion of "served" and "service" spaces—have influenced MLTW's thinking. They have devised two house types—the aediculae and "saddlebag" house, which both rely on Kahn's notion of service and served spaces. The aediculae house, as exemplified by Moore's own house in Orinda, California, of 1962, contains a central space marked off by four posts around which are disposed service and served spaces; in Moore's house this is doubled to two aediculae. Moore relates that he became interested in the type when reading in John Summerson's *Heavenly Mansions* of 1948 that medieval statues of saints were placed under four-posted aedicula and that Egyptian pharoahs renewed themselves by sitting under such structures. The primitive hut with its posts and central hearth provides another inspiration for the aediculae house. Robert Venturi's Pearson House project of 1957, organized as a series of layers of

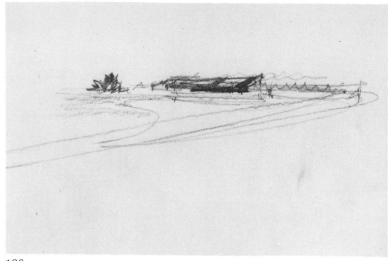

180

enclosure, provides conceptual parallels to Moore's aediculae house.

The "saddlebag" house was developed in 1961 at the Bonham Cottage on Big Sur and elaborated on in the Talbert House (179) of 1962 in Oakland. This house type contains a large central vertical space around which are hung servant spaces. The Talbert House is built on a sharply sloping site and is connected to the street by a long stairway. One enters the house on a bedroom level. A shed roof bathroom or servant space is hung out the side of this level in a "saddlebag." Stairs extend to the dining level where the kitchen is attached as a saddlebag. At the bottom of this snaking space is the fireplace and seating area. Balconies are other saddlebags, which jut out from the house on the north and south. The exterior is sheathed in painted plywood striated more frequently on the saddlebags.

The Sea Ranch Condominium development (178) of 1964 sponsored by Oceanic Properties was designed by MLTW with Lawrence Halprin as landscape architect. The office of Joseph Esherick (page 250) has also designed units there. MLTW's units have been admired and widely imitated, stimulating the growth of a new vacation vernacular all over America. MLTW's intention on Sea Ranch's 10-mile long, narrow site above the sea was to create a complex in total harmony with the idiosyncrasies of a microenvironment as studied in depth by Lawrence Halprin Associates. Ten great rooms, or houses, faced in wood siding are situated around courtyards under one sloping roof, which echoes the configuration of the land. The houses are grouped to serve as breaks against the wind and to provide views of the sea from each dwelling. The decision to group the units together creates a building in scale with the open site. The forms of the buildings, their materials, and informal siting recall the barns and small houses located there, first when it was a logging town and then when over a 50-year period it was developed for ranching.

Each condominium unit is a development of the aediculae house and is essentially one room. Almost every one contains two little houses, one a four-poster over a hearth supporting a bedchamber, which can be made private by lowering a canvas tent; the other a miniature house containing a kitchen on the lower level and in some cases a sleeping loft above. The interior furniture is finished in smooth painted wood and creates the feeling of a cabinet or doll house. Special seating and sleeping areas are conceptually outside the building's core.

As an element of the master plan of Sea Ranch, two athletic clubs with pool and tennis court were planned by MLTW and Lawrence Halprin Associates in 1966 and 1970. The illustrated site plan (181) was the first conception and is different from the constructed complex, although the relationship between tennis court and swimming pool is the same. In the completed facility the swimming pool is L-shaped and the buildings have been consolidated along one end of the site with a more complex massing.

The first scheme for the University of California Faculty Club at Santa Barbara (180), like Sea Ranch and many of MLTW's works, recalls the massing of vernacular buildings. This image, which precludes a direct and assertive association with High Style architecture, is combined in the completed Faculty Club and in the firms other buildings with complex spatial manipulations. This approach is characteristic of the "Bay Area tradition," which MLTW has strengthened in the last 15 years.

181

180   Charles W. Moore
*First scheme for the Faculty Club, University of California at
Santa Barbara*
Perspective, 1967
Pencil, 11 x 14" (27.9 x 35.6 cm)
University of California at Santa Barbara
Santa Barbara, California

181   William Turnbull
Sea Ranch Athletic Club I, Sea Ranch, California
Site plan, 1964
935 black Prismacolor pencil on tracing paper
32¾ x 42" (83.2 x 106.7 cm)
Collection of Moore, Lyndon, Turnbull, Whitaker Archives
San Francisco, California

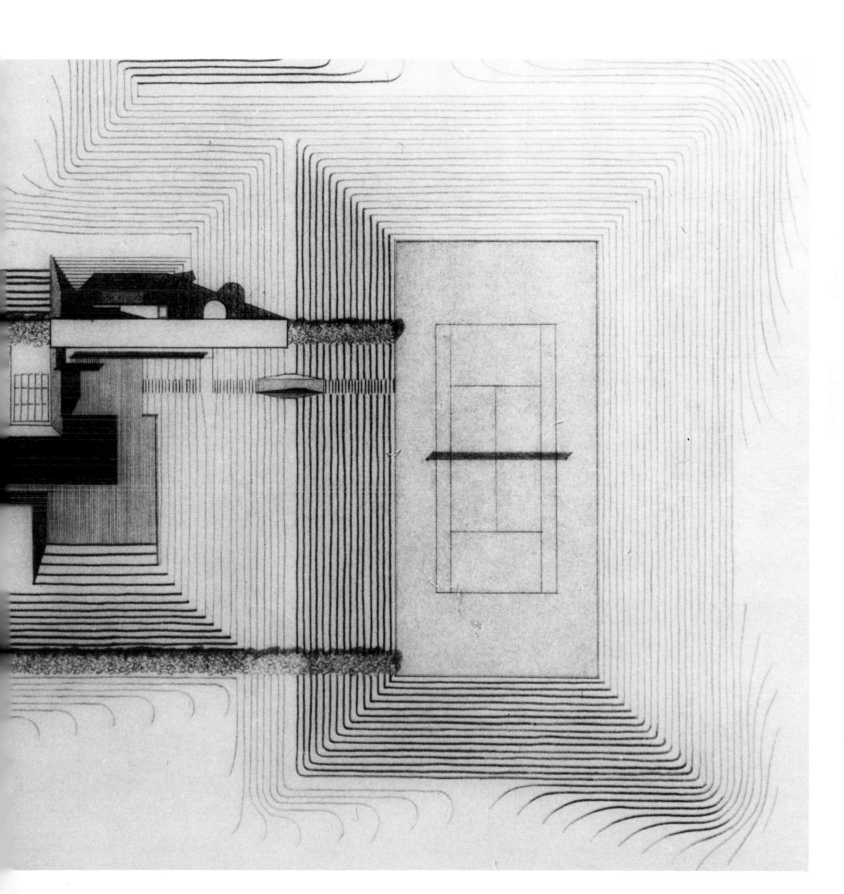

The critic Lewis Mumford wrote that Matthew Nowicki would probably have become the outstanding architect in America in the post–World War II era if he had not tragically lost his life in a plane crash while returning from India after a long *charette* on the plan of Chandigarh. Mumford was prompted to make this comment because of Nowicki's innovative and humanistic approach to planning, his imaginative and effective use of new structural techniques and his concern for architectural education during the time he taught at North Carolina State College (now the University of North Carolina) from 1948 to 1950.

Nowicki was born in Siberia where his father, a Polish diplomat, was assigned. He graduated in 1936 from the Polytechnic in Warsaw and in the same year married Stanislova Sandecka, who became his frequent collaborator and was awarded with her husband the Gold Medal for graphics at the 1937 Paris Fair. In Warsaw from 1936 to 1945 he taught at the Polytechnic; constructed several office buildings and a "Corbusian" home for his parents; was the city planner; and placed in several important competitions. In 1945 he was assigned to the Polish consulate in Chicago; from 1947 to 1949 he represented Poland on the committee for the design of the United Nations and advised Wallace K. Harrison on planning problems for its construction.

In late winter of 1950 in America, Nowicki and Alfred Mayer of Mayer & Whittlesey laid out the general scheme for Chandigarh, whose details would be determined by Nowicki in India. Superblocks consisting of individual houses were designed to encourage the development of individual neighborhoods. Nowicki particularized this plan to suit the environmental needs and sociological traditions of India: houses were organized to make the most of wind conditions; exterior detailing, done in a modern idiom, conformed to the intricate ornament of much traditional Indian architecture; markets were centralized (in the plan carried out under the design of Le Corbusier these were eliminated). This was one of the first instances in modern planning of the consideration and adaptation of new forms to the structure of a non-Western society, vernacular architecture, and local environmental conditions. Until that time, modern planners had been largely antihistorical and antiregional in their search for universally applicable solutions.

In 1950 Nowicki collaborated with William Dietrick and William Henley on the North Carolina State Fairgrounds. The project entailed general planning of the fairgrounds; construction of exhibit buildings and the Dorton Arena, or livestock judging pavilion; enlargement of the grandstand; and refacing of several older structures. The sketch for the Dorton Arena (182), which seats 5,500 people, presents a structure of sloping brick walls, with glass infilled to the cable roof, thus allowing a great deal of natural light to illuminate the interior. Seating is intended to be grandstand fashion along the sloping walls. The exhibition areas, as indicated in the drawing, are arranged around the arena and protected from the elements by a cable roof system. The arena was constructed to Nowicki's specifications following his death. Its walls, constructed entirely of glare-reducing glass, are divided at 6-foot 11-inch/19.8-meter intervals by steel columns that serve both as support for two intersecting concrete parabolic arches and as mullions for the glass. A two-way tension-cable system to solve roof flutter problems

182

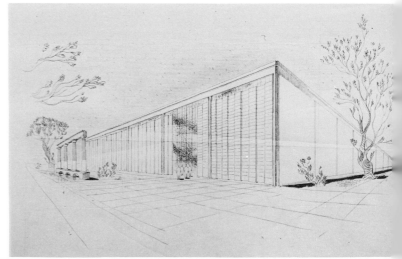

183

supports the corrugated steel roof. This was one of the first large-scale catenary cable roofs constructed since that designed by John Holabird at the 1933 Century of Progress Exhibition in Chicago. It becomes apparent on comparison of the sketch and the actual building that the primary determinant of Nowicki's form was the introduction of light into a large arena; from this developed his imaginative structural solution.

In 1950 Nowicki and William Dietrick designed a project for the North Carolina Museum of Art (183) on a site near the Classical Revival State Capitol by Ithiel Town. In scale with the Capitol, Nowicki conceived of a building, rectangular in massing, whose elevation on three sides was composed of large rectangular blocks of stone. The fourth side, the principal entrance to the museum, was formed of small stone sections. The articulation of all four elevations, recalling the modular proportioning of classical structures, set in juxtaposition to a fragment of a Doric colonnade, provides a foil to the Capitol. Their scheme was contextual in approach, designed in sympathy with the 19th-century Capitol.

182 Dorton Arena, North Carolina State Fairgrounds
Raleigh, North Carolina
Perspective study, c. 1950
Pastel, 17 x 23" (43.2 x 58.4 cm)
North Carolina Chapter
American Institute of Architects
Raleigh, North Carolina

183 North Carolina Museum of Art, Raleigh, North Carolina
Perspective, c. 1950
Pencil and crayon, 30 x 42" (76.2 x 106.7 cm)
North Carolina Museum of Art
Raleigh, North Carolina

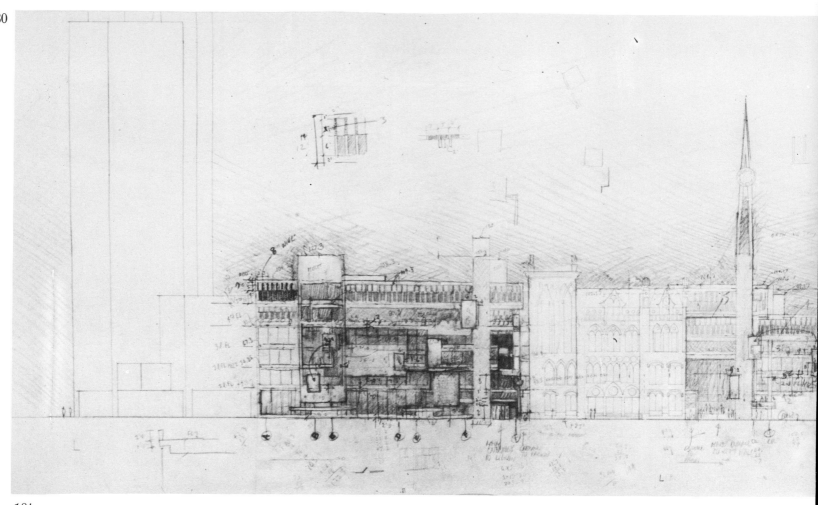

184

184   New Haven Government Center
Elevation study, 1976
Colored pencil on vellum, 18 x 48" (45.7 x 121.9 cm)
Collection of Paul Rudolph
New York, New York

185   Art and Architecture Building, Yale University
New Haven, Connecticut
Perspective studies and detail, c. 1959
Pencil on yellow sketch pad, 12 x 16" (30.5 x 40.6 cm)
Collection of Paul Rudolph
New York, New York

Paul Rudolph (b. 1918)

Paul Rudolph, one of the major personalities in post–World War II architecture and a powerful force in the history of the architecture school at Yale where he was chairman between 1958 and 1965, has produced a large *oeuvre* of outstanding and provocative structures for every building type. The monumental, sculptural buildings of his mature period, beginning in the late fifties, of rough and smooth cast concrete sometimes in combination with brick, introduced a powerful and romantic alternative to the International Style of sheer transparent glass, metal curtain walls, and boxlike forms. Rudolph is interested in what he has called a "beautiful game of space." His concern is with "the creation of living, breathing, dynamic spaces of infinite variety, capable of helping man forget something of his troubles." Rudolph's mature buildings are spatially dynamic, drawing much of their inspiration from the later works of Le Corbusier and Frank Lloyd Wright (page 234). They have also been concerned with giving expressive form to the structural facts of a building and, as Vincent Scully has written in *American Architecture and Urbanism* of 1969, not with "the snappy technological package but the basic humanistic image."

Rudolph's attitudes are in contrast with those espoused at Harvard University's Graduate School of Design under Walter Gropius's direction where Rudolph received a Master of Architecture degree in 1947. Gropius stressed the team method in design conception and execution, with a primary emphasis on functional planning and the use of industrialized technology and standardized materials in the development of form. Individualistic design expression was anathema. Rudolph rejected most of Gropius's philosophy except for his interest in industrialized materials and technology, areas which have constantly fascinated Rudolph. Rudolph's own approach to architectural education at Yale, consistent with attitudes expressed in his own work, are summarized by his statement that the architecture student "must understand that in the exhilarating, awesome moment when he takes pencil in hand and holds it poised above a white sheet of paper, that he has suspended there all that will ever be. The creative act is all that matters."

Rudolph was born in Kentucky and educated at Alabama Polytechnic Institute, 1935–1940, before studying at the Harvard Graduate School of Design. During World War II as an officer in the Navy he was involved with ship construction at the Brooklyn Navy Yard. Between 1948 and 1952 Rudolph was in partnership in Sarasota, Florida, with Ralph Twitchel, producing primarily domestic work in an orthodox Modernist idiom that was distinguished by technological innovation unusual for domestic design at the time. For example, in Siesta Key, Florida, the Healy Guest House of 1948–1949 was waterproofed with a plastic spray developed in the Navy for moth-balling ships, while at the Ingraham Hook House of 1951–1952 Rudolph pioneered the use of bent plywood as a spanning material. In the Walker Guest House at Sanibel Island, Florida, of 1952–1953, his first independent professional work, spherical weights raise hinged glass walls out and upward to a horizontal position.

In 1958 when Rudolph assumed his post at Yale, he moved his practice to New Haven. This was also the beginning of the period in which he produced his most important works, such as the Yale University School of Art and Architecture, 1958–1963; the New Haven Parking Garage, 1962; the Endo Laboratories building, Long Island, 1962; Crawford Manor Housing for the Elderly, New Haven, 1962–1966; the Boston Government Service Center of 1963; and many outstanding residences.

The Art and Architecture Building at Yale was designed and built between 1958 and 1963. The original seven-story structure was divided into 37 different levels grouped in a pinwheel. A central two-story space with drafting areas for each year of the architecture program was the main focus of the interior design. The painters' studios were located in the top beam section; the lower levels contained additional studios, exhibition spaces, a library, and an auditorium. Because of a fire in 1969 and pressure from groups within the school, much of the interior organization of the building has been altered. The primary construction elements of the building are poured-in-place concrete with rough vertical striations; smooth-faced concrete is used for floors, horizontal interior elements, and other detailing.

The drawing (185), one of approximately 1,000 that were done in the development of this building, represents one of the earliest of six schemes developed before a final one was selected. The lower perspective describes the building at the corner of York and Chapel streets; the other perspective describes the same facade looking up York Street. (The small insert on the page is unrelated to the other studies.) Urbanistic context and structure as a primary formal device are the two essential problems studied here. In an effort to create a strong relationship among his building, its corner site, and the larger context of the Yale campus, Rudolph visually anchored the building to the corner with a heavy pier. The four-story porch with two stories above at once unifies the building and creates a large-scaled structure that can be read from a distance. In the final scheme this porch was eliminated and the columns became piers.

The Graphic Arts Center (186) of 1967 was proposed to be built out from the existing Manhattan land mass and into the Hudson River. It is a megastructure containing 4,000 dwelling units, office buildings, recreational facilities, plazas, and parking. The modular housing units are mobile homes hung off trusses cantilevered from huge hollow pylon tubes housing vertical transportation of stairs, elevators, and mechanical services. The trailers were used in part because their lightweight, minimized demands on the foundation. The lower levels of the complex contain parking, pedestrian plazas, shops and restaurants, schools, and a small hotel. Rudolph grouped the modules, which he has called "20th-century bricks," like "a clustering of grapes." This sculptural deployment of the modules around the structural cores is in contrast with the free-span office towers. Rudolph has thereby emphasized the variation in program through form.

In 1968 Paul Rudolph received the commission for a new government center including a City Hall and library for the city of New Haven (184). The site for the complex is along Church Street, facing the Green and sandwiched between a new bank, the old Victorian Gothic City Hall, and the Classic Revival post office (separated from the site by narrow Court Street). Moving from left to right on the drawing is the proposed new bank, the new library, the old City Hall, the new City Hall, Court Street, and the post office. In 1956 Rudolph wrote an article entitled "The Six Determinants of Architectural Form" for

Architectural Record in which he warned against the creation of a new eclectic architecture as the result of a too literal correspondence between new and old buildings. Rudolph's answer to integrating the new and the old in this complex is through scale, not an eclectic vocabulary.

Rudolph originally planned a tall, thin tower for the new City Hall to replace the tower that had once adorned the old one. He decided to move the tower away from the Victorian building, as it would be overshadowed by the bank in that position. Subsequent to the execution of this drawing, a shift in attitudes toward the preservation of 19th-century buildings caused the city to rebuild the old tower. As the new City Hall has only a 75-foot/229-meter frontage on the street, Rudolph's tower is a vehicle to augment the importance of the new City Hall in the totality of the block and to link the Victorian Gothic and Classical buildings together. Rudolph makes the connection over Court Street between his City Hall and the post office by creating a "gateway" over Court Street, which is read as a single unit paralleling the one-story reading of the four-story post office. This "tall door," as Rudolph has called it, is studied on the lower right of the drawing. Rudolph is continually conscious of questions of urban design in this complex. He notches the new building next to the rebuilt tower to allow sky through the facade and to link the New Haven Green and the courtyard behind the complex. In an unpublished interview between the architect and Carl Black, Rudolph says that "the intention is to connect the room of New Haven with the smaller courtyard back of the existing City Hall" and that this "sieve of space" helps "to clearly define the rebuilt tower itself so that it becomes much more of a free standing element." In the drawing this "sieve of space" is marked in blue; glass is indicated in green; and depth is indicated by red.

To further connect the old and the new, Rudolph scales the top of the new City Hall on its right side to the beginning of the raking of the pediment of the post office; the height of the building jogs up to the other side so that it parallels the height of the Victorian facade. Finally, as indicated on the elevation and in the study at the upper left, the scale of the windows is related to the proportions and scales of both older structures. The lower spacings in the study are related to the spacings of the post office columns; the spacings above these relate to the proportions of the windows in the Victorian building.

186   *Graphic Arts Center, project, New York City*
Perspective, 1967
Pencil on vellum, 24 x 36" (61 x 91.4 cm)
Collection of Paul Rudolph
New York, New York

186

187

187   Dulles Airport, Washington, D.C.
Elevation study, c. 1958–1960
Pencil on yellow notebook paper, 8½ x 11" (21.6 x 27.9 cm)
Art and Architecture Library
Yale School of Architecture
Yale University
New Haven, Connecticut

Eero Saarinen (1911–1961)

Eero Saarinen, the son of Eliel Saarinen (page 223), came to full artistic maturity in the late forties, and in the short span of time before his death in 1961, he produced some of the most provocative buildings of the post–World War II era. The prevailing Modern style of the forties and fifties was characterized by the International Style esthetics of simple rectangular plans, planar facades with large expanses of glass, and revealed structure, and is best typified by the work of Mies (page 215). Saarinen broke from this mold, relying on few precedents, and produced buildings in which program and structure were dramatically expressed through highly personal and varied forms.

When Saarinen studied at Yale's School of Architecture in the 1930s, its educational philosophy was grounded in that of the École des Beaux-Arts. This approach, which put primary emphasis on the expression of structure and program in the creation of form (page 269), is directly related to Saarinen's mature buildings. His father's work, romantic in character (page 223), shows a more direct and forceful expression of structure and becomes more simply ornamented when Eero joins him in 1938.

The first plan and complex of buildings that Saarinen executed, the General Motors Technical Institute at Warren, Michigan, was completed in 1953 after a decade of design and construction. This project had originally been awarded to both Saarinen and his father, but the elder architect's death in 1950 placed full design responsibility with Eero. Although these buildings are particularly influenced by the work of Mies, in particular the siting and design of his Chicago campus for the Illinois Institute of Technology executed between 1940 and 1956, Saarinen begins to make a very personal statement here. Saarinen brought to the Miesian formula a brilliant palette of red, green, yellow, and blue glazed brick and a predilection for dramatic statement, as in the design of a circular showroom placed at one end of the plan and in the handling of the huge water tower and reflecting pools. His work subsequent to this moved toward a very personal structural expressionism—as in the Jefferson

Memorial Arch, the David Ingalls Rink at Yale University, 1953
–1959; the Dulles Airport in Washington, 1958–1962; and the
TWA Terminal, at John Fitzgerald Kennedy Airport in New
York—and toward romanticism, as in Stiles and Morse Colleges
at Yale, which recall a medieval town in their planning and
materials.

The general oval plan of the Ingalls Rink (188) c. 1953 was
determined by the program of a collegiate ice hockey rink that
could be converted into an auditorium. Saarinen enclosed the
rink with a hanging roof suspended by cables from a central
arch (189). In the constructed building the ends of the arch are
pulled upward, whereas in the drawing they are pulled
outward. This design change gives a sweeping, energized feeling
to the building. A goalie's comment that the building makes him
"go, go, go" was a compliment that Saarinen often quoted. The
curved, sloping roof is in plan like the section of the central
spanning arch. This formal manipulation of structure creates an
almost theatrical expression of the program's essence: speed on
ice.

Dulles Airport (187) of 1962 outside Washington was the first
commercial airport to be planned from its inception for the jet.
It is again a dramatic formalization of the structural forces and
utilitarian needs of the building. Saarinen developed a mobile
waiting-departure lounge that eliminated the long walks
passengers had to make between terminal and airplane. He
unified all the other functions of the terminal in one building.
The roof projection was designed to serve as a continuous
marquee to protect pedestrians; and he related that the unusual
curved, suspended roof, lower in the back, was a development
from the conceptualization early in the design development of
the need for such a sheltering element. The roof is made of
precast concrete slabs, joined with lightweight cables. Heavy
concrete piers supporting the roof are sloped outward in an
exaggerated manner, emphasizing the outward pull of the
cables. The dimensions of the piers are enlarged beyond the size
needed for pure physical function to dramatize their supportive
role. This system has a purely pragmatic advantage as well in
that it can be extended to meet the future needs of the terminal
for more space. The roof and the piers combine to give the

building its soaring image, which recalls the flight of a plane in
takeoff.

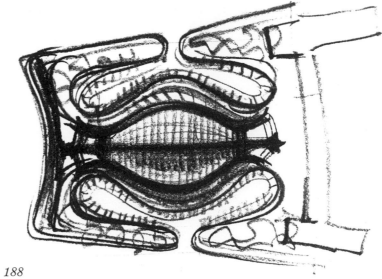

188

188   *Ingalls Rink, Yale University, New Haven, Connecticut*
Plan study, c. 1953
Dark pencil on yellow notebook paper, 8½ x 11" (21.6 x 27.9 cm)
Art and Architecture Library
Yale School of Architecture
Yale University
New Haven, Connecticut

189   *Ingalls Rink, Yale University, New Haven, Connecticut*
Perspective study, c. 1953
Dark pencil on yellow notebook paper, 8½ x 11" (21.6 x 27.9 cm)
Art and Architecture Library
Yale School of Architecture
Yale University
New Haven, Connecticut

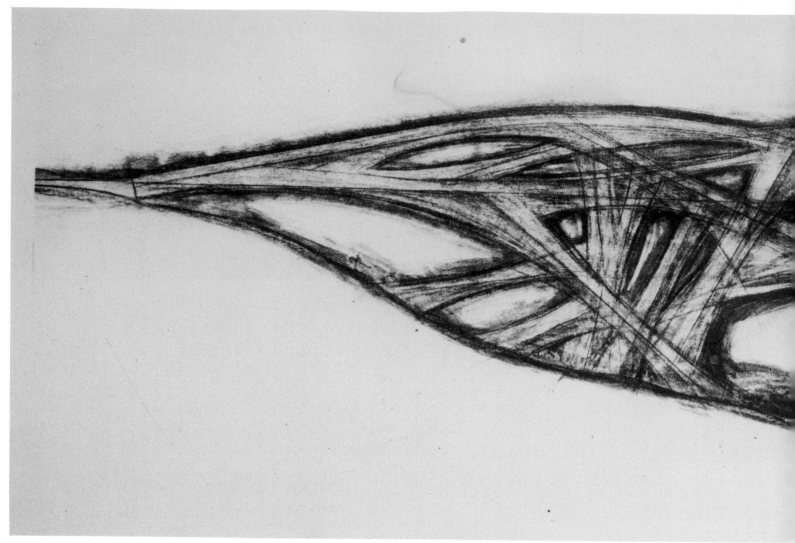

190

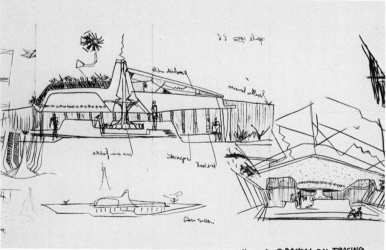

191

Paolo Soleri (b. 1919)

Paolo Soleri, architect of a futuristic visionary city he calls Arcology (a conflation of architecture and ecology) and director of the Cosanti Foundation in Scottsdale, Arizona, since 1961, was born in Turin, Italy, and earned a doctorate in architecture at the Torino Politecnico in 1946. Between 1947 and 1949 he studied at Taliesin with Frank Lloyd Wright whose advocacy of design in harmony with the nature of materials had a profound effect on Soleri's thinking. His first commission, a desert house for Mrs. Leonora Woods designed with Mark Mills in 1951 at Cave Creek, Arizona, had a domed movable roof. His only large constructed design is the spiral-formed Solimene Ceramics factory of 1954 at Vietri-Sul-Mare, Italy, whose walls are embedded with chips of colored tile and glass.

In 1956 Soleri settled in Arizona. In 1970, 14 years of developing and presenting his ideas for the Arcology and other projects culminated in a huge one-person exhibition at the Corcoran Gallery in Washington.

The arcologies developed by Soleri are megastructures that are cities containing all the services needed for humanity. Yet despite the high density of this city and its controlled technology, some freedom over the design of his private environment is given to individuals. By concentrating the human-made world, it is Soleri's contention that much more of the environment will be left inviolate. The prelude to the Arcology was "Mesa City" of 1959–1964, which Soleri has since rejected because as a linear development it spread too far into the landscape. Since 1970, Soleri and students who have come to study with him are constructing a mini-arcology 70 miles north of Phoenix for 2,500 to 3,000 people called Arcosanti.

In 1956 Soleri constructed the first earth house (191) that has become the model for his buildings at Arcosanti. The earth house is consistent with his Wright-inspired credo, "the builder must mold the earth, farm the land"; it is a house made from the materials of the Arizona landscape, and its method of construction and finish are consistent with the natural properties of those materials. A mound of earth is constructed

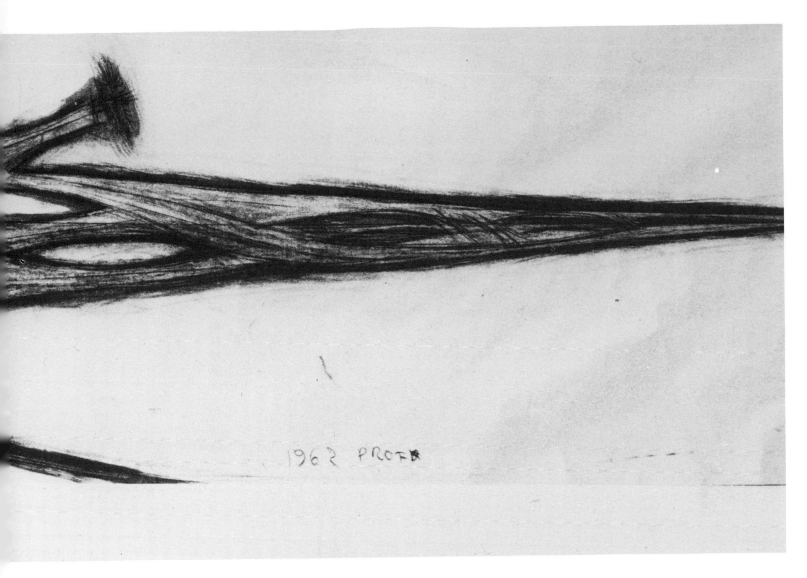

1962 PROTB

for the earth house, which is then covered with a 3- to 4-inch/8- to 10-centimeter layer of sprayed or poured concrete, the house is then hollowed out. The building is subterranean but open through the roof to light and the environment.

Soleri expressionistically manipulates and exploits structure in his cantilever bridge project (190) of 1962 for esthetic ends. Thus a form is produced that plays both on the intrinsic nature of a bridge as a spanning element and on complex 20th-century technology. One of Soleri's first great bridge designs was his "The Beast," conceived for Elizabeth Mock's *The Architecture of Bridges* of 1949.

190   *Cantilever bridge, project*
Elevation, 1962
Crayon and ink on butcher paper, 48 x 188" (121.9 x 477.6 cm)
Collection of Paolo Soleri
Scottsdale, Arizona

191   *Earth house studies*
Elevations and sections, 1956
Crayon on tracing paper, 21 x 47" (53.3 x 119.4 cm)
Collection of Paolo Soleri
Scottsdale, Arizona

BRANT · JOHNSON HOVSE   1975~.   VAIL VILLAGE · COLORADO

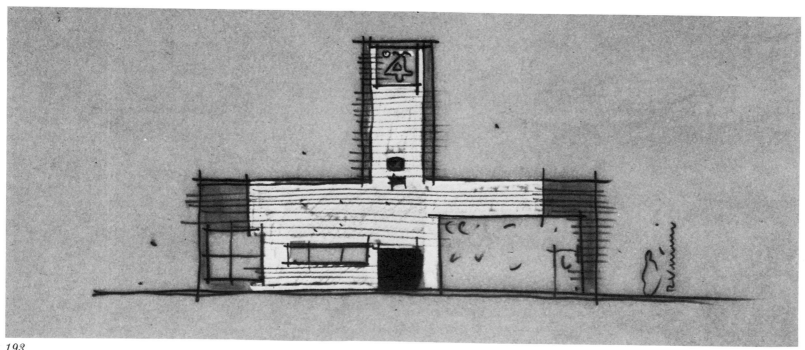

Robert Venturi (b. 1925)

One of the most provocative and influential post–World War II American architect-theorists is Robert Venturi, a partner with Denise Scott Brown and John Rauch in Venturi & Rauch in Philadelphia and author of *Complexity and Contradiction in Architecture*, published in 1966 by The Museum of Modern Art. His second book, *Learning from Las Vegas* of 1972, was written in collaboration with Denise Scott Brown and Steven Izenour. These books present an architectural theory that accepts formal ambiguity and contradictions in architecture and is in contrast with the purist, exclusivist attitudes of the International Style. As a method of learning more about architectural problem solving, Venturi and his collaborators analyze vernacular architecture and High Art buildings of the past.

Denise Scott Brown, an architect and planner, has made a significant theoretical contribution to the firm's production and has been particularly involved with the development of large planning projects and exhibitions. The architect, John Rauch, has been an important force in the implementation and design development of the firm's built work.

Venturi & Rauch have produced buildings that are compelling, continually polemical, and often highly controversial. To date the greatest volume of their built work is domestic, including the provocative Trubeck and Wisolocki houses on Nantucket of 1970 and the elegant Brant houses in Greenwich, Connecticut, of 1970 and in Bermuda of 1976. They have also built the Humanities Building at the State University of New York at Purchase and the poetic Benjamin Franklin Museum in Philadelphia in 1976. Robert Venturi's 1958 renovation for the New York University Institute of Fine Arts of the Duke Mansion in New York designed by Horace Trumbauer and Julien Abele (page 232) has provided a model of sensitive and understated renovation and recycling.

Venturi & Rauch have also been involved in exhibition design and development. Their exhibitions include one documenting their own work at the Whitney Museum in 1971; "Signs and Symbols of American Life" at the Renwick Gallery in Washington, D.C., in 1976; and the installation of the Whitney Museum's "200 Years of American Sculpture" in 1976.

Although Venturi & Rauch have been prolific in their production of new projects, many of them, especially their nondomestic work, have remained unbuilt. Yet many of these projects have had a major influence on American architecture. The Beach House project of 1959 by Robert Venturi, with the 1962 house for his mother, Vanna Venturi, built in Chestnut Hill, Pennsylvania, has engendered a modern domestic idiom, which includes strong references to the Shingle Style architecture (pages 137, 142) of the 1880s as well as to other more distant historical modes.

Complexity and Contradiction in Architecture is a polemic for an attitude toward architecture, not for a particular style. For Venturi, complexity occurs in architecture when all levels of a building's program and relationship to both its physical and cultural environment are considered and given recognition through form. This inclusivist approach produces a complex, sophisticated, sometimes difficult physical solution tied to the particularized realities of a specific program. Venturi expresses these ideas in his book by analyzing a large number of historical examples as case studies for complexity and contradiction in architecture. In 1966 the use of history as a text for finding parallels for design solutions of the present was near heresy for most modern architects; today, however, history is again relevant and this is due largely to Venturi's book. In it Venturi quotes the eminent architectural historian, Henry-Russell Hitchcock, who wrote in *Perspecta:* ". . . it [the investigation of architectural history] is with no idea of repeating its forms, but rather in the expectation of feeding more amply new sensibilities that are wholly the product of the present." Venturi's book could have been called *Learning from the Past.*

The use of history as a model for architectural problem solving of the present, as outlined by Venturi in 1966, is the prelude to both *Learning from Las Vegas* and articles in periodicals by Venturi and Denise Scott Brown that analyze on a perceptual and conceptual level a part of America's recent past and continuing present—the commercial vernacular of Las Vegas and the highway. This analysis was undertaken in order to use the principles of design found in the ad hoc planning and

192   *Brant-Johnson House, Vail Village, Colorado*
Perspective, 1975
KC 5 print with Pantone, 21½ x 28" (54.6 x 71.1 cm)
Collection of Venturi & Rauch
Philadelphia, Pennsylvania

193   *Fire Station #4, Columbus, Indiana*
Elevation, 1966
Colored pencil on buff tracing paper, 8 x 12" (20.3 x 30.5 cm)
Collection of Venturi & Rauch
Philadelphia, Pennsylvania

194

194 *Allen Memorial Art Museum Addition, Oberlin College*
Oberlin, Ohio
Elevation, January 23, 1974
Contact print on positive film with Pantone
15 x 51½" (38.1 x 130.8 cm)
Collection of the Allen Memorial Art Museum
Oberlin, Ohio

symbolism of the strip, as Vincent Scully says in *American Architecture and Urbanism*, "to make it function better as a general environment." The authors of *Learning from Las Vegas* analyze not only the use of signage as an informational tool and as symbol, but also the relationships among car, strip, parking, and building, and they discover that in the culture and environment of the highway strip, the sign is most often more powerful as image and more important than the building that it fronts or points to.

Fire Station No. 4 (193) in Columbus, Indiana, of 1965 is an attempt to emphasize the symbolic nature of a fire station. Venturi makes the white-glazed and red-brick facade larger than functionally necessary to increase its importance within the environment; this building, like many Main Street structures, is actually lower than the real facade in front. The tower with its "Fire Station 4" is a simple image of the archetypal firehouse.

Venturi & Rauch were commissioned to renovate the Allen Memorial Art Museum (194) designed by Cass Gilbert (page 164) and completed in 1917 at Oberlin College and to add a new wing to it, housing a new gallery, studio space for artists, art library, offices, and laboratories for the Intermuseum Conservation Association. The architects set the new wing back from Cass Gilbert's Renaissance Revival building with its bay system of modulation and its deep arcaded porch so that the new wing does not compete with but rather contrasts with the older museum. A checkerboard of pink granite and rose sandstone analogous in color to the older building covers the main elevation of the new wing. In an unpublished paper on the museum Venturi states that the facade was conceived of as "a medieval banner hanging from a Renaissance balcony during the Palio [in Siena]." The buff-brick rear elevation of the building refers to another building of the same material on the other side of the campus; the material also appears as a small portion of the front facade. A 10-inch/25.4-centimeter vertical strip of gray granite at the joint of the new and old walls and the strip windows, with their bottom edges at the cornice lines of the old building, makes visual links between the buildings. The building is simple in form inside and out: the gallery is almost a square; the studios and offices of the conservation center are in a three-story loft, inaccessible from the gallery in front, with regular bays, continuous strip windows, and a central corridor; the top floor is the art library. This building, simple in form,

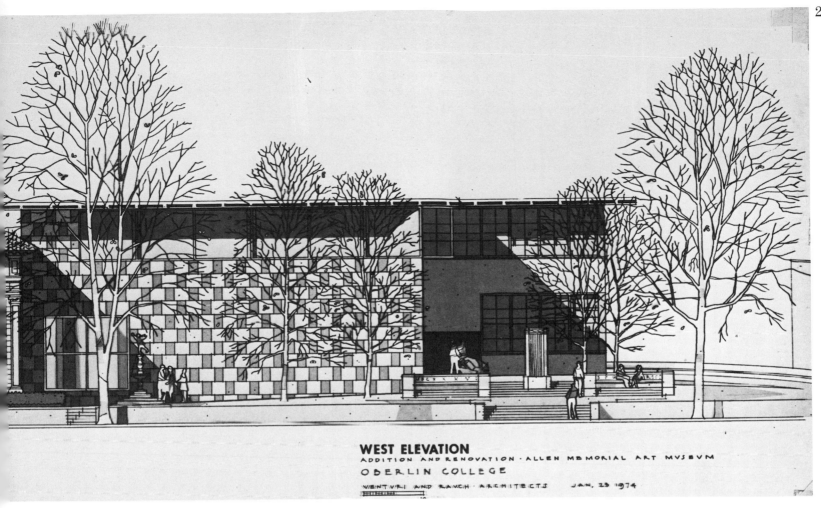

WEST ELEVATION
ADDITION AND RENOVATION · ALLEN MEMORIAL ART MVSEVM
OBERLIN COLLEGE
VENTVRI AND RAVCH · ARCHITECTS   JAN. 23 1974

derives its imagery from the surface treatment of the facades. Venturi has described this kind of building as a "decorated shed." This is in opposition to what Venturi calls a "duck," a building that takes its symbolic meaning from the form itself. The most blatant example of the duck is a roadside dairy store built in the form of a milk bottle; a less obvious duck is Chartres Cathedral.

The wooden Brant-Johnson House (192) in Vail Village of 1977 is located on a hilly site in this Colorado ski resort. The building's form emphasizes the fact of its location on a slope. Its materials and form recall vernacular European wooden architecture, a reference appropriate for the house's location and use. One enters the house through the stairs, half hidden from view, to utility and changing spaces on the first level. The highest level is a single space—a living room with built-in seating that double as beds, surrounded on four sides by semicircular windows, in conception not unlike Thomas Jefferson's circular domed "sky room" surrounded by windows at Monticello.

Notes

1. Reginald Blomfield, *Architectural Drawing and Draughtsmen* (London: Cassell & Co., 1912), p. 9. There has been surprisingly little published on the relationship between architectural drawings and architecture. Blomfield's 1912 volume is still one of the best. An excellent, much more recent discussion of the question is contained in an article by James Smith Pierce, "Architectural Drawings and the Intent of the Architect," *Art Journal* **27** (Fall 1967), pp. 48–59. Eileen [Manning] Michels has also explored aspects of the subject in *A Developmental Study of the Drawings Published in the American Architect and in Inland Architect through 1895*, (Ph.D. thesis, University of Minnesota, 1972) and in her article, "Late Nineteenth-Century Published American Perspective Drawings," *Journal of the Society of Architectural Historians* **31** (December 1972), pp. 291–308. Additional literature on the subject includes William Burges's paper, "Architectural Drawings," presented in 1860, which is one of the earliest and was published in the *Papers of the Royal Institute of British Architects*, London, 1861, pp. 15–28. Others that followed are James Burford, "The Historical Development of Architectural Drawings to the End of the Eighteenth Century," *Architectural Review* [London] **54** (1923), pp. 1–5, 59–65, 83–87, 141–145, 156–160, 222–227; Martin S. Briggs, *The Architect in History* (London: Oxford, 1924); "A Cross-Section of the Present State of the Art of Delineation in America" *Pencil Points* **21** (July 1940), pp. 398–430, 442–446; H. S. Goodhart-Rendel, "Architectural Draughtsmanship of the Past," *Journal of the Royal Institute of British Architects* **58** (February 1951), pp. 127–136; Frank Jenkins, *Architect and Patron* (London: Oxford University Press, 1961). Both Claudius Coulin's *Drawings by Architects from the Ninth Century to the Present Day* (New York: Reinhold, 1962) and Alfred M. Kemper's *Drawings by American Architects* (New York: Wiley, 1973) are picture books and nothing more. In his Introduction to *The Drawings of Frank Lloyd Wright* (New York: Horizon, 1962), Arthur Drexler speculates on the relationship between Wright's drawings and his built buildings. James F. O'Gorman discusses the general question of architectural drawings and architecture in his Introduction to *Selected Drawings: Henry Hobson Richardson and His Office* (Cambridge, Mass.: Harvard University Press, 1974), pp. 16–18. Other recent catalogs of architectural drawings tend to avoid any general discussion. See Richard P. Wunder, "The Architect's Eye," *The Cooper Union Museum Chronicle* 3 (September 1962), pp. 3–49; James C. Massey, ed., *Two Centuries of Philadelphia Architectural Drawings* (Philadelphia: Philadelphia Museum of Art, 1964); William B. O'Neal, *Architectural Drawing in Virginia* (Charlottesville, Va.: University of Virginia Press, 1969). Spiro Kostof's (ed.) recent volume, *The Architect: Chapters in the History of the Profession* (New York: Oxford University Press, 1976), touches on various aspects of drawings and their relationship to the practice of architecture.
2. Reginald Blomfield, *op. cit.*, p. 9
3. *Ibid.*, p. 5.
4. *Ibid.*, pp. 4–5; for a view on the relationship of 20th-century High Art painting and architecture see Henry-Russell Hitchcock's *Painting toward Architecture* (New York: Duell, Sloan & Pierce, 1948).
5. John Dixon Hunt and Peter Willis, eds., *The Genius of Place: The English Landscape Garden, 1620–1820* (London: Paul Elek, 1975); Carroll L. V. Meeks, "Henry Austin and the Italian Villa," *Art Bulletin* **30** (June 1948), pp. 22–31.
6. Reginald Blomfield, *op. cit.*, pp. 4–6; Briggs, *op. cit.*, pp. 3–5; Jenkins, *op. cit.*, xiii–xvi; Barrington Kaye, *The Development of the Architectural Profession in Britain* (London: George Allen & Unwin, 1960), pp. 22–31.
7. Minard LaFever published five pattern books between 1829 and 1856. The first of these was *The Young Builder's General Instructor* (Newark: W. Tuttle & Co., 1829); the latest and best known was *The Architectural Instructor* (New York: Putnam, 1856). See Jacob Landy's volume, *The Architecture of Minard LaFever* (New York: Columbia University Press, 1970).
8. Hugh Ferriss, *The Metropolis of Tomorrow* (New York: I. Washburn, 1929); Walter Dorwin Teague, *Design This Day* (New York: Harcourt, Brace, 1940); V. Vorsanger, "Loewy's Latest," *Art and Industry* **25** (September 1938), pp. 106–111; Norman Bel Geddes, *Horizons* (Boston: Little, Brown, 1832) and *Magic Motorways* (New York: Random House, 1940).
9. James F. O'Gorman, *Selected Drawings: Henry Hobson Richardson and His Office* (Cambridge, Mass.: Harvard University Press, 1974).
10. Arthus Drexler, ed., *The Drawings of Frank Lloyd Wright* (New York: Horizon, 1970).
11. Though some photographs of Richardson's work were published in the *American Architect and Building News* and other American architectural magazines, most illustrations of his work published before his death were drawings. Wright always liked to use architectural drawings to convey his designs. When Robert C. Spencer, Jr., presented Wright's work in the pages of *The Architectural Review* 7 (June 1900), pp. 61–72, he relied on drawings. Later publication of Wright's work in the special issues of the *Architectural Forum* were organized around his drawings, not the photographs of his built buildings.
12. Eileen [Manning] Michels, *The Architectural Designs of Harvey Ellis* (Master's thesis, University of Minnesota, Minneapolis, 1953).
13. Arline Leven, *Hugh Ferriss: Drawings and Architects' Vision* (exhibition catalog, Gallery of Art, Washington University, St. Louis, 1976).
14. Eileen Michels, *op. cit.*, 1972, p. 300.
15. Published drawings that influenced American and European architecture at and before the turn of the century were Johann Winkelmann, *History of Ancient Art* (1764; reprint ed., Boston: Osgood, 1880.); G. P. M. Dumont, *Temples of Paestum: 1764* (London: [J. de Darren?], 1769); Robert Wood, *The Ruins of Palmyra* (1757; reprint ed., Boston: Gregg Press, 1971).
16. Bellicard, Jérôme C., *Observations upon the Antiquities of the Town of Herculaneum, Discovered at the Foot of Mount Vesuvius* (London: Jombert, 1753); Robert Adam, *Ruins of the Palace of the Emperor Diocletian at Spalatra in Dalmatia* (London, 1764).
17. James Stuart and Nicholas Revett, *Antiquities of Athens* (London: J. Haberkorn, 1762, 1788, and 1794).
18. J. C. Loudon, *The Suburban Gardner and Villa Companion* (London, 1838); A. J. Downing, *A Treatise on the Theory and Practice of Landscape Gardening* (New York: G. P. Putnam, 1849).
19. R. Phene Spiers, *Architectural Drawing* (New York: Cassell & Co., 1887), pp. 45–46; "The Custody of an Architect's Drawings," *American Architect and Building News* 3 (June 15, 1878), pp. 206–208; "The 'Blue' Copying Process," *American Architect and Building News* 4 (Aug. 3, 1878), p. 44.
20. Martin S. Briggs, *op. cit.*, pp. 23, 42.
21. *Ibid.*, pp. 88–89, 165–166, 223–265.
22. *Ibid.*, p. 362; Frank Jenkins, *op. cit.*, pp. 123–124, 209; J. Wilton-Ely, "The Architectural Model: 1. English Baroque," *Apollo* **88** (October 1968), pp. 250–259; J. Wilton-Ely, "Architectural Model," *Architectural Review* [London] **142** (July 1967), pp. 26–32.
23. "The Small Scale Model in Architecture," *American Architect and Building News* **95** (Mar. 31, 1909), pp. 105–108; Frederic C. Hirons, "The Use of Scale Models," *Pencil Points* **1** (November 1920), pp. 4–9; 2 (December 1920), pp. 4–9; 3 (January 1921), pp. 22–24; Kenneth Reed, "Architectural Models," *Pencil Points* **20** (July 1929), pp. 206–412; R. Pfaeudler, "Architectural Models," *Architectural Review* [London] **140** (July 1966), pp. 68–76; J. Physick and M. Darby, "The Architectural Model during the Victorian Period," *Architectural Review* [London] **140** (July 1966), pp. 68–76; J. Physick and M. Darby, "The Architectural Model during the Victorian Period," *Marble Halls* (exhibition catalog published by the Victoria and Albert Museum, London, 1973), pp. 13–16.
24. Two examples of the use of study models in American architecture are Raymond M. Hood, "The American Radiator Building, New York," *American Architect* **126** (Nov. 19, 1924), pp. 266–474; Morgan, Walls, and Clements, "The Richfield Building," *American Architect* **139** (May 1931), pp. 44–45.
25. Study models have been extensively used by Robert Venturi and especially by Charles Moore.
26. See the axonometric drawings of William Turnbull in Charles Moore, Gerald Allen, and Donlyn Lyndon's *The Place of Houses* (New York: Holt, Rinehart, & Winston, 1974).
27. William Burges, *op. cit.*, pp. 15–28; Reginald Blomfield, *op. cit.*, pp. 8–10; James Smith Pierce, "Architectural Drawing and the Intent of the Architect," *Art Journal* 27 (Fall 1967), p. 59.
28. The technique of presentation, i.e., the style of rendering utilized in architectural drawings, remained basically parallel to that of High Art painting through the early 1900s. With the introduction of avant garde painting, from Cubism on, most (although not all) styles of architectural drawings remained quite conservative. See Henry-Russell Hitchcock, *op. cit.*
29. The 10 to 11 years between 1886 and 1897 represent a high point in the quality of architectural drawings that were published in the *American Architect and Building News, The Inland Architect*, etc. This was the period when formal presentation drawings of Harvey Ellis, David Gregg, Henry Kirby, and others were published. See Eileen [Manning] Michels, *op. cit.*, 1972.
30. While European Expressionism in architecture has been studied [see Dennis Sharp, *Modern Architecture and Expressionism* (New York: Braziller, 1966), and Wolfgang Pehnt, *Expressionist Architecture* (New York: Praeger, 1973)], American Expressionism has hardly been looked at. Some published drawings of American Architectural Expressionism are to be found in Arthur Drexler, ed., *op. cit.*, pls. 95–105; David Gebhard, *Schindler* (New York: Viking Press, 1972), pls. 31, 39, 73; Mori Takenobu, ed., *Bruce Goff in Architecture* (Tokyo: Takenobu, 1970), especially the sketches printed in the Introduction (unnumbered); Esther McCoy, "John Lautner, West Coast Architects, V," *Arts and Architecture* **82** (August 1965), pp. 22–26.
31. Hugh Morrison, *Early American Architecture* (New York: Oxford University Press, 1952). The original drawings of Independence Hall were published in Thomas Brabazon, "Our Earliest Civic Center," *Architectural Record* **35** (July 1913), p. 2. Two mid-18th century drawings are illustrated in Fiske Kimball's *Domestic Architecture of the American Colonies and of the Early Republic* (1922; reprint ed., New York: Dover, 1966). These are a drawing by Benjamin Wyatt (fig. 32) and by Richard Monday (fig. 45).
32. Thomas T. Waterman, *Mansions of Virginia* (Chapel Hill, N.C.: University of North Carolina Press, 1946), pp. 243–247.
33. Carl Bridenbaugh, *Peter Harrison, First American Architect* (Chapel Hill, N.C.: University of North Carolina Press, 1949), p. 158.
34. Fiske Kimball, *Thomas Jefferson, Architect* (New York: Da Capo, 1968); Frederick Doveton Nichols, *Thomas Jefferson's Architectural Drawings* (Boston: Massachusetts Historical Society, 1960).
35. Harold Kirker, *The Architecture of Charles Bulfinch* (Cambridge, Mass.: Harvard University Press, 1969); Fiske Kimball, *Mr. Samuel McIntire, Carver, the Architect of Salem* (Gloucester, Mass.: Peter Smith, 1966).
36. Helen Park, *A List of Architectural Books Available in America before the Revolution* (Los Angeles: Hennessey, 1973); Alexander Wall, *Books on Architecture Printed in America, 1775–1830* (Cambridge, Mass.: Harvard University Press, 1925); Henry-Russell Hitchcock, *American Architectural Books: A List of Books, Portfolios and Pamphlets on Architecture and Related Subjects Published in America before 1895* (New York: Da Capo, 1975).
37. Helen Park, *op. cit.*, Foreword by Adolf K. Placzek, pp. ix–xii.
38. *Ibid.*, pp. 1-130.
39. *Ibid.*, pp.16–18, 26, 27–28.
40. James Ackerman, "Architectural Practice in the Italian Renaissance," *Journal of the Society of Architectural Historians* 13 (October 1954), p. 8; James Smith Pierce, *op. cit.*, p. 49.
41. In their popular, much used volume, *The American Builder's Companion* (Boston: Etheridge, 1806), Asher Benjamin and Daniel Raynerd followed the usual 18th century practice of pattern books by first presenting details and then, at the end, plans of town and country houses, churches, meeting halls, summer houses, etc. All these drawings were orthographic projections.
42. Fiske Kimball, *op. cit.*, 1940.
43. Hugh Morrison, *op. cit.*, p. 292; John Trumball, *Autobiography, Reminiscences and Letters* (New York: Wiley & Putnam, 1841).
44. Harold Kirker, *op. cit.*, pls. 10, 13, 17, 82, 136, 158.
45. *Ibid.*, pl. 14; Fiske Kimball, *op. cit.*, 1940, fig. 158.
46. *Ibid.*, pls. 3, 56, 136, 154.
47. Fiske Kimball, *op. cit.*, 1916; Frederick Doveton Nichols, *op. cit.*
48. Frederick Doveton Nichols, *op. cit.*, figs. 1–4.
49. Peter Collins, "Origin of Graph Paper as an Influence on Architectural Design," *Journal of the Society of Architectural Historians* 21 (December 1962), pp. 159–162.
50. Peter Collins, *op. cit.*, pp. 161–162.
51. Frederick Doveton Nichols, *op. cit.*, figs. 29, 30; L. M. Watson, "Thomas Jefferson's Other Home: Poplar Forest," *Antiquities* **71** (April 1957), pp. 342–346.
52. Talbot Hamlin, *Benjamin Henry Latrobe* (New York: Oxford University Press, 1955).
53. Talbot Hamlin, *op. cit.* See Latrobe's drawings for the Penitentiary at Richmond (pl. 11), Proposed West Elevation of the United States Capitol, Washington (pl. 24), Proposed Library at Baltimore (pl. 32), and the Front Elevation of the Second Bank of the United States in Philadelphia (pl. 34). See also Latrobe's sketches for a house for Robert Liston, illustrated in Fiske Kimball, *op. cit.*, fig. 45.
54. A. J. Downing, *op. cit.*, p. 320.
55. A. J. Downing, *ibid.*; see figs. 40–60.
56. Roger Hale Newton, *Town and Davis: Architects* (New York: Columbia University Press, 1942), pls. 27, 28.
57. Agnes Addison Gilchrist, *William Strickland, Architect and Engineer 1768-1854* (New York: Da Capo, 1963); H. M. Pierce Gallagher, *Robert Mills* (New York: Columbia University Press, 1935).
58. Thomas U. Walter and J. Jay Smith, *Two Hundred Designs for Cottages and Villas* (Philadelphia: Carey & Hart, 1846).
59. E. Steese, "Villas and Cottages by Calvert Vaux," *Journal of the Society of Architectural Historians* 6 (January 1947), pp. 1–12; Jacob Landy, *The Architecture of Minard LeFever* (New York: Columbia University Press, 1970).
60. Everard M. Upjohn, *Richard Upjohn, Architect and Churchman* (New York: Columbia University Press, 1939).
61. *Ibid.*, fig. 14.
62. *Ibid.*, figs. 76, 77, 106, 108.
63. The decade of the 1870s was *the* period when architectural journals began to be published in the United States. *The American Architect and Buildings News* (1876) was the most prestigious of these. Earlier journals, such as *The Builder and Woodworker* (1868) and *Carpentry and Building* (1877) were oriented, like the pattern books of the time, to the carpenter-builder.
64. Architectural practice at the time is outlined in two articles published in the *Inland Architect and News Record*. These are "A City Architect's Office" **15** (July 1890), pp. 85–86; and in H. E. Perkins' "System in Architect's Offices" **17** (February 1891), pp. 3–4.
65. George E. Woodward and F. W. Woodward, *Woodward's Country Homes* (New York: Woodward, 1866), see figs. 14, 19, 24, 28, etc.; Samuel Sloan, *Homestead Architecture* (Philadelphia: J. P. Lippincott, 1861), see figs. 23, 27, 30, 32, etc.
66. Louis H. Gibson, *Convenient Houses with Fifty Plans for the Housekeeper* (New York: Thomas Y. Crowell, 1889). One edition of this pattern book even used a photograph on the outside of the front cover.
67. Eileen [Manning] Michels, *The Architectural Designs of Harvey Ellis* (Master's thesis, University of Minnesota, Minneapolis, 1953).
68. George E. Thomas and James F. O'Gorman, *The Architecture of Frank Furness* (New York: Museum of Modern Art, 1973).
69. George E. Thomas and James F. O'Gorman, *op. cit.*, pl. 2, figs. 34, 4–5, 5–1.
70. Eileen [Manning] Michels, *op. cit.*, 1953, pp. 5–12.
71. *Ibid.*, pp. 26–54.
72. *Ibid.*, pp. 12–19; also see Jean R. France, "Harvey Ellis Architect," in *A Rediscovery: Harvey Ellis Architect, Artist* (catalog published by the Memorial Art Gallery of the University of Rochester, Rochester, N.Y., 1972), pp. 5–24.
73. Henry-Russell Hitchcock, *The Architecture of H. H. Richardson and His Times* (New York: Museum of Modern Art, 1936); James F. O'Gorman, *op. cit.*, 1974; also Henry-Russell Hitchcock, *Richardson and His Office as a Victorian Architect* (Northampton: Smith College, 1965).
74. Marianna Griswold Van Rensselaer (Mrs. Schuyler Van Rensselaer), *Henry Hobson*

Richardson (New York: Dover, 1969); James F. O'Gorman, *op. cit.*, 1974.

75. James F. O'Gorman, *op. cit.*, 1974.

76. *Ibid.*, p. 20.

77. *Ibid.*, pp. 18–21.

78. For illustrations of Richardson's Andrews House and for Price's "The Craig," see Vincent Scully, *The Shingle Style* (New Haven, Conn.: Yale University Press,1955), pls. 4, 40; for McKim, Mead, and Bigelow's Alden House see *American Architect and Building News* 6 (Aug. 30, 1879).

79. Vincent Scully, *op. cit.*, pls. 46–50, 86, 91, 99; for Emerson also see Cynthia Zaitzevsky's, *The Architecture of William Ralph Emerson* (exhibition catalog by the Fogg Museum, Harvard University, Cambridge, Mass., 1969).

80. See the catalog for the exhibition "The Architecture of the Beaux Arts" (An exhibition organized for the Museum of Modern Art, New York, by Arthur Drexler, David Van Zanten, Neil Levine, and Richard Chafee. See also A. D. F. Hamlin, "Ecole des Beaux-Arts and Its Influence on Our Architecture," *Architectural Record* 23 (April 1908), pp. 241–247. For the importance of being able to quickly express oneself via drawings within the Beaux-Arts system, see *Les Esquisses de 24 heures, 1890 a 1905* (Paris: Auguste Vincent, 1905).

81. *A Monograph on the Work of McKim, Mead and White: 1879–1915*, 4 vols. (New York: Architectural Book Publishing Co., 1918); Charles Moore, *Daniel H. Burnham, Architect Planner of Cities*, 2 vols. (Boston: Houghton-Mifflin, 1921); Thomas S. Hines, *Burnham of Chicago* (New York: Oxford University Press, 1974).

82. Robert C. Spencer, Jr., "The Work of Frank Lloyd Wright," *Architectural Review* 7 (June 1900), pp. 61–72.

83. Frank Lloyd Wright, "In the Cause of Architecture," *Architectural Record* 23 (March 1908), pp. 155–221.

84. Frank Lloyd Wright, *Ausgeführte Bauten und Entwürfe von Frank Lloyd Wright*, 2 vols. (Berlin: Wasmuth, 1910); H. Allen Brooks, "Frank Lloyd Wright and the Wasmuth Drawings," *The Art Bulletin* 48 (June 1966), pp. 193–202.

85. *The Western Architect* 19 (January 1913); 19 (August 1913); 21 (January 1915); 21 (February 1915); 22 (July 1915).

86. *The Western Architect* 19 (January 1913). The layout of the pages was by William Gray Purcell. George Grant Elmslie provided the designs for the pages.

87. Wilson Eyre, "House in Downington," *American Architect and Building News* 13 (Mar. 10, 1883); Wilson Eyre, "Pepper House, Jenkintown," *American Architect and Building News* 41 (Aug. 12, 1893).

88. Stickley employed both pencil and ink and wash drawings in the *Craftsman* magazine and in his pattern books. A good number of these drawings were from his hand. The best of the drawings presented in the *Craftsman* were those produced between 1903 and 1904 by Harvey Ellis.

89. Ernest Coxhead, "Whittell House, San Francisco," *California Architect and Building News* 15 (April 1894); "A Study for a Residence," *Architect and Engineer* 23 (January 1911), p. 39; Willis Polk, "Boericke House, San Francisco,"*California Architect and Building News* 15 (May 1894); and "Sketch for Mausoleum at San Mateo," *Western Architect* 30 (December 1921), pl. 7. Few of John Galen Howard's drawings were published. See William C. Hays, "Some Architectural Work of John Galen Howard," *Architect and Engineer* 40 (January 1915), pp. 47–82.

90. Bernard Maybeck was a skilled draftsman and delineator, but few of his drawings were ever published. His collection of drawings is located at the Library of the School of Environmental Design, University of California at Berkeley.

91. Joan Elaine Draper, *John Galen Howard and the Beaux-Arts Movement in the United States* (Ph.D. thesis, University of California, Berkeley).

92. Walter Steilberg, "Some Examples of the Work of Julia Morgan," *Architect and Engineer* 15 (November 1918), pp. 38–107; John Beach, *Architectural Drawings by Julia Morgan: Beaux-Arts Assignments and Other Drawings* (catalog for an exhibition at the Oakland Museum, 1976).

93. Bernard Maybeck, "Three Houses," *Architectural Record* 40 (November 1916), pp. 488–489. For a published example of Maybeck's drawings, see Ruth Newhall, *San Francisco's Enchanted Palace* (Berkeley: Howell-North, 1967), p. 13.

94. The French Classical approach to drawing on the part of these architects can be seen in Harold Van Buren Magonigle, *Architectural Rendering in Wash* (New York: Scribners & Sons, 1921). The vision of the Beaux-Arts and the City Beautiful movement reached a culmination in the large scale formal presentation drawings of Jules Guerin.

95. "Cass Gilbert, Master of Style," *Pencil Points* 15 (November 1934), pp. 541–556; "Bertram Grosvenor Goodhue, Architect, Design and Draftsman," *Pencil Points* 5 (June 1924), pp. 42–61; Charles Harris Whitaker, ed., *Bertram Grosvenor Goodhue. Master of Many Arts* (New York: The Architecture Book Publishing Co., 1925).

96. "Cass Gilbert, Detroit Public Library," *The Architect* 44 (July 1921), pls. 33–37.

97. Bertram Grosvenor Goodhue, "The Nebraska State Capitol," *American Architect* 118 (July 21, 1920); "The Los Angeles Public Library," *Western Architect* 36 (February 1927), pls. 19–26.

98. Ralph Adams Cram, *The Builder and Woodworker* 4 (March 1882), p. 41; 4 (May 1882), p. 80; 4 (July 1882), pp. 122, 123. Examples of later drawings by Cram are illustrated in Douglass Shand Tucci, *Church Building in Boston 1720–1970. An Introduction to the Work of Ralph Adams Cram and the Boston Gothicists* (Concord, Mass.: Rumford Press, 1974).

99. The first issue of *Pencil Points* was published in June 1920. It was planned that the magazine would be devoted to architectural practice and especially to the uses of drawing within the practice of architecture.

100. *The International Competition for a New Administration Building for the Chicago Tribune, MCMXXII* (Chicago: Chicago Tribune, 1922).

101. Herbert Croly, "Recent Work of John Russell Pope," *Architectural Record* 29 (June 1911), pp. 441–511; Royal Cortissoz, *The Architecture of John Russell Pope* (New York: William Helburn, 1925).

102. Paul Cret, "Integrity Trust Company, Philadelphia," *Architectural Record* 66 (October 1929), pp. 290–306. Harold Van Buren Magonigle, "A Half Century of Architecture, A Biographical Review," *Pencil Points* 14 (November 1933), pp. 477–480; 15 (1934), pp. 223–228, 357–359, 464–466, 563–565. *Contemporary American Architects: Raymond Hood* (New York: Whittlesey, 1931). *Contemporary American Architects: Ely Kahn* (New York: Whittlesey, 1931).

103. Paul Cret's conceptual drawings for the Pan American Union Building, Washington, D.C., of 1912–1913 were published in C. Matlack Price, "The Pan American Union and Its Annex, Washington, D.C.," *Architectural Record* 34 (November 1913), pp. 386–387. Cret's finished presentation drawings for the same building are on pp. 388–401; Francis S. Swales, "Draftsmanship and Architecture: As Exemplified by the Work of Paul P. Cret," *Pencil Points* 9 (November 1928), pp. 688–704.

104. Talbot F. Hamlin, *The American Spirit in Architecture* (New Haven, Conn.: Yale University Press, 1926), pp. 229–230; also *The Architect* 55 (January 1927), pp. 1–8.

105. Harold Van Buren Magonigle, "The Liberty Memorial, Kansas City," *Journal of the American Institute of Architects* 9 (August 1921), pp. 266–270.

106. Hugh Ferriss, *The Metropolis of Tomorrow* (New York: I. Washburn, 1929).

107. "Hugh Ferriss," *Pencil Points* 1 (December 1920), p. 25; Hugh Ferriss, "Three Stages of Rendering," *Pencil Points* 2 (January 1921), pp. 6–9; Hugh Ferriss, "Re-Rendering," *Pencil Points* 21 (July 1940), pp. 401–403.

108. Myron Bement Smith, "Master Draftsman—XX: Claude Bragdon," *Pencil Points* 8 (April 1927), pp. 201–216.

109. Walter H. Kilham, Jr., *Raymond Hood Architect* (New York: Architectural Book Publishing Co., 1973); Francis S. Swales, "Draftsmanship and Architecture: As Exemplified by the Work of Raymond M. Hood," *Pencil Points* 9 (May 1928), pp. 258–269.

110. Francis S. Swales, *op. cit.*, 1928, p. 261.

111. *Ibid.*, p. 268.

112. Royal Barry Wills, *Houses for Homemakers* (New York: Franklin Watts, 1945) and *Living on the Level* (Cambridge, Mass.: Riverside Press, 1955).

113. Samuel Chamberlain's prints and drawings were continually published from the mid-1920s on in *Pencil Points*. Characteristic of his work is his print of Faneuil Hall, Boston, published in *Pencil Points* 9 (January 1930), p. 43. One of his most popular picture books of the 1930s was *A Small House in the Sun* (New York: Hastings House, 1936).

114. None of George Grant Elmslie's sketches or drawings was published during the 1920s.

115. As with his former partner George Grant Elmslie, William Gray Purcell's work of the 1920s was not published in any of the national architectural journals.

116. Sally Anderson Chappell, "Barry Byrne Architect: His Formative Years," *Prairie School Review* 3 (1966). Also see Byrne's drawing for the Church of Christ King, Cork, Ireland, in H. Allen Brooks, *The Prairie School* (Buffalo: University of Toronto Press, 1972), fig. 241. Mori Takenobu, ed., *Bruce Goff in Architecture* (Tokyo: Takenobu, 1970). David Gebhard and Harriet Von Breton, *Lloyd Wright, Architect* (Santa Barbara: The Standard Printing Co., 1971).

117. Arthur Drexler, *The Drawings of Frank Lloyd Wright* (New York: Horizon Press, 1962), pls. 58–123.

118. "Frank Lloyd Wright," *Architectural Forum* 68 (January 1938).

119. David Gebhard, *Schindler* (New York: Viking Press, 1971); Esther McCoy, *Richard Neutra* (New York: Braziller, 1960).

120. David Gebhard and Harriet Von Breton, *L. A. in the 30s* (Salt Lake City: Peregrine Smith, 1975), pp. 114–115, figs. 143–154.

121. Esther McCoy, *op. cit.*, figs. 29, 154–159.

122. David Gebhard and Harriet Von Breton, *op. cit.*, figs. 149, 150, 152.

123. William Lescaze, "Brooklyn Children's Museum," *Pencil Points* 18 (May 1937), p. 20; "House for Mrs. George French Porter, Ojai, California," *American Architect* 137 (March 1930), p. 56.

124. Carl Koch, "Koch House, Belmont, Mass.," illustrated in John McAndrew, ed., *Guide to Modern Architecture Northeast States* (New York: Museum of Modern Art, 1940).

125. Philip Johnson, "House in Cambridge, Mass.," *Architectural Forum* 76 (December 1943), pp. 89–93.

126. Ludwig Glaeser, *Ludwig Mies Van der Rohe: Drawings in the Collection of the Museum of Modern Art* (New York: Museum of Modern Art, 1969).

127. Marcus Whiffen, ed., *The History, Theory and Criticism of Architecture* (Cambridge, Mass.: MIT Press, 1965).

128. Susan King, *The Drawings of Eric Mendelsohn* (Berkeley, Calif.: University Museum, University of California, 1969), pp. 104–106.

129. Edward D. Stone, *The Evolution of an Architect* (New York: Horizon Press, 1962), pp. 138, 149.

130. Bruce Harold Schafer, ed., *Writings and Sketches of Matthew Nowicki* (Charlottesville, Va.: University of Virginia Press, 1973).

131. Allen Temko, *Eero Saarinen* (New York: Braziller, 1962); Eero Saarinen and Aline B. Saarinen, eds., *Eero Saarinen on His Work* (New Haven, Conn.: Yale University Press, 1962).

132. Esther McCoy, *Modern California Houses: Case Study Houses 1945–1962* (New York: Rinehart, 1962).

133. Charles Eames, "Case Study House, Pacific Palisades," *Arts and Architecture* 66 (May 1949), pp. 38–39; (September 1949), p. 33; (December 1949), pp. 26–39.

134. Thomas D. Church, *Gardens Are for People* (New York: Rinehart, 1955); Lawrence Halprin, "Houses and Landscape," *Progressive Architecture* 41 (May 1960), pp. 140–181; as an example of Halprin's work with William Wurster, see *Progressive Architecture* 39 (May 1958), pp. 95–103.

135. As an example see the drawings in Frank Lloyd Wright's *A Testament* (New York: Horizon Press, 1957).

136. "Frank Lloyd Wright," *Architectural Forum* 91 (January 1948).

137. "Frank Lloyd Wright's Concrete and Copper Skyscraper in the Prairie for H. C. Price Co.," *Architectural Forum* 98 (May 1953), p. 99 and cover.

138. Mori Takenobu, ed., *op. cit.*; "Bauten und Entwürfe von Bruce Goff 1935–1937," *Bauwelt* 27 (January 1958), pp. 77–88; Robert Kostka, "Bruce Goff and the New Tradition," *The Prairie School Review* 7 (1970), pp. 5–15.

139. Sibyl Moholy-Nagy, *The Architecture of Paul Rudolph* (New York: Praeger, 1970); Yukio Futagawa and Paul Rudolph, ed., *Paul Rudolph: Drawings* (Tokyo: ADA Edita, 1972).

140. Vincent Scully, *Louis I. Kahn* (New York: Braziller, 1962); Richard S. Wurman and Eugene Feldman, eds., *Louis I. Kahn Notebooks and Drawings* (Cambridge: MIT Press, 1973); Romaldo Giurgola, *Louis I. Kahn* (Boulder, Colo.: Westview Press, 1976).

141. Peter Eisenman, et al., *Five Architects: Eisenman, Graves, Gwathmey, Hejduk, Meier* (New York: Oxford University Press, 1975), pp. 15–37; "On Reading Architecture," *Progressive Architecture* 53 (March 1972), pp. 67–87; "House at Lakeville, Conn.," *Progressive Architecture* 55 (May 1974), pp. 92–99.

142. Peter Eisenman, et al., *op. cit.*

143. *Ibid.*, pp. 87–109; "The Bye House, Second Wall House," *Progressive Architecture* 55 (June 1974), pp. 98–102.

144. Mitchell/Giurgola Assoc., "Three Projects," *Architectural Record* 152 (October 1972), pp. 105–114.

145. Mitchell/Giurgola Assoc., "Student Union, State University College, Plattsburgh, New York," *Progressive Architecture* 56 (April 1975), pp. 66–71.

146. Hardy, Holzman, Pfeiffer, "Survey of the Firm's Work," *Progressive Architecture* 56 (February 1975), pp. 41–59.

147. Charles W. Moore, "Where Are We Now, Vincent Scully?" *Progressive Architecture* 56 (April 1975), pp. 78–83.

148. "A Summation of Parts, Profile: Daniel, Mann, Johnson and Mendenhall," *Progressive Architecture* 53 (June 1972), pp. 72–83; Gruen Assoc., "Shopping Center; Enclosed Civic Space, Columbus, Indiana," *Architectural Record* 153 (March 1973), pp. 128–132; Gruen Assoc., "City Hall, San Bernardino, California," *Progressive Architecture* 55 (February 1974), pp. 66–71.

149. "Frank O. Gehry: The Search for 'No-rule' Architecture," *Architectural Record* 159 (June 1976), pp. 95–102.

150. Robert Venturi, *Complexity and Contradiction in Architecture* (New York: Museum of Modern Art, 1966); Robert Venturi, Denise Scott Brown, and Steven Izenhour, *Learning from Las Vegas* (Cambridge, Mass.: MIT Press, 1972).

151. Robert Venturi, Denise Scott Brown, and Steven Izenhour, *op. cit.*, pp. 170–171; "Some Decorated Sheds or Towards an Old Architecture," *Progressive Architecture* 54 (May 1973), pp. 86–89.

152. Charles W. Moore, "You Have to Pay for the Public Life," *Perspecta* 9/10 (1965), pp. 57–106; "MLTW/Moore, Lyndon, Turnbull: Pembroke College Dormitories, Brown University, Providence, Rhode Island," *Progressive Architecture* 51 (January 1970), pp. 130–135; Charles Moore, Gerald Allen, Donlyn Lyndon, with drawings by William Turnbull, *op. cit.*

The listing of books and articles that follows are those which specifically contributed to our understanding of drawings within the practice of architecture. This bibliography, therefore, is not a compilation of histories of American architecture. It is fascinating though to note how those who have written on American architecture have or have not utilized illustrations of drawings in their texts. The inclusion and exclusion of drawings provide us with at least a hint of how important or insignificant the authors have considered drawings in the design process.

Fiske Kimball, in his numerous monographs and in his classic *Domestic Architecture of the American Colonies and of the Early Republic* (New York: Scribner's, 1921), allowed drawings a prominent place among his illustrations. Later histories, such as Talbot F. Hamlin's *The American Spirit in Architecture* (New Haven: Yale University Press, 1926), G. H. Edgell's *The American Architecture of Today* (New York: Scribner's, 1928), or Thomas E. Tallmadge's *The Story of Architecture in America* (New York: Norton, 1927), used only a limited number of formal perspective presentation drawings. Plans and even sketches were important for Kimball, whereas they are sparsely reproduced in the other publications.

The more recent histories of the 1950s and 1960s do not present a consistent pattern in the way they approach and reproduce drawings. Though Wayne Andrews in his *Architecture, Ambition and Americans* (New York: Harper, 1955) illustrated only a limited number of plans, the ones he included are of major import. John Burchard and Albert Bush-Brown in *The Architecture of America: A Social and Cultural History* (Boston: Little, Brown, 1961) rejected drawings altogether, while Alan Gowans in *Images of American Living* (New York: Harper & Row, 1964) found that site plans, cutaway isometric drawings, and interior and exterior drawings were essential to his analysis of architecture and its relation to culture. The use of drawings as illustration has become increasingly prevalent in recent years. Vincent Scully relied heavily on them in his *American Architecture and Urbanism* (New York: Praeger, 1969). William H. Pierson, Jr., and William H. Jordy in their four-volume series *American Buildings and Their Architects* (New York: Doubleday, 1972) often found drawings more essential to their argument than photographic illustrations. The new preeminence of drawings can be sensed in the writing of our present theorists, historians, architects—that of Robert Venturi and Charles W. Moore, for instance. The current concern for intent in American architecture has necessitated a renewed reliance on drawings. The use of drawings as illustration coupled with a discussion of them has now become central to any general history of American architecture and to monographs by and about individual practitioners. The most recent example is Henry-Russell Hitchcock and William Seale's *Temples of Democracy: The State Capitals of the U.S.A.* (New York: Harcourt Brace Jovanovich, 1976).

General References

Ackerman, James. "Architectural Practice in the Italian Renaissance." *JSAH* **13** (October 1954), pp. 3–11.
Beach, John. "The Bay Tradition, 1890–1918." *Bay Area Houses.* Edited by Sally Woodbridge. New York: Oxford University Press, 1976, pp. 23–98.
Bel Geddes, Norman. *Magic Motorways.* New York: Random House, 1940.
———. *Horizons.* Boston: Little, Brown, 1932.
"Bertram Grosvenor Goodhue: Architect, Designer and Draftsman." *Pencil Points* **5** (June 1924), pp. 42–61.
Blomfield, Reginald. *Architectural Drawing and Draughtsmen.* London: Cassell & Co., 1912.
"The 'Blue' Copying Process." *American Architect and Building News* **4** (Aug. 3, 1878), p. 44.
Briggs, Martin S. *The Architect in History.* London: Oxford University Press, 1924.
Burford, James. "The Historical Development of Architectural Drawings to the End of the Eighteenth Century." *Architectural Review* [London] **54**, pp. 1–5, 59–65, 83–87, 141–145, 156–160, 222–227.
Burges, William. "Architectural Drawings." *Transactions of the Royal Institute of British Architects* (1861), pp. 15–28.
"Cass Gilbert, Master of Style." *Pencil Points* **15** (November 1934), pp. 541–566.
Collins, Peter. "The Origin of Graph Paper as an Influence on Architectural Designs." *JSAH* **21** (December 1962), pp. 159–162.
Coulin, Claudius. *Drawings by Architects from the Ninth Century to the Present Day.* New York: Reinhold, 1962.
"A Cross-Section of the Present State of the Art of Delineation in America." *Pencil Points* **21** (July 1940), pp. 398–430, 442–446.
"The Custody of an Architect's Drawings." *American Architect and Building News* **3** (June 15, 1878), pp. 206–208.
Draper, Joan Elaine. *John Galen Howard and the Beaux-Arts Movement in the United States.* Master's thesis, University of California, Berkeley, 1972.
Drexler, Arthur. *The Drawings of Frank Lloyd Wright.* New York: Horizon, 1970.
Ferriss, Hugh. *The Metropolis of Tomorrow.* New York: I. Washburn, 1929.
Garvin, Anthony. *Architecture and Town Planning in Colonial Connecticut.* New Haven: Yale University Press, 1951.
Goodhart-Rendel, H. "Architectural Draughtsmanship of the Past." *Journal of the Royal Institute of British Architects* **58** (February 1951) pp. 127–136.
Hamlin, Talbot F. *The American Spirit in Architecture.* New Haven: Yale University Press, 1926.
Hitchcock, Henry-Russell. *American Architectural Books*, 3d rev. ed. New York: Da Capo, 1975.
Jenkins, Frank. *Architect and Patron.* London: Oxford University Press, 1961.
Jenson, J. Norman. "Early History of Blue Printing." *Architectural Record* **71** (May 1932), p. 335.
Kaye, Barrington. *The Development of the Architectural Profession in Britain: A Sociological Study.* London: George Allen & Unwin, 1960.
Kemper, Alfred M. *Drawings by American Architects.* New York: Wiley, 1973.
Kimball, Fiske. *Domestic Architecture of the American Colonies and of the Early Republic.* 1921. Reprinted. New York: Dover, 1966.
———. *Mr. Samuel McIntire, Carver, the Architect of Salem.* Salem, Mass.: P. Smith, 1949.
———.*Thomas Jefferson, Architect.* 1916. Reprint. New York: Da Capo, 1968.
King, Susan. *The Drawings of Eric Mendelsohn.* Berkeley: University Museum, University of California, Berkeley, 1969.
Kirker, Harold. *The Architecture of Charles Bulfinch.* Cambridge, Mass.: Harvard University Press, 1969.
Kostof, Spriro, ed. *The Architect: Chapters in the History of the Profession.* New York: Oxford University Press, 1977.
Magonigle, Harold van Buren. "A Half Century of Architecture, a Biographical Review." *Pencil Points* **14** (1933), pp. 477–480; **15** (1934), pp. 223–233, 357–359, 464–466, 563–565.
Massey, James C. *Two Centuries of Philadelphia Architectural Drawings.* Philadelphia: Philadelphia Museum of Art, 1964.
———. *Sources for American Architectural Drawings in Foreign Collections: A Preliminary Survey Carried out under a Grant from the Ford Foundation.* Washington, D.C., January 1969. Copy in Avery Library, Columbia University, New York.
Michels, Eileen. *A Developmental Study of the Drawings Published in the American Architect and in Inland Architect through 1895.* Ph.D. thesis, University of Minnesota, Minneapolis, 1972.
———. "Late Nineteenth-Century Published American Perspective Drawings." *JSAH* **31** (December 1972), pp. 291–308.
Morrison, Hugh. *Early American Architecture.* New York: Oxford University Press, 1952.
Nichols, Frederick Doveton. *Thomas Jefferson's Architectural Drawings.* Boston: Massachusetts Historical Society, 1960.
O'Gorman, James F. *Selected Drawings: Henry Hobson Richardson and His Office.* Cambridge, Mass.: Harvard University Press, 1974.
O'Neal, William B. *Architectural Drawings in Virginia.* Charlottesville: University of Virginia Press, 1969.
Pfaendler, R. "Architectural Models." *Architectural Review* [London] **140** (July 1966), pp. 68–76.
Physick, J., and Darby, M. "The Architectural Model during the Victorian Period." *Marble Halls.* Exhibition catalog, Victoria and Albert Museum, London, 1973, pp. 13–16.
Pierce, James Smith. "Architectural Drawings and the Intent of the Architect." *Art Journal* **27** (Fall 1976), pp. 48–59.
Spiers, Richard Phene. *Architectural Drawings.* London: Cassell & Co., 1887.
Stickley, Gustav. *Craftsman Houses.* New York: Craftsman Publishing Co., 1910.
Swales, Francis S. "Draftsmanship and Architecture: As Exemplified by the Work of Paul P. Cret." *Pencil Points* **9** (November 1928), pp. 688–704.
Swales, Francis S. "Draftsmanship and Architecture: As Exemplified by the Work of Raymond M. Hood." *Pencil Points* **9** (May 1928), pp. 259–269.
Teague, Willer Dorwin. *Design This Day.* New York: Harcourt, Brace, 1940.
Waterman, Thomas T. *The Mansions of Virginia.* Chapel Hill, N.C.: University of North Carolina Press, 1946.
Wilton-Ely, J. "The Architectural Model: l. English Baroque." *Apollo* **88** (October 1968), pp. 250–259.
———. "Architectural Models." *Architectural Review* [London] **142** (July 1967), pp. 26–32.
Withey, Henry and Elsie. *Biographical Dictionary of American Architects (Deceased).* Los Angeles: New Age Publishing Co., 1956.
Wright, F. A. *Architectural Perspective for Beginners.* New York: Comstock, 1885.
Wunder, Richard P. "The Architect's Eye." *The Cooper Union Museum Chronicle* **3** (September 1962), pp. 3–49.

1776–1976

The following is a selected bibliography providing both the best general introduction to an architect's career and titles relating specifically to the illustrated drawings. General histories of American architecture are included when they contain either the only or a particularly illuminating discussion of an architect's work. There exist no monographs for many of the architects in this book—just one example of the need for more in-depth study of those who have shaped our architectural heritage. The only abbreviations used are *AIAJ* for the *American Institute of Architects Journal* and *JSAH* for *Journal of the Society of Architectural Historians.*

Gregory Ain

Gebhard, David, and von Breton, Harriet. *L.A. in the Thirties.* Salt Lake City: Peregrine Smith, 1975.
——— and Winter, Robert. *A Guide to Architecture in Southern California.* Los Angeles: The Los Angeles County Museum of Art, 1965.
"The Logic of Levels in Reverse." *Architectural Record* **95** (April 1944), 64–67.
The Museum of Modern Art. *The Museum of Modern Art–Woman's Home Companion Exhibition House, Gregory Ain, Architect.* New York: Museum of Modern Art, 1950.
"Step-back Planning Gives Privacy in the Dunsmuir Flat Building, Erected on a 49-foot Los Angeles Inside Lot: Designer Gregory Ain." *Architectural Record* **87** (May 1940), 45–47.

Albert Bendernagel

Christovich, Mary L., and Toledano, Roulhac. *The American Sector.* New Orleans Architecture, vol. 2, Gretna, La.: Pelican, 1972.

Asher Benjamin

Benjamin, Asher. *The Works of Asher Benjamin: Boston, 1806–1853.* 7 vols. 1797–1843. Reprinted with new introductions. New York: Da Capo Press, 1973.
Cummings, Abbott Lowell. "An Investigation of the Sources, Evolution and Influence of Asher Benjamin's Building Guides." Ph.D. dissertation, Ohio State University, 1950.
Hamlin, Talbot. *Greek Revival Architecture in America.* New York: Dover, 1964. Reprinted from New York: Oxford University Press, 1944.
Howe, Florence Thompson. "More about Asher Benjamin." *JSAH* **13** (October 1954), pp. 16–19.
O'Donnell, Thomas E. "Asher Benjamin: A Pioneer Writer of Architectural Books." *Architecture* **54** (December 1926), pp. 375–378.

Andrew Binney

Gilchrist, Agnes Addison. *William Strickland, Architect and Engineer, 1788–1845.* Enlarged ed. New York: Da Capo Press, 1969. Reprinted from Philadelphia: University of Pennsylvania Press, 1950.
Summerson, John. *The Classical Language of Architecture.* 3d ed. Cambridge, Mass.: MIT Press, 1971.

Arnold W. Brunner

Aitken, Robert Ingersoll, ed. *Arnold W. Brunner and His Work.* With contributions by Edwin H. Blashfield, Daniel C. French, Clayton Hamilton, J. Horace McFarland, Brander Matthews, Charles Harris Whitaker, and Brand Whitlock. New York: Press of the American Institute of Architects, 1926.

Charles Bulfinch

Kirker, Harold. *The Architecture of Charles Bulfinch.* Cambridge: Harvard University Press, 1969.
———, and Kirker, James. *Bulfinch's Boston: 1787–1817.* New York: Oxford University Press, 1964.
Pierson, William H., Jr. *The Colonial and Neo-Classical Styles.* American Buildings and Their Architects, vol. 1. Garden City, N.Y.: Doubleday, 1970.
Place, Charles A. *Charles Bulfinch: Architect and Citizen.* New York: Da Capo Press. 1968. Reprinted from Boston: Houghton-Mifflin, 1925.

John Byers
Edla Muir

Byers, John. "Adobe Construction." *American Architect* **127** (May 20, 1925), pp. 469–473
"An English Farm House." *California Arts and Architecture* **27** (December 1935), p. 17.
Goodnow, Marc N. "Ancient Adobes for Modern Homes." *The Architect and Engineer* **49** (November 1929), pp. 35–46.
Harris, Allen. "The Essence of Architecture." *Pacific Coast Architects* **30** (August 1926), pp. 9–37.
Irving, Jean. "Some of John Byers' Houses." *The Architect and Engineer* **95** (October 1928), pp. 34–44.
"Larry Crabe House." *Arts and Architecture* **57** (September 1940), p. 35.
Morrow, Irving F. "Folk Songs." *The Architect and Engineer* **79** (December 1924), pp. 74–93.
Newcomb, Rex Ford. "John Byers, Architect." *The Western Architect* **38** (January 1929), pp. 3–4.

Francis Barry Byrne

Brooks, H.[Harold] Allen. *The Prairie School: Frank Lloyd Wright and His Midwest Contemporaries.* Buffalo: University of Toronto Press, 1972.
Chappell, Sally Anderson. "Barry Byrne." *Inland Architect* **11** (January 1968), pp. 6–10.
———. "Barry Byrne, Architect: His Formative Years." *The Prairie School Review* **3** (1966).

Serge Chermayeff

Chermayeff, Serge. "Architects' Studio and a Group of Vacation Houses at Wellfleet, Massachusetts." *House and Home* **6** (July 1954), pp. 120–125.
———, and Alexander, Christopher. *Community & Privacy; Toward a New Architecture of Humanism.* 2d ed. Garden City, N.Y.: Doubleday, Anchor Books, 1969.
———, and Tzonis, Alexander. *The Shape of Community: Realization of Human Potential.* Baltimore, Md.: Penguin, 1971.

Nicholas J. Clayton
Barnstone, Howard. *The Galveston That Was.* New York: MacMillan, 1966.
Turner, Drexel, and Fox, Stephen. *The Architecture of Nicholas J. Clayton and Galveston: 1870–1900.* College Station, Tex.: Texas A & M University Press, forthcoming.
Grieff, Constance M. *Lost America: From the Mississippi to the Pacific.* Princeton, N.J.: Pyne Press, 1972.

Ernest Coxhead
Beach, John. "The Bay Tradition: 1890–1918." In *Bay Area Houses,* edited by Sally Woodbridge. New York: Oxford University Press, 1976.
Coxhead, Almeric. "The Telephone Exchange, San Francisco." *Architect and Engineer* **18** (August 1909), pp. 34–36.
Coxhead, Ernest. "Phoebe Hearst Architectural Competition for the University of California." *Architect and Engineer* **30** (September 1912), pp. 97–101.

Ralph Adams Cram
Cram, Ralph Adams. *My Life in Architecture.* Boston: Little, Brown, 1936.
———. "A Note on Architectural Style." *Architectural Review* **12** (October 1905), pp. 181–195.
Maginnis, Charles D. *The Work of Cram & Ferguson, Architects: Including Work by Cram, Goodhue, & Ferguson.* New York: Pencil Points Press, 1929.
North, Arthur Tappan. *Contemporary American Architects: Ralph Adams Cram (Cram and Ferguson).* New York: McGraw-Hill Book Co., 1931.
Schuyler, Montgomery. "The Architecture of West Point." *Architectural Record* **14** (December 1903), pp. 463–492.
———. "The Works of Cram, Goodhue and Ferguson . . . 1892–1910." *Architectural Record* **29** (January 1911), pp. 1–112.
Tucci, Douglas Shand. *Ralph Adams Cram—American Medievalist.* Boston: The Boston Public Library, 1975.

Paul Philippe Cret
Cret, Paul. "The Ecole des Beaux-Arts and Architectural Education." *JSAH* **1** (April 1944), pp. 12–15.
———. "The Ecole des Beaux-Arts: What Its Architectural Teaching Means." *Architectural Record* **23** (May 1908), pp. 367–371.
White, Theo B. *Paul Philippe Cret, Architect and Teacher.* Philadelphia: Art Alliance Press, 1973.

James H. Dakin
Scully, Arthur, Jr. *James Dakin, Architect: His Career in New York and the South.* Baton Rouge, La.: Louisiana State University Press, 1973.

Alexander Jackson Davis
Andrews, Wayne. "Alexander Jackson Davis." *The Architectural Review* [London] **109** (May 1951), pp. 307–312.
Davies, Jane. "A.J. Davis' Projects for a Patent Office Building, 1832–1834." *JSAH* **24** (October 1965), pp. 229–251.
———. "Six Letters by William Elliott to Alexander J. Davis; 1834–1838." *JSAH* **20** (March 1961), pp. 71–73.
Hamlin, Talbot. *Greek Revival Architecture.* New York: Dover, 1964. Reprinted from New York: Oxford University Press, 1944.
Newton, Roger Hale. *Pioneers in American Revivalist Architecture, 1812–1870, Including a Glimpse of Their Times and Their Contemporaries.* New York: Columbia University Press, 1942.
Tatum, George Bishop. "Alexander Jackson Downing: Arbiter of American Taste, 1815–1852." Ph.D. dissertation, Princeton University, 1950.

Alden Ball Dow
Dow, Alden. "An Architect's View of Creativity." *AIAJ* **31** (February 1959), pp. 19–26.
———. *Reflections.* Midland, Mich.: Northwood Institute, 1970.
Hamlin, Talbot F. "The Architect and the House, No. 8, Alden B. Dow of Michigan." *Pencil Points* **23** (May 1944), pp. 268–286.
———. "Profiles in Design: Alden Dow," *House and Home* **19** (February 1961), pp. 110–123.
"Houses in Midland, Michigan, Alden Dow, Architect." *Architectural Forum* **65** (September 1936), pp. 191–200.

Charles Eames
"Case Study Houses 8 and 9 by Charles Eames and Eero Saarinen, Architects." *Arts and Architecture* **62** (December 1945), pp. 44–51.
"Case Study House, A House Designed and Built for the Magazine Arts and Architecture." *Arts and Architecture* **67** (July 1950), pp. 26–39.
"Case Study House No. 8 and 9: Charles Eames and Eero Saarinen, Assoc. Archts." *Arts and Architecture* **65** (March 1948), pp. 40–41.
Drexler, Arthur. *Furniture from the Design Collection.* New York: Museum of Modern Art, 1973.
Kaufmann, Edgar, Jr. "Chairs, Eames, and Chests." *Art News* **49** (May 1960), pp. 36–40.
McCoy, Esther. "Arts and Architecture Case Study Houses." *Perspecta* **15** (1975), pp. 54–73.
Noyes, Eliot. "Charles Eames." *Art and Architecture* **63** (September 1946), pp. 26–44.
Smithson, Alison; Smithson, Peter; Brawne, Michael; Holroyd, Geoffrey; and Eames, Charles. "Eames Celebration." *Architectural Design* (London) **36** (September 1966). Whole issue.

Leopold Eidlitz
Brooks, H. [Harold] Allen. "Leopold Eidlitz 1823–1908." Master's thesis, Yale University, 1953.
Eidlitz, Leopold. *The Nature and Function of Art, More Especially of Architecture.* London: Sampson Low, Marston Searle and Rivington, 1881; New York: A. C. Armstrong & Son, 1881.
Jordy, William H. Introduction to Montgomery Schuyler, *American Architecture and Other Writings,* edited by William H. Jordy and Ralph T. Cox. 2 vols. Cambridge, Mass.: Harvard University Press, 1961.
Schuyler, Montgomery. "A Great American Architect: Leopold Eidlitz." *Architectural Record* **24** (September 1908), pp. 164–179; (October 1908), p. 277; (November 1908), p. 365.

Peter Eisenman
Eisenman, Peter. "House I 1967"; "House II 1969." In Peter Eisenman et al., *Five Architects: Eisenman, Graves, Gwathmey, Hejduk, Meier.* New York: Oxford University Press, 1975, pp. 15–17, 25–27.
———. "House III: Miller Residence, Lakeville, Conn." *Progressive Architecture* **55** (May 1974), pp. 92–99.
———. "Notes on Conceptual Architecture: Towards a Definition." *Casabella* **35** (December 1971), pp. 48–58.
Gandelsonas, Mario. "On Reading Architecture: Eisenman & Graves: An Analysis." *Progressive Architecture* **53** (March 1972), pp. 68–88.

Harvey Ellis
Bragdon, Claude. "Harvey Ellis: A Portrait Sketch." *Architectural Review* **15** (November 1908), pp. 173–183.
Kennedy, Roger G. "The Long Shadow of Harvey Ellis." *Minnesota History* **40** (Fall 1966), pp. 97–108.
Michels, Eileen. *A Developmental Study of the Drawings Published in the American Architect and in Inland Architect through 1896.* Ph.D. thesis, University of Minnesota, Minneapolis, 1972.
Wade, Karen Graham. "Harvey Ellis' Contribution to the Arts and Crafts Movement in America." *JSAH* **33** (October 1972), p. 229.

Craig Ellwood
Blake, Peter. "Craig Ellwood, Architect." *Zodiac* (1959), pp. 162–167.
Heyer, Paul. *Architects on Architecture: New Directions in America.* New York: Walker & Co., 1966.
McCoy, Esther. *Craig Ellwood; Architecture.* Foreword by Peter Blake. New York: Walker & Co., 1968.
"A Ponte, in California: Edifico universitario a Pasadena." *Domus* (April 1975), pp. 18–21.

George Grant Elmslie
William Gray Purcell
Brooks, H. (Harold) Allen. *The Prairie School: Frank Lloyd Wright and His Midwest Contemporaries.* Buffalo: The University of Toronto Press, 1972.
Elmslie, George Grant. "The Chicago School: Its Inheritance and Bequest." *AIAJ* **37** (July 1952), pp. 32–38.
Gebhard, David. "A Guide to the Architecture of Purcell and Elmslie." *Prairie School Review* **2** (First Quarter, 1965).
———. "Louis Sullivan and George Grant Elmslie." *JSAH* **19** (1960), pp. 62–68.
———. "William Gray Purcell and George Grant Elmslie and the Early Progressive Movement in American Architecture from 1900 to 1920." Ph.D. dissertation, University of Minnesota, 1957.
———, ed. "The Work of Purcell & Elmslie." *The Western Architect* (January 1913, January 1915, July 1915). Reprinted as one volume, Park Forest, Ill.: The Prairie School Press, 1965.
Purcell, William G. "Lincoln as a Greek God." *The Independent* **22** (Feb. 8, 1912), pp. 320–322.
———. Elmslie, George G. "American Renaissance?" *The Craftsman* **21** (January 1912), pp. 430–435.

Joseph Esherick
Esherick, Joseph. "Architectural Education in the Thirties and Seventies: A Personal View." In *The Architect: Chapters in the History of the Profession.* Edited by Spiro Kostof. New York: Oxford University Press, 1976.
"Joseph Esherick and His Use of Form, His Use of Space, His Use of Site." *House and Home* **1** (January 1952), pp. 124–135.
"Joseph Esherick: Theory and Practice." *Western Architect & Engineer* **222** (December 1961) pp. 20–37.

Wilson Eyre, Jr.
Githeus, Alfred Morton. "Wilson Eyre, Jr.: His Work." *The Architectural Annual of 1900.* Edited by Albert Kelsey. Philadelphia: The Architectural Annual and The Architectural League of America, 1900, pp. 121–184.
Harbeson, John. "Wilson Eyre 1858–1944." *AIAJ* **5** (March 1946), pp. 129–135.
Millard, Julian. "The Work of Wilson Eyre." *Architectural Record* **14** (October 1903), pp. 280–325.

Richard Fourchy
No significant references exist.

Frank Furness
Levine, Neil. "The Idea of Frank Furness' Building." Master's thesis, Yale University, 1967.
Massey, James. "Frank Furness in the 1870's: Some Lesser Known Buildings." *Charette* **43** (January 1963), pp. 13–16.
———. "Frank Furness in the 1880's. *Charette* **43** (October 1963), pp. 25–29.
———. "Frank Furness: The Declining Years 1890's–1912." *Charette* **46** (February 1966), pp. 8–13.
———. "The Provident Trust Buildings 1879–1897." *JSAH* **19** (May 1960), pp. 79–81.
O'Gorman, James F. *The Architecture of Frank Furness.* Philadelphia: Philadelphia Museum of Art, 1973.
Robinson, Cervin. "Furness in '73." *Architecture Plus* **1** (August 1973), pp. 26–33.

James Gallier, Jr.
James Gallier, Sr.
Cullison, William R. "Gallier House—The House of a Nineteenth Century New Orleans Architect." *Antiques* **102** (September 1972), pp. 471–475.
Gallier, James, Sr. *Autobiography of James Gallier, Architect.* Introduction by Samuel Wilson, Jr. New York: Da Capo Press, 1973. Reprinted from Paris: Briere, 1864.
Hamlin, Talbot. *New Orleans and Its Environs.* New York: William Helburn, 1938.
Toledano, Roulhac, et al. *Suburb Marigny.* New Orleans Architecture, vol. 4 Gretna, La.: Pelican, 1974.
Wilson, Samuel, Jr. *James Gallier, Architect: An Exhibition of His Work.* New Orleans: Louisiana Landmarks Society, 1950.
———, and Lemann, Bernard, *The Lower Garden District.* New Orleans Architecture, edited by Mary L. Christovich and Roulhac Toledano, vol. 1. Gretna, La.: Pelican, 1971.

Frank O. Gehry
Goldberger, Paul. "Studied Slapdash." *The New York Times Magazine*, Jan. 18, 1976.
Nairn, Janet. "Frank Gehry: The Search for a 'No Rules' Architecture." *Architectural Record* **159** (June 1976), pp. 95–102.
Ryder, Sharon Lee. "A Rousing Place." *Progressive Architecture* **57** (February 1976), pp. 58–63.
Skura, Norma. "Paper Furniture for Penny Pinchers." *The New York Times Magazine*, April 9, 1972, pp. 90–91.

Cass Gilbert
"Cass Gilbert, Master of Style." *Pencil Point* **15** (November 1934), pp. 541–556.
Cornfield, Richard. "The Poetic Vision: The Design of the St. Louis World's Fair." *Classical America* **3** (1973), pp. 56–66.
Gilbert, Cass. "Festival Hall and the Cascades: Louisiana Purchase Exposition, St. Louis, Missouri." *American Architect and Building News* **85** (Aug. 27, 1904), p. 71.
Plotts, Donald A. "Cass Gilbert, 1859–1934." Master's thesis, Columbia University, undated.
Thompson, Neil B. *Minnesota State Capitol: The Art and Politics of a Public Building.* St. Paul: Minnesota Historical Society, 1974.

Romaldo Giurgola
Giurgola, Romaldo. "Reflections on Buildings and the City: The Realism of the Partial Vision." *Perspecta* **9/10** (1965), pp. 107–130.
Nakamura, Toshio, ed. "Mitchell/Giurgola: Special Feature." *Architecture & Urbanism* [Japan] **5** (December 1975), pp. 62–123. Entire issue; includes Paul Goldberger, "Works of Mitchell/Giurgola," pp. 121–123.

Bruce Goff
Delong, David. *The Architecture of Bruce Goff; Buildings and Projects, 1916–1974.* New York: Garland, 1976.
Futagawa, Yukio, ed. *Bavinger House, Norman, 1950; Price House, Bartlesville, Oklahoma, 1957–1966/Bruce Goff.* Tokyo: ADA Edita, 1975.
Goff, Bruce. "Bauten and Entwürfe von Bruce Goff, 1935–1957." *Bauwelt* **27** (January 1958), pp. 77–88.
———. *Bruce Goff: A Portfolio.* Compiled and designed by William Murphy and Louis Muller. New York: The Architectural League of New York, 1970.
———. "A Young Architect's Protest for Architecture." *Perspecta* **13/14** (1971), pp. 330–357.
Kostka, Robert, "Bruce Goff and the New Tradition." *The Prairie School Review* **7** (1970), pp. 5–15.
Takenobu, Mori, ed. *Bruce Goff in Architecture.* Tokyo; Takenobu, 1970.
Waechter, H. H. "The Architecture of Bruce Goff." *AIAJ* **32** (December 1959), pp. 32–36.

Bertram Grosvenor Goodhue
"Bertram Grosvenor Goodhue, Architect, Designer and Draftsman." *Pencil Point* **5** (June 1924), pp. 42–61.
Goodhue, Bertram Grosvenor. *A Book of Architectural and Decorative Drawings.* New York: The Architectural Book Publishing Co., 1914.
Maginnis, Charles D. *The Work of Cram & Ferguson, Architects: Including Work by Cram, Goodhue, & Ferguson.* New York: Pencil Points Press, 1929.
Mumford, Lewis. "B. G. Goodhue." *The New Republic* **44** (Oct. 28, 1924), pp. 259–260.
Schuyler, Montgomery. "The Architecture of West Point." *Architectural Record* **14** (December 1903), pp. 463–492.
———. "The Works of Cram, Goodhue and Ferguson . . . 1892–1910." *Architectural Record* **29** (January 1911), pp. 1–112.
Tucci, Douglass Shand. *Ralph Adams Cram: American Medievalist.* Boston: The Boston Public Library, 1975.
Whitaker, Charles Harris, ed. *Bertram Grosvenor Goodhue, Master of Many Arts.* New York: The Architectural Book Publishing Co., 1925.

Michael Graves
Carl, Peter. "Towards a Pluralist Architecture." *Progressive Architecture* **54** (February 1973), pp. 82–89.
Frampton, Kenneth. "Frontality vs. Rotation." In *Five Architects: Eisenman, Graves, Gwathmey, Hejduk, Meier.* New York: Oxford University Press, 1975.
Graves, Michael. "The Swedish Connection." *Journal of Architectural Education* **29** (1975), pp. 12–13.
LaRiche, William. "Architecture as the World Again?" In Peter Eisenman et al., *Five Architects: Eisenman, Graves, Gwathmey, Hejduk, Meier.* New York: Oxford University Press, 1975.

Charles Sumner Greene
Henry Mather Greene
Bangs, Jean Murray (Mrs. Harwell H. Harris). "Greene and Greene." *Architectural Forum* **89** (October 1948), pp. 80–89.
Current, William and Karen. *Greene & Greene; Architects in the Residential Style.* Fort Worth: Amon Carter Museum of Western Art, 1974.
David, Arthur C. "An Architect of Bungalows." *Architectural Record* **20** (October 1906), pp. 306–315.
Greene, Charles Sumner. "Bungalows." *The Western Architect* **12** (July 1908) pp. 3–5.
———. "Impressions of Some Bungalows and Gardens." *Homes and Gardens* **1** (January 1916), pp. 9–11.
Hopkins, Una Nixson. "The California Bungalow." *Architect and Engineer* **4** (April 1906), pp. 33–39.
Jordy, William H. *Progressive and Academic Ideals at the Turn of the Twentieth Century.* American Buildings and Their Architects, vol. 3. Garden City, N.Y.: Doubleday, 1972.
Lancaster, Clay. *The Japanese Influence in America.* New York: Walton H. Rawls, 1963.
Makinson, Randell L. *A Guide to the Work of Greene & Greene.* Salt Lake City: Peregrine Smith, 1974.
———. "Greene and Greene." In Esther McCoy, *Five California Architects.* New York: Reinhold, 1960.
Strand, Janaan. *A Greene & Greene Guide.* Pasadena: Grant Dahlstrom/The Castle Press, 1974.
Winter, Robert W. "The Arroyo Culture." *California Design 1910.* Edited by Timothy J. Andersen, Eudorah M. Moore, Robert W. Winton. Pasadena: California Design Publications, 1974.
Yost, Lloyd M. "Greene and Greene of Pasadena." *JSAH* **9** (March 1950), pp. 11–19.

Marion Mahony Griffin
Walter Burley Griffin
Berkon, Susan Fondiler, and Kay, Jane Holz. "The First Lady: Marion Mahony (Later Marion Mahony Griffin)." *Feminist Art Journal*, May 16, 1975.
Birrell, James. *Walter Burley Griffin.* Brisbane: University of Queensland Press, 1964.
Brooks, H. (Harold) Allen. *The Prairie School: Frank Lloyd Wright and His Midwest Contemporaries.* Buffalo: University of Toronto Press, 1972.
McCoy, Robert E. "Rock Crest/Rock Glen: Prairie School Planning in Iowa." *Prairie School Review* **5** (Third quarter, 1968), pp. 1–2, 5–39, 51.
Torre, Susana, ed. *Women in American Architecture: A Historic and Contemporary Perspective.* New York: Whitney Library of Design, 1977.
Van Zanten, David T. "The Early Work of Marion Mahony Griffin." *Prairie School Review* **3** (1966), pp. 1–2, 5–23, 27.
———, ed. *Walter Burley Griffin, Selected Designs.* Palos Park, Ill.: Prairie School Press, 1970.

Hugh Hardy
Malcolm Holzman
Norman Pfeiffer
Cohen, Stuart. "Hardy Holzman and Pfeiffer on America." *Progressive Architecture* **56** (February 1975), pp. 42–59.
Hardy, Hugh; Holzman, Malcom; and Pfeiffer, Norman. "Hardy Holzman & Pfeiffer." *L'Architecture d'Aujourd'Hui* (November–December 1973), pp. 79–98.
Pfeiffer, Norman. "Una Alternativa Non-estetica." *Casabella* **37** (August–September 1973), pp. 127–132.

Harwell Hamilton Harris
Gebhard, David, and Von Breton, Harriette. *L. A. in the Thirties: 1931–1941.* Salt Lake City: Peregrine Smith, 1975.
Harris, Harwell Hamilton. "A Collection of His Writings & Buildings." *Student Publication of the School of Design North Carolina State University at Raleigh* **14** (1965).
———. "Rhythmic Integration of Panel Elements." *Perspecta* **2** (1953), pp. 37–44.
"Wood." *California Arts and Architecture* **55** (May 1939), pp. 17, 40.
"Houses by Harwell Hamilton Harris." *Architectural Forum* **72** (March 1940), pp. 171–185.

John Haviland
Baigell, Matthew. *John Haviland.* Ph.D. Thesis, University of Pennsylvania. Ann Arbor, Mich.: University Microfilms, 1965.
———. "John Haviland in Philadelphia, 1818–1826." *JSAH* **25** (October 1966), pp. 197–208.
———. "John Haviland and the Picturesque Taste in America." *The Architectural Review* (London) **139** (March 1966), pp. 215–216.
Gardner, Albert Ten Eyck. "A Philadelphia Masterpiece: Haviland's Prison." *The Metropolitan Museum of Art Bulletin* **51** (December 1955), pp. 103–108.
Hamlin, Talbot. *Greek Revival Architecture in America.* New York: Dover, 1964. Reprinted from New York: Oxford University Press, 1944.
Johnston, Norman B. "John Haviland, Jailer to the World." *JSAH* **23** (May 1964), pp. 101–105.

John Hejduk
Eisenman, Peter, et al. *Five Architects: Eisenman, Graves, Gwathmey, Hejduk, Meier.* New York: Oxford University Press, 1975.
Frampton, Kenneth. "Notes from the Underground." *Artforum* **10** (April 1972), pp. 40–47.
———. "Renovation Foundation Building, Cooper Union." *Domus* **551** (October 1975), pp. 11–15.
John Hejduk. "Hors du Temps dans L'Espace." *L'Architecture d'Aujourd'hui* **35** (September–November 1965), pp. 21–23.
———, and Oswald, Franz. *Projects/John Hejduk, Architect.* Paris: Fondation Le Corbusier, 1972.
———, and Sadek, George. *Three Projects.* New York: Cooper Union School of Art & Architecture with the Graham Foundation for Advanced Studies in the Fine Arts and The Architectural League of New York, 1969.
Morton, David. "Second Wall House." *Progressive Architecture* **55** (June 1974), pp. 98–103.
Nakamura, Toshio, ed. "John Hejduk: Special Feature." *Architecture & Urbanism* **5** (May 1975), pp. 73–154. Entire issue; includes Kenneth Frampton, "John Hejduk and the Cult of Humanism," pp. 141–142; and John Hejduk, "Out of Time and into Space," p. 3.

Richard Morris Hunt
Burnham, Alan. "The New York Architecture of Richard Morris Hunt." *JSAH* **11** (May 1952), pp. 9–14.
Montgomery, Schuyler. "The Works of the Late Richard M. Hunt." *Architectural Record* **5** (October–December 1895), pp. 97–134.

Thomas Jefferson
Adams, William Howard, ed. *The Eye of Jefferson.* Washington, D.C.: The National Gallery of Art, 1976.
Collins, Peter. "The Origin of Graph Paper as an Influence on Architectural Design." *JSAH* **21** (December 1962), pp. 159–162.
Guiness, Desmond, and Sadler, Julius. *Thomas Jefferson, Architect.* New York: Viking Press, 1973.
Hersey, George. "Replication Replicated." *Perspecta* **9/10** (1965), pp. 211–248.
Kimball, (Sidney) Fiske. *Thomas Jefferson, Architect.* Introduction by Frederick D. Nichols. New York: Da Capo Press, 1968.
Lehman-Hartleben, Karl. *Thomas Jefferson, American Humanist.* New York: Macmillan, 1947.
Nichols, Frederick D. *Thomas Jefferson's Architectural Drawings.* 3d ed. Boston: The Massachusetts Historical Society and Charlottesville, Va.: The Thomas Jefferson Memorial Foundation and the University of Virginia, Press, 1961.
Pierson, William H., Jr. *The Colonial and Neo-Classical Styles.* American Buildings and Their Architects, vol. 1. Garden City, N. Y.: Doubleday, 1970.

Ely Jacques Kahn
Bletter, Rosemarie Haag, and Robinson, Cervin. *Skyscraper Style: Art Deco New York* New York: Oxford University Press, 1975.
Kahn, Ely Jacques. *Ely Jacques Kahn.* Foreword by Arthur Tappan North. New York: McGraw-Hill, 1931.

Louis I. Kahn
Giurgola, Romaldo, and Mehta, Jaimini. *Louis I.Kahn.* Boulder, Colo.: Westview Press, 1975.
Jordy, William H. *The Impact of European Modernism in the Mid-Twentieth Century.* American Buildings and Their Architects, vol. 4. Garden City, N.Y.: Doubleday, 1972.
———. "The Span of Kahn." *Architectural Review* **155** (June 1974), pp. 318–342.
Kommendant, August. *18 Years with Architect Louis I. Kahn.* Englewood, N.J.: Aloray, 1975.
Rowan, Jan C. "Wanting to Be." *Progressive Architecture* (April 1961), pp. 130–149.
Scully, Vincent J., Jr. *Louis I. Kahn.* New York: George Braziller, 1962.
Wurman, Richard Saul, and Feldman, Eugene. *The Notebooks and Drawings of Louis I. Kahn.* 2d ed. Cambridge, Mass.: MIT Press, 1973.

George Fred Keck
Cohen, Stuart E. *Chicago Architects.* Introduction by Stanley Tigerman. Chicago: Swallow Press, 1976.
Keck, George Fred. "House of Tomorrow, Century Homes, Inc., Chicago." *Architectural Record* **75** (January 1934), p. 29.
———."Insulation & House Design." *Pencil Points* **25** (February 1944), pp. 76–82.
Slade, Thomas. "The Crystal House of 1934." *JSAH* **29** (December 1970), pp. 350–353.
"Sliding Roof Gives House Year-Round Use of Patio." *Architectural Record* **137** (February 1965), pp. 157–160.

Benjamin Henry Latrobe
Daiker, Virginia. "The Capitol of Jefferson and Latrobe." *Library of Congress Quarterly* (Spring 1975), pp. 25–32.
Hamlin, Talbot. *Benjamin Henry Latrobe.* New York: Oxford University Press, 1955.
"Latrobe Drawings." *AIAJ* **5** (February 1946), pp. 66–67.
Norton, Paul Foote. "Benjamin Henry Latrobe: A Bibliography." *American Association of Architectural Bibliographers* **9** (1972), pp. 53–84.
———. *Latrobe, Jefferson and the National Capitol.* Ph.D. thesis, Princeton University, 1952.
Pierson, William H., Jr. *The Colonial and Neo-Classical Styles.* American Buidlings and Their Architects, vol. 1. Garden City, N.Y.: Doubleday, 1970.

William Lescaze
Barbey, Gilles. "William Lescaze: Sa carrère et son oeuvre de 1915–1939." *Werk* **58** (August 1971), pp. 559–563.
Howard, William. *On Being an Architect, William Lescaze.* New York: G. P. Putnam's Sons, 1942.
Jordy, William H. *The Impact of European Modernism in the Mid-Twentieth Century.* American Buildings and Their Architects, vol. 4. Garden City, N.Y.: Doubleday, 1972.
———."PSFS: Its Development and Its Significance in Modern Architecture." *JSAH* **21** (May 1962), pp. 47–83.
Stern, Robert A. M. *George Howe: Toward a Modern American Architecture.* New Haven: Yale University Press, 1975.
———."PSFS: Beaux-Arts Theory and Rational Expressionism." *JSAH* **21** (May 1962), pp. 284–295.

Thomas Lewinski
Downing, Alexander Jackson. *The Architecture of Country Houses.* Introduction by J. Stewart Johnson. New York: Dover, 1969. Reprinted from New York: D. Appleton, 1950.
Lancaster, Clay. *Ante Bellum Suburban Villas and Rural Residences of Fayette County Kentucky.* Lexington, Ky.: Thoroughbred Press, 1955.
———. "Italianism in American Architecture before 1860." *American Quarterly* **4** (Summer 1952), pp. 127–148.
———. "Major Thomas Lewinski: Emigre Architect in Kentucky," *JSAH* **11** (December 1952), pp. 13–20.
———. "Palladianism in the Blue Grass." *Gazette des Beaux-Arts* **25** (June 1944), pp. 347–370.

John McComb, Jr.
Gilchrist, Agnes Addison. "Notes for a Catalogue of the John McComb (1763–1853) Collection of Architectural Drawings in the New-York Historical Society." *JSAH* **28** (October 1969), pp. 201–210.
Lancaster, Clay. "The New York City Hall Reconsidered." *JSAH* **29** (March 1970), pp. 33–39.
Schuyler, Montgomery. "A Piece of Architectural History." *Architectural Record* **23** (May 1908), pp. 387–390.
Stillman, Damie. "New York City Hall: Competition and Execution." *JSAH* **23** (October 1967), pp. 129–142.

Samuel McIntire
Cousins, Frank, and Riley, Phil M. *The Wood-Carver of Salem: Samuel McIntire, His Life and Work.* New York: AMS Press, 1970.
Kimball, (Sidney) Fiske. *Mr. Samuel McIntire, Carver, the Architect of Salem.* Portland, Maine: The Southworth-Anthoensen Press for the Essex Institute, Salem, Mass. 1940.
Larbaree, Benjamin, ed. *Samuel McIntire, a Bicentennial Symposium, 1757–1957.* Salem, Mass.: The Essex Institute, 1957.
Pierson, William H., Jr. *The Colonial and Neo-Classical Styles.* American Buildings and Their Architects, vol. 1. Garden City, N.Y.: Doubleday, 1970.

Bernard Maybeck

Bakewell, John, Jr. "The San Francisco Civic Center Competition: How the Successful Architects Arrived at Their Solutions." *The Architect and Engineer* 29 (July 1912), pp. 47–53.

Cahill, B. J. S. "The San Francisco City Hall Competition." *The Architect and Engineer* 29 (July 1912), pp. 54–75.

Howard, John Galen. "The San Francisco Civic Center." *The Architect and Engineer* 33 (July 1913), pp. 41–61.

———. "The Significance of the Civic Center." *The Architect and Engineer* 29 (June 1912), pp. 79–86.

Jordy, William H. *Progressive and Academic Ideals at the Turn of the Twentieth Century.* American Buildings and Their Architects, vol. 3. Garden City, N.Y.: Doubleday, 1972.

Maybeck, Bernard. *Palace of Fine Arts and Lagoon: Panama-Pacific International Exposition, 1915.* San Francisco: Paul Elder, 1915. Excerpts in *AIAJ* 15 (May 1951), pp. 225–228.

———, and Maybeck, Ann White. *Programme for the Development of a Hillside Community.* Berkeley, Calif.: Bulletin of the Hillside Club, 1906–1907. Excerpts in *AIAJ* 15 (May 1951), pp. 225–228.

Woodbridge, Sally, ed. *Bay Area Houses.* Contributions by John Beach, David Gebhard, Charles Moore, Roger Montgomery, Richard C. Peters. New York: Oxford University Press, 1976.

Richard Meier

Eisenman, Peter, et al. *Five Architects: Eisenman, Graves, Gwathmey, Hejduk, Meier.* New York: Oxford University Press, 1975.

Toshio, Nakamura, ed. "Spatial Structure: Richard Meier." *Architecture & Urbanism* [Japan] 64 (April 1976), pp. 45–120. Entire issue; includes Rosemarie H. Bletter, "Recent Work by Richard Meier, the Shamberg Pavilion and the Bronx Developmental Center," pp. 101–103.; Ching-Yu-Chang, "Meier's Whitness," p. 117; Mario Gandelsonas, "Analysis: Richard Meier's Work," pp. 85–86.

Meier, Richard. *Richard Meier, Architect.* Introduction by Kenneth Frampton. New York: Oxford University Press, 1976.

Arthur Ingersoll Meigs

Eberlein, Harold D. "Examples of the Work of Mellor, Meigs and Howe." *Architectural Record* 39 (March 1961), pp. 212–246.

Price, C. Matlack. "The Country House in Good Taste." *Arts and Decoration* 23 (October 1925), pp. 42–44, 95.

Stern, Robert A. M. *George Howe: Toward a Modern American Architecture.* New Haven: Yale University Press, 1975.

Wister, Owen. *A Monograph of the Work of Mellor, Meigs and Howe.* New York: The Architectural Book Publishing Co., 1923.

Ludwig Mies van der Rohe

Blake, Peter. *Mies van der Rohe, Architecture and Structure.* Baltimore: Penguin, 1964.

Blaser, Werner. *Mies van der Rohe: The Art of Structure.* New York: Praeger, 1972.

Carter, Peter. *Mies van der Rohe at Work.* New York: Praeger, 1974.

Drexler, Arthur. *Ludwig Mies van der Rohe.* New York: Braziller, 1960.

Glaeser, Ludwig, ed. *Ludwig Mies van der Rohe: Drawings in the Collection of the Museum of Modern Art.* New York; Museum of Modern Art, 1969.

Hilberseimer, Ludwig. *Mies van der Rohe.* Chicago; P. Theobald, 1956.

Johnson, Philip C. *Mies van der Rohe.* New York: Museum of Modern Art, 1953.

Jordy, William H. *The Impact of European Modernism in the Mid-Twentieth Century.* American Buildings and Their Architects, vol. 4. Garden City, N.Y.: Doubleday, 1972.

Speyer, James A. *Mies van der Rohe.* Chicago: Art Institute of Chicago, 1968.

Robert Mills

Ames, Kenneth. "Robert Mills and the Philadelphia Row House." *JSAH* 27 (May 1968), pp. 140–146.

Federal Writers' Project. *South Carolina: A Guide to the Palmetto State.* New York: Oxford University Press, 1941.

Gallagher, Helen Pierce. *Robert Mills: Architect of the Washington Monument, 1781–1855.* New York: Columbia University Press, 1935.

Pierson, William H., Jr. *The Colonial and Neo-Classical Styles.* American Buildings and Their Architects, vol. 1. Garden City, N.Y.: Doubleday, 1970.

Charles W. Moore
William Turnbull

Cook, John W., and Klotz, Heinrich. *Conversations with Architects.* New York: Praeger, 1973.

Moore, Charles; Allen, Gerald; Lyndon, Donlyn. *The Place of Houses.* New York: Holt, Rinehart, & Winston, 1974.

Ryder, Sharon Lee. "Outside in: Zimmerman House." *Progressive Architecture* 57 (February 1976), pp. 72–75.

Turnbull, William, Jr. *MLTW Charles Moore and William Turnbull, Sea Ranch, California.* Edited and photography by Yukio Futagawa. Global Architecture. Tokyo: A.D.A. Edita, 1966.

Woodbridge, Sally, ed. *Bay Area Houses.* New York: Oxford University Press, 1976.

Julia Morgan

Longstreth, Richard. "Julia Morgan: Some Introductory Notes." *Perspecta* 15 (1975), pp. 74–86.

Morgan, Julia. "San Simeon, The Refectory." *American Architect* 145 (September 1934), pp. 37–42.

Steilberg, Walter T. "Some Examples of the Work of Julia Morgan." *The Architect & Engineer* 55 (November 1918), pp. 38–83, 84–104.

Torre, Susana, ed. *Women in American Architecture: A Historic and Contemporary Perspective.* New York: Whitney Library of Design, 1977.

Richard Joseph Neutra

Boesiger, Willy, ed. *Richard Neutra, Buildings and Projects:* vol. 1 (1923–1950), 1954; vol. 2 (1950–1960), 1960; vol. 3 (1961–1966), 1966. Zurich: Girsberger.

Gebhard, David. *Architecture in California: 1868–1968.* Santa Barbara: Standard Printing, 1968.

McCoy, Esther. *Richard Neutra.* New York: Braziller, 1960.

Neutra, Richard J. *Life and Shape.* New York: Appleton-Century-Crofts, 1962.

———. *Survival through Design.* New York: Oxford University Press, 1954.

———. "Terminals—Transfers." *Architectural Record* 68 (August 1930), pp. 98–104.

———. *Wiebaut Amerika?* Stuttgart: J. Hoffman, 1927.

Zevi, Bruno. *Richard Neutra.* Milan: Il Balcone, 1954.

John Notman

Dallett, Francis James. "John Notman, Architect." *Princeton University Library Chronicle,* Spring 1959.

Early, James. *Romanticism and American Architecture.* New York: A. S. Banner, 1965.

Lancaster, Clay. "Italianism in American Architecture before 1860." *American Quarterly* 4 (Summer 1952), pp. 127–148.

Tatum, George B. *Penn's Great Town.* Philadelphia: University of Pennsylvania Press, 1961.

White, Theo B. ed. *Philadelphia Architecture in the 19th Century.* Cranbury, N.J.: Associated University Press, 1973.

Matthew Nowicki

Brandt, James L., ed. "Matthew Nowicki." *Student Publications of the School of Design, North Carolina State College* 1 (Winter 1951). Whole issue.

Drew, Jane. "On the Chandigarh Scheme." *MARG* (India) 6 (1953), pp. 19–25.

Mumford, Lewis. "The Life, the Teaching & the Architecture of Matthew Nowicki." *Architectural Record* 115 (June 1954), pp. 139–149; 116 (July 1954), pp. 128–135; 117 (August 1954), pp. 169–175; 118 (September 1954), pp. 153–159.

———. "Matthew Nowicki." *Architectural Forum* 93 (October 1950), pp. 200–201, 206–207.

Nowicki, Matthew. *The Writings & Sketches of Matthew Nowicki.* Charlottesville: University of Virginia Press, 1973.

Henry Hobson Richardson

Hitchcock, Henry-Russell, Jr. *The Architecture of H. H. Richardson and His Times.* Hamden, Conn.: Archon Books, 1961. Reprinted from New York: Museum of Modern Art, 1936.

Mumford, Lewis. "The Regionalism of Richardson." In *Roots of Contemporary American Architecture.* New York: Reinhold Publishing Corp., 1952, pp. 117–131.

O'Gorman, James F. *H. H. Richardson and His Office.* Cambridge: Harvard College Library, 1974.

Price, Charles. "Henry Hobson Richardson: Some Unpublished Drawings." *Perspecta* 9/10 (1965), pp. 199, 210.

Van Rensselaer, Mariana Griswold. *Henry Hobson Richardson.* Introduction by William Morgan. New York: Dover, 1969. Reprinted from Boston: Houghton, Mifflin, 1888.

Christian Francis Rosborg

No significant references exist.

Paul Rudolph

Black, Carl John. *Human Space and the Constructions of Paul Rudolph.* New York: Harper & Row, forthcoming.

Black, Carl, Jr. *Paul Rudolph.* Global Architecture, edited by Yukio Futagawa, vol. 20. Tokyo: ADA Edita, 1973.

Cook, John W., and Klotz, Heinrich. *Conversations with Architects.* New York: Praeger, 1973.

Franzen, Ulrich, and Rudolph, Paul. *The Evolving City: Urban Design Proposals.* Text by Peter Wolf. New York: The Whitney Library of Design for The American Federation of Arts, 1974.

Futagawa, Yukio, and Rudolph, Paul, eds. *Paul Rudolph: Drawings.* Tokyo: ADA Edita, 1972.

Schwab, Gerhard. *The Architecture of Paul Rudolph.* Introduction by Sibyl Moholy-Nagy; commentary by Paul Rudolph. New York: Praeger, 1970.

Rudolph, Paul. "6 Determinants of Architectural Form." *Architectural Record* 120 (October 1956), pp. 183–190.

Spade, Rupert. *Paul Rudolph.* New York: Simon & Schuster, 1971.

Stern, Robert A. M. "Yale 1950–1965." *Oppositions* 4 (October 1974), pp. 35–62.

Eero Saarinen

Carter, Peter. "Eero Saarinen: 1910–1961." *Architectural Design* 31 (December 1961).

Saarinen, Eero. "Interview." *Perspecta* 7 (1961), pp. 29–42.

———, and Saarinen, Aline B., eds. *Eero Saarinen on His Work: A Selection of Buildings Dating from 1947–1964.* Rev. ed. New Haven, Conn.: Yale University Press, 1968.

Spade, Rupert. *Eero Saarinen.* London: Thames & Hudson, 1971.

Temko, Allen. *Eero Saarinen.* New York: Braziller, 1962.

Eliel Saarinen

Christ-Janer, Albert. *Eliel Saarinen.* Foreword by Alvar Aalto. Chicago: University of Chicago Press, 1948.

"Cranbrook Academy of Art, Bloomfield Hills, Michigan." *Architectural Record* 68 (December 1930), pp. 444–451.

Creese, Walter. "Saarinen's Tribune Design." *JSAH* 6 (July–Dec. 1947), pp. 1–5.

Ditchy, Clair W. "Eliel Saarinen, 1873–1950." *Forum Amsterdam* 6 (February 1951), pp. 34–46.

Jackson, Paul. "Tribune Tower Competition, 1922." *Dicta* (January 1963), pp. 92–106.

Ryder, Sharon Lee. "Saarinen Atelier." *Progressive Architecture* 55 (July 1974), pp. 71–75.

Saarinen, Eliel. *The City, Its Growth, Its Decay, Its Future.* New York: Reinhold Publishing Corp., 1943.

———. *Search for Form: A Fundamental Approach to Art.* New York: Reinhold Publishing Corp., 1945.

Rudolph M. Schindler

Gebhard, David. "Ambiguity in the Work of R. M. Schindler." *Lotus* 5 (1968), pp. 106–121.

———. *R. M. Schindler: An Exhibition of the Architecture of R. M. Schindler (1887–1953).* Introduction by Esther McCoy. Santa Barbara: The Art Galleries, the University of California, Santa Barbara, 1967.

———. *Schindler.* New York: Viking Press, 1972.

Paolo Soleri

Kostof, Spiro. "Soleri's Arcology." *Art in America* 59 (March–April 1971), pp. 90–95.

Soleri, Paolo. *Arcology: The City in the Image of Man.* Cambridge, Mass.: MIT Press, 1967.

———. *The Sketchbooks of Paolo Soleri.* Cambridge, Mass.: MIT Press, 1971.

Wall, Donald. *Visionary Cities: the Arcology of Paolo Soleri.* New York: Praeger, 1971.

Wilcoxen, Ralph. *Paolo Soleri: A Bibliography.* Monticello, Ill.: Council of Planning Librarians, 1969.

George Washington Smith
Lutah Maria Riggs

Allen, Harris. "Spanish Atmosphere." *Pacific Coast Architect* 29 (May 1929), pp. 5–33.

Gebhard, David. *George Washington Smith, 1876–1930; The Spanish Colonial Revival in California.* Santa Barbara: The Art Galleries, University of California, Santa Barbara, 1964.

———; Montgomery, Roger; Winter, Robert; Woodbridge, John; and Woodbridge, Sally. *A Guide to Architecture in San Francisco and North California.* Salt Lake City: Peregrine Smith, 1973.

Lane, Jonathan. "The Period House in the 1920's." *JSAH* 20 (December 1961), pp. 169–178.

Morrow, Irving F. "A Dialogue Which Touches upon Mr. Smith's Architecture." *Architect and Engineer* 78 (July 1924), pp. 53–97.

John Goddard Stearns
Robert Swain Peabody

Holden, Wheaton A. "The Peabody Touch: Peabody and Stearns of Boston, 1870–1917." *JSAH* 32 (May 1973), pp. 114–137.

Sturgis, Russell. "Great American Architects Series: Peabody and Stearns." *Architectural Record* (Supplement, July 1896), pp. 53–97.

John Calvin Stevens

Scully, Vincent, J., Jr. *The Shingle Style.* 2d rev. ed. New Haven: Yale University Press, 1974.

Stevens, John Calvin, and Cobb, Albert Winslow. *Examples of American Domestic Architecture.* New York: W. T. Comstock, 1889.

Isaac Newton Phelps Stokes

Goodyear, William. "The Columbia University Chapel." The Brickbuilder 15 (December 1906), pp. 261–269.

Lubore, Roy. "I. N. Phelps Stokes: Tenement Architect, Economist, Planner." *JSAH* 23 (May 1964), pp. 75–87.

Stokes, Isaac Newton Phelps. *The Iconography of Manhattan Island.* New York: R. H. Dodd, 6 vols. 1915–1928.

300 ———. *Recollections of a Happy Life*. New York. 40 copies for private distribution; copy at Avery Library, Columbia University, New York, 1941.

William Strickland
Gilchrist, Agnes Addison. "Additions to William Strickland, Architect and Engineer, 1788–1854." *JSAH* 13 (October 1954).
———. *William Strickland, Architect and Engineer, 1788–1854.* Enlarged ed. New York: Da Capo Press, 1969. Reprinted from Philadelphia: University of Pennsylvania Press, 1950.
Pierson, William H., Jr. *The Colonial and Neo-Classical Styles.* American Buildings and Their Architects, vol. 1. Garden City, N.Y.: Doubleday, 1970.
Senkevitch, Anatole, Jr. "Nineteenth-Century Public Buildings in Nashville." *Antiques* 100 (August 1971), pp. 222–227.
Strickland, William. "Journal of a Tour in the United States of America, 1794–1795." Edited by Reverend J. E. Strickland with a facsimile edition of *Observations on the Agriculture of the United States of America*, by William Strickland. Collections of the New-York Historical Society 83 (1971). Entire issue.

Louis Henry Sullivan
Brooks, H. [Harold] Allen. *The Prairie School: Frank Lloyd Wright and His Midwest Contemporaries.* Buffalo: University of Toronto Press, 1972.
Bush-Brown, Albert. *Louis Sullivan.* New York: Braziller, 1960.
Gebhard, David. "Louis Sullivan and George Grant Elmslie. *JSAH* 19 (May 1960), pp. 62–68.
Hitchcock, Henry-Russell, Jr. "Sullivan and the Skyscraper." *The Builder* 185 (Aug. 7, 1953), pp. 197–200.
Hope, Henry. "Louis Sullivan's Architectural Ornament." *The Architectural Review* 102 (October 1947), pp. 111–114.
Jordy, William H. *Progressive and Academic Ideals at the Turn of the Century.* American Buildings and Their Architects, vol. 3. New York: Doubleday, 1970.
Kaufmann, Edgar, Jr., ed. *Louis Sullivan and the Architecture of Free Enterprise.* Chicago: The Art Institute of Chicago, 1956.
Morrison, Hugh. *Louis Sullivan: Prophet of Modern Architecture.* New York: Museum of Modern Art and W. W. Norton, 1935.
Scully, Vincent, Jr. "Louis Sullivan's Architectural Ornament." *Perspecta* 5 (1959), pp. 73–80.
Sullivan, Louis Henry. *Autobiography of an Idea.* Foreword by Claude Bragdon. New York: Dover, 1956. Reprinted from American Institute of Architects Press, 1926.
———. *Kindergarten Chats.* Lawrence, Kans.: Scarab Fraternity Press, 1934.
———. *A System of Architectural Ornament.* Introduction by Ada Louise Huxtable. New York: Eakins Press, 1967. Reprinted from New York: American Institute of Architects Press, 1924.
Szarkowski, John. *The Idea of Louis Sullivan.* Minneapolis: University of Minnesota Press, 1956.
Wright, Frank Lloyd. *Genius and the Mobocracy.* Enlarged ed. New York: Horizon Press, 1971.

Thomas Alexander Tefft
Cady, John Hutchins. *The Civic and Architectural Development of Providence 1636–1950.* Providence: The Book Shop, 1957.
Clark, I. Edwards. "Thomas A. Tefft and Brick Architecture in America." *American Architect and Building News* 19 (June 12, 1886), pp. 282–283.
Hitchcock, Henry-Russell, Jr. *Rhode Island Architecture.* 2d ed. New York: Da Capo Press, 1968. Reprinted from Providence: Rhode Island Museum Press, 1939.
Wriston, Barbara. "The Architecture of Thomas Tefft." *Rhode Island School of Design Bulletin* 28 (November 1940), pp. 37–45.
———. "Thomas Alexander Tefft: Architect and Economist." Master's thesis, Brown University, 1942.

Horace Trumbauer
Julien F. Abele
Kidney, Walter C. *The Architecture of Choice: Eclecticism in America: 1880–1930.* New York: Braziller, 1974.
"A New Influence in the Architecture of Philadelphia." *Architectural Record* 15 (February 1904), pp. 93–121.
Tatum, George B. *Penn's Great Town.* Philadelphia: University of Pennsylvania Press, 1961.
Underwood, Eric. "A Great American University." *Country Life* 110 (Oct. 26, 1951), pp. 1366–1369.

John Trumbull
Jaffe, Irma B. *John Trumbull, Patriot-Artist of the American Revolution.* Boston: New York Graphic Society, 1975.
Sizer, Theodore. "John Trumbull, Amateur Architect." *JSAH* 8 (July–December 1949), pp. 1–6.
———. *The Work of Colonel John Trumbull, Artist of the American Revolution.* Rev. ed. New Haven: Yale University Press, 1967.
Trumbull, John, and Sizer, Theodore, eds. *The Autobiography of Colonel John Trumbull, Patriot, Artist: 1756–1843.* New Haven: Yale University Press, 1953.

Richard Upjohn
Stanton, Phoebe B. *The Gothic Revival and American Church Architecture, an Episode in Taste: 1840–1856.* Baltimore: Johns Hopkins University Press, 1968.
Upjohn, Everard Miller. *Richard Upjohn, Architect and Churchman.* New York: Da Capo Press, 1968. Reprinted from New York: Columbia University Press, 1939.
Upjohn, Richard. *Upjohn's Rural Architecture; Designs, Working Drawings and Specifications for a Wooden Church and Other Rural Structures.* New York: Da Capo Press, 1975. Reprinted from New York: George P. Putnam, 1852.

Calvert Vaux
Barlow, Elizabeth, and Alex, William. *Frederick Law Olmstead's New York.* New York: Praeger, 1972.
Sigle, John David. "Bibliography of the Life and Works of Calvert Vaux." *American Association of Architectural Bibliographers*, Papers 5 (1968), pp. 69–106.
Steese, Edward. "Villas & Cottages by Calvert Vaux, Condensed by Edward Steese." *JSAH* 6 (January–June 1947), pp. 1–12.
Vaux, Calvert. *Villas and Cottages.* Introduction by Henry Hope Reed. New York: Da Capo Press, 1968. Reprinted from New York; Harper & Brothers, 1857.

Robert Venturi
Schulz, Franz. "Chaos as Architecture." *Art in America* 58 (July–August 1970), pp. 88–96.
Scully, Vincent, Jr. *The Shingle Style Today or The Historians' Revenge.* New York: Braziller, 1974.
Venturi, Robert. *Complexity and Contradiction in Architecture.* New York: The Museum of Modern Art, 1966.
———. "Essays in the Ugly and Ordinary: Some Decorated Sheds." *Architecture and Urbanism* [Japan] 1 (October 1971), pp. 9–118. Entire issue.
———; Brown, Denise Scott; and Izenour, Steven. *Learning from Las Vegas.* Cambridge, Mass.: MIT Press, 1972.

Thomas Ustick Walter
Hamlin, Talbot. *Greek Revival Architecture in America.* New York: Dover, 1964. Reprinted from New York: Oxford University Press, 1944.
Huxtable, Ada Louise. "Jayne Building 1849–50." *Progressive Architecture* 37 (November 1956), pp. 133–134.

Peterson, Charles E.; Cooper, E. Newbold; and Gilchrist, Agnes Addison. "The Girard College Architectural Competition, 1832." *JSAH* 16 (May 1957), pp. 20–27.
Pierson, William H., Jr. *The Colonial and Neo-Classical Styles.* American Buildings and Their Architects, vol. 1. Garden City, N.Y.: Doubleday, 1970.

Whitney Warren
Warren, Whitney. Obituary. *The New York Times*, Jan. 25, 1943.

Peter Bonnet Wight
Burchard, John, and Bush-Brown, Albert. *The Architecture of America.* Boston: Little, Brown, 1961.
"The Mercantile Library, Brooklyn." *New York Sketch-Book of Architecture* 3 (February 1876).

Frank Lloyd Wright
Brooks, H. [Harold] Allen. *The Prairie School: Frank Lloyd Wright and His Midwest Contemporaries.* Buffalo: University of Toronto Press, 1972.
———. "Frank Lloyd Wright and the Wasmuth Drawings." *Art Bulletin* 48 (June 1966), pp. 193–202.
Drexler, Arthur, ed. *The Drawings of Frank Lloyd Wright.* New York: Horizon Press, 1962.
Eaton, Leonard K. *Two Chicago Architects and Their Clients: Frank Lloyd Wright and Howard Van Doren Shaw.* Cambridge: MIT Press, 1969.
Hitchcock, Henry-Russell, Jr. *In the Nature of Materials.* New York: Da Capo Press, 1975. Reprinted from New York: Hawthorn Books, 1942.
Jordy, William H. *Progressive and Academic Ideals at the Turn of the Twentieth Century.* American Buildings and Their Architects, vol. 3, Garden City, N.Y.: Doubleday, 1972.
———. *The Impact of European Modernism in the Mid-Twentieth Century.* American Buildings and Their Architects, vol. 4. Garden City, N.Y.: Doubleday, 1972.
Kaufmann, Edgar, Jr. *Taliesin Drawings: Recent Architecture of Frank Lloyd Wright Selected from His Drawings.* New York: Wittenborn, Schultz, 1952.
Scully, Vincent J., Jr. *Frank Lloyd Wright.* New York: Braziller, 1960.
Sergeant, John. *Frank Lloyd Wright's Usonian Houses: The Case for Organic Architecture.* New York: Whitney Library of Design, 1976.
Smith, Norris Kelly. *Frank Lloyd Wright: A Study in Architectural Content.* Englewood Cliffs, N.J.: Prentice-Hall, 1966.
Wasmuth, Ernst, ed. *Ausgeführte Bauten und Entwürfe, von Frank Lloyd Wright* ("The Wasmuth Portfolio"). Berlin: Wasmuth, 1910. Reprinted as *Buildings Plans and Designs of Frank Lloyd Wright.* New York: Horizon Press, 1963.
Wright, Frank Lloyd. *An Autobiography.* New York: Duell, Sloan & Pearce, 1943.
———. *Writings and Buildings* (with list of executed works). Edited by Edgar Kaufmann, Jr., and Ben Raeburn. New York: Horizon Press, 1960.

Lloyd Wright
Gebhard, David, and von Breton, Harriette. *Lloyd Wright, Architect: 20th Century Architecture in an Organic Exhibition.* Santa Barbara: The Standard Printing Company, 1971.
McCoy, Esther. "Lloyd Wright." *Arts and Architecture* 83 (October 1966), pp. 22–26.
Schindler, Pauline [Gibling]. "Modern California Architects." *Creative Arts* 10 (February 1932), pp. 111–115.
———. "The Samuel House, Los Angeles." *Architectural Record* 67 (June 1930), pp. 520–530.

Index

Illustrations are indicated by italics; bold numerals refer to the major discussion of the architect's work. Buildings are listed under the city in which they were built.